U.S. LEGAL REASONING, WRITING, AND PRACTICE FOR INTERNATIONAL LAWYERS

U.S. LEGAL REASONING, WRITING, AND PRACTICE FOR INTERNATIONAL LAWYERS

JOHN B. THORNTON
Clinical Assistant Professor of Law
Northwestern University School of Law

LexisNexis®

ISBN: 978-0-7698-5656-8 (print)
ISBN: 978-0-3271-7980-1 (ebook)

Library of Congress Cataloging-in-Publication Data

Thornton, John Brendan, author.

U.S. legal reasoning, writing, and practice for international lawyers / John B. Thornton, Clinical Assistant Professor of Law; Northwestern University School of Law.

pages cm

Includes index.

ISBN 978-0-7698-5656-8

1. Law--United States. 2. Legal research--United States. 3. Practice of law--United States. 4. Legal composition. 5. Lawyers, Foreign--United States--Handbooks, manuals, etc. I. Title. II. Title: United States legal reasoning, writing and practice for international lawyers.

KF386.T483 2014

349.73--dc23

2014008737

NOTE TO USERS

To ensure that you are using the latest materials available in this area, please be sure to periodically check the LexisNexis Law School web site for downloadable updates and supplements at www.lexisnexis.com/lawschool.

Editorial Offices
121 Chanlon Rd., New Providence, NJ 07974 (908) 464-6800
201 Mission St., San Francisco, CA 94105-1831 (415) 908-3200
www.lexisnexis.com

MATTHEW BENDER

(2014–Pub.3371)

Dedication

To Gosha, Sean, and Paulina, with all my love.

Acknowledgments

I would like to thank all of my present and former colleagues in the Communication and Legal Reasoning program at Northwestern University School of Law, from whom I've learned so much about how to teach legal reasoning, writing, and research. In particular, I would like to thank Professors James McMasters, Christopher Martin, Dana Hill, Brian Silbernagel, Grace Dodier, Martha Kanter, Deborah Borman, Elizabeth Inglehart, Kathleen Dillon Narko, Michelle Falkoff, Sue Payne, Susan Provenzano, Judy Rosenbaum, Margaret Curtiss Hannon, and Ellen Mulaney for graciously sharing their knowledge, insights and materials with me, and for being willing to discuss both teaching and the contents of this book. Thanks also to my research and teaching assistant Suzanne Alton, for her diligent, timely research, and her positive spirit.

I would also like to thank Lawrence S. Schaner, Christopher J. Karacic, and Mark E. Wojcik for their help and excellent advice, and thanks to those who gave copyright permissions. Finally, I would like to thank Leslie Levin and Jennifer Beszley of LexisNexis for helping me to make this book a reality.

Preface

In recent years, many law schools across the United States have seen a large increase in the number of students from other countries who are studying for Masters of Laws degrees ("international LL.M. students"). These students are the primary audience for this book.

International LL.M. students arrive at U.S. law schools from around the world, coming from countries with a great diversity of legal systems and cultures. You also arrive with great differences in your levels of legal practice experience. Some students may have already been practicing law for five to ten years, while others may have recently graduated from law schools in your countries.

Of the students with experience practicing law, some of you may have worked exclusively in your native language, while others may have created attorney work product both in English and in your first language. Still others may have worked at U.S.- or U.K.-based international law firms.

Despite these differences, international LL.M. students share an important similarity: attending law school in the United States will be a challenging new experience for everyone. Part of the purpose of this book is to guide international LL.M. students as you adjust to studying law in a new country, in a different legal system, and likely in a new language as well.

What This Book Contains

This book is designed for a class that teaches U.S. legal reasoning, writing, and research skills (a "legal writing class") to international LL.M. students. Whatever your law school might call the class, it is designed to teach you how to function as an attorney in the U.S. legal system and how to reason and write in the style that U.S. legal audiences expect.

Thus, this book introduces you to the common law system that exists in the United States; it teaches you how to identify the appropriate rules for a legal issue, whatever their source; how to analyze a legal issue by applying the relevant rules of law to the facts at issue; and how to clearly and efficiently communicate this analysis in the writing style that U.S. lawyers expect to see.

As we will learn, the writing style that a U.S. legal audience expects is likely to be somewhat different from the type of legal writing that you do in your country and in your native language. Indeed, it may well be different from the legal writing that you may have already done in your country in English for English-speaking clients. This is because what each legal system and each language considers to be good legal writing may vary greatly. To learn how to write well here, in English and within the context of the U.S. legal system, it is important to be flexible, and to be willing to write in a style that is likely different from the style that you are familiar with and comfortable using.

It is not easy to learn to write in a different rhetorical style while writing in a different language and while adapting to a different legal system. Accordingly, this book contains chapters with exercises that will help you to master the type of legal writing in English that U.S. lawyers expect. We will practice using the rhetorical style of U.S. legal writing, and legal English vocabulary for the U.S. legal system. The book also covers grammar and usage problems that are common for lawyers who speak English as a second language.

Also, the book discusses certain aspects of U.S. law firms and legal culture, such as the hierarchy, economics and culture within firms, and what partners expect from associate attorneys, as well as from the international counsel with whom they work.

Moreover, the book teaches study skills that will enable you to succeed in a U.S. law school, including how to write case briefs and course outlines, and how to take final examinations.

Each chapter begins with a preview that introduces the areas that the chapter will cover, and ends with a review that summarizes the main concepts in the chapter. Key legal terms are written in bold, and defined in the chapter and in a glossary at the back of the book.

Finally, the book contains numerous examples of good U.S. legal writing, to help you to understand better what it looks like. The appendixes at the back of the book contain several types of legal writing that U.S. attorneys commonly produce: formal office memoranda, more informal email memos, letters to clients and opposing counsel, basic contracts, and trial and appellate briefs. These writing samples are real U.S. attorney work product that has been redacted for the book.

In conclusion, this book is designed to help you to master the legal reasoning and writing skills that will help you to succeed in a U.S. law school, as well as the skills that will enable you to practice law with a U.S.- or U.K.-based international law firm. In addition, these skills will help you to work as local counsel in your country in matters where U.S.- or U.K.-based international law firms may work with your firm to represent the same client, or where they may represent the opposing party. Also, these skills will help you to work as in-house counsel for a company that does business internationally. In short, using this book and taking a legal writing course at a U.S. law school will help you to gain U.S. legal expertise and to add value for your clients as an attorney who is familiar with the U.S. legal system, and with how U.S. lawyers think, write, and behave.

John B. Thornton
Chicago, October 2013

Table of Contents

Chapter 1

A BRIEF HISTORY OF THE COMMON LAW IN THE UNITED STATES

Chapter Preview

This chapter provides a background for our study of the common law system that we use in the United States. The chapter discusses:

- The origin of the common law system in England;
- The reception of English common law by the United States and the early development of American common law; and
- The different meanings of the term "common law."

A. THE ORIGINS OF THE COMMON LAW SYSTEM IN ENGLAND

Traditionally, the United States is viewed as a member of the common law family of nations, along with the United Kingdom, Canada, Australia, New Zealand, and to greater and lesser extents, many other former colonies of England that are now members of the British Commonwealth.

If you are an international LL.M. student who is studying at a law school in the United States, you are likely from a country that is a member of the civil law family of nations, or you may be from a country that has a mixed legal system, with certain civil law features and certain common law features. Perhaps your country has a legal system that contains certain aspects of one of those systems as well as certain traditional aspects of your country's culture, whether socio-ethnic traditions, religious traditions, or a mix of the two. Thus, you may either be unsure of what the term "common law" means, or you may have a somewhat different conception of the term than a U.S. lawyer does.

Thus, to understand what we mean when we describe the United States as a common law country, it is helpful to begin by looking briefly at the origins of the common law system in England, and then at how that system was received in the United States, and how it has evolved in this country. Finally, we will look at the different ways that lawyers here use the term "common law."

1. The Norman Conquest

What we think of today as the English common law system began after one event in 1066 — the Norman Conquest. William the Conqueror provided a centralized form of government that led to the development of the common law system.[1]

A millennium before the Norman Conquest, the Roman Empire had occupied England for several hundred years, but Roman law largely left England when Rome's soldiers did. Even during the Roman occupation, Roman law governed only the Roman occupiers and had little effect on the local people. After the Romans left, the country was dominated by various tribal groups such as the Angles, Saxons, and Jutes, as well as the Danes, each with their own customs and laws.

Although William left the patchwork of local customary laws mostly intact and allowed local issues to continue to be decided by local courts, he established a central government at Westminster. William also took possession of all of the land, distributing it among his most trustworthy followers after they had pledged their loyalty to him. In addition, he established a royal judicial authority called the Curia Regis, which was composed of a council of the king and certain trusted advisors. These judicial powers were later given to the royal courts at Westminster.

---

[1] For a more in-depth treatment of this topic, *see Overview of U.S. Law* 2–10 (Ellen S. Podgor & John F. Cooper eds., LexisNexis 2009). *See also* Mary Ann Glendon, Michael Wallace Gordon & Christopher Osakwe, Comparative Legal Traditions 438–447 (2d ed., West Group, 1994).

2. The Royal Courts at Westminster

Over the next several hundred years, the royal courts at Westminster came to hear tax and revenue matters that affected the government directly, other matters that directly affected the power of the king and the central government, and matters that resolved disputes between individuals. These courts included the Court of Exchequer, which dealt with taxes, revenue, and matters that affected the royal treasury; the King's Bench, which dealt with both political and criminal matters; and the Court of Common Pleas, which dealt with lawsuits between private individuals.

The Curia Regis, and later the King's Bench, had the authority to review cases from the Court of Common Pleas. Although these courts did not completely replace the old local courts, **litigants** generally preferred them, because they saw them as fairer and more progressive.[2]

3. The Development of Equity

Nevertheless, these courts had their own problems. Bringing suit in the early courts was not an easy process: It involved purchasing a **writ** from the Curia Regis. The writ was a letter from the Curia Regis that directed the court to hear the case. The system was complex, and the results were often harsh. For example, if there was no type of writ that addressed his or her problem, the **plaintiff** could not sue, and if a plaintiff purchased the wrong type of writ, the case would be dismissed.

If this occurred, the **party** who was left without a remedy could petition the king to compel the defendant "to act as morality and good conscience required."[3] The king would pass the petition to the Chancellor, a high government official who was familiar with the writ process and the developing common law. The Chancellor was also connected to the church, and thus familiar with **canon law** — the ecclesiastical law of the church. Eventually, petitions went directly to the Chancellor, and these petitions were heard in the High Court of Chancery.

The Chancellor had the flexibility to rule in accordance with principles of justice and fairness, without having to strictly apply common law. These legal principles, known as **equity**, drew from ancient Greek and Roman traditions, and also from Christianity. Unlike the common law, which provided monetary **damages** for relief, equitable relief included **injunctions** (where the court orders the **defendant** not to act in a way that will harm the plaintiff) and **specific performance** (where the court orders the defendant to perform under the provisions of the contract at issue).

Although the High Court of Chancery became increasingly popular, courts of equity did not replace the common law courts. Instead, they co-existed, and it would be more accurate to describe the work of the High Court of Chancery as filling in the holes in the common law and compensating for its sometimes harsh results.

Over time, courts of equity began to more closely resemble the common law courts in an important way: the importance of **precedent.** When equity was a relatively new

---

[2] *See* Glendon, Gordon & Osakwe, *supra* note 2, at 440–441.

[3] *See* Podgor & Cooper, *supra* note 2, at 8.

legal concept in England, the Chancellor was able to rule on a case in whatever way he thought was fair. However, over time, the Chancellor came to feel bound by the decisions of earlier cases (precedent) in the same way that the common law courts were.[4]

4. The Heart of the Common Law — Precedent

As we have discussed so far, the term *common law* arose from the court system of medieval England that developed after the Norman Conquest of 1066, and it was called the "common law" because the decisions of those royal courts became the unified law of the land throughout the entire kingdom. Thus, unlike the patchwork collections of local laws that had existed in England before that time, or the patchwork collections of local laws that existed elsewhere on the continent of Europe at that time, the rules were not local in nature, but common to everyone in the kingdom — hence, *common law*.

For a legal system to be accepted by its citizens, however, and for the legal system to serve as the basis for a successful, well-functioning society, a legal system must be more than just "common to all" in its application. The people need to have some understanding of what the law is and how it will affect their lives, and they need to believe that their nation's legal system is fair and that it is not controlled by the needs and moods of its rulers.

In other words, a legal system must be *consistent*, so that if different courts are given the same legal issues with the same facts, they are likely to reach the same rulings. A legal system must also be *predictable*, so that when people make important decisions, they can predict what the legal consequences of their actions will be. First, they need to know whether or not the proposed actions are legal. Second, they should also understand what the legal consequences of those actions will be: for example, what the tax consequences will be, or whether, if another party sues them, a court would likely rule in their favor. Without this information, it is difficult for businesses to make informed decisions, and it is difficult for a society to prosper.

The English common law courts solved this problem by applying the legal doctrine of **stare decisis**, which is loosely translated from Latin as "the decision stands." Under this doctrine, courts resolve cases with similar legal issues and similar facts in consistent and similar ways by applying precedent. This means that the judge in a new case considers (1) the facts and legal issues in the case, and also (2) the facts and legal issues in a similar case that has already been decided (the precedent). If the facts and legal issues in the new case are similar to those of the previous case, then the court should resolve the new case in the same way that the earlier court resolved the precedent. In short, under the doctrine of stare decisis, courts must follow precedent.

Over time, as new cases arise, courts rule on them by analyzing the facts and legal issues, determining the appropriate law, and applying it to the facts of the case. In

---

[4] *See id.* at 8–9.

cases in the common law system, "determining the appropriate law" includes analyzing precedent.

As time goes on, legal rules continue to develop and to evolve because there are new cases each year, and lawyers and courts have an ever-increasing body of precedent to compare their new cases to. Thus, at least in theory, as the "database" of precedent continues to develop and grow, courts should be able to reach decisions that are more consistent, and the law should become more predictable because the legal system has more precedent to guide it.

QUESTIONS FOR DISCUSSION

1. The writing focuses on several important developments in the law of England after the Norman Conquest. How did those developments lead to the common law system?

2. The concept of precedent is central to the common law system. How important is the concept of precedent in your country's legal system? Do cases have precedential value? Are they a primary source of law?

B. EARLY DEVELOPMENT OF THE COMMON LAW IN THE UNITED STATES

1. The Development of Law in the Thirteen Colonies

The first permanent English settlers crossed the Atlantic Ocean and landed on what is now the east coast of the United States in the early seventeenth century. They established settlements at Jamestown in Virginia in 1607 and at Plymouth in Massachusetts in 1620. Over the course of that century, English settlers established 13 colonies along the east coast, from Massachusetts in the north to Georgia in the south.

At first, the population of each colony was small, and the earliest settlers were not lawyers. As a result, they established untrained laymen's versions of English legal institutions, and they brought with them the average person's understanding of English common law.[5]

As the seventeenth century progressed, the population of the colonies grew due to continued immigration and to natural growth, and the colonies developed rapidly. By the first half of the eighteenth century, colonial administrations, courts, and law had become increasingly professional, particularly in the larger and more financially successful colonies. Landowners had property rights to secure. As commerce increased, business people traded within their own colonies, but also with other colonies and with England. They needed to have regular, consistent, predictable laws to protect their interests and rights, and this required lawyers.

---

[5] Eva H. Hanks, Michael E. Herz & Steven S. Nemerson, *Elements of Law* 5 (2d ed., LexisNexis 2010).

When the first lawyers arrived, they helped their clients to structure transactions, and to secure property rights and financial interests. They also helped to develop the colonial administrations and courts, all according to the general legal principles of the English common law, with its precedent-based legal reasoning and its adversarial common law courts.[6]

However, the reception of English common law by the American colonies was never complete, because England and its American colonies had societies with different social structures, different needs, and different perspectives. For example, there was no aristocracy in the American colonies, and the highly stratified nature of English society and institutions did not exist there. Also, the legal systems of the colonies developed at first without the lawyers, and the American colonists maintained a pragmatic, independent nature. Thus, the colonies drafted their own statutes and tended to follow their own precedents.[7]

It is more helpful to think of lawyers in the American colonies not as receiving and applying a particular body of English legal doctrine, but rather adopting the English common law *approach* to dealing with legal issues, and pragmatically using that approach — those general legal principles — to fit the circumstances of life in the new colonies.

2. Law in the New United States

As the 13 colonies continued to grow and to develop, the English Parliament and the King found them to be a valuable source of revenue, and levied increasingly heavy taxes on them. The American colonists, many of whom had never been to England, grew unhappy and began to protest.

When the English government showed no interest in, or sympathy for, the colonists' concerns and demands for greater self-governance, representatives of the 13 colonies met at Philadelphia in 1776. They drafted the Declaration of Independence, which established the 13 colonies as the United States of America. A seven-year long war of independence from England ended in victory in 1783, and after six difficult years under the unsuccessful Articles of Confederation, the 13 states ratified the United States Constitution in 1789.

While these new developments were wonderful achievements for the former colonists, they also posed great challenges. For example, now that the United States was an independent country, there was no reason for English common law to carry any more authority than the law of France, Italy, or any other country. Moreover, there was even some question as to whether the new country could accurately be described as a common law country.

Unlike England, the new United States had a written constitution, and a system of government that was divided into three separate but equal branches: the executive, the legislative, and the judicial. Following the lead of the U.S. Constitution and the

---

[6] *See id.* at 5–6.

[7] For a more in-depth treatment of this topic, *see* Edgar Bodenheimer, John B. Oakley & Jean C. Love, *An Introduction to the Anglo-American Legal System* 51–56 (4th ed., Thomson West 2004).

federal (national) government, each state quickly drafted its own constitution and also divided its government into executive, judicial, and legislative branches. Moreover, the legislatures of the federal government and each of the state governments drafted laws that we call **statutes**. Some of the statutes **abrogated** (rejected or invalidated) traditional English common law, particularly in areas where English law involved aristocracy and the social class system, such as family law and real property law — laws that preserved privilege and wealth among the aristocracy and the wealthy.

To define the legal systems of the 13 new states, each state drafted constitutional provisions or statutes which typically said that as of a date approximately at the time of the American Revolution (often around 1775 or 1776), the common law of England and Great Britain, and the statutes passed by the colonial legislature, would continue to be the law of the new state. Although some of the drafters of these "reception statutes" may have wanted them to state more specifically how limited the reception of the common law was in scope, state legislators may not have agreed on how much of the English common law they wanted to adopt, so the reception statutes typically contained general language.

In practice, U.S. lawyers continued to operate under the common law principles that they had received from England. Where there were no U.S. federal or state statutes that discussed an area of law, courts and lawyers would look to common law decisions, and although English legal opinions may not have had binding authority, U.S. courts could and did still look to them for guidance, particularly when the United States was a new country and there was little U.S. precedent that had accumulated.

Depending upon the other law courses that you are taking, you may have noticed that some of the oldest judicial opinions in your U.S. law school casebooks are from England, including ones that are more recent than the American Revolution (such as cases from the 1840s, 1850s, or even the 1860s). That is because, although leading English cases of the late eighteenth century and the nineteenth century had no **binding** authority in U.S. courts, they were still seen as **persuasive** and worthy of respect, and U.S. courts felt free to adopt rules from the English cases that they found to be useful. Indeed, for the first 60 to 70 years of the nineteenth century, the United States Supreme Court and lower courts often cited to English cases. Then, as the body of U.S. precedent continued to increase in size and scope, U.S. courts found it less useful to look at English cases, and the practice gradually decreased.

C. "COMMON LAW" AND THE UNITED STATES

1. Different Meanings of the Term "Common Law"

You may have noticed that in this chapter, the term "common law" has been used in more than one way. In its most general sense, we use the term "common law" as a name for a type of legal system: the type of legal system that originated in England and that has spread to certain other countries such as the United States. When we say that the United States has a common-law legal system or that it is a member of the common law family of countries, we are using the term in this very broad way.

Second, as shown above, the term "common law" was historically used to describe the body of decisions of the English common law courts because these decisions were common to (and applied to) everyone in the kingdom. In those cases, the legal rules were judge-made and not based on statutes. Through the use of the doctrine of stare decisis, the English common law courts followed precedent by applying the rules that they derived from older cases to the facts of new cases.

The third usage of "common law" from this chapter is how U.S. lawyers typically use the term today. As stated above, the United States legal system contains both a federal Constitution and 50 state constitutions, and there are federal and state statutes as well. Most cases in the federal and state court systems today involve at least one claim that is based on a federal or state statute or constitutional provision. However, even now, there are still many cases that are based wholly or partially upon judge-made rules of law. U.S. lawyers typically refer to these cases or claims as "common law cases" or "common law claims," and when they do so, they are commenting on the source of the law. The term "common law" refers to judge-made law, not to laws that were written by legislatures. Even today, this body of judge-made law covers many traditional areas of the law, such as torts, contracts, property, and family law.

2. The United States Is a Mixed Common Law Country

As we have seen, lawyers have traditionally described the United States as a member of the common law family of nations because of the country's origin as 13 colonies of England, and because the colonies all developed their court systems and procedures, laws, and administrations in keeping with general English common law rules and principles.

After independence, various state reception statutes note the continued acceptance of English common law as part of the law of the state. Finally, even today, many lawsuits are based in whole or in part on judge-made law, and both federal and state courts employ the doctrine of stare decisis so that new cases follow the decisions of older cases that have similar facts.

Despite all of these common law features, however, it is more accurate to describe the United States as having a mixed common–law system. Unlike England, the United States has written constitutions for the federal government and the 50 state governments. Moreover, there are large and ever-growing bodies of statutes pertaining to both federal law and to the laws of each state, and in many areas of the law, these bodies of statutory law are similar to the codes of civil law countries. Indeed, as the new nation continued to grow through immigration and new citizens arrived from countries with European civil law legal systems, it made sense that the developing United States legal system would reflect the influences of other countries as well as the "mother country."

Nevertheless, despite this mixed legal heritage, it is still accurate to consider the United States as a common law country. Even when courts consider cases involving statutory law, judges **construe** (interpret) the meanings of the statutes. Those opinions may create new rules that the courts use to explain and apply general statutory language to the facts before them.

Moreover, through the use of stare decisis, cases that involve statutes follow precedent, so later courts must look at both the relevant statutes *and* at the precedent that interprets those statutes. Over time, the way that courts interpret a statute may evolve somewhat, as each subsequent opinion must consider precedent, and new cases may add new rules. Thus, there can be a "common law-like" evolution of the law even where judicial opinions interpret statutes.

QUESTIONS FOR DISCUSSION

1. Legal historians generally agree that the 13 American colonies never completely adopted English common law. To what extent did the 13 American colonies adopt English common law? What prevented them from adopting it more completely? Could the attitude of the colonists have played a role?

2. What challenges did the former colonists encounter in creating a legal system for the United States after the American Revolution? How did the legal system reflect the growing population of the country?

3. Has your country ever been a colony of another country at some time during its history? If so, how did it create a new legal system after independence? Was the process similar to or different from the process in the United States, and in what ways?

Chapter Review

- Along with the United Kingdom, other English-speaking nations such as Canada and Australia, and many former colonies of England that are now members of the British Commonwealth, the United States is traditionally considered a member of the common law family of nations.
- The common law system originated in England after the Norman Conquest of 1066, when the decisions of certain royal courts established rules of law for the whole kingdom. Under the doctrine of stare decisis, those judge-made rules had to be followed by later courts that considered legal issues with similar facts.
- The rules were common to everyone in the kingdom — hence the term "common law." The term "common law" also refers to the system of judge-made law that is recorded in precedent (judicial opinions that have to be followed by later courts considering similar facts).
- In England's 13 colonies on the east coast of North America, the early colonists generally tried to follow English common law traditions. Later, as the colonies grew and became more successful, lawyers arrived and helped the colonists to protect their interests and rights, and to set up administrations and courts that followed general English common law rules, principles, and procedures.
- English common law rules were not completely adopted in the 13 American colonies, and were used more as general principles.

- Shortly after the American Revolution, the new United States retained the general English common law approach, but drafted a written Constitution and federal statutes. Each state did the same.
- The United States today has a mixed common law system in which courts apply statutes or constitutional provisions where relevant, but common law (i.e., judge-made law) still covers many areas of the law, and courts still follow precedent under the doctrine of stare decisis.

Chapter 2

SIMILARITIES AND DIFFERENCES BETWEEN CIVIL LAW SYSTEMS AND THE U.S. LEGAL SYSTEM

Chapter Preview

This chapter completes the introduction to two of the world's major legal systems by looking briefly at civil law systems, and by comparing and contrasting them with the common law system as we use it in the United States. The chapter discusses:

- The history and development of the civil law system;
- Similarities and differences between the civil law and common law systems; and
- Suggestions for how lawyers who are trained to think in the context of a civil law system can approach their legal studies in the U.S. legal system.

A. BRIEF OVERVIEW OF THE HISTORY OF THE CIVIL LAW SYSTEM

If you are an international LL.M. student who is studying at a U.S. law school, you are likely either a lawyer from a civil law system, or a graduate of a law school from a country that has a civil law system. Just as there are differences among the legal systems of countries that are members of the common law family of nations, the differences among the legal systems of countries that are members of the civil law family of nations can also be great. The chapter thus begins with a brief look at the development of civil law systems throughout the world, to help everyone to gain a proper context for the discussion of the similarities and differences between the civil law and common law systems.

1. Roman Law and Its Revival

"Roman law" describes a period of legal development in ancient Rome that lasted for nearly a thousand years (from approximately 450 B.C. to the Justinian compilations of Roman law circa 534 A.D.) — a length of time that is similar to the entire history of the common law, from 1066 A.D. to the present time.[1] During the Roman Republic, the first professional lawyers arose, a group of men called Jurisconsults. Over the next several centuries, their case-by-case opinions established legal principles that were set forth in treatises; Roman law moved from fixed rules to more flexible standards; and the reasoning became increasingly abstract.[2]

Although the Western Roman Empire fell, Roman law was preserved in the East by the Byzantine Emperor Justinian in the sixth century, but it was not preserved perfectly, as the Byzantine lawyers preserved the parts of Roman law with which they agreed and rejected others. Also, Roman law was preserved in at least some fashion by the Germanic tribes which conquered Rome, as their laws became a blend of customary tribal laws with Roman laws. Finally, Roman law survived to a certain extent in the canon law of the Catholic Church, which was influenced by ancient Roman law.

At about the same time that the common law was beginning to develop in medieval England, ancient Roman law was revived in northern Italy, as legal scholars at the University of Bologna began to study the Justinian texts, which were more than 500 years old at that time. Thousands of students from across Europe studied there over the next several hundred years, and over time, what they brought back home from Bologna was a blend between the revived Roman law (which was often hard to understand due to the difference in societies and the passage of hundreds of years) and the medieval Romano-Germanic law. This shared legal background of lawyers that spread across Europe led to, in effect, a received "common law" (*jus commune*) of continental Europe — "common" not in the sense of judge-made law or the use of precedent, but "common" in the sense that it was shared by all — a common

---

[1] For a more in-depth treatment of this topic, *see* Glendon, Gordon & Osakwe at 44–64.

[2] *See id.* at 44–45.

approach, with a shared body of law, a shared legal vocabulary, and a shared form of legal education.[3]

What made it easier for this to occur was that Europe did not have strong, unified nations at the time, so that there were many different jurisdictions and many types of courts: ecclesiastical courts that applied canon law, merchant guilds that applied the developing business and commercial law, called the "law merchant," and judges in local courts in cities and towns who would look for appropriate legal rules from either local custom or the received *jus commune*.

Some English law students returned from Italy, and brought Roman law back with them to the English universities, where it became a popular subject of study. Although the English courts refused to accept the influence of Roman law, England traded extensively with the continent, and so the law merchant eventually became an internationally-accepted body of commercial rules.[4]

2. The Codification of European Law

Several trends from the 16th through 18th centuries led to the move away from the received *jus commune* and to the development of national codes of law. First, as the center of legal scholarship moved from Italy to France and Holland, Roman law became seen more as a historical text rather than "living law," and the Dutch Natural Law School's conception of a system of law based on a "universal law of nature" helped to prepare the way for national codes.[5]

Also, political developments throughout Europe led to the gradual replacement of smaller royal kingdoms and territories with modern nation-states. Political power began to centralize; local languages replaced Latin in universities; and the Reformation led to the development of other Christian churches that separated from the Catholic Church in Rome. As power centralized, it also led to the rise of **public law**[6] — a term that lawyers from civil-law systems use to refer to the laws that pertain to governments and administrative/regulatory law. All of these developments led to the rise of national law and a decline in the influence of Roman law and canon law.

The first national codes were influenced by the *jus commune*, but replaced it as the basic source of national law.[7] However, the two national codes that have arguably had the greatest influence on the development of civil law systems around the world were not created until the 19th century: the French Civil Code of 1804 (sometimes called

---

[3] *Id.* at 48–49.

[4] *Id.* at 49.

[5] *See id.* at 51–52.

[6] "Public law" has a different meaning to U.S. lawyers, who describe almost *all* law enacted by legislatures as public law (e.g., laws affecting the relationships between governments and the citizens, laws affecting the general public, and laws dealing with the structure and procedure of government). In the U.S., "private law" refers only (1) to legal documents that are drafted by, and are binding upon, individuals or parties, such as contracts, or (2) "special law" (a narrow class of statutes that is typically enacted to provide compensation for an individual or specific group of individuals).

[7] *See id.* at 52.

the "Code Napoleon"), at the beginning of the century, and the German Civil Code of 1896, at the end.

Although it was written when Napoleon was in power, the French Civil Code of 1804 showed the influence of the ideas that animated the French Revolution, especially in the area of family law, where it rejected the old laws that had supported the aristocracy's ability to pass on land and wealth from generation to generation. Other goals were to protect freedom of contract and private property. Thus, similar to the ancient Roman law, the French Civil Code of 1804 focused on **private law**,[8] as civil-law attorneys use the term: law that focuses on private rights, duties, and obligations (e.g., property law, contract law, and family law). The style of writing of the French Civil Code of 1804 was similar to that of the U.S. Constitution of 1789: it was written for citizens to be able to read, so it was concise and clear, and provided general rules.

In contrast, the German Civil Code of 1896 took a very different approach: scientific, precise, with technical language used throughout, the German Civil Code of 1896 attempted to provide a scientific logical system that was designed for legal professionals, not the general public.[9]

3. The Spread of Civil Law Systems Throughout the World

As he marched east in his conquests, Napoleon brought the French Civil Code of 1804 with him, and it influenced several of the European countries that his army occupied. Then, during the colonial era, French colonial expansion brought the Code to much of Africa, the Middle East, and parts of Asia and the Americas. Moreover, its clear style and its sweeping away of the old aristocratic order led the French Civil Code to become influential and admired in many countries that had never been French colonies, such as many Latin American countries.

In contrast, the German Civil Code did not travel so easily, because it was more technical and had more challenging language, and also because it did not appear until 1896, by which time many countries had already begun to develop their own civil codes. Nevertheless, the German Civil Code of 1896 influenced a number of other European codes and the Japanese Civil Code, and it also had some influence on the Brazilian Code of 1916, and South Korean law.[10]

Today, countries that fall within the civil-law family of nations include most European and Latin American nations, and many nations throughout Asia and Africa.

4. Different Meanings of the Term "Civil Law"

Just as the term "common law" is used in several ways, this is also true with the term "civil law." In its most general sense, we use the term "civil law" as a name for a type of legal system: the type of legal system that existed in ancient Rome and that

[8] *See* note 6 *supra.*

[9] *See generally* Glendon, Gordon & Osakwe at 53–57.

[10] *See id.* at 58–60.

has spread to many nations in Europe, Latin America, Asia, and Africa. When we say that France has a civil-law legal system or that it is a member of the civil law family of nations, we are using the term in this very broad way.

Lawyers from many civil law nations use the term "civil law" in a narrower sense. They use the term to refer only to the civil codes and related laws, and typically, the civil codes refer only to private law — law that pertains to private duties, obligations, and rights. Also, even though these nations may now have legal systems that include many areas of law that may fall outside the civil codes, such as public law, administrative law, and regulatory law, lawyers from many civil-law legal systems often still see the civil code as forming the core of the legal system — its fundamental root.[11]

Lawyers in the United States use the term "civil law" in a very different way in the U.S. legal system. Here, it refers to all law that is not criminal law. For example, if Company A sues Company B, the lawsuit is "civil litigation" because it does not involve criminal law. For civil litigation, federal courts use a body of rules known as the Federal Rules of Civil Procedure, and the rules apply to all cases in the federal court system that do not involve criminal law (federal courts apply the Federal Rules of Criminal Procedure to criminal law cases).

Finally, depending upon the American cases that you read, you might find an opinion that discusses "civility," and whether or not the parties or opposing counsel are "civil" to each other. In this situation, the courts are referring to politeness and professional behavior, and the opinion likely criticizes one or both of the parties and their lawyers for behavior that is impolite and/or unprofessional.

QUESTIONS FOR DISCUSSION

The *jus commune* was a blend of ancient Roman law principles and customary medieval law. Similarly, during the codification period, many countries drafted and adopted civil codes that were a blend of received law and local, customary law.

1. If you come from a country that is in the civil law family of nations, how would you describe your country's civil code to lawyers from other countries? Is it a blend of received law and customary law?

2. Was your country's civil code influenced by another country's civil code, such as the French Civil Code of 1804 or the German Civil Code of 1896?

3. In the 20th and 21st centuries, U.S. law has influenced the law of many civil-law nations. Has it influenced the law of your country? If so, in what areas of the law?

---

[11] *See id.* at 61–62.

B. COMPARING AND CONTRASTING CIVIL LAW SYSTEMS AND THE U.S. LEGAL SYSTEM

In the previous chapter, we described the U.S. legal system as a "mixed" common law system because it shares many of its characteristics with civil-law systems. For example, both the United States and almost all countries with civil-law systems have written constitutions. Like the United States, some civil-law systems also have federal systems, with both national and regional or state governments, and perhaps national and regional or state constitutions as well. Also, like civil-law systems, federal and state legislatures in the United States have drafted large bodies of statutory law, some of which are even called codes. For example, the body of federal statutes is compiled under the name "United States Code," and there is also the "Uniform Commercial Code" (UCC), a comprehensive codification of commercial contract law that 49 of the 50 states have enacted, and the other state has partially enacted.[12]

Nevertheless, as shown below, there are many differences between civil-law systems and the U.S. legal system, from the sources of law to the court system, trial procedures, and the roles of judges and attorneys in the system. While the sub-sections below summarize features that are common to many civil-law countries, the great variety among the legal systems in the civil-law family of nations means that these features may or may not be true for any particular civil-law country.[13]

1. Sources of Law

a. Primary Sources of Law

Civil Law Systems: Almost all civil-law countries have a code as the basis of their law. Countries may describe their bodies of statutory law as a compilation of separate codes (e.g., a civil code, a commercial code, a criminal code, etc.), and/or they may generally refer to the entire body of statutory law as "the Code."[14] Codes are typically both comprehensive and systematic, and they are enacted at one time. Revisions may be periodic, and new additions to the Code are enacted as they are needed. Almost all civil-law nations have a written national or federal constitution, and some also have written regional or state constitutions.

U.S. Legal System: The U.S. has more sources of law than civil-law nations. In addition to the federal Constitution and the 50 state constitutions, as well as the federal and state bodies of statutes and administrative regulations, court decisions are a source of primary law. Amendments to constitutions and new statutes are drafted as needed. Unlike civil law systems, the bodies of state and federal statutes are not comprehensive. For example, most tort and contract law is still common law, although

---

[12] Louisiana is the only state that has not completely adopted the UCC. Louisiana is also highly unusual because it has a hybrid civil-law/common-law system and a body of statutes that was originally based on the French Civil Code of 1804.

[13] If you come from a country that has a civil law system, consider this as you read: Does my country's legal system share these "general" civil-law features?

[14] For convenience, we will refer to the entire body of a civil-law nation's statutory law as "the Code."

states have enacted the UCC for commercial contract law.

b. Secondary Sources of Law

Civil Law Systems: Jurists, who are important legal experts, publish commentaries on the meanings of Code provisions, and on how the courts should interpret and apply the Code. Although their texts are not a primary source of law, they are doctrine and form an essential part of the law. Students study jurists' writing to learn what the law is; judges study it to ensure the consistency of their opinions; and legislators use it to ensure that any new additions to the Code will be consistent with the existing parts.

U.S. Legal System: There is nothing similar to jurists in the U.S. system. Although law professors and other legal scholars conduct legal research and publish many scholarly articles and books on the law, their work is typically not seen as very authoritative by U.S. courts or practicing attorneys. Attorneys use legal encyclopedias, treatises, hornbooks, digests, and articles to learn about areas of the law that are less familiar to them, and they also use these secondary sources as "finding tools" to locate the primary sources of law that they need to persuade a court or draft a document.

2. Court Systems

a. Structure

Civil Law Systems: Court systems are often specialized and independent of each other, and each system may have its own trial and appellate courts. For example, there may be constitutional courts, administrative courts, and courts for specialized areas of practice, such as family law or commercial law.

U.S. Legal System: There are courts of general jurisdiction in both the state and federal court systems, and they typically each have three levels: a trial court, an intermediate appellate court, and the highest appellate court, usually called the Supreme Court. There are also administrative courts and specialized courts in both the state and federal systems, but they are usually related to the three-level system of courts of general jurisdiction and may "feed into" them when parties appeal their decisions.

b. The Role of Courts in the Legal System

Civil Law Systems: Courts apply the relevant Code provision(s) to the case before them. The courts follow established doctrine and principles of jurisprudence in a legally scientific process that does not focus on a judge's discretion or power to interpret the law.

U.S. Legal System: Courts interpret the relevant statutory or constitutional provision(s) and apply them to the case before them, generally by analyzing the language of the statute and by looking at precedent to understand how courts have interpreted and applied the statute.

Where there is no statute that is relevant to the issue, the court determines what the most relevant common-law precedent is and applies the relevant common-law rules to the case. There is more emphasis on a judge's discretion or power to interpret the law, and judges also have the power to make law though their opinions.

c. The Legal Effects of Courts' Opinions

Civil Law Systems: A court's opinion resolves the issue for the parties before the court, but does not bind the decisions made by future courts. In other words, cases typically do not have precedential value and are not considered primary sources of law.

More recently, judicial opinions have become more important in many civil-law systems. In effect, the decisions provide commentary on the meaning of the Code section that is at issue. The concept of precedent is thus developing in some civil-law systems, at least in a limited way, but judicial decisions typically do not bind other courts. Rather, courts may look at earlier decisions for guidance and try to keep the new decisions consistent with the older ones, although it is not mandatory.

U.S. Legal System: A court's opinion resolves the issue for the parties before the court, and may also bind the decisions made by future courts. Cases have precedential value and are considered primary sources of law. Even when there is a statute that is relevant to a legal issue, courts also look to precedent to understand how to interpret and apply the statute.

This leads to another major difference between the systems: Because courts in the United States must follow precedent, and because the body of case law in American jurisdictions is both huge and constantly evolving, legal research is typically more complicated and time-consuming in the U.S. legal system than it is in civil-law systems.

3. Trial Procedures

a. Trial Courts

Civil Law Systems: The judge plays the central role as both the questioner and finder of fact. There is no jury in most civil-law systems. The parties submit their evidence to the court, and the judge asks the questions. Thus, lawyers have a comparatively limited role at trial. A series of hearings takes place over a period of time.

U.S. Legal System: The lawyers for each party play a central role at trials. Before the trial, they conduct the factual investigations, exchanging evidence with each other in a process called **discovery**, which can last for months or even several years. The judge plays a more limited role, more like the referee in a sports match.

At trial, the lawyers for each party question their own witnesses and cross-examine each other's witnesses. Defendants have a constitutional right to a jury in criminal trials, and each party has a constitutional right to a jury in many types of civil trials (although there is no right to a jury with equitable claims).

A jury trial is a continuous event which could last from as little as one day to many months, depending upon the number and complexity of the legal and factual issues in dispute. Judges "run" the trial, as a referee runs a sports match, by controlling the proceedings. They make legal rulings during the trial and instruct the jury as to what the relevant law is, and the jury determines the facts. In a **bench trial**, there is no jury, and the judge determines both the law and the facts.

b. Appellate Courts

Civil Law Systems: Appellate courts consider both the facts and the law, granting little deference to the trial court's rulings. In some cases, intermediate appellate courts might ask for new testimony, evidence, and expert opinions. The highest courts, however, only hear questions of law and do not investigate the facts further.

U.S. Legal System: Appellate courts have no authority to collect new evidence. They may only review the issues, facts, and evidence that have been preserved for their review in the trial court record. There are different standards of review for findings of fact and findings of law. The appellate court's review of the trial court's factual findings is highly deferential, but the standard of review for the legal findings is **de novo**, meaning it is a "new" determination and there is no deference.

4. The Roles of Practicing Attorneys

Civil Law Systems: Many civil law systems use the terms "Advocates" and "Notaries" to describe different legal functions. Advocates represent clients in court and give them legal advice. Notaries draft, authenticate, and preserve legal documents.

U.S. Legal System: Unlike England's common law system, where "barristers" go to court and "solicitors" perform non-courtroom work such as drafting legal documents and preparing for trial, all American lawyers with active bar licenses may perform the full range of attorney work. In other words, all practicing lawyers in the U.S. may go to court, advise clients, and draft legal documents. Usually, lawyers tend to specialize in either **litigation** (work related to lawsuits and trials) or **transactional law** (advising and representing clients in business transactions and drafting legal documents), but nothing prevents a lawyer from doing both kinds of legal work.

C. COMMON LAW/CIVIL LAW CONTRASTS: A CONCLUSION

Although the previous section has shown that there are many differences between the legal systems of civil-law countries and the common law system that we use in the United States, there are also many similarities, particularly in substantive law.

Both types of systems work with constitutions, statutes, and regulations. The bodies of statutes in U.S. state law and federal law are not as comprehensive as the Code of a civil-law country, because they have "holes" that are filled by the common law. Nevertheless, legislatures continue to write new statutes every year, and most **cases** that are in the U.S. state and federal court systems today involve at least one claim that is based on statutory law. Indeed, some federal court and state court opinions even refer to the common law in the past tense, by which the judges are referring to the time when, unlike today, the law in the United States was based more on common law than on statutes. Similarly, although cases in civil-law systems generally do not have precedential value, their importance is increasing, and the concept of precedent is developing. Thus, over time, the two great legal systems are increasingly beginning to resemble each other.

Moreover, as international trade, international organizations and rule-making bodies, and international law continue to develop and expand, national laws are harmonizing in many areas, such as intellectual property. In the European Union ("EU"), for example, many laws of the individual nations are harmonizing with each other, and the EU's growing legal regime is arguably a hybrid of civil-law and common-law doctrines, approaches, and structures.

Thus, while you study law in the U.S., you will likely find that the substantive legal doctrines that you are learning are often similar to those of your country, or at least will not seem very surprising. What *will* seem different, however, is the approach to analyzing and resolving legal issues.

You will be reading many judicial opinions.[15] This may be a relatively new experience for you. At first, it may seem strange: you might wonder *why are they having me read so many cases? Where is the law*? It's important to always remember that you will find the legal rules that you need to learn in the cases, whether the rule is (1) a statute or regulation that is quoted in the case, (2) a judge-made rule that helps the court to interpret the statute or regulation and apply it to the facts of the case, or (3) a judge-made common law rule. All of these are the law.

It's also important to understand that simply memorizing rules of law is not the main focus of studying law here. Rather, U.S. law schools focus on the process of analyzing and resolving legal issues, or what lawyers in the United States like to call "thinking like a lawyer."[16] How do we find the relevant rules of law, understand what they mean, and apply them to the facts of our legal issue? That's really the focus. Over time, the law that pertains to a legal issue may change, but the process of analyzing and resolving legal issues is consistent, and you will do well in your U.S. law school classes if you follow the approach to analyzing and resolving legal issues that U.S. lawyers use.

---

[15] U.S. lawyers often refer to written judicial opinions as "cases," and they refer to the judge-made rules of law that come from cases as "case law."

[16] As a student who already has a law degree and perhaps many years of legal practice experience in your country, you already know very well what it means to think like a lawyer in your legal system. However, in the context of the mixed common law system that we use in the United States, the process of thinking like a lawyer may be somewhat similar to what you do in your country, but it will not be the same. Flexibility and a willingness to try something new and different will greatly help you here.

QUESTIONS FOR DISCUSSION

In Section B of this chapter, we compared and contrasted features that many civil-law systems share with the mixed common-law system that we use in the United States.

1. Due to the great variety of legal systems that fall within the civil law family of nations, the general descriptions here may or may not be completely accurate for any individual civil-law country.

If you come from a civil-law country, does the general description of civil-law system features here accurately describe your country's legal system? If not, what does your country do differently?

2. These descriptions of certain features of the U.S. legal system were general introductions, and you will learn about each of these areas in greater depth in later chapters. Did you find any of these descriptions surprising? If so, what was surprising about them?

Chapter Review

- Roman law was preserved by the Byzantine Emperor Justinian in the sixth century, and to some extent by the Germanic tribes who conquered Rome and mixed it together with their own customary law. It also influenced the canon law of the Catholic Church. Roman law helped to form the civil-law system.
- In medieval Europe, the study of ancient Roman law was revived at the University of Bologna in Italy, and students who studied there spread throughout Europe for centuries. The resulting mixture of the received Roman law and local customary law was known as the *jus commune.*
- In the 17th and 18th centuries, the development of national codes of law began, and began to spread throughout the world.
- The French Civil Code of 1804 and the German Civil Code of 1896 influenced the codes of many countries.
- Civil codes initially focused on the rights, obligations, and duties of individuals, and dealt with such areas as property, contract law, and family law. More recently, codes have expanded with the development of public law and regulatory law.
- The term "civil law" refers to civil-law legal systems in general, and more specifically to the civil codes. In the United States, "civil law" refers to non-criminal law. Also, "civility" refers to professional, polite behavior of counsel and parties.
- The United States has growing bodies of statutes that are similar to civil-law codes, but less comprehensive. Similarly, cases are becoming more important in many civil-law nations, and the concept of precedent is beginning to emerge. Moreover, some national law is harmonizing due to increases in international trade, governance, and law. Thus, the common-law and civil-law legal systems are growing more similar. Some important differences between civil-law systems and the U.S. legal system include:

(1) Sources of law: The U.S. system considers judge-made rules to be law as well as statutes, and precedent can bind later courts;

(2) Court systems: Unlike specialized civil-law courts, U.S. state and federal court systems feature three-tier courts of general jurisdiction, although some specialized courts also exist;

(3) Trial procedures: Civil-law courts collect evidence and question the parties, while counsel play this role in the U.S.; there is a right to jury trials for criminal defendants and both parties in many civil trials in the U.S.; and intermediate appellate courts may sometimes ask for new evidence in some civil-law countries, but not in the U.S.; and

(4) In many civil-law countries, Advocates represent clients in court and give them legal advice, while Notaries draft, authenticate, and preserve legal documents. In the United States, all active members of the bar can represent clients in court, counsel clients, and draft legal documents, although many lawyers specialize either in litigation or in transactional work.

Chapter 3

THE CONSTITUTION AND THE U.S. SYSTEM OF GOVERNMENT

Chapter Preview

This chapter describes the system of government of the United States. The chapter discusses:

- The early pre-Constitution government, and how the Constitution set out the structure of the government;
- The country's two levels of government — the federal government and the 50 state governments;
- The functions of the executive, legislative, and judicial branches of government, at both the federal and state levels; and
- The relationships between each of the three branches, as well as the relationships between the federal and state governments.

As law students in a U.S. law school, you are learning about the laws and legal system of the United States. Before you can understand those laws, however, you must first understand the design and structure of the United States government. Without that essential context, nothing that you learn will make sense.

Although the United States has one system of government, it is in another sense 51 governments — the federal government at the national level, and each of the 50 state governments at the state level. All 51 governments have three co-equal branches: legislative, executive, and judicial.[1] We will look at the three branches of government, and discuss the role of each, and their relationships with each other.

We will also use two terms that you may hear in other classes — **federalism** and **separation of powers**. Federalism refers to the division of the U.S. governmental system into two levels, federal and state, and the relationships between those two levels of government. Separation of powers refers in part to the division of governmental responsibilities among each of the three branches of government, but it also refers to the relationship between them and the principle that no one branch may completely control the other two branches. The Constitution grants specific powers to each branch to allow it to prevent the other branches from exceeding their Constitutionally-granted powers. This democracy-protecting principle is also known as "checks and balances." After looking at how the Constitution lays out the structure of the government, we will consider federalism and the separation of powers.

A. HOW THE CONSTITUTION ESTABLISHES THE GOVERNMENT

1. Pre-Constitution

The Second Continental Congress, which met in 1776, included delegates from all 13 colonies who opposed British authority over the American colonies. The delegates unanimously signed and adopted the Declaration of Independence, and they also adopted a resolution to prepare a document that would become the Articles of Confederation, which they eventually ratified in 1781. The heading over the opening sentence of the Declaration of Independence describes it as "The unanimous Declaration of the thirteen united States of America."[2]

Modern Americans read this heading without any surprise because they are citizens of the United States of America, and assume that the term had the same meaning then. In 1776, however, there was no such country; rather, there were 13 colonies which were attempting to unite to gain their independence from England. Note that the delegates who met in 1776 formed the "Second Continental Congress," with "continent" referring generally to North America, rather than to a specific term for the 13 colonies.

---

[1] There are also governments for parts of the United States that do not belong to any state, such as Washington, D.C. (the nation's capital), and certain islands. In addition, there are local governments for counties and cities, some of which also contain legislative, executive, and judicial branches.

[2] The Declaration of Independence is available online at http://usconstitution.net/declar.html.

Although we should not place too much importance on capitalization rules, perhaps, the Declaration of Independence's heading referred to the 13 colonies as the "united States," not the "United States." Is there a difference? Without the capital letter, "united" is an adjective describing the 13 "States," which suggests that at least some of the founders may have seen it more as a federation of 13 different states than a unified country (in other words, more like the European Union is today: a confederation of independent countries).

The 13 colonies fought together to defeat England, and we name July 4, 1776 as the founding date of the United States because the Declaration of Independence was signed on that date. However, it took five years for the Congress to draft, debate, and ratify the first attempt to set forth the system of government for the new nation.

Congress ratified the Articles of Confederation two years before the fighting ended, and three years before the Revolutionary War officially ended with the signing of the Treaty of Paris in 1784. Although the war was over, the new country's problems were just beginning. The Articles of Confederation was the product of revolutionaries who passionately disliked central authority because of their fight with Parliament and King George III. They distrusted a strong central government so much that the only national government that the Articles of Confederation created was Congress. There was no chief executive such as a president or a prime minister, and any action required the agreement of 9 out of the 13 states, each of whom had different economies and different interests.[3] Because the revolutionaries had resented the British government's control over the economy and the high taxes that it imposed on the colonists, the Articles of Confederation gave the new government no power to tax or to regulate commerce. Moreover, the Congress had no authority to enforce its laws.

Because of the extraordinarily weak "central government," the new country had serious problems from the beginning. Some of the states ignored provisions of the Treaty of Paris of 1784, and the government had no way to enforce the provisions and to make the states follow them. As a result, the British also ignored many of the treaty's provisions, and other friendly foreign countries such as France would not enter into treaties with a new country that did not have an effective central government.

Even worse, trade wars broke out between the states because there was no governmental structure that had authority to regulate trade. States made high tariffs that protected their businesses against competition from businesses in other states, and trade between the states actually decreased, at a time when the new country needed it to increase.

Americans are a pragmatic people, and given that the problems were so severe — indeed, they threatened the future of the new country — the states decided to meet in Philadelphia in 1787 to discuss a new governmental charter that could fix the problems. The meeting became the Constitutional Convention.

---

[3] The Northern States (also known as New England) had more urban, industrial economies. The Southern States had large farms and little industry, and the Mid-Atlantic States had a mixture of industrial cities and smaller farms.

2. The Constitution

Experience had shown the delegates to the Constitutional Convention that a very weak central government did not work, but they had great disagreements about just how strong the new government should be. There were two groups: the Federalists, who wanted a strong national government, and their opponents, the Anti-Federalist or "states' rights" delegates, who wanted to strengthen the national government just enough to address the great problems caused by the Articles of Confederation, but no more.

Although the Federalists generally prevailed and the Constitution was ratified on March 4, 1789, the Federalists had to make numerous compromises on its language (just as legislatures in the United States often still must do today to pass major new laws). Many Anti-Federalists opposed the Constitution because it did not contain a Bill of Rights. Federalists at first opposed a Bill of Rights because they were concerned that, over time, citizens' rights would be limited only to those contained in the Bill of Rights.[4] The Constitution went to the 13 states for ratification, but 5 of 13 states demanded a Bill of Rights along with their votes to ratify it. James Madison drafted the Bill of Rights, and it was ratified in 1791 as the first 10 Amendments to the Constitution.

The Constitution is the world's oldest written constitution, and it is also one of the shortest. Depending upon the format of how it is printed (i.e., the font, the size of the print, the margins, and the spacing), the seven Articles of the Constitution are approximately nine pages long, and the 27 Amendments are another seven pages.

The first three Articles lay out the structure of the federal government: Article I concerns the Legislative Branch, Article II the Executive Branch, and Article III the Judicial Branch. Article IV declares that the government shall guarantee a republican form of government to each of the states, and it sets out obligations of the states to each other, such as that they must honor each other's laws. Article V describes the difficult process of amending the Constitution. Article VI contains provisions that include the Supremacy Clause, which states that the Constitution, laws, and treaties of the United States are the supreme law of the land and that they are binding upon all judges in state courts, regardless of what that state's constitution or laws might state. Finally, Article VII states that nine of the 13 states must ratify the Constitution for it to take effect.

Article I is the longest and most detailed of the first three Articles (it has 10 sections, while Article II has 4, and Article III has only 3). The order and the number of sections for each of the first three Articles likely say something about how the Founding Fathers who drafted the Constitution (often called the "Framers") viewed each of the three branches of government. It is no accident that the Legislature is described first and in the most detail, because the Framers were concerned about the possibility of a strong executive becoming a new king and gaining the powers of a tyrant. Thus, they saw a strong Congress as an essential protector of liberty.

---

[4] This problem was addressed in the Bill of Rights, where the Ninth Amendment states that the rights of the people are not limited to the rights enumerated in the Constitution.

Article I sets out: the bicameral Congress, with two houses (the House of Representatives and the Senate); how long the terms of office are and the minimum age requirements for legislators; the procedures for how Congress drafts laws; the powers that Congress shall have and the limits on those powers; and the powers that the states are prohibited from exercising (which are generally powers that belong to Congress and to the federal government). It ends by granting Congress authority to ". . . make all Laws which shall be necessary and proper for carrying into Execution the foregoing Powers, and all other Powers vested by this Constitution in the Government of the United States, or in any Department or Officer thereof."[5]

Articles II and III are less detailed. Among other things, Article II lays out the main powers and duties of the President, such as Commander-in-Chief of the armed forces; the power to make treaties, with the Senate's advice and consent; and the power to appoint federal judges and government officers, such as the heads of departments. Article III does not set out the full system of federal courts that exists today. Instead, it simply vests power in the Supreme Court and "in such inferior Courts as the Congress may from time to time ordain and establish."[6] It also gives a description of the Supreme Court's original and appellate jurisdiction.

B. THE THREE BRANCHES OF GOVERNMENT

As stated above, the federal, state, and even many local (county and **municipal** (city)) governments have three branches: legislative, executive, and judicial. We generally describe their functions as follows: the Legislative Branch *enacts* the law, the Executive Branch *enforces* the law, and the Judicial Branch *interprets* the law. As we will discuss in the next section, this is an over-simplification, but it accurately describes the fundamental purpose of each branch.

1. The Legislative Branch

a. Numbers of Representatives and Terms of Office

The Congress has two houses as a result of a compromise made between the "large" states and the "small" states. The states with large populations wanted Congress to be based on population, so that states with larger populations would have more representatives. The states with small populations were worried that if representation in Congress were based solely on population, they would have no voice in debates, and the laws that Congress enacted would tend to favor the large states.

As a result of the compromise that the Framers reached between the two types of states, Congress has two houses, the House of Representatives (the "House") and the Senate. The representation in the House is based on population, and in the Senate, each state has two senators,[7] regardless of their population. Thus, there are 100 senators because there are 50 states. Senators were originally chosen by state

[5] U.S. Const. art.I, § 18.

[6] U.S. Const. art. III, § 1.

[7] Representatives in the Senate are called "senators." Representatives in the House are called

legislatures, but the 17th Amendment, which was ratified in 1913, provided for their direct election by popular vote.

In the House, there are 435 representatives, and they are proportional to the population. Each state must have at least one representative, and some states have many. For example, California, the state with the largest population, currently has 53 of the 435 representatives, whereas Wyoming, which has the smallest population, has only one.

The current number of 435 representatives was fixed by law early in the 20th century, and as the U.S. population continues to increase, it is measured every 10 years by a census. Based on the 2010 census, the average size of a congressional district is currently about 710,000 residents. Depending on the results of the census, most states keep the same number of representatives that they had in the previous decade, but some states may slightly gain or lose representatives.[8]

The Framers were concerned with avoiding the "tyranny of the majority," so they designed the terms of office for members of Congress so that not everyone in Congress is elected at the same time. For example, House representatives have two year terms, and all 435 House seats are up for election every two years. In contrast, senators serve for six years, and only one-third of them are up for reelection in any two-year period. Also, as the President has a four-year term, there is not a presidential election every time that there is an election in the House. This way, if a dramatic event causes the people to vote overwhelmingly for one party in the following election, only one-third of senators will be elected. The other two-thirds of the senators, who were elected in previous elections, are likely to provide stability, as is the President, if he or she is not up for reelection.

b. Powers of Congress

In another compromise between the Federalists and the Anti-Federalists, Section 8 of Article I sets out the "enumerated" (explicitly stated) powers of Congress. The Framers gave Congress the power to legislate in areas where they saw problems in having the states legislate, such as those seen under the Articles of Confederation. For example, the Constitution gives the Congress power to collect taxes, to issue money, to regulate commerce between the states, to raise a military, to declare war, to spend money for the general welfare of the country, to establish a postal system to deliver the mail, to confirm or reject Presidential appointments, and to create federal courts below the Supreme Court.

"congressmen," "congresswomen," or "representatives."

[8] Thus, the district boundaries for the House of Representatives must be redrawn every 10 years to keep the number of residents per district similar. The party who is in charge of each state's legislature tends to draw the boundary lines for that state in ways that are favorable to their party's chances of winning the most seats. Political scientists believe that one of the main reasons why Congress is presently so polarized between the Democrats and the Republicans is that the parties are using computers to scientifically design districts that are either more conservative (favoring Republicans) or liberal (favoring Democrats). If the candidates have less need to be moderate to win election, perhaps they are also less moderate after arriving in the House.

The 10th Amendment reserves the powers that are not delegated to the federal government in the Constitution (or prohibited to the states by the Constitution), to the states or to the people. This means that the states have the residual power that is not explicitly granted to the federal government, or prohibited to the states, by the Constitution.

The Constitution did not need to enumerate the states' powers because all of the states already had state constitutions before the drafting of the Constitution. The only thing that the Constitution did was to limit some state powers and give them to the federal government, and to require state court judges to follow the Constitution and laws passed by Congress, even if they conflicted with existing state laws. Other than that, the states retained the powers that they already had. The 10th Amendment merely confirmed this situation.

c. Committees, Sub-Committees, Agencies, and the Legislative Process

Congress has the power to draft legislation and to investigate, and it uses committees and sub-committees for both purposes. The Senate has 17 committees with 70 sub-committees, and the House has 23 committees, with 104 sub-committees. Congress also has a small number of agencies, such as the Government Accountability Office ("GAO"), formerly known as the General Accounting Office; the Library of Congress; the Congressional Budget Office, and the Government Printing Office.

The legislative process begins with a proposed law called a **bill**. Although anyone can write a bill, a member of Congress must propose it. The bill goes to the appropriate sub-committee, which holds hearings on it, investigates it, possibly amends it, and votes on it. If the sub-committee approves the bill, it then moves on to the full committee, where the same process is repeated. If the bill passes out of the committee, the leadership of the House or Senate decides whether to introduce it to the full house, where it is debated, possibly amended, and voted on. House and Senate debate rules are very different — debate is limited in the House, but senators may discuss a bill for hours or delay it with a process called a **filibuster**, which may be defeated with a supermajority of 60 votes. In both houses of Congress, a simple majority vote is all that is needed to pass the bill.

Before a bill goes to the President, both houses of Congress must approve it. If the bill has different language in the two houses due to amendments in one of the houses, a committee that comprises members of both houses works out a final version of the bill, which both houses then vote on.

When both houses have approved a bill, it goes to the President for his or her signature. If the President likes the bill, he or she signs it and it becomes a law. If the President does not like the bill, he or she **vetoes** it, and it does not becomes law unless Congress can **override** the veto. They do so by having two-thirds of each house vote for the law again. If the bill gets two-thirds of the votes in both houses, it becomes law without the President's signature.

The President has two other options: If he or she does nothing, the bill becomes law 10 days later. However, if the President does nothing and Congress adjourns (ends its session) when fewer than 10 days have passed, the bill does not become law. This is called a **pocket veto**. Then the bill dies, and Congress would have to start all over again after it returns.

d. State Legislative Branches

Like the U.S. Congress, 49 of the 50 states have bicameral legislatures, with a house of representatives and a senate (only one state, Nebraska, has a unicameral legislature).

2. The Executive Branch

a. The Federal Government

Although all three branches of the federal government have evolved since the founding of the country, perhaps no branch has evolved as much as the Executive Branch. The Constitution refers to the President, the Vice President, the "public Ministers and Consuls," "all other Officers of the United States," and "Heads of Departments."[9]

Perhaps due to disagreements between the Framers, the Constitution did not specify the departments of the Executive Branch, but left their creation to Congress. So far, Congress has created 15 Executive Branch departments,[10] and the head of each department is called a "secretary." Collectively, the secretaries form a body of senior advisors to the President called the "Cabinet."[11] Also, because the President is Commander-in-Chief of the armed forces, the Army, Navy, Air Force, and Marines are part of the Executive Branch.

Finally, the Executive Branch contains organizations that were never mentioned in the Constitution. For example, the Executive Office of the President contains a dozen organizations such as the Office of Management and Budget and the Council of Economic Advisers, and there are several dozen executive agencies and government corporations: the Central Intelligence Agency ("CIA"), Federal Communications Commission ("FCC"), Federal Trade Commission ("FTC"), Securities and Exchange Commission ("SEC"), United States Postal Service, and many others. Legislation enacted by the Congress often gives these agencies the authority to **promulgate** regulations that they use to enforce or implement the legislation.

All told, the Executive Branch currently has more than four million employees, including the military.[12] Given that the United States only had about seven million people at the time that the Constitution was drafted, the Framers would certainly be

---

[9] U.S. Const. art. II, § 2, cl. 2.

[10] The 15 Executive Branch departments are: Agriculture, Commerce, Defense, Education, Energy, Health and Human Services, Homeland Security, Housing and Urban Development, Interior, Justice, Labor, State, Transportation, Treasury, and Veterans Affairs.

[11] In parliamentary systems, the heads of departments are called "ministers." For example, the counterpart of the U.S. Secretary of State is called the Foreign Minister.

[12] http://www.whitehouse.gov/our-government/executive-branch.

shocked if they could see the size of the federal government today!

b. State Executive Branches

As with the Executive Branch in the federal government, each state has a chief executive called the **governor**, and various departments with the authority to promulgate regulations. Unlike the federal government, however, not all of the department heads are appointed by the governor. Many states have their residents elect important state officials such as the Secretary of State or the Attorney General, and it is possible for them to be from a different political party than the governor. Thus, it is fair to say that governors are not as powerful at the state level as Presidents are at the federal level, because they do not have the ability to appoint many of the most powerful state officials.

3. The Judicial Branch

As shown above, the Constitution created the United States Supreme Court and such lower federal courts as the Congress may establish. Since then, Congress has established a three-tiered federal court system, with federal trial courts and intermediate federal appellate courts below the Supreme Court, as well as a limited number of specialized federal courts.[13]

Similarly, at the state level, most state court systems have three tiers as well, although nine states with smaller populations currently have no intermediate courts of appeal.[14] In the trial courts, the judge or jury hears the evidence, determines what the facts are, and enters a judgment.[15] Appellate courts determine whether the trial court applied the correct law and whether the decision had sufficient evidence to support it. Appellate courts do not hear evidence in a trial; they must rely on the record that was developed in the trial court.

The highest courts, the United States Supreme Court and the highest state courts (also known as the "courts of last resort"), hear only the most important cases from the lower courts (typically from the intermediate appellate courts at the federal level and in 41 states, or from the trial courts in the other 9 states). Although the state courts of last resort are usually called the "Supreme Court," there are exceptions such as New York, where the highest appellate court is called the New York Court of Appeals.

Typically, trial court decisions bind only the parties before the court and do not have precedential value. The decisions of the intermediate appellate courts and the courts of last resort *do* have precedential value and are sources of primary law.

---

[13] Chapter 4 will cover the federal and state court systems in greater detail.

[14] The nine states without intermediate courts of appeal are Maine, Montana, Nevada, New Hampshire, Rhode Island, South Dakota, Vermont, West Virginia, and Wyoming.

[15] There are a limited number of situations in both federal and certain state courts where a trial court may function as an appellate court by hearing an appeal from an administrative court or another court of limited jurisdiction.

QUESTIONS FOR DISCUSSION

As shown above, the federal government, each of the 50 state governments, and even some local governments all have legislative, executive, and judicial branches. At the local level, city government is called "municipal government," the chief executive is generally called the "mayor," the legislature is called the "City Council," and local statutes are called **ordinances**.

Although many local governments do not have judicial branches because the courts are part of the state court system, some cities or counties may have local courts of limited jurisdiction such as traffic courts or small claims courts.

1. As we have seen, federalism arose in the United States because the country began as 13 colonies who joined together to rebel against the central government in England and who wanted to retain as much local government control as possible after independence. While the Framers saw the need to have a unified national government, they also wanted the states to preserve their authority over many aspects of daily life.

Does your country have a federal system of government similar to that of the United States? If so, how does it allocate (assign) power between the federal government and the state/regional government?

2. Is your country's system of government divided into legislative, executive, and judicial branches? Are they seen as co-equal?

3. What do you see as the advantages of a federal system of government? What are the disadvantages?

C. RELATIONSHIPS BETWEEN THE BRANCHES: SEPARATION OF POWERS AND CHECKS AND BALANCES

1. Separation of Powers

As stated above, we traditionally say that the Legislative Branch *enacts* the law, the Executive Branch *enforces* the law, and the Judicial Branch *interprets* the law, but this is an over-simplification. In fact, it was never completely accurate, and it's even less accurate today.

As society has grown more complex and the role of government in society has increased, the limited government that is envisioned in the Constitution no longer exists. Each branch of government performs multiple functions, and as we shall see, they often overlap. Thus, "separation" of powers is a misleading term. Perhaps it would be better to refer to a *distribution* of powers that spreads them among the three branches.

a. All Three Branches Make the Law

Only the Legislative Branch enacts law, meaning that only a legislature can draft and pass statutes for the executive (President or governor) to sign. However, the Legislative Branch and the Judicial Branch both make law as well.

The Executive Branch does so in two ways. First, pursuant to authority given to them by statutes, Executive Branch agencies promulgate regulations. Agencies employ experts in that field, and unlike the typically general rules that statutes provide, the regulations are likely to be specific.

For example, Congress has drafted a statute to protect domestic animals from dangerous or worthless medicines or other biologic agents. This statute is found in Title 21 of the United States Code, which is divided into 51 areas of law called "titles." Title 21 contains statutes that deal with food and drugs. Section 151 prohibits the preparation and sale of any worthless, contaminated, dangerous, or harmful virus, serum, toxin, or analogous product intended for use in the treatment of domestic animals, and no person, firm, or corporation shall prepare, sell, barter, exchange, or ship as aforesaid any virus, serum, toxin, or analogous product manufactured within the United States and intended for use in the treatment of domestic animals unless and until the said virus, serum, toxin, or analogous product shall have been prepared, under and in compliance with regulations prescribed by the Secretary of Agriculture, at an establishment holding an unsuspended and unrevoked license issued by the Secretary of Agriculture as hereinafter authorized.[16]

While the language of the statute may at first sound fairly specific, it is really not. Notice that it delegates to the Department of Agriculture the responsibility to promulgate regulations prescribing how the medicine or biologic agent shall be prepared, and also the responsibility to license and regulate the businesses that prepare and sell the medicines.

The Department of Agriculture (an agency in the Executive Branch) employs experts in this field, who write the specific regulations prescribing the conditions under which the medicines must be manufactured. Other experts in the Department of Agriculture write the regulations that pertain to licensing and regulating these businesses. Typically, federal and state agencies publish new regulations before they become effective, to provide for a "comment" period, where interested individuals, corporations, or other organizations have a chance to comment on the proposed regulations. Like the statutes that enable them, these regulations are primary law as soon as they take effect.

The federal government's regulations are published in the Code of Federal Regulations, which is much larger than the already-large United States Code. Thus, the Executive Branch works together with the Legislative Branch to make law by providing the regulations that the statutes envision. Together, both branches of government create the law — the Legislative Branch enacts the statutes that state the law, and Executive Branch agencies promulgate the regulations that specifically flesh out the law and enable its enforcement.

---

[16] 21 U.S.C. § 151 (2006).

Second, the Executive Branch also makes law when the President, with the assistance of the State Department, negotiates and signs treaties, which take effect after the Senate **ratifies** them by a two-thirds majority.

Finally, as we have already discussed, the Judicial Branch also makes law through its judicial opinions. Obviously, judges make law in common law decisions, where there are no statutes and judge-made rules constitute the law. But judges may also make law even when they interpret statutes. Here's how: Just as legislatures often enact statutes that delegate authority to agencies to promulgate regulations, legislatures also "delegate" authority to courts to give more specific meaning to general statutory language. Unlike statutes that expressly delegate authority to agencies, however, statutes generally do not expressly delegate authority to courts to interpret statutes. Rather, that authority exists because it is a core function of the Judicial Branch to interpret the law.

For example, statutes often use the word "reasonable," as when they require the government or private parties to make "reasonable efforts" or to take "reasonable measures," but the drafters of the statute typically do not provide a definition of "reasonable" in the statute. Instead, legislators expect judges to determine what constitutes "reasonable efforts" or "reasonable measures" in a given context. Statutes may intentionally have general, somewhat vague language, either because the legislators defer to the courts to work out the meaning of the statute in practice, or because the different legislators could not agree on more specific language, and kept the language vague in order to pass the bill.

Accordingly, judges often develop tests with several parts to help them to determine whether or not private parties or the government have met the requirements of the statute. If a statute requires "reasonable efforts," a court may develop, for example, a three-part test that determines what would constitute "reasonable efforts" in a given situation. These judge-made tests become rules of law that courts employ together with the relevant statute when analyzing a legal issue.

b. All Three Branches Enforce the Law

While it is the main responsibility of the Executive Branch to enforce the law, the other branches have some authority to enforce the law as well. It is the Judicial Branch's role to interpret the law in the context of civil disputes between parties, or when criminal defendants have been charged with crimes. However, when it "interprets the law," the court does more than simply explain what the law is — it pronounces a judgment that is legally binding upon the parties. By its very nature, a judgment enforces the law, whether by sending a defendant to prison, or by ordering one party to pay another a sum of money.

Similarly, the Legislative Branch sometimes plays a judicial role, and thus has authority to enforce the law in this way. For example, Congressional committees have the power to conduct investigations and issue subpoenas for witnesses to testify before them. Individuals who ignore congressional subpoenas to testify are subject to "contempt of Congress." More dramatically, if the House of Representatives votes to impeach the President, there is a trial in the Senate, and all Senators vote to convict or to acquit the President (a two-thirds vote is necessary to convict the President).

c. All Three Branches Interpret the Law

While it is the main responsibility of the Judicial Branch to interpret the law, the other branches have some authority to interpret the law as well. As described above, agencies have the power to make rules and to enforce them. Agencies also have the power to adjudicate whether parties have followed their regulations, through hearings before an administrative law judge of the relevant agency. Indeed, several agencies, such as the National Transportation Safety Board, do not promulgate regulations and have adjudication as their only purpose.

As described above, Congress also plays a judicial role in certain circumstances, such as the impeachment of the President, and interprets the law in accordance with that role.

More broadly, each branch of government must interpret the law in order to carry out their core functions. For example, Executive Branch agencies must interpret the law in order to carry out their enforcement functions, promulgate regulations, and adjudicate them. Similarly, Congress must interpret the law when it drafts new legislation, which must be constitutional and legal, and which should work together with existing law in a consistent and coherent way.

2. Checks and Balances

As we have seen, the Framers distributed power among the three branches of government to ensure that no one branch could threaten the freedom of the citizens by grabbing too much power. We commonly refer to this power-sharing plan by the name of "checks and balances." Under this design, the branches of government need to work together to carry out their work. The following are examples of checks and balances:

- Although the Senate and the House of Representatives can work together to pass a bill, the President has the power to veto the bill.
- Although the President has the authority to veto a bill, Congress can override the veto if each house votes to pass the bill by a two-thirds margin, thus making the bill become law without the President's signature.
- However a bill becomes law, the Executive Branch is responsible for enforcement, but it has some discretion as to how actively it will enforce the law.[17]
- Although the President is the Commander-in-Chief of the armed forces,

[17] For example, Colorado and Washington have recently passed laws that legalize the private use of marijuana by citizens who are over 21, and several other states have laws that allow the use of marijuana for medical purposes. All of these laws potentially conflict with federal law, which makes marijuana illegal. Because of the Constitution's Supremacy Clause, federal law preempts inconsistent state law. However, President Obama has indicated that the Justice Department has higher priorities than enforcing the federal law prohibiting marijuana in states that have legalized it, implying that the Justice Department will not enforce the federal law prohibiting marijuana in those states.

Congress has the power to declare war and to appropriate funds to pay for the war.

- The President has the power to appoint Supreme Court justices, judges on the lower federal courts, ambassadors, and other officers, but the Senate must vote to confirm the appointments.
- The President has the power to negotiate treaties, but the Senate must ratify them by a two-thirds margin, and Congress may also have to pass laws to give some of them effect in the United States.
- With "judicial review," courts have the power to invalidate laws by determining that they are unconstitutional. Although this power is not explicitly granted in the Constitution, an early Supreme Court decision, *Marbury v. Madison*,[18] held that judicial review is implicit in the Constitution.
- Congress may "overrule" judicial opinions by drafting or amending legislation so that a particular judicial opinion is no longer good law. Of course, this does not actually overrule the opinion — it changes the law going forward. Thus, while the opinion itself is still valid and binding on the parties, it will not have precedential value because the law has changed. Congress may not legislatively "overrule" opinions that concern the Constitution, however.
- The House of Representatives may vote to impeach the President, Vice President, and all civil officers of the United States, including Supreme Court justices and other federal judges, for "Treason, Bribery, or other High Crimes and Misdemeanors."[19] The trial is held in the Senate, and two-thirds of the Senators who are present must vote to convict.[20]

Finally, although this is not generally viewed as a check or balance, the government of the United States differs from parliamentary democracies by not requiring one party to have both a legislative majority and the chief executive.[21] While the President may be a member of the same political party as the majorities of the Senate and the House of Representatives, this is not a requirement. For example, in 2013, the President was a Democrat and Democrats controlled the Senate, but Republicans controlled the House. The possibility of a "divided government" in which no one political party has complete control, and the fact that not all of the government is elected in any one election due to different terms of office, further show the effort of the Framers to avoid the "tyranny of the majority."

---

[18] 5 U.S. 137 (1803).

[19] U.S. Const. art. II, § 4.

[20] U.S. Const. art. I, § 6.

[21] Typically, in a parliamentary democracy, if a party wins the majority of the seats or is able to form a coalition that has the majority of the seats in the legislature, it can place its leader as Prime Minister. In the United States, because there are separate elections for the President, the Senate, and the House of Representatives, a "divided government" can exist.

QUESTIONS FOR DISCUSSION

As we have seen, the Framers worked hard to achieve a balance in which the federal government had sufficient power to overcome the problems caused by the Articles of Confederation, but it did not dominate state governments and it did not have tyrannical power. With the Constitutional principles of separation of powers and checks and balances, the Framers tried to ensure that the three branches of government would need to work together to do the will of the people, and no one branch could dominate.

1. Over the past 100 years, we have seen a great increase in the size and power of the Executive Branch.

Do you think that Constitutional principles such as separation of powers and checks and balances still work, or has the Executive Branch become too powerful?

2. Are separation of powers and checks and balances constitutional principles in your country's government? Do they exist in a non-constitutional form? If they do not exist in any form, does your country's system of government have any other mechanisms to prevent a strong executive or political party from gaining absolute control of the government? If so, what does it have?

Chapter Review

- The Continental Congress ratified the Articles of Confederation in 1781, during the Revolutionary War. To ensure that a new tyrannical government could not arise in the new United States, representatives designed a weak central government that had no power to tax, to regulate commerce, or even to enforce its laws.
- The new United States struggled without an adequate central government, and representatives agreed on a new Constitution, which was ratified in 1789, along with the Bill of Rights (the first 10 Amendments), which was ratified in 1791.
- The Constitution balanced the desires of those who wanted a strong federal government with the desires of those who wanted to keep most authority in the hands of the state governments.
- The Constitution set up a system of government with three branches, the executive, the legislative, and the judicial. It gives the federal government certain limited and enumerated powers such as the ability to raise taxes, to regulate commerce between the states, to raise a military and to declare war, and to make all laws that are necessary and proper to exercise its powers.
- Broadly speaking, the Legislative Branch enacts the law, the Executive Branch enforces the law, and the Judicial Branch interprets the law. In practice however, these functions overlap.
- Federalism refers to the division of the U.S. governmental system into two levels, federal and state, and the relationships between those two levels of government.

- Like the federal government, all 50 states have constitutions and three branches of government.
- Over the past 100 years, the federal government, especially the Executive Branch, has grown in size and power, which causes tension with the Constitution.
- Under the Supremacy Clause of the Constitution, the Constitution, laws, and treaties of the United States are the supreme law of the land and bind all judges in state courts, regardless of what that state's constitution or laws might state.
- Separation of powers refers to the division of governmental responsibilities among each of the three branches of government, to the relationship between them and to the principle that no one branch may completely control the other two branches.
- The Constitution grants specific powers to each branch to help it to prevent the other branches from exceeding their Constitutionally-granted powers. The branches also need to work together to accomplish certain goals. This democracy-protecting principle is known as "checks and balances."

Chapter 4

THE THREE-TIERED U.S. COURT SYSTEM

Chapter Preview

This chapter concludes the introduction to the U.S. legal system by focusing on the federal and state court systems and how they work. The chapter discusses:

- The three-tiered court system, for both the federal courts and most state courts;
- The hierarchy of sources of law;
- The difference between mandatory (binding) and persuasive authority; and
- State-court and federal-court jurisdiction.

If you are a lawyer and/or law school graduate from a civil-law country, you may not have read many judicial opinions ("cases") in your legal studies. In a U.S. law school, however, you will spend much of your time reading and analyzing cases. Why? In the U.S. legal system, case law forms an essential part of the law for two reasons: (1) many areas of the law are still based on common law and the relevant rules of law come entirely from the cases; and (2) even when the law comes from statutes, lawyers must look both at the relevant statutes and at cases that construe the meanings of those statutes.

Cases that construe statutes show us how courts interpret the meaning of the statutes. Because of the principle of stare decisis, the cases also guide lawyers as to how future courts are likely to rule on that issue. Also, the cases often provide rules that the courts use to interpret the statute and to analyze the legal issues. Thus, an American lawyer cannot stop researching the law after he or she finds a relevant statute. Instead, he or she must also research case law to find out whether courts have developed rules for the statute, and to understand how courts interpret the statute.

Because you will be reading many cases, it is necessary to understand their context: whether it is a federal or state court case, what the level of the court is, what the source of the legal rule is, and in the context of a specific legal issue, whether the case is mandatory (binding) or persuasive precedent.

A. THE HIERARCHY OF SOURCES OF LAW

As we discussed in Chapter 2, the U.S. legal system has a variety of sources of law, ranging from the Constitution to the common law at the federal level, and from state constitutions to state common law at the state level. Because of the Supremacy Clause, federal law ranks higher than state law. Figure 4.1 shows the hierarchy of all sources of law from highest to lowest, with the federal Constitution at the top and state common law at the bottom.

Figure 4.1 Hierarchy of Sources of Law[1]

1. The federal Constitution
2. Federal statutes, court rules, and treaties
3. Federal agency rules and regulations
4. Federal common law
5. State constitutions
6. State statutes and court rules
7. State agency rules and regulations

[1] Hierachy taken from William Burnham, *Introduction to the Law and Legal System of the United States* 41 (5th ed., West 2011).

8. State common law

When different kinds of law share the same level, the more recent law prevails. For example, if the language of a federal statute (level 2) conflicts with the language of an international treaty that the United States has signed (also level 2), courts look to the more recent law to resolve the conflict. If the treaty is more recent than the statute, the treaty's terms prevail, but if the federal statute is more recent, its language would prevail.[2]

1. Where Does Case Law Fit on the Hierarchy?

This hierarchy lists federal common law at the bottom of the federal hierarchy (level 4), and state common law at the bottom of the state law hierarchy (level 8). As we've discussed, "common law" refers to judge-made law in this context, so cases that involve federal common law rules are in level 4, and cases that involves state common law rules are in level 8. Where do cases that interpret enacted law fall in the hierarchy? They share the same level of hierarchy as the enacted law that they interpret.

In other words, cases that interpret the federal Constitution are on the highest level, as we see when a court writes an opinion that states that a federal statute (level 2) is invalid because it violates the Constitution. Similarly, cases that interpret a federal statute are on level 2, cases that interpret federal regulations are on level 3, cases that interpret a state constitution are on level 5, and so forth.

Do not assume that this hierarchy implies that all law from a higher level is "more important" than law from a lower level. For example, the laws that govern the daily lives of most Americans, such as tort law, contract law, and criminal law, are the laws of the state in which they reside. If the law is from a state statute, it's on level 5, or if it's based on a common law rule, it's on level 8. These state laws are generally far more "important" to most citizens than, say, an international treaty, even though that is on level 2.[3]

Also, do not assume that conflicts between different laws are equally likely between all different levels. For example, conflicts between state and federal statutes or regulations are somewhat common, but conflicts between federal regulations and state constitutions would be very unlikely.[4] This is because regulations and constitutions generally deal with different aspects of the law, and state constitutions are likely to be similar to the federal Constitution. Thus, if a federal regulation conflicted with a state constitutional provision, there is a good chance that it would also conflict with a federal Constitutional provision.

---

[2] In practice, it would be unusual for Congress to draft a bill whose language conflicts with the terms of an existing international treaty.

[3] *See id.* at 41–42.

[4] *See id.*

EXERCISE 4 A

For each problem below, assume that the given laws conflict with each other. Based on the hierarchy of law, write the letter of the law that would prevail (A or B):

1.	A:	The Illinois Constitution (1970)	
	B:	The United States Constitution (1789)	________
2.	A:	A California statute	
	B:	A federal regulation	________
3.	A:	A federal regulation that took effect on January 30, 2009	
	B:	A state regulation that took effect on June 1, 2012	________
4.	A:	An international treaty that took effect on January 30, 2009	
	B:	A federal statute that took effect on June 1, 2012	________
5.	A:	A Texas court rule that took effect on December 1, 2008	
	B:	A Texas statute that took effect on May 1, 2006	________

B. THE FEDERAL AND STATE COURT SYSTEMS

As we stated in the discussion of federalism in Chapter 3, the United States has two different and largely parallel systems of government — the federal government and each of the 50 state governments.

Each system is similar in form: like the federal government, each of the 50 states has a constitution and executive, legislative, and judicial branches. Each branch of government is similar as well. In Chapter 3, we focused on similarities between the federal and state executive branches and legislative branches. This is also true with the judicial branch, where 41 out of 50 states resemble the federal court system by having a three-tiered court system, with trial courts, intermediate appellate courts, and the highest appellate courts, also known as the "court of last resort."

1. The Federal Court System

The federal court system has a three-tiered hierarchy, which consists of trial courts called United States District Courts; intermediate appellate courts of appeals known as the United States Circuit Courts of Appeals; and the highest appellate court, which is called the United States Supreme Court. *See* Figure 4.2 below. The general rule is that federal courts hear disputes that involve the application of federal law, but they can sometimes hear state-law issues as well. *See* Section D below for the general rule and its exceptions.

a. The United States District Courts (Trial Courts)

There are 96 trial courts in the federal court system, 94 of which are geographically-based courts called United States District Courts. There are 89 U.S. District Courts in the 50 states, with at least one district in each state. The 24 states that have the largest populations are geographically divided into two, three, or four districts each. For example, California is divided into the Northern District, the Central District, the Southern District, and the Eastern District, and Illinois is divided into the Northern District, the Central District, and the Southern District. There are also five U.S. District Court jurisdictions that are not within the boundaries of any state: the District of Columbia (Washington, D.C.), Puerto Rico, the Virgin Islands, Guam, and the Northern Mariana Islands.

In addition to the 94 geographically-based U.S. District Courts, there are two special federal trial courts with nationwide jurisdiction: the U.S. Court of International Trade and the U.S. Court of Federal Claims. The Court of International Trade deals with international trade and customs issues, and the Court of Federal Claims handles claims for money damages against the United States government, federal government contract disputes, unlawful "takings" of private property by the federal government, and other similar claims.

Federal courts have **exclusive jurisdiction** over bankruptcy, which means that bankruptcy claims cannot be filed in state courts. Due to the high volume of bankruptcy filings, there are separate federal bankruptcy courts for the geographically-based U.S. District Courts.

Trials in the U.S. District Courts take place before a judge, and a jury if the parties request one. In most civil and criminal matters, parties have a constitutional right to have the case heard by a jury. In a **jury trial**, the jury makes determinations regarding the factual issues, and is called the "finder of fact." The judge makes determinations regarding the law, such as which laws apply and what evidence is admissible. If there is no jury, the judge makes determinations of both the law and the facts in a **bench trial**.

b. The United States Circuit Courts of Appeal (Intermediate Appellate Courts)

There are 13 intermediate appellate courts in the federal court system, divided into "circuits." Twelve of them are geographically-based, and 11 of them are in circuits that are numbered first through eleventh. As shown in Figure 4.3, the numbered circuits each contain several states. For example, the United States Court of Appeals for the Second Circuit contains New York, Vermont, and Connecticut; the United States Court of Appeals for the Third Circuit contains Pennsylvania, New Jersey, and Delaware; and the United States Court of Appeals for the Seventh Circuit contains Illinois, Wisconsin, and Indiana. Lawyers usually refer to these courts by their short names: the "Second Circuit," the "Third Circuit," and the "Seventh Circuit." The twelfth geographically-based circuit is the United States Court of Appeals for the District of Columbia Circuit, known for short as the "D.C. Circuit." Each appellate court hears appeals from the U.S. District Courts within its circuit, and appeals from the decisions of the federal administrative agencies.

The thirteenth intermediate appellate court, the Federal Circuit, has nationwide jurisdiction. It hears appeals from the U.S. District Courts of certain intellectual property cases such as patent cases, and it also hears appeals from the U.S. Court of International Trade and the U.S. Court of Federal Claims.

In civil cases, parties who are not satisfied with the decision in the trial court have a right to appeal to the intermediate appellate court. In criminal cases, convicted defendants may appeal, but if the prosecution (i.e., the government) loses, it may not appeal, because this would constitute **double jeopardy**. Parties appeal by claiming that the trial court made errors in its factual or legal determinations. The party who appeals is called the **appellant**, and the other party is called the **appellee** or **respondent**.

Appeals are generally heard before three-judge panels, although occasionally certain important matters are heard before larger panels, which may include all of the appellate judges in that circuit. These decisions from these special cases are called ***en banc*** decisions.

Appeals have a different procedure from trials; no witnesses testify and no new evidence is submitted to the court. Instead, the appellate panel reviews the written record and exhibits from the trial court. There may be a short hearing known as **oral argument**, usually less than an hour long, where the three-judge panel asks the attorneys questions about their clients' positions. Often, the appellate panel does not want to hear oral arguments, and it rules based on the appellate briefs of the parties and the written record and exhibits from the trial court.

The **standard of review** that the appellate panel uses is very important to an appellant's chance for success. This refers to the way that the appellate court must review and consider the issue. If the appellant claims that the judge or jury made an error in a finding of fact, the appellate panel must defer to the trial court's decision and it can only reverse the trial court's decision if it was "clearly erroneous," an "abuse of discretion," or a similar standard. This is because the appellate panel was not present at trial and did not hear the witnesses. Because it must rely only upon the parties' briefs and the written record from the trial and the exhibits, it defers to the fact finder, who was present at the trial.

If the appellant claims that the trial court judge erred in a finding of law, however, the standard of review is **de novo**. This means that the appellate panel is, in effect, making a new decision, and owes no deference to the trial court's decision. This is because appellate court judges are presumed to know the law as well as, or better than, trial court judges. Accordingly, lawyers understand that they have a better chance of winning their appeal if they can find a legal issue to appeal than if they can only find a factual issue to appeal.

c. The United States Supreme Court

The United States Supreme Court consists of a panel of nine judges called justices — the Chief Justice and eight Associate Justices. As with federal judges from the lower courts, Supreme Court justices are appointed by the President and confirmed by the Senate, and they have lifetime appointments to the bench.[5]

Like the intermediate appellate courts, the Supreme Court hears appeals from the lower federal courts. It also has **original jurisdiction** of a limited number of types of cases, such as "Cases affecting Ambassadors, other public Ministers and Consuls, and those in which a State shall be a Party."[6] Unlike the appeal as of right to the 13 circuit courts, however, appeals to the Supreme Court are discretionary. The Court is not required to hear cases, and chooses the cases that it will hear.

Parties who wish to appeal to the Supreme Court must first file a "petition for certiorari" — a petition in which the parties attempt to convince the Court that their cases are important and should be heard. Four of the nine justices must agree that the case should be heard; when they do so, they **grant certiorari**, and agree to hear the case.

Over the past five years, the Supreme Court has granted certiorari fewer than 100 times per year, with an average of only 83 cases per year.[7] Meanwhile, it has typically disposed of almost 8,000 cases a year: approximately 78 cases per year through written opinions, 3 through unwritten **per curiam** opinions, and the great majority through denying certiorari and refusing to hear the case.[8] Each of the past five years, the Court has only disposed of 1 or 2 cases in which it had original jurisdiction.[9] Thus, the Court only agrees to hear approximately 1% of the petitions for certiorari that it receives each year.

The Supreme Court may hear appeals from either the lower federal courts or the state courts that involve the United States Constitution or issues of federal law, but it takes very few state cases, and has no power to review state cases that only have issues of state law. Instead, it typically hears cases from the lower federal courts that involve federal law or the United States Constitution.

The Supreme Court is generally not interested in reviewing issues of fact; it reviews issues of law, typically in important and new or unsettled areas of the law. For example, it often agrees to hear cases where the law is unsettled and different circuits have rulings that conflict with each other, known as "circuit splits." The Supreme Court frequently hears cases to resolve circuit splits, thereby ensuring that federal law is as consistent as possible in its application.

---

5 Because this is set out in Article III of the Constitution, federal judges are often called "Article III judges."

6 U.S. Const. art. III, § 2, cl. 2.

7 *Judicial Business of the United States Courts, 2012 Annual Report of the Director*, Table A-1, http://www.uscourts.gov/Statistics/JudicialBusiness/2012/statistical-tables-us-supreme-court.aspx.

8 *Id.*

9 *Id.*

Figure 4.2 The United States Federal Court System

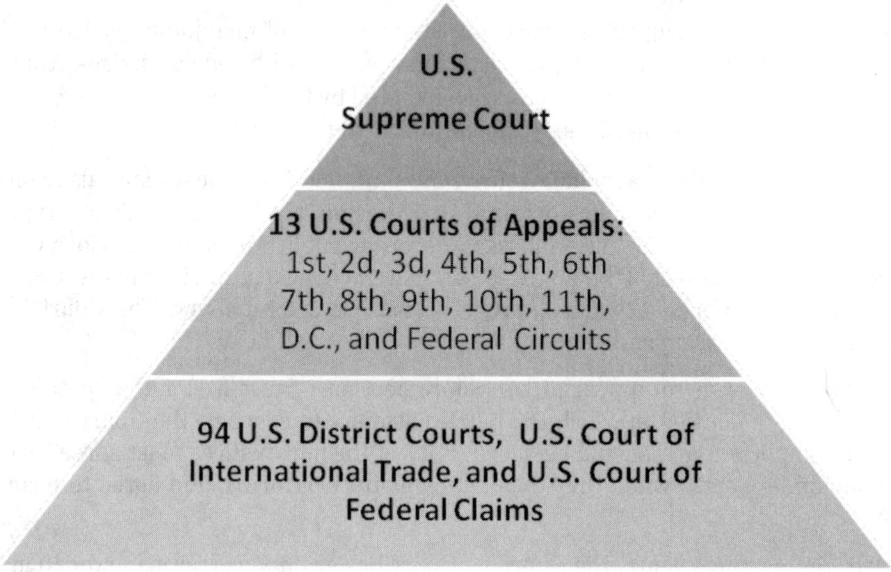

Figure 4.3 Map of the United States Federal Court System

Source: Administrative Office of the United States Courts, http://www.uscourts.gov/images/CircuitMap.pdf

2. State Court Systems

Forty-one out of 50 states have three-tiered court hierarchies, with trial courts of general jurisdiction, intermediate appellate courts, and the highest appellate court, which is usually, but not always, called the Supreme Court (in New York, for example, an intermediate appellate court is called the Supreme Court, and the highest court is called the Court of Appeal). *See* Figure 4.3 below, which shows the Illinois state court system.

a. State Trial Courts

There are two kinds of trial courts at the state level — courts of general jurisdiction, and courts of limited jurisdiction. Only certain types of cases can be heard in courts of limited jurisdiction, which include traffic courts, juvenile courts (which hear matters involving troubled or dependent children), probate courts (which deal with the distribution of property after death), small claims courts (which hear cases involving small amounts of money, and where parties often appear **pro se**— without lawyers), and criminal courts. These courts are sometimes generally referred to as municipal (city or local) courts.

Trial courts of general jurisdiction typically exist at the county level, and the trial court's jurisdiction may consist of one county, if the county has a large population, or several counties, if the counties have small populations. In Illinois, for example, the 102 counties are divided into 23 trial court regions called "circuits."[10] Depending upon the state, these courts may be called "Circuit Courts," "Superior Courts," "District Court of Common Pleas," etc.

These trial courts have general jurisdiction, meaning the ability to hear many types of cases. They can hear cases and claims arising under state constitutional, statutory, and common law, and they can also hear cases that have multiple claims arising under both state law and federal law. In addition to having original jurisdiction to hear state law claims, state trial courts of general jurisdiction may sit as appellate courts to review the decisions of state courts of limited jurisdiction.

As we have seen, the Constitution sets out a system of government in which the federal government has limited and enumerated powers, and the states have retained the residual power. Thus, even though the volume of federal law and the power of the federal government have grown significantly in the past 100 years, most laws that govern citizens' lives still tend to be state laws. As a result, if two residents of a state have a contractual dispute, or one alleges that the other has harmed him or her under a principle of tort law, or if a citizen is arrested for murder, theft, or drunk driving, the dispute is likely to be adjudicated in state court, unless a particular federal law has allegedly been violated. Indeed, approximately 95% of all cases filed in courts across the United States are initiated in state courts.[11] For each of the seven years from 2003

---

[10] http://www.state.il.us/court/general/proceed.asp.

[11] Court Statistics Project, *Examining the Work of State Courts, An Analysis of 2010 State Court Caseloads*, A Comment from the Chair (R. Lafountain et al. eds, 2011), available at http://www.courtstatistics.org/FlashMicrosites/CSP/images/CSP2009.pdf.

through 2009, the total number of state court caseloads was more than 100 million cases.[12]

Let's consider Illinois: there were 3.38 million cases filed in 2011, of which only 7,826 cases were filed in the intermediate appellate courts.[13] There were 1,799 petitions for leave to appeal filed with the Illinois Supreme Court, and it agreed to hear only 78 (about 4%) of the petitions.[14] Thus, of the huge volume of cases filed in each state, only a tiny percentage of those cases reach the intermediate appellate courts, and only a small percentage of *those* cases are heard by the state supreme court.

b. State Appellate Courts

In the 41 states that have intermediate appellate courts, most appeals are heard as of right (meaning that the appellate court must hear the case), and they are appeals from the trial courts and the state administrative agencies. Depending upon the population of the state, there may be several appellate jurisdictions. For example, California has six appellate districts. Similarly, Illinois is divided into five appellate judicial districts, as shown in Figure 4.4 below.

Like the United States Supreme Court, state supreme courts generally have discretion to hear most cases, and parties must file a petition for leave to appeal if they want the state supreme court to hear their case. Certain cases, such as appeals in states that have the death penalty, are reviewed as of right, and there may be a limited number of types of cases where the state supreme court has original jurisdiction. State supreme courts often consist of a panel of seven justices — the Chief Justice and six Associate Justices.

---

[12] *Id.* at 1.

[13] How Cases Proceed Through the Court System, available at http://www.state.il.us/court/general/proceed.asp.

[14] 2011 *Annual Report of the Illinois Courts, Statistical Summary* 142, available at http://www.state.il.us/court/SupremeCourt/AnnualReport/2011/StatsSumm/default.asp.

Figure 4.4 The Illinois State Court System

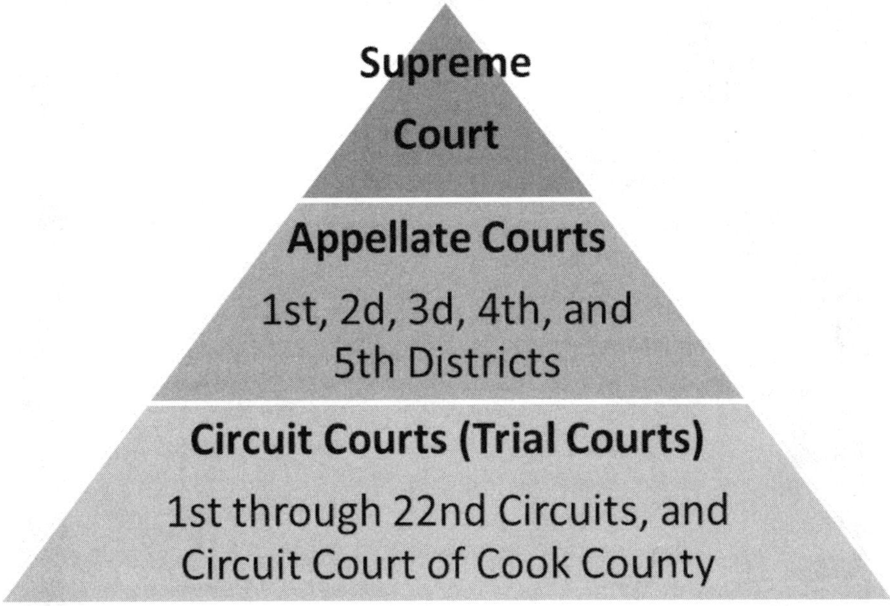

State trial court opinions are generally not published and have no precedential value, but they constitute the overwhelming majority of all cases in a given state court system. Intermediate state appellate decisions have precedential value, but not all decisions are considered significant enough to publish, while full opinions in the state supreme court are generally published. The practice in federal courts is slightly different: certain trial court decisions are published, as are many decisions in the intermediate federal appellate courts, where anywhere from approximately 10% to 50% of the **dispositions** are published.[15]

[15] Stephen L. Wasby, *Unpublished Court of Appeals Decisions: A Hard Look at the Process*, 14 S. Cal. Interdisc. L.J. 69 (2004–2005).

Figure 4.5 Illinois Appellate Court Districts

Source: 2011 Annual Report of the Illinois Courts, Statistical Summary 128, available at http://www.state.il.us/court/SupremeCourt/AnnualReport/2011_Amap.pdf.

In conclusion, in both the federal and state court systems, the great majority of cases occur in the trial courts, and those cases are rarely published because they do not have precedential value. Similarly, although cases in the intermediate appellate courts have precedential value, many are unsigned memorandum dispositions or are not considered sufficiently important to publish. Only the United States Supreme Court or a state supreme court is highly likely to publish a full opinion, and even there, some cases are disposed of with very short one-sentence opinions that announce the disposition rather than full opinions.

Why is this important? You will spend much of your time as an LL.M. student in a U.S. law school reading judicial opinions, and many U.S. lawyers (particularly litigators) will read thousands of judicial opinions in their careers, so it is essential to understand the context: As shown in figure 4.5 below, only a small minority of all U.S. judicial opinions are published. Thus, the cases that you will read are not typical: they are important cases that have likely broken new ground in some way. Perhaps they have announced a new legal rule, clarified an existing rule, or harmonized different rules from lower courts.

Figure 4.6 The Universe of State and Federal Court Opinions

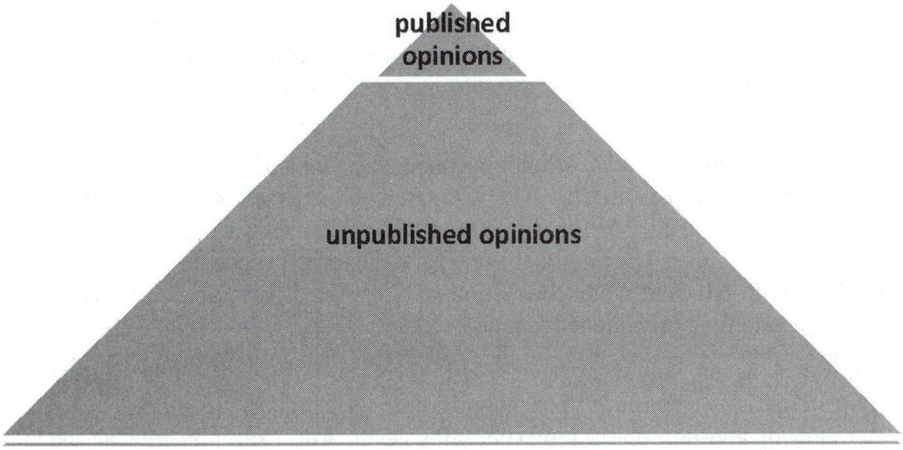

C. BINDING AND PERSUASIVE PRECEDENT

As we have learned, the common law operates through the principle of stare decisis: new decisions must follow the rules and reasoning of earlier decisions, known as precedent. However, courts are not bound by *all* precedent — much of it is merely persuasive. Unlike binding precedent, which must be followed, persuasive precedent is entitled to respect and consideration, but courts can choose whether to follow it or not.

To determine whether precedent is binding or persuasive, lawyers must consider the following: (1) court hierarchy; (2) the jurisdiction; and (3) whether the facts and legal issues of the precedent are similar.

The general rule for both state and federal courts is that a court is bound by the decisions of a (1) higher court (2) within its jurisdiction.

1. State Courts

State trial courts are bound by the decisions of the higher courts within their jurisdictions for issues arising from that state's law, and they are bound only by decisions of the United States Supreme Court for federal constitutional and statutory issues (the decisions of the lower federal courts are persuasive). State trial court decisions have no precedential value and are typically not published.

When states have more than one intermediate appellate district (such as California and Illinois), there are two different possibilities. In California, the trial courts are bound only by the holdings of the intermediate appellate court for the district in which they sit. In Illinois, the trial courts are bound by the decisions of all intermediate appellate courts in the state, but if there is a conflict between the law of two districts, the precedent of the appellate court for the trial court's own district will prevail.

For example, the Superior Court of California for Los Angeles County (the state trial court in Los Angeles) is in the Second Appellate District of California. Under the rule that California follows, only appellate decisions from the Second Appellate District are binding on the trial court in Los Angeles — decisions from the intermediate appellate courts of the other five California appellate districts are persuasive.

In Illinois, which takes the other approach, the Cook County Circuit Court (the trial court in Chicago) is in the First District. The decisions of the intermediate appellate courts in all five of the Illinois appellate districts are binding on the trial court in Chicago, unless they conflict with First District precedent. In that situation, the trial court in Chicago would be bound only by the First District precedent, and not by the conflicting precedent from the other district.

Courts are never bound by the decisions of lower courts, so an intermediate appellate court is not bound by precedent from a trial court. Nor can it be bound by the decision of another district of the same level. For example, in California, the Second Appellate District is not bound by the decisions of the Third Appellate District (and vice versa), and in Illinois, the First District is not bound by the decisions of the Second District (and vice versa). State appellate courts are bound by their own earlier decisions due to stare decisis, but they can generally overrule their own decisions from earlier cases. For federal constitutional and statutory issues, intermediate state appellate courts are bound only by decisions of the United States Supreme Court (the decisions of the lower federal courts are persuasive).

A state's highest court (usually called its supreme court) is bound only by its own decisions for issues of state law, unless it chooses to overrule them, and by decisions of the United States Supreme Court for federal constitutional and statutory issues (the decisions of the lower federal courts are persuasive).

legal issues of the precedent are similar.

The general rule for both state and federal courts is that a court is bound by the decisions of a (1) higher court (2) within its jurisdiction.

1. State Courts

State trial courts are bound by the decisions of the higher courts within their jurisdictions for issues arising from that state's law, and they are bound only by decisions of the United States Supreme Court for federal constitutional and statutory issues (the decisions of the lower federal courts are persuasive). State trial court decisions have no precedential value and are typically not published.

When states have more than one intermediate appellate district (such as Ohio and Illinois), there are two different possibilities. In Ohio, the trial courts are bound only by the holdings of the intermediate appellate court for the district in which they sit. In Illinois, the trial courts are bound by the decisions of all intermediate appellate courts in the state, but if there is a conflict between the law of two districts, the precedent of the appellate court for the trial court's own district will prevail.

For example, the Cuyahoga County Court of Common Pleas (the state trial court in Cleveland, Ohio) is in the Eighth District of Ohio. Under the minority rule that Ohio follows, only appellate decisions from the Eighth District are binding on the trial court in Cleveland — decisions from the intermediate appellate courts of the other eleven Ohio appellate districts are persuasive, not binding.

In Illinois, which takes the majority approach (i.e., the approach of most states), the Cook County Circuit Court (the trial court in Chicago) is in the First District. The decisions of the intermediate appellate courts in all five of the Illinois appellate districts are binding on the trial court in Chicago, unless they conflict with First District precedent. In that situation, the trial court in Chicago would be bound only by the First District precedent, and not by the conflicting precedent from the other district.

Courts are never bound by the decisions of lower courts, so an intermediate appellate court is not bound by precedent from a trial court. Nor can it be bound by the decision of another district of the same level. For example, in Ohio, the Eighth District is not bound by the decisions of the Tenth District (and vice versa), and in Illinois, the First District is not bound by the decisions of the Second District (and vice versa). State appellate courts are bound by their own earlier decisions due to stare decisis, but they can generally overrule their own decisions from earlier cases. For federal constitutional and statutory issues, intermediate state appellate courts are bound only by decisions of the United States Supreme Court (the decisions of the lower federal courts are persuasive).

A state's highest court (usually called its supreme court) is bound only by its own decisions for issues of state law, unless it chooses to overrule them, and by decisions of the United States Supreme Court for federal constitutional and statutory issues (the decisions of the lower federal courts are persuasive).

2. Federal Courts

Like the state courts, federal courts are bound by the decisions of higher courts within their jurisdiction for matters of federal law. If they consider an issue of state law, they are bound by the decisions of the highest court of that state, but not by lower state courts.

Like the state trial courts, the decisions of federal district courts (the federal trial courts) do not have precedential value. They are sometimes published, but even when published they do not bind other courts. A judge who sits on the bench of a federal district court, such as the Central District of California or the Northern District of Illinois, must consider the published decisions of other judges within the same district, but is not bound by them.

Federal district courts are bound by the decisions of the circuit court of the federal circuit in which they sit, and by the United States Supreme Court. For example, the Central District of California is in the Ninth Circuit, so it is bound by Ninth Circuit opinions (but not by the opinions of the other circuits). Similarly, the Northern District of Illinois is in the Seventh Circuit, so it is bound by Seventh Circuit opinions, but not by the opinions of the other circuits.

The federal intermediate appellate courts are bound by their own decisions, but they can overrule them if the circuit's judges sit together en banc. They are not bound by the decisions of the other circuits — for example, the Ninth Circuit is not bound by Seventh Circuit opinions, and vice versa. All of these courts, however, are bound by the United States Supreme Court's decisions.

For state-law issues, federal courts are bound by the opinions of the highest court of that state, but not by the lower courts. For example, if the Ninth Circuit is reviewing a ruling by the Central District of California on an issue of California state law, it would be bound by a ruling of the California Supreme Court on that issue. If there is no California Supreme Court holding on that issue, the Ninth Circuit must try to predict how the California Supreme Court would rule on that issue. It could do so by looking at an opinion of a California appellate court, but that opinion is persuasive; the Ninth Circuit could determine that the California Supreme Court would rule differently than the appellate court did.

Like a state supreme court, the United States Supreme Court is not bound by the opinions of lower courts. It is bound by its own prior decisions due to stare decisis, but it also has the authority to overrule its prior decisions.

In brief, the general rule is that courts are bound by the holdings of higher courts in their own jurisdictions, and the holdings of courts in other jurisdictions are only persuasive. When a state court considers a federal-law issue, it is bound only by holdings by the U.S. Supreme Court. Similarly, when a federal court considers a state-law issue, it is bound only by holdings by that state's supreme court.

Whenever a U.S. lawyer reads a case, he or she must quickly determine whether or not that case constitutes binding or persuasive precedent for the legal issue that the lawyer is analyzing. When you read cases in U.S. law school courses, however, you will not have clients, unless you are working with a hypothetical problem that provides you with a fictional client. Nevertheless, as you read cases in law school, it is important to learn to be an "active reader" and to read cases as a U.S. attorney would. This means that you should do more than to try to memorize legal rules. You should ask yourself which courts the decision would bind, and which courts it would not bind. For example, if you are reading an opinion from the Delaware Supreme Court, you should remember that it is binding upon Delaware state courts, and upon federal courts that are adjudicating an issue involving Delaware law.

If you have a hypothetical problem, think about the facts of the problem as you read the cases. In which jurisdiction is the problem set? Does the problem involve litigation in a particular court? If so, does the case that you are reading bind that court's decision? In order to understand the significance of the cases that you are reading, it is necessary to ask questions such as these.

EXERCISE 4 B

For each problem below, decide whether the precedent that is described would be binding or persuasive on the court listed in the problem. Write "B" if the precedent is binding, and "P" if it is persuasive. Be able to explain the reason(s) for each answer.

1. The United States District Court for the Central District of California, sitting in Los Angeles, decided a case based on federal law and wrote an opinion that was published. Is that opinion binding or persuasive on the following courts?
   a. U.S. District Court for the Eastern District of California ____________
   b. U.S. District Court for the Central District of California ____________
   c. The Superior Court of California for Los Angeles County, applying federal law ____________
2. The United States Court of Appeals for the Seventh Circuit, sitting in Chicago, applied Illinois law in deciding a case in which it had diversity jurisdiction. Is that opinion binding or persuasive on the following courts?
   a. Cook County Circuit Court ____________
   b. Illinois Appellate Court for the First District ____________
   c. U.S. District Court for the Northern District of Illinois, applying Illinois law ____________
3. The Illinois Supreme Court decided a case, applying Illinois law. Is that opinion binding or persuasive on the following courts? ____________
   a. Cook County Circuit Court ____________
   b. Illinois Appellate Court for the First District ____________
   c. Wisconsin Supreme Court ____________
   d. The United States Court of Appeals for the Seventh Circuit, applying Illinois law ____________

e. The United States Court of Appeals for the Second Circuit, applying Illinois law ____________

4. The United States Court of Appeals for the Seventh Circuit decided a case based on federal law. Is that opinion binding or persuasive on the following courts?

a. U.S. District Court for the Northern District of Illinois ____________

b. U.S. District Court for the Southern District of New York ____________

c. The United States Court of Appeals for the Second Circuit ____________

d. Cook County Circuit Court, applying federal law ____________

e. The United States Court of Appeals for the Seventh Circuit ____________

5. The Illinois Appellate Court for the First District decided a case, applying Illinois law. Is that opinion binding or persuasive on the following courts?

a. Cook County Circuit Court (in the First District) ____________

b. DuPage County Circuit Court (in the Second District) ____________

c. U.S. District Court for the Northern District of Illinois, applying Illinois law) ____________

d. Illinois Appellate Court for the Second District ____________

D. JURISDICTION

To understand how the state and federal court systems work, we must understand which types of cases can be heard in federal court, and which types of cases can be heard in state court. As we have seen, the general rule is that federal courts typically hear issues involving federal law and state courts typically hear issues involving state law. However, we have also learned that there are certain situations where federal courts can hear issues involving state law, and state courts can hear issues involving federal law. These rules can be very complex: U.S. law schools have entire courses on this subject. Although a complete analysis of the issue is thus outside the scope of this book, it is essential for students to have a basic understanding of how these federalism principles work in the nation's federal and state court systems.

1. Jurisdiction

The key term for this discussion is **jurisdiction**, a word that has several different meanings. So far, we have used the word to refer to a specific geographic area over which a judicial or political authority has power. For example, a state is a jurisdiction: The executive, legislative, and judicial branches of Illinois have authority over that state. The term also applies to smaller judicial or political divisions within a state, such as a county. The First District is an appellate court jurisdiction at the north end of the state that comprises only Cook County, which has a very large population, whereas the Fifth District is an appellate court jurisdiction at the south end of the state that comprises 37 counties with small populations. *See* figure 4.4 above. For federal courts, the Central District of California and the Northern District of Illinois are district court jurisdictions, and the Ninth Circuit and Seventh Circuit are appellate jurisdictions.

Another meaning of "jurisdiction" involves a government's power over the people who live within its geographical area. For a court, it refers both to the court's authority to hear a certain type of claim and to grant the appropriate relief (**subject-matter jurisdiction**), and its authority to bring a defendant into court and subject the defendant to its authority (**personal jurisdiction**). For any trial to occur in either the state or federal court systems, the court must have (1) personal jurisdiction over the defendant(s) and (2) subject-matter jurisdiction over the nature of the dispute.

a. Personal Jurisdiction

The rules that apply to personal jurisdiction are very complex, and different jurisdictions have different rules. It is enough for now to understand these rules at their most general: a jurisdiction has the authority to bring an individual or corporate defendant into court and to enforce a judgment against the defendant if the defendant (1) lives in the jurisdiction or (2) has sufficient minimum contacts with the jurisdiction that the suit would not offend "traditional notions of fair play and substantial justice."[16] A defendant may also consent to jurisdiction, even if he, she, or it has no contacts with the forum jurisdiction.

b. Subject-Matter Jurisdiction

In addition to having personal jurisdiction over the defendant(s), a court must have the authority to decide the particular type of controversy at issue in the lawsuit, known as subject-matter jurisdiction. As state courts have subject-matter jurisdiction over many (but not all) areas of federal law, and federal courts may have subject-matter jurisdiction over state-law issues given certain circumstances, it is sometimes possible for a plaintiff to have the choice of bringing the lawsuit in either state or federal court. In this situation, the state and federal courts have **concurrent jurisdiction**, which means that both courts have the authority to hear the case. If only one type of court has the authority to hear the case, it has **exclusive jurisdiction.**

i. State Courts

State courts have plenary (full) subject-matter jurisdiction. This means that they can hear all matters of state law (involving state constitutions, statutes, regulations, and common law), and all matters of federal law (involving the United States Constitution, federal statutes, regulations, and common law) except for certain areas where federal courts have exclusive jurisdiction (such as bankruptcy or immigration).

---

[16] *International Shoe Co. v. Washington*, 326 U.S. 310, 316 (1945).

ii. Federal Courts

Federal Courts have limited subject-matter jurisdiction. They may only hear certain types of cases that have been set out in Article III, Section 2 of the United States Constitution or in federal statutes. These types of cases include:

- Cases arising under the United States Constitution, federal statutes and regulations, and treaties (**federal question jurisdiction**);
- Cases between citizens of different states (**diversity jurisdiction**);
- Cases affecting ambassadors and other official representatives of foreign sovereigns;
- Admiralty and maritime cases;
- Controversies to which the United States is a party;
- Controversies between states and between a state and citizens of another state;
- Cases between citizens of the same state claiming lands under grants of different states; and
- Cases between a state or its citizens and foreign states and their citizens.

For most U.S. lawyers, the most important types of jurisdiction here are federal question jurisdiction and diversity jurisdiction. Other than federal question jurisdiction, the types of claims that may be heard in federal court generally involve claims that do not involve any state's territory (such as an accident on a ship at sea), or they involve claims in which there is a concern that a state court might be biased in favor of a local resident (such as a lawsuit between a resident of the forum state and a resident of a different state).

Under the federal diversity jurisdiction statute, a federal court has subject matter jurisdiction over a dispute that only involves issues of state law where (1) there is complete diversity among the parties such that no plaintiff shares state citizenship with any defendant; and (2) the amount in controversy exceeds $75,000.[17] For corporate defendants, complete diversity means that there must be diversity in two areas: (1) the state under whose laws the corporation is incorporated, and (2) the state in which the principal place of business is located.[18] If the plaintiff and the defendant share residency in either area, diversity is destroyed.

EXERCISE 4 C

For each problem below, decide whether the case may be heard by a federal court, a state court, or both courts. Write "F" if the case may only be heard by a federal court, "S" if the case may only be heard by a state court, or "B" if the case may be heard by both courts. Be able to explain the reason(s) for each answer.

---

[17] 28 U.S.C. § 1332 (2006).

[18] *Id.*

1. There was a car accident in California. The plaintiff is from California and the defendant is from Arizona. The plaintiff is seeking $60,000 in damages. ______________

2. Company A sues Company B for breach of contract, and is seeking $150,000 in damages. Company A has its headquarters in Virginia, and Company B has its headquarters in New York. Both Companies are incorporated under Delaware law. ______________

3. Joe's Tire Co. is owed $50,000 by Jim's Trucking, Inc., which has filed for bankruptcy. ______________

4. A guest at a hotel in Miami, Florida is suing the hotel company for injuries he sustained when he fell off the balcony of his hotel room. He is suing for $500,000. The guest lives in New York City. The hotel company has its headquarters in Chicago, and it is incorporated under Delaware law. ______________

5. An office-supply company based in California and incorporated under the laws of Delaware is suing all four members of a partnership to whom it had sold office equipment and furniture. Three of the partners live in Nevada and the fourth partner lives in California. ______________

Chapter Review

- In the U.S. common law legal system, there are four main sources of primary law: constitutions, statutes and treaties, regulations, and case law.
- These sources of law exist in a hierarchy. For federal law, the hierarchy ranks the Constitution as the highest authority, followed in order by federal statutes and international treaties, federal agency regulations, and federal common law decisions. For state law, the order is the same: the state constitution is the highest authority, followed by state statutes, state agency regulations, and state common law decisions.
- Because the Supremacy Clause of the United States Constitution says that federal law ranks higher than state law, all four sources of federal law rank higher than the four sources of state law.
- Although common law (judge-made law) is at the bottom of each hierarchy, cases that construe the meanings of a constitution, a statute, or a regulation take the same hierarchical rank as the law that they interpret.
- The federal court system has three tiers, with the United States Supreme Court as the highest court, followed by the 13 intermediate courts of appeal, known as circuit courts of appeal, and the trial courts, known as district courts.

- Forty-one out of 50 states have a similar three-tiered structure, beginning with the highest state court (usually but not always called the "supreme court"), continuing with the intermediate appellate courts, and the trial courts, which have names such as the superior court, the circuit court, or the district court of common pleas. The nine states with the smallest populations have two levels of courts: the state supreme court and the trial courts.
- Below the state courts of general jurisdiction, there are local or municipal courts of limited jurisdiction, which only hear certain types of cases. Examples include traffic court, small claims court, and juvenile or family court.
- There are two types of authority: binding and persuasive. Courts must follow binding authority, but do not have to follow persuasive authority.
- The general rules regarding authority are that, for both the federal and state court systems, (1) the decisions of the trial courts do not have precedential value and are only persuasive, and (2) courts are bound by the decisions of higher courts in the same jurisdiction.
- When state courts consider matters of federal law, they are bound only by the decisions of the U.S. Supreme Court; the decisions of the lower federal courts are persuasive.
- When federal courts consider matters of state law, they are bound only by the decisions of the state's highest court; the decisions of the lower state courts are persuasive.
- Federal courts have limited jurisdiction, granted to them by the Constitution or by federal statutes. They may hear matters of federal law (federal question jurisdiction), matters of state law where the parties are from different states and the controversy is valued at more than $75,000 (diversity jurisdiction), and a limited number of situations where state courts might be more likely to favor one party over another.
- State courts have plenary (full) jurisdiction. They may hear all matters of state law, and all matters of federal law that have not been exclusively reserved for the jurisdiction of federal courts.

Chapter 5

READING CASES

Chapter Preview

This chapter helps us to understand how U.S. lawyers read judicial opinions by looking at a modern case. The chapter discusses:

- The differences between older cases and modern cases;
- Unanimous opinions, majority opinions, plurality opinions, concurrences, and dissents;
- The differences between the case excerpts that you read in law school casebooks and complete cases;
- The editorial enhancements preceding the actual opinion that exist in reporters and online legal research sources and that are designed to help lawyers find and understand the law; and
- The organization and parts of a typical case.

As we discussed in the introduction to Chapter 4, case law forms an essential part of U.S. law for two reasons. First, common law rules come entirely from cases. Second, even where legal rules come from enacted law such as constitutions, statutes, or regulations, lawyers must look both at the rules and at cases that construe the meanings of those rules in order to fully understand what the rules mean and how to apply them.

Whether you practice law in a civil-law system or a common-law system, you know from experience that enacted law is unavoidably somewhat general and abstract. Lawyers need expert guidance from jurists about the meaning of the law. In civil-law systems, jurists tend to be legal experts such as law professors who provide written commentaries about the law. In the U.S. legal system, however, we do not rely upon commentaries about the law. Instead, we rely on case law. Our jurists are our judges. When a lawyer needs to understand the meaning of a statute and how the law applies to the facts of the client's case, he or she must turn to case law.[1]

A. LEGAL OPINIONS: AN INTRODUCTION

1. Old Opinions

As we learned in Chapter 1, the common law system began in England approximately one thousand years ago. As one might expect, the nature of legal opinions has changed greatly over that period of time. Originally, judicial opinions were announced orally and not written down. Although they eventually became written, early opinions resemble transcriptions of oral opinions. If you take a course that begins with old historical cases, you may read a "seriatim" opinion, where the opinions of more than one of the judges on an appellate panel are given in sequence.

2. Votes Count: Majority Opinions, Plurality Opinions, Concurrences, and Dissents

Today, appellate court opinions do not consist of individual opinions by the judges on the panel, written one after another. Rather, one judge writes the opinion for the court, in the **majority opinion**. If all of the judges on the panel agree, the opinion is **unanimous**. If they do not, there may be two levels of disagreement:

- A judge may agree with the court's decision, but not with the court's reasoning for reaching that result. The judge *concurs* with the opinion, and may choose to write a separate opinion following the majority opinion called a **concurrence**.
- A judge may disagree with both the court's decision and with the court's reasoning for reaching the decision. The judge *dissents* from the opinion, and

---

[1] U.S. lawyers can also look at secondary legal sources such as legal encyclopedias, treatises, hornbooks, and law review articles for background knowledge, but these sources are not primary law, and thus not as authoritative as case law. In other words, it is insufficient for a lawyer in the United States to simply review enacted law and a secondary legal source that discusses that law.

may choose to write a separate opinion following the majority opinion (and any concurrence) called a **dissent**.

Often, judges choose not to write concurrences or dissents, so many appellate opinions that are not unanimous have only one part — the majority opinion. Appellate court decisions do not need to be unanimous; a majority is sufficient. For example, on a three-judge panel, if two or more judges agree with the trial court's decision in favor of the plaintiff, the court will affirm the decision. If two or more judges disagree with the trial court's decision, the court will **reverse** it. If the appellate court sends the case back to the trial court for further findings in accordance with its decision, it **remands** the case.

Where the court is more deeply divided, a majority of the judges might agree on the decision, but not on the reasoning for that decision. In that case, one of the judges writes a **plurality opinion**. This happens fairly often with the United States Supreme Court, which frequently deals with new or difficult legal issues.

For example, if six of the nine justices vote to affirm a decision, but only four of the six can agree on the reasoning for that result, one of the justices writes a plurality opinion that is joined by three other justices. The opinion will also state that two other justices concur in the result, and one or both of them may choose to write a separate concurrence that explains where they disagree with the plurality opinion's reasoning. Of the three justices who disagree with the result, one or more of them might choose to write a dissent that explains why they disagree with the result and the plurality opinion's reasoning, or one justice might write a dissent and the other two might join it. This partially explains why modern Supreme Court opinions are sometimes more than 100 pages long!

3. The Weight of Authority

As we learned, the opinions of higher courts carry more authority than the opinions of lower courts. But that is not all — the weight of authority may also depend on how the appellate panel voted. For example, unanimous opinions are seen as highly authoritative, whereas plurality opinions are seen as weak and with unclear precedential value. Therefore, the appellate court judges who form the majority on a case may agree to compromise on the reasoning to reach a majority opinion.

Concurrences and dissents have no precedential value and are not law. Only the majority (or plurality) opinion states what the law *is*; a concurrence or dissent states what it *should be*, according to the author. Do not be confused by this! Law school casebooks often include concurring and dissenting opinions, and many law professors like to ask students if they agree with the reasoning of the concurrence or the dissent. While these questions are interesting, and they help law students to develop the ability to explain and defend their legal positions, remember that a concurrence or dissent has no legal authority, no matter how reasonable it seems.

Given that concurrences and dissents have no legal effect, why would a busy appellate judge take the time and make the effort to write one? Generally, it is because he or she feels strongly about the issue. Also, because opinions can be overruled — and even the United States Supreme Court sometimes overrules its precedent — a judge with a passionate belief in a "losing" position may write a dissenting opinion that will persuade a future court to overrule the decision someday.

4. Modern Opinions

Modern opinions do not use the "spoken language" of older opinions. As a result, judges today are not likely to write a sentence like "I am of the opinion that the defendant was negligent." Instead, they are more likely to write "the defendant was negligent" without the introductory language.[2] Another difference is that modern opinions are written in a more tightly organized style, and often contain headings and sub-headings to make the opinion easier to read.

Modern opinions also contain many **citations** to legal authority. A citation to a constitution, statute, treaty, regulation, or case identifies the source of law by name, which allows the legal reader to understand the weight of authority, and it also contains information that allows the reader to find and read that source. In modern legal writing, all references to legal authority must be supported with citations, whether the writing is an opinion written by a judge, or a brief, a motion, a memorandum, or a letter written by an attorney. This is quite different from older legal writing, which may contain few citations to precedent or enacted law. Instead, old opinions may refer to legal principles or the law generally without giving specific citations for each legal assertion.

B. CASE EXCERPTS IN CASEBOOKS v. COMPLETE CASES

Your casebooks contain many "cases," but it is important to understand that casebooks typically contain case *excerpts* instead of the complete cases that practicing lawyers use. As a result, you are reading only what the author of the casebook wants you to focus on, and some of the context is missing.

1. Cases in Casebooks Are Edited

Casebooks typically give you heavily-edited excerpts from cases. When you are reading a case and you see a series of asterisks going across the page like this:

* * * * *

* * *

it means that the author of the book has edited the case and removed part of the opinion at that place. What is not clear (unless you use the case citation to get a complete version of the case) is how much of the opinion has been removed.[3] Those asterisks could represent as little as an edit of a few sentences, or as much as an edit

---

[2] A modern judicial opinion may still use "spoken language" to announce a ruling: "We hold that the defendant was negligent."

[3] After you receive your passwords at your law school, you can use one of the commercial online legal research companies such as LexisNexis, Westlaw, or Bloomberg Law to get a complete version of the case by typing a citation (e.g., 360 F.3d 125) into a search box.

of many pages. For example, a Supreme Court case that is over 100 pages long might be reduced to a case excerpt of only five or six pages.

Why do casebook authors edit cases so heavily? For two reasons:

- First, casebooks are often 800 to 1,300 pages long, even with all of the case edits. If the authors were to give the complete versions of every case, a 1,000 page book might easily become a 5,000 page book.
- Second, authors typically use a case to provide an illustration of one legal issue. For example, an author might decide to include an opinion in which the plaintiff has appealed the trial court's dismissal of three of its claims: breach of warranty, misrepresentation, and breach of contract. However, the author of the casebook only wants to use the opinion to illustrate the breach of warranty issue, so he or she removes the parts of the opinion that analyze the misrepresentation and breach of contract claims.

2. Cases in Casebooks Have No Editorial Enhancements

A second difference is that a practicing lawyer sees cases in a different form from the edited case excerpts in casebooks. Lawyers find cases either in books called **reporters** or online, where they exist in the databases of commercial online legal research companies such as LexisNexis, Westlaw, or Bloomberg Law, as well as certain free websites such as GoogleScholar and some federal and state court websites. Currently, very few practicing attorneys still use reporters; lawyers usually get cases online from one of the major commercial online legal research companies.

a. Reporters

Reporters are books that collect published cases from a certain jurisdiction or jurisdictions. In the federal court system, reporters include the United States Reports, which contains United States Supreme Court cases; the Federal Reporter, which contains decisions from federal intermediate appellate courts such as the Second Circuit; and the Federal Supplement, which contains published decisions from the federal district courts.

Similarly, most state court systems have their own reporters for decisions of the state supreme court and the state intermediate appellate courts (remember that state trial court decisions are not published in reporters). There are also "regional reporters" that collect certain state supreme court and appellate court decisions from the states in that region. For example, the North Eastern Reporter collects decisions from Illinois, Indiana, Massachusetts, New York, and Ohio; the Atlantic Reporter contains decisions from Delaware, the District of Columbia, and eight other states; and the Southern Reporter contains decisions from Alabama, Florida, Louisiana, and Mississippi. The other four regional reporters are the Pacific Reporter, which includes California appellate court cases and cases from 14 other states; the North Western Reporter, which includes cases from Michigan and six other states; the South Western Reporter, which contains cases from Texas, four other states and American Indian territorial jurisdictions; and the South Eastern Reporter, which contains cases from Virginia and four other states.

Reporters are numbered by the series. A series is typically 1,000 volumes of a reporter. For example, the Federal Reporter is currently in its third series, as are the North Eastern and Pacific regional reporters.

b. Citations to Cases in Reporters and Online

A citation for a case includes the name of the case, followed by the volume number of the reporter, an abbreviation for the reporter, the series number if there is more than one series, the page the case that begins on, information about the jurisdiction, and the year of the decision.

This chapter includes a 2004 case from the Second Circuit in which a famous restaurant in New Orleans, Brennan's, sued a well-known new restaurant in New York City for trademark infringement because the owners shared the same last name: Brennan. The citation for the case is:

Brennan's, Inc. v. Brennan's Rest., L.L.C., 360 F.3d 125 (2d Cir. 2004).

After the case name, "360" refers to the volume number of the reporter, "F" refers to the Federal Reporter (which contains cases from the Second Circuit because it is a federal appellate court), "3d" refers to the third series of the Federal Reporter, and "125" refers to the page on which the case begins. In other words, this 2004 case begins on page 125 of volume 360 of the third series of the Federal Reporter.

The online research systems use the same citations as the reporters, so if you are looking for the *Brennan's* case online, you can type "360 F.3d 125" and get the case that way. Online research systems also include some cases that are not published in reporters, and they use their own citation format for those cases. Recently, some states have begun publishing cases online rather than having reporters printed. Those states have devised their own citation formats for citation for the new cases.

c. Editorial Enhancements in Reporters and Online

As we have learned, lawyers need to review case law when they do legal research. In the days before computers, when lawyers had to find relevant cases in reporters, publishers designed a variety of tools called "editorial enhancements" that helped them to do legal research quickly and efficiently.

Editorial enhancements exist at the beginning of an opinion (which is usually an appellate case, except for federal district court cases in the Federal Supplement). The enhancements begin right after the name of the case, but they are not actually considered part of the opinion because they are written by editors, not judges.

First, there is a summary of the opinion that includes the procedural history of the case (what happened in the trial court, which party appealed, and why), and the evidentiary facts of the case (what happened to the parties and why they are in court). A lawyer can read the case summary and quickly decide, without actually reading the case, whether or not it might be relevant.

Then, there are headnotes, which contain the rules of law that the court applies in the case. If lawyers are looking for cases that discuss a particular rule of law, they can use the headnote to find other cases with a similar legal issue that use the same rule.

LexisNexis and Westlaw also have these editorial enhancements in their online cases, and they work even better online than they did in reporters because they contain hyperlinks to other legal authority. For example, if you find a case that you like, and realize that the most relevant rule is in headnote number five, you can click on that headnote, type in the jurisdiction that you want, and immediately find all of the published cases in that jurisdiction that contain that rule of law.

In the actual opinions, there are numbers which correspond to the headnotes, so if you click on headnote number five, it will immediately jump to the part of the case where that rule is. Also, in the actual opinion, when the court cites to precedent, the citation is a hyperlink, and if you click on it, you will see the precedent.

Thus, while you are reading cases in your casebook, it is useful to go online and find the complete case. If you use LexisNexis or Westlaw, you will see the case summary at the beginning, and you can also look at the headnotes to make sure that you have identified what the legal rules are in the opinion.

C. THE PARTS OF A CASE

There are no laws or regulations that tell judges exactly how to write opinions. Nevertheless, most modern opinions follow a similar pattern.

First, the opinion begins by giving the name of the judge who wrote the opinion. Then, it provides a background for the dispute. It names the parties, and gives the background facts. If it is an appellate case, the opinion gives the **procedural facts**, which describe what happened in the trial court: who won, what the holding was, and who appealed. The procedural facts also explain how the appeal reached the appellate court by describing the grounds for the appeal. In addition, the background provides the **evidentiary facts**, which describe the nature of the dispute: what happened between the parties, and why the plaintiff sued the defendant (or in a criminal case, why the government prosecuted the defendant).

After this factual introduction to the case, opinions often announce the issue or issues that the court must resolve. The issues for appeal may be centered on the law or the facts: a law-centered issue involves what the law means, and a fact-centered issue involves applying the law to the facts of the dispute. Often but not always, the opinion states the holding after it states the issues for appeal.

After this introduction comes the main part of the opinion, called the **discussion**. Here, the court methodically analyzes the issues one at a time. For each issue, the opinion first states what the relevant legal rules are for the issue, whether the rules come from constitutions, statutes or treaties, regulations, or case law. Rule sections typically begin with the general rules, and then move to more specific rules, which might provide definitions, exceptions, or explanations for the general rule. Opinions may also describe relevant precedent with similar facts, to show how the court applied the rules to the facts in the earlier case.

Then the opinion applies the rules to the facts of the case. Often, it mentions the parties' arguments for the issue, and considers whether they are accurate. Sometimes, the court directly applies the rules to the facts itself and does not discuss the parties' arguments. Then it provides its holding for the issue (how it resolved the issue), and its rationale — the reasons for its holding.

Opinions repeat this pattern for each separate issue, and then provide the **disposition** or **judgment** at the end. This is the action that the court has ordered, such as affirming the trial court's decision, reversing it, or reversing and remanding it.

The *Brennan's* case below is an example of a well-written modern opinion. It is clearly organized, and provides headings (Background and Discussion) and subheadings for each issue in the Discussion. To show you what a complete case looks like, including the editorial enhancements, this case comes from the LexisNexis online version, with one small edit: the hyperlinks have been removed from thc top of each headnote. There are also comments written along the side of the opinion to explain its organization.

Remember that the first part of the "case" is the editorial enhancements, which are very useful, but they are *not* actually part of the case. The opinion begins where it says, "CARDAMONE, Circuit Judge," the name of the author of the opinion.

Brennan's, Inc. v. Brennan's Rest., L.L.C., 360 F.3d 125	Case citation
United States Court of Appeals for the Second Circuit October 2, 2003, Argued; February 26, 2004, Decided Docket No. 03-7382	Court
Reporter: 360 F.3d 125 | 2004 U.S. App. LEXIS 3671 | 69 U.S.P.Q.2D (BNA) 1939	Reporters
BRENNAN'S, INC., Plaintiff-Appellant, v. BRENNAN'S RESTAURANT, L.L.C., 565 LEXINGTON AVENUE CO., LLC., Defendants-Appellees.	Complete case name
Prior History: [1] Plaintiff Brennan's, Inc., a New Orleans restaurant owner, appeals from the denial of its motion for a preliminary injunction in a memorandum and order of the United States District Court for the Southern District of New York (McKenna, J.) dated March 17, 2003 and entered March 20, 2003. Plaintiff made its motion during the pendency of its trademark infringement suit against defendants, owners of a New York City restaurant with a similar name. Brennan's, Inc. v. Brennan's Rest., LLC, 2003 U.S. Dist. LEXIS 3974 (S.D.N.Y., Mar. 17, 2003)	***Editorial enhance–ments begin here.*** *(Note: they are not part of the opinion.)*
Disposition: Affirmed.	Judgment
Core Terms restaurant, marks, proximity, geographic, district court, preliminary injunction, likelihood of confusion, consumer confusion, consumers, trademark infringement, reputation, trademark, secondary meaning, last name, user, first name, infringement, registration, customers, distant, likelihood of success, the Lanham Act, own name, registered, relevant market, incontestable, advertising, marketplace, injunction, diners	Search terms that can be used to find similar cases.
Case Summary	Case Summary
Procedural Posture Appellant trademark holder filed a trademark infringement suit against appellee alleged trademark infringer regarding the use of its name in its restaurant. The United States District Court for the Southern District of New York denied the holder's motion for a preliminary injunction during the pendency of the suit. The holder sought review.	Procedural facts
Overview The holder used its last name, which was registered as a	Evidentiary

trademark, for its New Orleans restaurant. The user had the same last name and used his first name and last name for a New York City restaurant. On appeal, the court affirmed the denial of a preliminary injunction, holding that there was no clear error in the district court's findings that the holder was not likely to succeed on the merits of showing a likelihood of consumer confusion. In particular, with respect to the strength of the holder's mark, although a proper name was not inherently distinctive, the holder had continuously used the registered mark for five consecutive years. However, as a common last name, the mark was inherently weak, and there was no showing that it had acquired distinctiveness in New York City. Further, the holder failed to show that the user's inconsistent use of the first name was confusing to consumers. In addition, the geographic remoteness between the parties was critical, particularly in the restaurant industry involving individual restaurants and not chains. The court noted that the holder failed to demonstrate that an appreciable number of relevant consumers were likely to be confused.

facts

Outcome

The court affirmed the district court's order denying the holder a preliminary injunction.

Decision

LexisNexis® Headnotes

Headnotes

HN1 See 15 U.S.C.S. § 1125(a)(1).

HN2 The key for a plaintiff in proving infringement of its trademark is to show the likelihood of consumer confusion.

HN3 A party seeking a preliminary injunction must establish (1) irreparable harm and (2) either (a) a likelihood of success on the merits or (b) a sufficiently serious question going to the merits and a balance of hardships tipping decidedly in the moving party's favor. In a trademark infringement case, proof of a likelihood of confusion establishes both a likelihood of success on the merits and irreparable harm.

HN4 An appellate court reviews a district court's denial of a preliminary injunction for an abuse of discretion.

HN5 To evaluate the likelihood of consumer confusion, courts apply a multi-factor test. This test requires analysis of several non-exclusive factors, including: (1) the strength of the mark, (2) the degree of similarity between the two marks, (3) the competitive proximity of the products, (4) actual confusion, (5) the likelihood the plaintiff will bridge the gap, (6) the defendant's good faith in adopting its mark, (7) the quality of the defendant's products, and (8) the sophistication of the purchasers. No single factor is dispositive, nor is a court limited to consideration of only these factors. Further, each factor must be evaluated in the context of how it bears on the ultimate

Headnotes are rules of law used in the case, given in the same order that they appear in the case below. Look in the opinion for the symbols "HN1," etc., and you will find the rule at that place.

When you do legal research, headnotes can also be used to find other cases question of likelihood of confusion as to the source of the product.

HN6 In reviewing a district court's evaluation of the factors to determine likelihood of consumer confusion in a trademark infringement action, each individual factor is reviewed under a clearly erroneous standard, but the ultimate determination of the likelihood of confusion is a legal issue subject to de novo review.

HN7 The strength of a mark refers to its ability to identify the source of the goods being sold under its aegis. There are two components of a mark's strength: its inherent distinctiveness and the distinctiveness it has acquired in the marketplace. The former, inherent distinctiveness, examines a mark's theoretical potential to identify plaintiff's goods or services without regard to whether it has actually done so. The latter, acquired distinctiveness, refers to something entirely different. This measure looks solely to that recognition a mark has earned in the marketplace as a designator of goods or services.

HN8 Courts assess inherent distinctiveness by classifying a mark in one of four categories arranged in increasing order of inherent distinctiveness: (a) generic, (b) descriptive, (c) suggestive, or (d) fanciful or arbitrary.

HN9 A proper name is descriptive because it does not by itself identify a product; however, if a name develops secondary meaning, it may come to identify a product as originating from a single source. The name of a person, therefore, like other descriptive marks, is protectible only if it has acquired secondary meaning.

HN10 A registered mark in continuous use for five consecutive years after registration, and still in use, becomes incontestable. 15 U.S.C.S. § 1065.

HN11 To achieve the status of a strong mark, a plaintiff must demonstrate distinctiveness in the relevant market, for if the mark is not recognized by the relevant consumer group, a similar mark will not deceive those consumers and thereby increase search costs.

HN12 The fact that a mark has selling power in a limited geographical or commercial area does not endow it with a secondary meaning for the public generally.

HN13 When evaluating the similarity of marks, courts consider the overall impression created by a mark. Each mark must be compared against the other as a whole; juxtaposing fragments of each mark does not aid in deciding whether the compared marks are confusingly similar. The fact that the two marks appear similar is not dispositive. Rather, the question is whether such similarity is more likely than not to cause consumer confusion.

that contain the same rule.

This case has 17 headnotes. Longer cases will likely have more, shorter cases less.

HN14 In trademark infringement litigation, the proximity inquiry asks to what extent the two products compete with each other. In assessing product proximity, courts look at the nature of the products themselves and the structure of the relevant market. The competitive proximity factor has two elements, market proximity and geographic proximity. Market proximity asks whether the two products are in related areas of commerce and geographic proximity looks to the geographic separation of the products. Both elements seek to determine whether the two products have an overlapping client base that creates a potential for confusion.

HN15 A geographically remote mark may nevertheless gain protection in a distant market, at least where there is extensive advertising or evidence of strong reputation in the distant market.

HN16 Although registration presumptively creates nationwide protection, the Lanham Act only permits an injunction against a party where that party's use of a similar mark is likely to cause confusion. 15 U.S.C.S. § 1114.

HN17 Substantial geographic separation remains a significant indicator that the likelihood of confusion is slight.

Counsel: EDWARD T. COLBERT, Washington, D.C. (William M. Merone, Kenyon & Kenyon, Washington, D.C.; Gregg A. Paradise, Kenyon & Kenyon, New York, New York, of counsel), for Plaintiff-Appellant.

List of attorneys for the parties.

ADAM M. COHEN, New York, New York (Dana M. Susman, Kane Kessler, P.C., New York, New York, of counsel), for Defendants-Appellees.

Judges: Before: CARDAMONE, MINER, and CALABRESI, Circuit Judges.

Opinion by: CARDAMONE

Names of the judges on the panel, and name of the author.

Opinion

[127] CARDAMONE, Circuit Judge:

This is an appeal from the denial of a preliminary injunction in a trademark infringement suit. The suit involves a dispute between two restaurant owners over the use of the name "Brennan's." The owner of a widely-renowned New Orleans restaurant named "Brennan's" moved for a preliminary injunction against the [2] owners of a New York City restaurant called "Terrance Brennan's Seafood & Chop House." Plaintiff's motion was denied by the United States District Court for the Southern District of New York (McKenna, J.) in a memorandum and order entered March 20, 2003.

The opinion begins here, on page 127 of the reporter.

The first paragraph describes the

This trademark infringement suit is focused on the protectability as a mark of plaintiff's use of the family name Brennan. In trademark law names are important identifiers of the source of goods or services marketed to the public consumer. [128] Names, of course, are not constant like the northern star, but are changeable, as some -- like show-business people, some newly married women, and recent immigrants -- shed their birth names like old coats and happily don new ones they prefer. But others, like plaintiff and defendant in this case, think their names are treasures to be safeguarded jealously. From the surname Brennan, plaintiff's predecessor coined a trademark he used for his restaurant. Defendant, also named Brennan, attached to that surname his first name of Terrance and used these names as a mark for his restaurant. Thus, the stage for the trademark litigation before us was set.

procedural facts.

This paragraph introduces the main issue of the case.

BACKGROUND

Plaintiff Brennan's, Inc. (Brennan's [3] New Orleans, plaintiff, or appellant) owns and operates the restaurant "Brennan's," founded in 1946 in New Orleans, Louisiana. Plaintiff registered the name Brennan's pursuant to the Lanham Act, 15 U.S.C. §§ 1051 et seq., as a trademark for its restaurant services. The validity of that mark is not disputed. Plaintiff operates one other restaurant, "Owen Brennan's Restaurant," in Memphis, Tennessee, but owns no restaurants in the New York City area. Terrance Brennan, so named at birth, is a New York City chef who, prior to this litigation, opened two restaurants in New York City, "Picholine" and "Artisanal." He is a well-known "name" chef whose reputation attracts customers. At the center of this controversy is his newest enterprise, "Terrance Brennan's Seafood & Chop House" (Terrance Brennan's), located in Manhattan. A corporation was formed called 565 Lexington Avenue Co., LLC to own and operate the restaurant. This corporation along with its sole managing member, Brennan's Restaurant, LLC, are the named defendants in this action. Defendants originally called the new restaurant "Brennan's Seafood & Chop House," but after receiving a cease-and-desist [4] letter from plaintiff's lawyers, they added the first name "Terrance" to their mark.

The opinion uses headings to help the reader.

This paragraph introduces the evidentiary (substantive) facts.

Brennan's New Orleans sought a preliminary injunction on the grounds that the name Terrance Brennan's Seafood & Chop House infringed its rights in the name Brennan's and was likely to cause consumer confusion. After expedited limited discovery and a two-day hearing, Judge McKenna denied the motion for a preliminary injunction. See Brennan's, Inc. v. Brennan's Rest., LLC, 2003 U.S. Dist. LEXIS 3974, No. 02-CV9858, 2003 WL 1338681 (S.D.N.Y. Mar. 18, 2003). This appeal followed. We affirm.

End of fact section and announce-ment of holding ("We affirm.")

DISCUSSION

I Preliminary Injunction Under the Lanham Act

The Lanham Act creates a cause of action against any person

Beginning

who, in connection with goods or services, uses in commerce any word, term, name, symbol, or device, or

HN1 any combination thereof, or any false designation of origin . . . which -- (A) is likely to cause confusion, or to cause mistake, or to deceive as to the . . . connection . . . of such person with another person, or as to the origin, sponsorship, or approval of his or her goods, [or] services . . . .
15 U.S.C. § 1125(a)(1). HN2 The key for a plaintiff [5] in proving infringement of its trademark is to show the likelihood of consumer confusion. See Restatement (Third) of Unfair Competition § 21 cmt. a (1995) ("The test for infringement is whether the actor's use of a designation as [129] a trademark . . . creates a likelihood of confusion . . . .").

HN3 A party seeking a preliminary injunction must establish (1) irreparable harm and (2) either (a) a likelihood of success on the merits or (b) a sufficiently serious question going to the merits and a balance of hardships tipping decidedly in the moving party's favor. See Jackson Dairy, Inc. v. H.P. Hood & Sons, Inc., 596 F.2d 70, 72 (2d Cir. 1979) (per curiam). In a trademark infringement case, proof of a likelihood of confusion establishes both a likelihood of success on the merits and irreparable harm. See Hasbro, Inc. v. Lanard Toys, Ltd., 858 F.2d 70, 73 (2d Cir. 1988).

Although appellant has properly invoked our jurisdiction on an interlocutory appeal pursuant to 28 U.S.C. § 1292(a)(1), we must observe that a decision on a motion for a preliminary injunction in a trademark dispute [6] is closely tied to the merits, especially where, as here, the validity of the registered mark is uncontested and the key question is whether there is consumer confusion. By taking an appeal after the denial of a preliminary injunction appellant asks us -- with only a limited factual record before us - in effect to decide the merits. Because HN4 we review a district court's denial of a preliminary injunction for an abuse of discretion, see Virgin Enterprises Ltd. v. Nawab, 335 F.3d 141, 145-46 (2d Cir. 2003), it is not surprising that appellant has a formidable hurdle to overcome.

Presumably Brennan's New Orleans seeks expedited review in hopes we will reverse the district court and grant the injunction. Yet, at this early stage, we have before us mostly conclusory allegations supported by facts that are generally contested. Infrequently will such prove to be a record on which an appellate court will find that a district court has abused its discretion by refusing to issue a preliminary injunction. The only result of an appeal in such circumstances is several months delay. It seems to us that if a party desires rapid resolution of the suit, after its motion for a [7] preliminary injunction has been denied, better practice would be to seek an expedited trial on the merits. With the parties then able to create a more substantial record, the district court would have an opportunity to make more extensive and reliable findings of fact and we would be in a better position to engage in meaningful appellate review.

of analysis of legal issues.

First issue (obtaining a preliminary injunction)

Key trademark infringement rule

Main rule for obtaining a preliminary injunction.

Court's suggestion that plaintiff was not wise to appeal denial of injunction now, on a limited record, with a difficult standard of review for plaintiff.

Given review standard, court notes that it is unlikely to reverse trial court with little

Plaintiff also brought dilution and state law unfair competition claims in the district court, but the only issue before us on appeal is the trademark infringement claim. On that issue, the district court ruled that plaintiff had not demonstrated a likelihood of success on the merits. In particular, it noted the minimal evidence of actual confusion, the use of Terrance Brennan's first name in his mark, the sophistication of the relevant consumer market, and the substantial geographic distance -- more than 1,000 miles -- separating the two Brennan restaurants. Although we are doubtful about certain aspects of the district court's findings, we are at the same time persuaded that Judge McKenna's ultimate determination that plaintiff was not entitled to a preliminary injunction did not constitute an abuse of his discretion.

evidence.

Summary of trial court issues and issue on appeal.

Court explains it does not agree with all of the findings, but it still affirms the decision.

II Trademark Infringement

[8] Plaintiff's claim of trademark infringement is brought under the federal trademark laws, 15 U.S.C. §§ 1114 (imitation of registered mark) and 1125(a) (false designation of origin). To prevail on a claim of trademark infringement, a plaintiff must show, first, that its mark merits protection, and, second, that the defendant's use of a similar mark is likely to cause consumer confusion. Gruner + Jahr USA Publ'g v. Meredith Corp., 991 F.2d 1072, 1075 [130] (2d Cir. 1993); see, e.g., Virgin, 335 F.3d at 146 (noting that the Gruner test applies to infringement claims brought under §§ 1114 and 1125(a)). The parties do not dispute that plaintiff has a valid, registered mark in the name Brennan's that has become incontestable by operation of law. See 15 U.S.C. § 1065. We turn therefore to consider the pivotal question: the likelihood of confusion.

Main issue of case: whether plaintiff can show a likelihood of customer confusion between two restaurants with the name Brennan's.

HN5 To evaluate the likelihood of consumer confusion, we apply the multi-factor test set forth by Judge Friendly in Polaroid Corp. v. Polarad Elecs. Corp., 287 F.2d 492, 495 (2d Cir. 1961). This test requires analysis of several non-exclusive [9] factors, including: (1) the strength of the mark, (2) the degree of similarity between the two marks, (3) the competitive proximity of the products, (4) actual confusion, (5) the likelihood the plaintiff will bridge the gap, (6) the defendant's good faith in adopting its mark, (7) the quality of the defendant's products, and (8) the sophistication of the purchasers. See Mobil Oil Corp. v. Pegasus Petroleum Corp., 818 F.2d 254, 256 (2d Cir. 1987) (citing Polaroid, 287 F.2d at 495); Gruner, 991 F.2d at 1077. No single factor is dispositive, nor is a court limited to consideration of only these factors. Polaroid, 287 F.2d at 495. Further, "each factor must be evaluated in the context of how it bears on the ultimate question of likelihood of confusion as to the source of the product." Lois Sportswear, U.S.A., Inc. v. Levi Strauss & Co., 799 F.2d 867, 872 (2d Cir. 1986).

Key 8–factor likelihood of confusion test.

Note that although the Lanham Act is a federal statute, this 8–factor test is a judge–made test.

HN6 In reviewing the district court's evaluation of the Polaroid factors, each individual factor is reviewed under a clearly erroneous standard, but the ultimate determination of the likelihood of confusion is a legal issue subject [10] to de novo review. Hasbro, 858 F.2d at 75-76; Banff, Ltd. v. Federated

Standard of review for

Dep't Stores, Inc., 841 F.2d 486, 490 (2d Cir. 1988). The district court's findings with respect to each factor were as follows: (1) plaintiff has a strong mark; (2) the marks are similar, but Terrance Brennan's use of the first name "Terrance" in its mark reduces their similarity and reduces potential confusion; (3) the competing restaurants are not proximate competitors since they are more than 1,000 miles apart; (4) there is no indication that Brennan's New Orleans has any intention of bridging the gap by operating in or near New York City; (5) there is little or no evidence of actual confusion; (6) diners in the high-end restaurants tend to be sophisticated, and thus less likely to be confused; (7) there is no evidence of bad faith on the part of defendants; and (8) the high quality of Terrance Brennan's restaurant is not likely to diminish the reputation of Brennan's New Orleans. The district court concluded that the first factor favored plaintiff, the second partially favored plaintiff, and the remaining factors favored defendant. Accordingly, it refused to grant an injunction.

trial court's use of *Polaroid* factors.

Summary of trial court's findings re all 8 factors.

[11] We find no clear error in most of the district court's findings, and we share its view that plaintiff has not at this point demonstrated a likelihood of confusion. We think, however, that three of the Polaroid factors warrant further discussion: the strength of plaintiff's mark, the degree of similarity of the two marks, and the proximity of the services.

Roadmap for Part III: the three factors where the court did not completely agree with the trial court's findings.

III Polaroid Factors

A. Strength of the Mark

HN7 The strength of a mark refers to its ability to identify the source of the goods being sold under its aegis. See Nora Beverages, Inc. v. Perrier Group of America, Inc., 269 F.3d 114, 123 (2d Cir. 2001). There are two components of a mark's strength: its inherent distinctiveness and the distinctiveness it has acquired [131] in the marketplace. See Streetwise Maps, Inc. v. VanDam, Inc., 159 F.3d 739, 743-44 (2d Cir. 1998). The former, inherent distinctiveness, examines a mark's theoretical potential to identify plaintiff's goods or services without regard to whether it has actually done so. The latter, acquired distinctiveness, refers to something entirely different. This measure looks solely to that recognition plaintiff's mark has [12] earned in the marketplace as a designator of plaintiff's goods or services. See TCPIP Holding Co. v. Haar Communications, Inc., 244 F.3d 88, 97 (2d Cir. 2001).

Introduction to rules for first factor.

1. Inherent Distinctiveness of Family Names

HN8 Courts assess inherent distinctiveness by classifying a mark in one of four categories arranged in increasing order of inherent distinctiveness: (a) generic, (b) descriptive, (c) suggestive, or (d) fanciful or arbitrary. Streetwise, 159 F.3d at 744; Estee Lauder Inc. v. The Gap, Inc., 108 F.3d 1503, 1508 (2d Cir. 1997). HN9 A proper name such as Brennan's is descriptive because it does not by itself identify a product; however, if a name develops secondary meaning, it may come

First part of rule for first factor and

to identify a product as originating from a single source. See Gruner, 991 F.2d at 1076; 4 Callmann on Unfair Competition, Trademarks and Monopolies § 22:42 (4th ed. 2003) ("An individual name is rather similar to a descriptive word, in the sense that it might properly be regarded as a convenient description of the fact that the named individual is or was affiliated with the firm."). The name of a person, therefore, like other descriptive [13] marks, is protectible only if it has acquired secondary meaning. Patsy's Brand, Inc. v. I.O.B. Realty, Inc., 317 F.3d 209, 217 (2d Cir. 2003).

application of rule to facts of case.

Of course, HN10 a registered mark in continuous use for five consecutive years after registration, and still in use, becomes incontestable. See 15 U.S.C. § 1065. Because of this statutory incontestability, Brennan's New Orleans, which would ordinarily be accorded only minimal protection as a descriptive mark, in the district court's view became a strong mark entitled to protection under the Lanham Act. See Gruner, 991 F.2d at 1076-77. This statutory incontestability was bolstered by the district court's finding that plaintiff's mark had acquired secondary meaning through its long history and numerous media reviews.

In the case at hand plaintiff and defendant have a common last name. And, it is one they share with many others. We take judicial notice that a current Manhattan telephone book lists 184 residences and 20 businesses with the name Brennan. Because the thrust of trademark law aims to avoid confusion as to the product's source it is unhelpful to draw rigid rules when dealing [14] with a common last name. For our purposes in deciding this appeal, for example, it would be incorrect to insist that defendant is always entitled to use his own name in business, and it is equally incorrect to maintain that defendant is never entitled to the use of his own name to compete with the same and perhaps more famous business name of plaintiff.

Court's conclusion and reasoning for Part 1 of first factor.

While the law recognizes the unfairness of letting one person trade on the reputation or the name of another, at the same time it also recognizes that one's surname given at birth creates associations attached to that name which identify the individual. As a consequence, courts generally are hesitant to afford strong protection to proper names, since to do so preempts others with the same name from trading on their own reputation. "To prevent all use of [a man's personal name] is to take away his identity; without it he cannot [132] make known who he is to those who may wish to deal with him; and that is so grievous an injury that courts will avoid imposing it, if they possibly can." Societe Vinicole de Champagne v. Mumm, 143 F.2d 240, 241 (2d Cir. 1944) (per curiam). Cf. Taylor Wine Co. v. Bully Hill Vineyards, Inc., 569 F.2d 731, 735-36 (2d Cir. 1978); [15] Conagra, Inc. v. Singleton, 743 F.2d 1508, 1515 n. 9 (11th Cir. 1984).

As a common last name, we think at this point and contrary to the district court that plaintiff's mark is inherently weak. Cf. Scott Paper Co. v. Scott's Liquid Gold, 589 F.2d 1225, 1231 (3d

Cir. 1978) ("Selection of a mark with a common surname naturally entails a risk of some uncertainty and the law will not assure absolute protection."). A common last name implicates both the minimal level of protection traditionally granted to descriptive marks and the policy of not protecting last names to a degree that unnecessarily precludes other users from trading on their own names' reputation. Further, the more common a last name is, the lower the likelihood that a competitor will effectively appropriate the goodwill of the senior user since consumers will be unlikely to assume that the two brands with the same name refer to the same goods.

2. Plaintiff Has Not Acquired Distinctiveness in New York

Nevertheless, even a common name mark may warrant protection as a strong mark if it has achieved distinctiveness in the marketplace, the second component of a mark's strength. [16] Yet, HN11 to achieve the status of a strong mark, plaintiff must demonstrate distinctiveness in the relevant market, for if the mark is not recognized by the relevant consumer group, a similar mark will not deceive those consumers and thereby increase search costs. Dawn Donut Co. v. Hart's Food Stores, Inc., 267 F.2d 358, 364 (2d Cir. 1959); 4 J. Thomas McCarthy, McCarthy on Trademarks and Unfair Competition § 26:25 at 39 (4th ed. 2003). In this case, the relevant market is the pool of actual and potential customers of Terrance Brennan's, for it is those patrons whose potential confusion is at issue.

Second part of rule for first factor and application of rule to facts of case.

To support its conclusion that plaintiff's mark was strong, the district court cited media notices regarding Brennan's New Orleans from various newspapers around the country, and observed that Brennan's New Orleans "has had almost two million customers and generated over $ 84 million in revenues, spending more than $ 4,600,000 on advertising and promotion." Brennan's, Inc., 2003 U.S. Dist. LEXIS 3974, 2003 WL 1338681, at *2 n.4. While media and advertising figures are relevant to the analysis, the district court made no findings with respect to advertising expenditures or [17] media exposure in New York City.

We do not doubt that Brennan's New Orleans's history is notable. But virtually all the articles and reviews discuss Brennan's New Orleans in the context of the City of New Orleans or a trip to New Orleans. This evidence in no way demonstrates that potential diners in New York City who find the word Brennan's on a restaurant awning will have any reason to think the restaurant is connected with Brennan's New Orleans, or even will have heard of Brennan's New Orleans. This is especially true because Brennan's New Orleans has not expanded in or near New York, defendant Terrance Brennan has his own reputation in New York, and Brennan is a common name.

We recognize, of course, that some last names do achieve such a degree of secondary meaning that they can become strong identifiers of source (e.g., Bacardi for rum, Ford for

automobiles, Smucker for jam). [133] Considering however the importance of permitting a person's good faith use of his own name, courts have taken great care to ensure that injunctions are no broader than necessary to preserve the senior user's rights. To enjoin Terrance Brennan's use of his own name, Brennan's New Orleans must make [18] a showing that its mark has achieved such potency in Terrance Brennan's market that his use of his own name will cause consumer confusion as to source.
The current record suggests to us at most that plaintiff has a strong mark among New Orleans diners and visitors to New Orleans. "However, HN12 the fact that a mark has selling power in a limited geographical or commercial area does not endow it with a secondary meaning for the public generally." Mead Data Cent., Inc. v. Toyota Motor Sales, U.S.A., Inc., 875 F.2d 1026, 1030 (2d Cir. 1989); see also Hartman v. Hallmark Cards, Inc., 833 F.2d 117, 121 (8th Cir. 1987); Truck Equip. Serv. Co. v. Fruehauf Corp., 536 F.2d 1210, 1219 (8th Cir. 1976).

Absent from the district court's analysis was any demonstration of acquired distinctiveness in the relevant market, namely the actual and potential New York City diners of Terrance Brennan's. Because the district court's legal analysis on this matter was insufficient, its findings do not at present support the conclusion that plaintiff has a strong mark. The district court may want to revisit this issue at trial in light of further proof [19] it may have before it.

Court's conclusion and reasoning for Part 2 of first factor.

B. Similarity of the Marks

HN13 When evaluating the similarity of marks, courts consider the overall impression created by a mark. Each mark must be compared against the other as a whole; juxtaposing fragments of each mark does not aid in deciding whether the compared marks are confusingly similar. See Universal City Studios, Inc. v. Nintendo Co., 746 F.2d 112, 117 (2d Cir. 1984). The fact that the two marks appear similar is not dispositive. Rather, the question is whether such similarity is more likely than not to cause consumer confusion. See Gruner, 991 F.2d at 1078.

Rules for second factor.

We agree with the district court that the addition of the first name "Terrance" to defendant's mark is meaningful. Judge McKenna found that Terrance Brennan, through his restaurants Picholine and Artisanal, has become a well-known chef in Manhattan, and that the use of his first name suggests a restaurant connected with the Terrance Brennan of Picholine and Artisanal instead of a restaurant connected with Brennan's in New Orleans. Brennan's, Inc., 2003 U.S. Dist. LEXIS 3974, 2003 WL 1338681, at *2. This finding is not clearly erroneous.

Application of rules to facts of case.

Because the ultimate [20] issue is the likelihood of confusion, analysis focuses on the particular industry where the marks compete. This is relevant because likelihood of confusion is related to consumer expectations. See TCPIP, 244 F.3d at 101. In the restaurant industry, it is not uncommon to name a restaurant after its chef, particularly with high-end restaurants where that chef has developed a reputation in the public's mind.

Instances would be: Nobu/Matsuhisa (New York/Los Angeles), Charlie Trotter's (Chicago), Daniel/Cafe Boulud (New York), Jean Georges (New York), Hamersley's Bistro (Boston), Morimoto (Philadelphia), and Emeril's (multiple locations). These examples suggest the awareness diners have when connecting the name of a restaurant to a particular chef. They also suggest the importance of permitting a chef to use his own name, since forcing a junior user to change his mark imposes costs that may be substantial in the high-class restaurant business.

[134] Plaintiff is concerned that the name Terrance Brennan's Seafood & Chop House will, in practice, simply be truncated to Brennan's in daily use. The district court found that on several occasions, people answering the telephone [21] at Terrance Brennan's identified the restaurant as Brennan's Seafood and Chop House or simply Brennan's. But the court credited Terrance Brennan's testimony that he has since instructed his staff that the first name Terrance is always to be used. Whether and to what extent the practice of truncation may play a role in increasing consumer confusion need not concern us here because plaintiff has not demonstrated that any truncation in this case is of a confusing nature.

Court's conclusion for the second factor.

C. Proximity of the Products

HN14 The proximity inquiry asks to what extent the two products compete with each other. See Cadbury Beverages, Inc. v. Cott Corp., 73 F.3d 474, 480 (2d Cir. 1996). In assessing product proximity we look at "the nature of the products themselves and the structure of the relevant market." Vitarroz Corp. v. Borden, Inc., 644 F.2d 960, 967 (2d Cir. 1981).

Rules for third factor.

The competitive proximity factor has two elements, market proximity and geographic proximity. Market proximity asks whether the two products are in related areas of commerce and geographic proximity looks to the geographic separation of the products. Both elements seek to determine whether the two [22] products have an overlapping client base that creates a potential for confusion. In the instant case the services have close market proximity since both are upscale restaurants. The district court found that the two restaurants would, without question, compete for customers were they in the same city. Brennan's, Inc., 2003 U.S. Dist. LEXIS 3974, 2003 WL 1338681, at *3. The court also recognized the significance of the fact that the restaurants are geographically distant, with more than 1,000 miles separating them.

It is well established that HN15 a geographically remote mark may nevertheless gain protection in a distant market, at least where there is extensive advertising or evidence of strong reputation in the distant market. See, e.g., Stork Rest. v. Sahati, 166 F.2d 348 (9th Cir. 1948) (recognizing that the Stork Club in New York had sufficient nationwide reputation that a new tavern in San Francisco of the same name infringed its mark); 4 McCarthy on Trademarks, supra, § 26:17 at 26-27. HN16

Although registration presumptively creates nationwide protection, the Lanham Act only permits an injunction against a party where that party's use of a similar mark is likely [23] to cause confusion. See 15 U.S.C. § 1114.

We agree with the district court that geographic remoteness is critical in this case. In the restaurant industry, especially where individual restaurants rather than chains are competing, physical separation seems particularly significant to the inquiry into consumer confusion. Even in this age of rapid communication and travel, plaintiff faces a high hurdle to demonstrate that a single restaurant in New Orleans and a single restaurant in New York City compete for the same customers. That is particularly the case here where the dining services require a customer's physical presence and cannot rely, for instance, on Internet or mail-order sales.

Application of the rules to the facts of the case.

To succeed on an infringement claim, plaintiff must show that it is probable, not just possible, that consumers will be confused. See Streetwise, 159 F.3d at 743. The district court concluded that, even crediting plaintiff's contention that over seven percent of its business comes from New York State, the substantial distance [135] between the restaurants coupled with the fact that plaintiff has never had an establishment in New York City meant it was unlikely [24] that an appreciable number of ordinarily prudent purchasers were likely to be confused.

Geography is relevant to our analysis of a mark's strength, particularly with marks requiring secondary meaning. Likewise, strength analysis can inform proximity analysis, for the more arbitrary or fanciful a mark, the more likely that geographically distant customers with knowledge of the senior mark might presume that two similar marks are related. With a common last name, we consider it less likely that consumers in a distant market would be surprised to find two unrelated entities using the same common last name.

Certain businesses such as hotels, and to a lesser degree restaurants, attract the traveling public. Courts have recognized that even businesses that are separated by large distances may attract overlapping clientele due to the ease of travel. See, e.g., Tisch Hotels, Inc. v. Americana Inn, Inc., 350 F.2d 609, 613 (7th Cir. 1965) (geographic separation is not dispositive if the nature of the business, e.g., hotels, is such that it attracts the traveling public). We do not disagree with this possibility, but only note that, in the absence of actual [25] confusion or bad faith, HN17 substantial geographic separation remains a significant indicator that the likelihood of confusion is slight. See Dawn Donut, 267 F.2d at 364 (where use of marks by registrant and new user are confined to distinct and geographically separate markets, and no likelihood that registrant will expand into junior user's market, registrant not entitled to enjoin junior user's use of the mark); John R. Thompson Co. v. Holloway, 366 F.2d 108, 114 (5th Cir. 1966) ("Where the unauthorized use of a conflicting mark is confined to a distinct and geographically separate market by the junior user, there may be no present likelihood of public confusion."). Geography alone is not decisive, but the plaintiff still has the burden to demonstrate that an appreciable number of relevant consumers are likely to be confused. We find no such demonstration on this record.

Court's conclusion for the third factor.

As to the remaining Polaroid factors, we agree with the district court for substantially the reasons set forth in its memorandum and order. Having failed at this early stage to establish a likelihood of success on the merits, plaintiff is not entitled to a preliminary injunction. [26]

CONCLUSION

The order denying a preliminary injunction is affirmed.

Summary of conclusions on other five factors and judgment.

QUESTIONS FOR DISCUSSION

1. What was the original name of the New York restaurant?
2. Did it change its name? Why?
3. What was the name of the restaurant in New Orleans?
4. In which jurisdiction did the plaintiff bring the lawsuit?
5. What claims (causes of action) did the plaintiff bring in the trial court?
6. What motion did it make in the trial court? Why?
7. What was the trial court procedure for hearing the motion?
8. What did the trial court rule? Why?
9. Had there been a final judgment in the trial court at the time of the appeal?
10. What was the issue on appeal?
11. Is trademark infringement law based on a statute or on common law?
12. What about the 8-factor test for the "likelihood of confusion" rule? What is the source of that rule?
13. Do you agree with the Second Circuit's decision? Why or why not?

Chapter Review

- A practicing attorney in the United States or a student in a U.S. law school is likely to read many cases, and needs to become a skilled legal reader.
- In law school, the cases at the beginning of the semester may be old, historical cases, which look quite different from modern opinions. Old opinions were originally given orally, by each judge on a panel, and early written opinions

were similar in style.

- Modern cases are more tightly organized, and typically do not resemble "spoken language" in style. They also contain citations to legal authority, no matter what the source — constitutions, statutes, treaties, regulations, or case law. Modern legal writing requires citations to support each assertion of law.
- Modern judicial opinions are typically written by one author. In an appellate case, when the majority of judges agree that one party should win and they agree on the reasoning, one judge in the majority is assigned to write the majority opinion. If all of the judges on the panel are in agreement, it is a unanimous opinion. If a majority agrees on who should win, but not on the reasoning, a judge is chosen to write a plurality opinion.
- The authority of the case depends in part upon the votes of the judges on the panel: a unanimous opinion is highly authoritative, but a plurality opinion is considered weak. Thus, judges may compromise on the reasoning so that a majority opinion can be written.
- A judge who agrees with the result but not the reasoning might choose to write a separate opinion called a concurrence. A judge who disagrees with both the result and the reasoning might choose to write a dissent. Concurrences and dissents follow the majority opinion.
- Concurrences and dissents have no legal effect and no precedential value. Judges may choose to write them if they feel passionately about an issue and hope to persuade judges in the future to overrule the majority opinion or to move the law in a different direction.
- Casebooks have heavily-edited cases. A 100-page opinion might be reduced to 3 pages.
- Practicing attorneys read complete cases, which they find in books called reporters or online, from commercial or free legal research websites. Today, lawyers usually find cases online rather than in reporters.
- Reporters, LexisNexis, and Westlaw contain editorial enhancements that help lawyers to quickly determine if the case is relevant and to find other relevant cases. These include case summaries and headnotes that provide each rule of law used in the case.
- For new law students who are unfamiliar with reading U.S. cases, it can be helpful to look online at the editorial enhancements for the cases in your case book to make sure that you have found all of the relevant rules of law and understand the procedural and evidentiary facts of the case. Remember, though, that the editorial enhancements are not considered part of the case: they are there to help lawyers.
- Although no laws require that opinions follow a certain pattern, they generally follow a common format: appellate cases begin with a summary of the procedural history of the case (what happened in the trial court and what issues were appealed) and the evidentiary facts (what happened and why one of the parties sued the other, or for criminal law, why the government

prosecuted the defendant). Then many opinions state the legal issues that the opinion will decide, followed by the decision.

- The second part of the case is called the discussion. In this section, courts analyze the legal issues one at a time, usually beginning with a section that provides the overall rules of law and provides a "roadmap" for the reader.
- The discussion then states the relevant rules of law for the first issue, and then it applies the rules of law to the facts of the case. Often, it states each party's arguments for the issue, and whether they are valid or not. Then it gives the holding for the issue, and the reasons for the holding.
- The opinion then repeats this pattern for each legal issue. At the end, it provides a summary of the issues and states the judgment.

Chapter 6

WRITING A CASE BRIEF

Chapter Preview

This chapter and the next cover skills that will help you to work with cases at a deeper and more efficient level. This chapter discusses:

- Strategies to use while reading cases; and
- Strategies for writing case briefs, which are case summaries that students use to remember key information about the cases that they read.

Professors in U.S. law schools frequently say that the goal of their classes, and of law school in general, is to teach law students to "think like a lawyer." Doing well in law school in the United States involves developing the ability to read and analyze cases and other sources of other primary law critically, in a two-step process.

In the first step, as we saw when we looked at the *Brennan's* case in the last chapter, you need to analyze cases by breaking them down and making sure that you understand each of their parts: the procedural and evidentiary facts, the legal issues, the rules of law, the court's application of the rules to the material facts (the relevant facts of the case that the court uses in reaching its decision), the holding, and the court's rationale or reasoning. Accordingly, this chapter focuses on successful strategies for reading cases, evaluating them, using them to analyze legal issues, and taking notes about them called "case briefs."

In the second step of the process, when a night's reading may easily include three or four cases or more for each class, you need to synthesize what you have learned. Synthesizing cases is the opposite process from the first step — rather than breaking down a case into its parts, you are combining cases, and determining their relationship to each other.

In a course that uses a casebook, your readings for a given class are likely to be in the same chapter or section of the casebook. Why did the author of the casebook choose those cases for the chapter? What is the relationship between them? Do the later cases continue to develop the rules that were set out in the earliest case? Do they follow the same lines of reasoning, or do they go in different directions? Do they refer to the rules in the earliest case as well-settled law, or do they call them into question? What is the present state of the law for that legal issue? These are examples of the types of questions that successful U.S. law students ask themselves as they study, and that practicing lawyers ask themselves as they resolve their clients' legal issues.

A. READING CASES CRITICALLY

All of us have been reading for many years. As lawyers and law students, we are also people who have been academically successful for many years. However, we may not be aware that when we read for different purposes, we read in different ways.

1. "Think Like a Lawyer" by Asking Questions as You Read

For example, when you read a novel or a magazine, you read to understand the content and to enjoy the writing style of the writer. Such reading is fairly passive; in other words, we are not actively working to understand the meaning by constantly asking questions about what we have just read. More likely, we let the meaning of the words wash over us, as when we watch a movie.

For much of your school career, you have read textbooks to understand the content and to memorize information that was likely to be on a test. Perhaps you have a similar plan for your law school reading in the United States: to memorize as many legal rules as you can, and to ask law professors to give you "the answer" to a legal problem. However, these methods are not sufficient to do well at a U.S. law school.

Remember that the goal of legal education here is to "think like a lawyer" in the United States. Thus, casebooks and classes are designed to help you to develop and to practice that ability, and final examinations test that ability.

Final examinations in U.S. law schools are generally essay examinations that provide you with a complicated fact pattern. You are expected to identify the various legal issues that the facts raise, to state the legal rules that are relevant to those issues, to apply the rules to the facts in the fact pattern, and to determine the likely outcome.

The final examination problems are often designed so that there is no clear "answer." Professors expect you to look at all sides of an issue, to state the arguments that the lawyers for either party could make, to evaluate the strengths and weaknesses of the arguments, and then to predict who has the strongest argument. All of this involves a reasoning process that, for short, we call "thinking like a lawyer."

The best way to do this is to begin practicing these skills from the beginning of your time in a U.S. law school. When you read case excerpts in your casebooks, do more than just trying to find and memorize rules. Instead, work actively with each part of the case, beginning with the title.

Look at the citation. Which court decided the case? What is the jurisdiction, and the level of the court? When was the case decided? Is it an old case or a recent case? As you look at these things, do what a U.S. lawyer would do: determine in which courts the case would be binding authority, and in which courts it would merely be persuasive. U.S. lawyers, before even reading the case, would immediately determine whether the opinion would be potentially binding in their client's matter.

Although you do not have a specific client, you should still ask yourself which courts the opinion would bind. For example, if the case that you are reading is from the Supreme Court of Delaware, you should understand that it would bind Delaware state courts, and it could potentially also bind state courts in other states *if* the lawsuit arose from a contract with a choice of law provision that stated that the agreement would be governed by the laws of the state of Delaware or if the court determined that Delaware law applied. The opinion could also be binding on a federal court if the court is sitting under diversity jurisdiction and applying the law of Delaware.

Remember that the holding is the only part of the case that is potentially binding. For example, if the opinion discusses a hypothetical situation, such as what it would likely hold if the facts were different, it is called **obiter dictum**,[1] and it is not binding because the court is not actually deciding that issue. However, a later court may find dicta persuasive if it is attempting to decide the issue that is discussed in dicta.

Also, although you may not be an expert in U.S. history or culture, try to place the opinion that you are reading in the context of when it was decided, by looking at the date. Is it a very old case? Have societal attitudes changed much since the time that the case was decided? Have government policies changed much since then?

---

[1] We often shorten the phrase to "dictum." The plural form is "obiter dicta," which is often shortened to "dicta."

2. Use English-English Dictionaries and Do Not Translate New Words

As an international student, you will often find the language of some opinions difficult not just because of the new legal terms that they contain, but also because English is likely your second or third language. It is tempting to do what you did at home by using a bilingual dictionary, whether electronic or a book, to look up unfamiliar words and translate them to your native language.

Please avoid this temptation. Translating leads to confusion, sleepless nights, and poor grades. You are not studying in your country, where English is a foreign language. You are studying in a U.S. law school, where English is the only language of communication.

To do well here, you must communicate fluently and well in English, and translating to your native language prevents you from doing that. It inevitably leads to mistakes and misunderstandings, as bilingual dictionaries are full of mistakes and inaccuracies. Instead, use English-English dictionaries: a legal dictionary such as Black's or Ballantine's, and a general English dictionary. Although you may not have enough time to look up every new word that you see, make sure that you understand all legal terms by using a legal dictionary. You can buy them, or use online dictionaries. For example, LexisNexis and Westlaw have online legal dictionaries.

3. Analyze Cases by Breaking Them Into Parts and Understanding Each Part

Continue with each part of the case as you did with the citation, starting with the factual background. Ask yourself questions such as these as you read: Who are the parties? What happened and why did the plaintiff sue the defendant? Who won and who lost in the trial court, and why? What were the reasons for the trial court's decision? Who appealed? What issues formed the grounds for the appeal?

Continue with the Discussion section of the opinion and ask questions such as these for each issue: What are the rules? Which evidentiary facts are material (highly relevant)? How does the court apply the rules to those facts? What is the outcome, and what are the court's reasons?

When you look at the opinion's reasoning, look for "policy" issues. "Policy"refers to the purpose of the legal rules. For example, what was the legislature's purpose when it drafted the statute? Was it trying to ensure the free operation of markets and to promote competition between businesses? Was it trying to protect the public? How does the law do that? Should courts read the law broadly in order to better protect the public? These are examples of policy issues, which law professors frequently discuss in class.

Finally, think critically about the opinion itself. Do you think that the judgment was correct? Did the court apply the rules fairly and accurately? Do you agree with the court's reasoning? Why or why not?

As they read cases, some students highlight the different parts of the opinions with differently-colored markers as they read them. If that helps you, please do so. However, that alone is likely not enough. If you read several cases each night, it can be difficult to remember what you read the previous night when you are sitting in the following day's class. Moreover, it can be frustrating and embarrassing if the professor asks you a question about the opinion, and you do not remember what you read the night before.

Therefore, to help you study, and to remember all of the answers to the questions that you have been asking yourself as you analyzed the opinion, it is important to take notes about the case in a format that we call a "case brief."

B. WRITING A CASE BRIEF

What is a case brief? It's a summary of your analysis of a judicial opinion.

1. Why Write a Case Brief?

It's a study aid and/or research tool for yourself, not an audience. A case brief helps you:

- To prepare for casebook classes so that you are ready to discuss the cases and/or answer the professor's questions in class;
- To summarize what you have read;
- To remember and review the significance of the cases you have read;
- To organize and keep track of research you have done; and
- To efficiently write memos and briefs that will use the cases that you summarize in each case brief.

2. What Does a Case Brief Contain?

Case briefs typically contain the five following parts, and you may choose to also write the "optional information" at the end.

1. **Case name, citation, court, year**
2. **Facts**

   Procedural Facts: The history of how the case got to the court that wrote the opinion (usually an appellate court) (i.e., what the trial court held, the grounds of the appeal, etc.).

   Evidentiary Facts: What happened that caused the plaintiff to sue the defendant, including the material facts (the relevant facts the court used in deciding the case), and helpful background facts.
3. **Issue(s):** The questions that the court must decide to resolve the dispute between the parties. Write separate issue questions if the court must decide more than one issue. Consider using the "under-does-when" format: "Under (state the law), does/is (state the issue) when/where (state the material

facts)?"

4. **Holding(s):** The court's ruling(s) on the issue(s). It should answer the question posed in the statement of the Issue(s). There should be a holding for each issue.
5. **Reasoning:** The rules that the court applied, and the court's reasons for how it reached its rulings. State rules as general principles; divide them into sub-rules if appropriate; show how the court applied the rules to the facts of the case.

Optional information:

- State any policy considerations that affected the court's decision.
- Summarize the concurring or dissenting opinions, if any exist.
- Summarize any dicta that seem important or relevant to you.
- Provide your evaluation of the case, including any comments, thoughts, or questionsthat you have about the case.

3. How Should I Prepare My Case Briefs?

First, read the opinion one or two times, asking yourself questions about each part of the case as shown above. Then, when you write the case brief, use the case brief format to help you remember to include the necessary information.

Name of Case and Citation

Facts: Insert the relevant procedural facts (How did this case get to this court? How did the trial court rule and what is being appealed?) and evidentiary facts (who, what, when, where, why?) You can further break it down that way:

PF: (procedural facts)

EF: (evidentiary facts)

Issue(s): Identify the question or questions that the court must decide to resolve the dispute between the parties. State it as a question using the "under-does-when" format: Start with the relevant law, followed by the issue that the court must decide, and then the most relevant facts that the court uses to decide the issue.

Holding(s): Answer the question or questions that you have identified in the issue section. Remember that a holding is a statement of the rule of law that comes from a particular case; it is the judgment in that case, plus the material facts. Begin with a simple yes or no and then briefly elaborate on that answer.

Reasoning: State the rule(s) of law that the court applied to reach its decision. Then include the court's reasoning by showing how it applied the rule(s) to the facts of the case.

You may also choose to add the optional information listed above, which includes policy issues and whether or not you agree with the opinion of the court and why/why not (remember that professors often ask students for their opinions regarding whether or not a case was decided correctly and the reasons for their opinions).

EXERCISE 6 A

On your computer or a piece of paper, write a case brief of the *Brennan's* case that you read in Chapter 5. The headings and subheadings for the parts of the case brief are here to help you, and the citation and statement of the issue have been filled in.

***Brennan's, Inc. v. Brennan's Restaurant, L.L.C.*, 360 F.3d 125 (2d Cir. 2004).**

Facts:

Procedural Facts:

Evidentiary Facts:

Issue:

Under the Lanham Act, 15 U.S.C. §§ 1114, 1125(a), is there a likelihood of confusion between the trademarks of two expensive restaurants, where both marks share the same common family name but the defendant's mark has added his first name, and where the restaurants are more than 1,000 miles apart?

Holding:

Reasoning (includes rules):

Optional sections of case brief:

Policy:

Evaluation:

Chapter Review

- To read cases well at a U.S. law school, learn to analyze the case as a U.S. lawyer would.
- Reading several cases per night for a law school course involves a two-step process: First, analyze a case by reading it critically, breaking it into parts and asking yourself questions about each part as you read. Second, synthesize what you have learned by reading the cases, which likely discuss a particular area of the law. Notice the relationships between the cases and how the rules evolve.
- Analyze cases by asking yourself many questions as you read, starting with the case's title and citation. Think about the jurisdiction and the level of the court, and which courts the decision would bind.
- Look at the date of the case, and place it into context with what you know about what the U.S. was like at that time, such as whether government policies or social attitudes have changed since the date of the opinion.
- Look up words that you don't understand, especially legal terms. Use English-English legal dictionaries or general dictionaries. Do not use bilingual dictionaries and do not translate vocabulary into your native language.

Practice reading, thinking, and writing in English to improve your skills.

- Continue to ask yourself questions as you read the cases, such as questions about the procedural and evidentiary facts, the grounds for the appeal, the issues the court needed to decide, and the holding.
- In the discussion section of the case, ask yourself questions about each issue, such as what the relevant legal rules were, what the most relevant facts were, and how the court applied the rules to the facts to analyze the issue.
- Also consider the policy issues that the court discussed, and whether or not you agree with the result and why.
- After you have read the case once or twice, write a case brief that summarizes your analysis of the case.
- First write the name of the case and the citation.
- Then write the procedural and evidentiary facts.
- For each issue, state the issue in the form of a question: "Under (state the law), does/is (state the legal issue) when/where (state the material facts)?"
- For each issue, state the holding by answering the question.
- In the Reasoning section, state the relevant rules, and how the court applied the rules to the facts to reach its decisions.
- If it seems relevant or important, include such "optional" areas as the summary of a concurrence or a dissent, policy issues, any dicta that seems important, and whether or not you agree with the decision.

Chapter 7

ORGANIZING INFORMATION FROM CASES

Chapter Preview

This chapter continues the discussion of skills that will help you to work with cases and other legal sources at a deeper and more efficient level. This chapter discusses:

- How to mark cases or other legal sources (both in paper form and online) to help you to find the key information quickly; and
- How to organize the relevant information from several legal sources, all of which deal with the same legal issue or issues, to make your legal writing task easier and more efficient.

In Chapter 6, we discussed how to write case briefs as a study method for your classes. We also briefly mentioned highlighting relevant case material. In this chapter, we will look at that in more detail, and then we will discuss how to organize material from several cases, all of which analyze the same legal issue, to efficiently prepare for discussing and/or writing about that issue.

A. HIGHLIGHTING MATERIAL AND MAKING NOTES IN INDIVIDUAL CASES OR OTHER LEGAL SOURCES

Law students often highlight key language from their cases in their case books. They may also use their student subscriptions to online legal research providers such as LexisNexis and Westlaw to find the complete versions of the cases online. As we discussed in Chapter 5, these versions are likely to have the added editorial enhancements of case summaries and headnotes.

For law students with civil law backgrounds who are learning to find legal rules in the cases they read, headnotes can be especially useful. Headnotes contain the rules, and they are numbered so that it is easy to locate the rules in the opinions. Rather than relying on the headnotes to find the rules, however, it is best to develop the skill of finding the rules in the cases by yourself, and using the headnotes as a way to check your work and find any rules that you may have missed.

1. Using Printed Material

With case books or printed-out copies of cases, it is a good idea to highlight the key areas of the cases that you have written down in your case briefs: the substantive facts and procedural history, the legal rules, the holding(s), and the reasoning.

Some students take highlighting a step further by using a different highlighter color for each type of information: e.g., green for facts, yellow for rules, blue for holdings, and pink or orange for reasoning. Of course, the colors are arbitrary — if you choose this approach, it makes no difference which colors you choose for each type of information, as long as you use them consistently.

As we know, the facts, the rules, the holding, and the reasoning together comprise judicial opinions. As a result, some law students make the mistake of highlighting almost the entire opinion, which makes highlighting much less useful. Whether you use one color of highlighter only, or you choose different colors for each type of information, make sure that you highlight only the most relevant information.

In addition to highlighting key information, it is a good idea to make notes in the margins. For example, you might draw a star next to the general rule or make other notes reflecting how the key language is important, whether for your law school class or for the written legal work that you will compose, such as a memorandum.

2. Using Online Material

These days, attorneys and law students tend to do much of their work on the computer, including their legal research. Although you can print out the cases or other legal materials that you find and work with the hard copies (i.e., the paper copies), the major online legal research providers now allow you to save and work with the legal materials that you find (such as cases, statutes, regulations, secondary sources, briefs from court dockets, etc.) online.

LexisNexis, Westlaw, and Bloomberg Law all permit you to create a folder in which to save your research. For example, let's return to the area of law that the *Brennan's* case discusses — trademark infringement, or more specifically, the likelihood of confusion under Section 43(a) of the Lanham Act, 15 U.S.C. § 1125.

Let's say that your law professor (or the partner, if you are practicing law) has assigned you to do legal research for a legal problem where two similar products have similar names. Is there a likelihood of confusion between the first product and the allegedly infringing product under the Lanham Act?

When you do your legal research, you may find something like this: five relevant cases from the jurisdiction in which the problem is set, Section 43(a), and material from a legal encyclopedia and from a law review article that discusses the likelihood of confusion. With LexisNexis, Westlaw, and Bloomberg Law, you can save these materials in a folder which you then name (e.g., "likelihood of confusion under Lanham Act," or simply "likelihood of confusion").

After you have saved the material in the folder, you are then able to work with it in a way that is similar to what you do with a hard copy. You can highlight key information, and make notes about it in a box that will appear in the margin. Even better, unlike notes that you have made by hand on paper, you can take the relevant passages and your notes from the case and cut and paste them into a Word document such as the memorandum that you are writing.

B. ORGANIZING RELEVANT INFORMATION FROM MULTIPLE SOURCES

After collecting the research results, attorneys often find that they have a great deal of information with which to work, even if much of that information will not ultimately show up in the final work product. In the previous example, five cases from a federal appellate court,[1] a section of a federal statute, and secondary material from a legal encyclopedia and a law review article are long enough that if they were all printed out, you would have a fairly thick stack of material on your desk. Each federal opinion is likely to be somewhere between 10 and 30 pages long, and a law review article can easily be 60 pages long!

---

[1] As the Lanham Act is federal law, a trademark infringement claim under the Lanham Act will likely be heard in a federal court.

If you are a practicing lawyer who also has a case file containing many documents that are relevant to the legal issue, the stack of information becomes even thicker. Thus, it is important for attorneys to organize the information that they have found during the research process so that they may use it more efficiently in their writing.

1. Organize the Material by Considering the Structure of the Assignment

Returning to the Lanham Act problem, the Second Circuit's *Polaroid* test for the likelihood of confusion lists eight non-exclusive factors.[2] Often, when a legal rule involves a test with many non-exclusive factors, the court that establishes the rule recognizes that the issue has many possible factors, and not all of them are likely to be particularly relevant in a given case.

In fact, the opinions that apply the *Polaroid* test often do not analyze all eight factors in detail. Instead, they are more likely to focus on the three to five factors that the court finds most relevant, and to either be silent about the remaining factors or to discuss them very quickly.

Similarly, if a partner asks an associate to analyze this issue, the partner may determine that several factors are not particularly relevant, or that the outcome of those factors is clear enough that it is not necessary for an attorney to spend time analyzing it. Thus, the partner may give a young associate an assignment to analyze how four of the eight *Polaroid* factors are likely to apply to the facts of the client's case, and to memorialize the analysis in a memorandum. For example, the partner could assign the associate to analyze the following four *Polaroid* factors: (1) the degree of the marks' similarity; (2) the products' competitive proximity; (3) the quality of the alleged infringer's products; and (4) the sophistication of each product's purchasers.[3]

U.S. legal writing is highly organized, so the memorandum would analyze these four factors of the "likelihood of confusion" test one factor at a time. In drafting the memorandum, the attorney would likely begin the Discussion section of the memorandum by (1) stating the legal issue, (2) providing the complete eight-factor *Polaroid* test and any other general rules that apply to the issue, (3) and giving a "roadmap" that tells the reader which factors the memorandum will analyze, and states the conclusion as to the probable outcome.

Then, the memorandum would analyze the issue one factor at a time. For each factor, the writer would state any rules for the factor that the writer has found in the five cases; describe one or more cases that show how the court applied the rule to the facts of the case; compare the facts of that case to the facts of our case to see how the facts are similar or different; apply the rules to the facts of our case; and predict how the court in our case is likely to rule on that factor. Therefore, the writer will be using the five cases that he or she has found carefully and extensively — looking at the rules, the facts, and the reasoning of each.

---

[2] *Brennan's, Inc. v. Brennan's Restaurant, L.C.C.*, 360 F.3d 125, 130 (2d Cir. 2004).

[3] *Id.*

2. Putting the Most Important Information in a Chart

Because U.S. legal writing is so tightly organized, the writer should organize the information that is contained in each of the five cases so that it is easy to extract the rules, the facts, the holdings, and the reasoning from them and to include that information in the memorandum. Lawyers often do this by putting the relevant material from the cases into a grid, as follows:

Figure 7.1 Case Chart (Likelihood of Confusion)

Case	Winner of factor	Similarity of Marks	Competitive Proximity of Products	Quality of Def. Product	Sophisti-cation of Buyers
Case #1					
Case #2					
Case #3					
Case #4					
Case #5					

In the first column on the left, the attorney writes the name of the case. In the second column, the attorney writes who won the factor — the plaintiff or the defendant. The four remaining columns are for each of the four factors that the attorney will analyze in the memorandum.

If the case discusses that factor in depth, the attorney can fill the box with the most important information that he or she will use in the memorandum, such as the rules that apply to the factor, the key facts for the factor, and the court's reasoning for that factor. If the case provides little or no analysis for that factor, the attorney leaves it blank.

If the writer has filled out the chart with this information — how each of the five cases deals with that particular factor — he or she will have a much easier job when writing the memorandum because the most important information for each factor is right there at the writer's fingertips. This kind of preparation saves time and stress, and likely leads to a stronger memorandum.

Chapter Review

- Organizing key information from the cases that you read is an important skill for law students and attorneys to master.
- With case excerpts in case books or print-outs of complete cases from the online research providers, highlight the most important information that you would write in a case brief: the substantive facts, procedural history, rules of law, holdings, and reasoning. Also, make notes that reflect your analysis or understanding while reading the case.
- You may use different highlighter colors for the different parts of the case, or one color. Make sure not to highlight large portions of the case, because it defeats the purpose of highlighting.
- When doing research online, you can save the cases and other legal materials in an online folder, which you can then name.
- You can highlight and make electronic notes on the saved material, and then cut and paste that material into written documents such as legal memoranda or briefs.
- When you have researched a legal issue, you will likely have numerous documents, including cases, statutes, secondary sources, and client documents. It is important to organize the information from these documents to improve the efficiency of your legal writing.
- Legal writing in the United States legal system is highly organized, and the analysis of legal issues often involves a significant amount of work with case law.
- For example, the analysis of a factor or element from a statute or a judge-made rule typically involves finding rules from the cases; describing the facts of a case and showing how the court applied the rule to the facts of the case; comparing the facts of that case and the facts of our problem to determine whether they are similar or different; applying the rule from the case to our facts; and predicting how our court is likely to rule on that factor or element.
- Lawyers and law students can prepare efficiently for this type of analysis by making a chart whose headings show the relevant cases and the relevant factors, elements, or other legal issues. Then the writer fills in the key rules, facts, and reasoning for each box.
- Having the key information available in one location makes it easier to write a complete, logical memorandum or brief more quickly and with less stress.

Chapter 8

THE CIVIL LITIGATION PROCESS IN THE UNITED STATES

Chapter Preview

This chapter describes the civil litigation process in the United States from the moment that a client walks in your office door until a final decision can no longer be appealed. The chapter discusses:

- Client intake and case evaluation;
- Attempts to settle a dispute before litigation begins;
- The filing of a complaint and service of process;
- The pleading stage;
- The discovery process;
- Pre-trial attempts to settle the case or limit the scope of the dispute;
- The trial;
- The appeals process; and
- When res judicata attaches and what that means to the parties.

Many U.S. law school courses require students to read a large number of excerpts from appellate court opinions. The opinions usually begin with a paragraph or two of procedural facts that explain what happened at the trial court level, but they generally provide little information about the actual trial, or the pre-trial process. Moreover, as a lawyer or law graduate from a civil-law country (or even another common-law country), you may be unsure about the civil litigation process in the United States. Thus, in order to fully understand an appellate decision, it's important to be familiar with the complete civil litigation process in the United States, from the moment a potential client first walks into your office until the time when a court's decision may no longer be appealed.

A. BEFORE LITIGATION BEGINS

1. Client Intake and Interviewing

A potential client walks into your office with a legal problem, one which may or may not lead to litigation.

Perhaps he or she is having a problem with another person or a business and wants to file a lawsuit, or perhaps he or she has just been sued and needs a lawyer. Perhaps the client does not want to go to court at all, but needs to negotiate a business deal, and wants the help of an attorney to obtain the most favorable deal possible, and to properly memorialize the terms of the deal in a contract.

Before you decide whether to represent this potential client, you interview him or her to learn more about the legal problem. You need to learn the important background facts that relate to the representation. One way that less experienced attorneys can help to ensure that their information is comprehensive is to use the full range of question words in their questions (i.e., who, what, when, where, why, which, how, etc.).

For example, you would like to know what the nature of the legal issue is (what happened), who the parties are in the dispute or deal, when and where the event at issue occurred or when and where the negotiation will take place, and what the potential client is hoping that you can help him or her to achieve. For each of these questions, you want as much specific information as possible: addresses, phone numbers, dates, amounts, and all of the relevant documents that he or she can give you.

If the potential client is considering whether or not to sue a person or an organization, he or she may be looking for one of several possible **remedies**: money (called **damages**), performance in accordance with the terms of a contract (called **specific performance**), or a demand that the other party not do something (called a **temporary restraining order, preliminary injunction**, or **permanent injunction**, depending upon the duration of the remedy).[1]

---

[1] Injunctive relief is typically in the form of a court order that prevents the other party from doing something (such as destroying a historic building) for a certain period of time. Although it is also possible

2. Case Assessment

Often, attorneys prefer not to tell new potential clients that they agree to represent them at the initial meeting. Instead, they tell the clients that they will do some case assessment, after which they will communicate with the potential client and let them know about the strength of their case.

After the initial meeting, the attorney looks at the facts and considers what the possible causes of action are. Then the attorney (more likely a younger associate) conducts legal research into the potential causes of action, determining the relevant rules of law and how courts interpret the rule. The attorney compares the facts of the potential client's legal problem with the facts in the precedent. Did plaintiffs in cases with the most similar facts to those of the potential client win or lose?

The associate then drafts a memorandum that sets out the relevant law, describes the most relevant precedent, compares the facts of the precedent to the potential client's facts, and applies the rules of law to the facts to determine the strength of the potential client's case.

Based on the analysis, the attorney decides whether to represent the potential client, and informs him or her about the strength of the case.

3. Pre-Litigation Attempts to Resolve Dispute

If the attorney agrees to represent the client and the client wishes to proceed, the attorney will choose from among several options for how to advance. Often, the attorney begins by writing a letter to the opposing party that states the client's demands (a "demand letter") and/or proposes to meet to negotiate a possible settlement. If the opposing party is represented by counsel and the attorney knows the opposing counsel's identity, the attorney would send the demand letter directly to the opposing counsel.

A somewhat more aggressive strategy involves writing a demand letter with an attached proposed **complaint**, stating that if the opposing party fails to respond to the demand letter in a satisfactory manner by a certain date, the attorney will file the proposed complaint.

The third option is to write a letter that proposes that the parties use a form of **alternate dispute resolution** ("ADR"), such as binding **arbitration** or non-binding **mediation**. If the litigation arises from a contract, the contract may have a clause that requires the parties to use ADR, or it may at least require a party to propose using ADR before filing a lawsuit.

The fourth option is to file a complaint with the appropriate court without speaking to opposing counsel first. A plaintiff may consider this option if there is a concern about the defendant's disappearing, leaving the country, or doing something that would frustrate the purpose of the litigation.

---

to obtain an order that requires a party to *do* something, it is less common, perhaps because courts are sometimes uncomfortable about ordering parties to act in a certain way.

A plaintiff who especially worried about this may seek an injunction on an emergency basis. This type of injunction, which is called a temporary restraining order ("TRO"), is typically heard within 24 hours of filing, and may even be heard on an **ex parte** basis if the defendant cannot be reached in time. If granted, the TRO provides relief for a very short period of time — often 10 days to 14 days — until the parties have had time to brief a motion for a preliminary injunction, which generally provides relief during the pendency of the trial.

Attorneys for the plaintiff often prefer to begin with a demand letter or by making some effort to reach out to the defendant to settle the matter before litigation begins, partly because in many jurisdictions, parties are required to make some effort to settle the dispute prior to trial, and partly because judges are likely to view plaintiffs who have made genuinely good-faith efforts to settle in a favorable light.

B. THE PLEADING STAGE

1. Choosing the Court

As the party that initiates the lawsuit, the plaintiff chooses the appropriate court in which to file the complaint. However, although the plaintiff has the first choice, the defendant may be able to move the suit to a different court. For example, if the plaintiff files in state court, but there is a basis for a federal court being able to hear the case, such as diversity jurisdiction or subject matter jurisdiction (i.e., a claim based on federal law), the defendant may **remove** the case to federal court.

If the defendant cannot remove the case to federal court, it may still be able to change the **venue** by filing a **forum non conveniens** motion, in which it states that a court in a different part of the state would be more convenient than the court in which the plaintiff filed the lawsuit. A defendant may also make a motion to change the venue in order to receive a more fair trial. For example, if the media coverage of a dispute has made the local population likely to be biased against the defendant, the defendant might make a motion to change venue so that it could find a jury that is more likely to listen to the case without bias.

Whatever court the plaintiff chooses, the court must be able to establish both (1) personal jurisdiction over the defendant (the power to require the defendant to appear in court and the power to enforce a judgment against the defendant), and (2) subject matter jurisdiction over the matter (the power to hear the disputed claims). If the plaintiff has the option to file the suit in different courts (e.g., federal and state courts, or state courts in different counties), it may engage in "forum shopping." This refers to determining which forum is most likely to render a favorable decision. For example, the attorney for a poor plaintiff who sues a rich defendant may decide that a jury is more likely to be sympathetic in a large urban county than in a rich suburban county.

2. Choice of Law

State courts usually apply the law of the state in which they sit. They apply federal law in hearing a federal-law issue, and they may apply the law of a different state if it is appropriate.

Federal courts apply federal law under federal question jurisdiction, but state law when they hear state-law claims. For state-law claims, a federal court may apply the law of the state in which it sits, or the law of a different state where appropriate.

When the parties and the transactions or events that give rise to the claims have connections to more than one state, courts must decide which state's substantive law will govern the dispute, an issue called "choice of law." Each state has its own choice of law rules, and federal courts apply the choice of law rules of the states in which they sit.

Although the rules vary somewhat from state to state, they are generally fairly similar. In Illinois tort cases, the law of the state where the injury occurred controls unless Illinois has a "more significant relationship" with the parties and with the event.[2] When applying the most significant relationship test, Illinois courts consider "(1) where the injury occurred; (2) where the injury-causing conduct occurred; (3) the domicile of the parties; and (4) where the relationship of the parties is centered."[3]

If the lawsuit is based on a contract, the agreement may have a choice of law clause that states that the laws of a certain state (often New York or Delaware) shall govern all matters relating to the agreement. Courts generally enforce a contract's choice of law position, unless the court feels that the parties had unequal bargaining power and the terms were particularly unfair to one party.

3. Service of Process

State laws differ on how litigation begins. In some states, simply filing a complaint with the court is enough, but in many states, it begins only after all of the defendants have received a copy of the complaint and a summons to appear in court (collectively, "service of process").[4] The service of process rules differ from state to state, and there are federal court service of process rules as well,[5] so attorneys who are serving process on out-of-state defendants must carefully research and follow the proper procedures for serving process in the other state. In some jurisdictions, special process servers working for private companies may serve process; in others, a special department of the local county police must do so.

The complaint includes the basis for the court's jurisdiction, why venue is proper, the factual basis of the claims (set forth in short numbered paragraphs that are often only one sentence long), the causes of action, and the prayer for relief.

---

[2] *Esser v. McIntyre*, 169 Ill. 2d 292, 298 (1996) (*citing Ingersoll v. Klein*, 46 Ill. 2d 42, 45 (1970)).

[3] *Id.*

[4] Deborah B. McGregor & Cynthia M. Adams, *The International Lawyer's Guide to Legal Analysis and Communication in the United States* 35 (Aspen 2008).

[5] Fed. R. Civ. P. 4.

Within a given period of time, depending on the jurisdiction but typically within 20 to 30 days, the defendant(s) must respond. If the defendant fails to respond within the given response time, the court enters a default judgment in favor of the plaintiff. If the defendant agrees to waive service of process, the time period which it has to respond to the complaint doubles. Thus, many corporate defendants regularly agree to waive service of process to receive the extra 20 to 30 days to respond.

4. Answers and Motions to Dismiss

Defendants may respond in one of several ways: they may file a responsive pleading called an **answer**, they may challenge the complaint by filing a **motion to dismiss** ("MTD"), or they might do both. A defendant who chooses to file an MTD generally waits until the court rules on the motion, and then files the answer if the court denies it.

A motion to dismiss alleges that the complaint is legally defective and that the court cannot find in favor of the plaintiff even if all of the allegations are true. For example, the plaintiff has not asserted sufficient facts under which relief can be granted; the claim is missing an essential element; or the court has no personal jurisdiction over the defendant. The plaintiff files a **response** to the MTD, and the defendant files a **reply** to the response. The reply brief should not repeat the arguments in the original motion; rather, it should respond to the plaintiff's arguments in the response. Typically, the court then holds oral argument on the motion, and then makes its ruling.

The court has three possible rulings: it can deny the motion to dismiss, or it can grant it either **with prejudice** or **without prejudice**. If the court denies the MTD, the defendant then has the typical 20 to 30 day period of time in which to answer the complaint. If the court grants the motion without prejudice, it gives the plaintiff another chance to file an amended complaint that would cure the defects of the original complaint, which lawyers describe as having "another bite at the apple." If the court grants the MTD with prejudice, the plaintiff cannot file an amended complaint, and the decision is final (and appealable). Courts often prefer to grant MTDs without prejudice because judges may be reluctant to deny a plaintiff its "day in court" because of defects in the pleadings. Judges thus often give the plaintiff a chance to cure any defects before a final dismissal.

If the court denies the motion to dismiss, the defendant must then draft and file an answer to the complaint. Answers repeat each of the complaint's factual allegations line by line. The defendant admits or denies each allegation, partially admits and partially denies it and then explains why, or states that it is without sufficient information to admit or deny the allegation, and therefore denies it (to preserve it as a factual issue for trial).

After it deals with each factual allegation, the answer then states any affirmative defenses, as well as any counterclaims or cross-claims. If the defendant can establish it, an affirmative defense defeats the plaintiff's claim and requires the court to find in favor of the defendant for that issue. There are many affirmative defenses, including assumption of risk, contributory negligence, fraud, waiver, and statutes of limitations.[6]

A counterclaim is a claim that the defendant asserts against the plaintiff, making the defendant a counter-plaintiff. It is possible for a court to rule against all of the plaintiff's claims and to rule in favor of at least one of the defendant's counterclaims, so that the losing plaintiff would have to pay damages to the defendant (the successful counter-plaintiff).

A cross-claim is a claim that one defendant makes against another co-defendant. A cross-claim states that the defendant is without liability, but that if the court finds in favor of the plaintiff, the defendant is entitled to a contribution of some or all of the amount of liability from the co-defendant.

Either party can move for judgment on the pleadings, in which the **movant** (the moving party) asserts that based on the pleadings, it is entitled to judgment as a matter of law. If the court agrees, it enters judgment in the movant's favor. If it denies the motion, the parties begin the discovery process, or continue it if it has already begun.

EXERCISE 8 A

For each of the three problems below, consider three issues discussed in this section: removing a case to federal court, making a forum non conveniens motion to change the venue, and choice of law.

1. There was a car accident in San Francisco, California, which is 344 miles (554 kilometers) north of Los Angeles, California. The plaintiff, who lives in Los Angeles, sues in the Superior Court of California for Los Angeles County. The complaint alleges that California law applies. You represent the defendant, who lives in San Francisco.

Should you attempt to remove the case to federal court?

Should you make a forum non conveniens motion to change the venue from Los Angeles to San Francisco?

Should you consider contesting the plaintiff's choice of law assertion?

2. Two people from Chicago, Illinois were hurt in an accident on the balcony of their hotel room in Los Angeles, California. The hotel company has its principal place of business in California, and it is incorporated under California law. The plaintiffs sue in the Northern District of Illinois under diversity jurisdiction. You represent the California-based defendant.

Should you make a forum non conveniens motion to change the venue?

Do we know if California law, Illinois law, or federal law will likely apply to the plaintiffs' cause(s) of action? What do you think is most likely?

3. Two people from Chicago, Illinois were hurt in an accident on the balcony of their hotel room in Los Angeles, California. The hotel company has its principal place of business in Chicago, and it is incorporated under Illinois law. The plaintiffs sue in

[6] Fed. R. Civ. P. 8(c) contains a non-exhaustive list with 19 affirmative defenses.

the Cook County Circuit Court in Chicago. The complaint alleges that Illinois law applies. You represent the defendant.

Should you attempt to remove the case to federal court? If so, where — in California or in Illinois?

Should you consider making a forum non conveniens motion to change the venue? If so, what would you consider?

Should you consider contesting the plaintiff's choice of law assertion? If so, what would you consider?

C. DISCOVERY

If at least one of the plaintiff's claims has survived the pleading stage, the plaintiff has "stated a claim," and the discovery process begins. If several claims have been dismissed, discovery proceeds only on the claims that survive. Because discovery is time-consuming and expensive, defendants often make their first serious offer to settle the case at this point.

Discovery is the process by which the parties learn the facts that they need to present their case at trial. The discovery system that we use in the United States is one of the central distinguishing features of the U.S. legal system. Not only is it fundamentally different from the judicial investigation process that the civil law system uses, but it is different in scope even from the discovery that is conducted in other common-law systems such as those of Canada or England.

Attorneys or law graduates from civil-law legal systems are often surprised to learn that discovery practice in the United States is conducted by the attorneys for the parties and not by the court. That is by design: it is a commonly-held belief in common-law countries, particularly the United States, that fact investigation by the court, a branch of the government, would be unnecessarily intrusive and potentially dangerous. Thus, the system relies on counsel for each party to conduct the factual investigation, with the trial judge serving as a neutral referee whose primary purpose is to resolve discovery disputes between the parties. Overall, discovery in the United States is more "liberal" (open and extensive) than in other countries, even than in other common-law countries.

1. Types of Discovery

The main types of discovery are document requests, requests for admission, interrogatories, and depositions.

a. Document Requests

With document requests, parties ask each other for documents that are relevant to the issues in the case, and relevance is defined more broadly at the discovery stage than it is at trial, so that the parties are able to receive the full universe of relevant documents.

Often, parties make general requests that ask the other party to "produce all documents that address, concern, refer, or relate to ___." In its response, the opposing party typically objects that the request is overbroad and burdensome, but generally produces the requested documents. The requested documents could include letters, contracts, memoranda, charts, spreadsheets, emails, notes, photographs, graphics, and virtually anything that exists in written form, physically or electronically.

Well-drafted document requests include instructions and definitions that make the scope of the requests clearer and that reduce the chances for objections and non-responsive documents. Well-drafted document requests are also specific enough to avoid the production of thousands and thousands of irrelevant documents that add to litigation costs.

Parties do not produce documents that are covered by the attorney-client privilege or attorney work product doctrine, but they must produce a "privilege log," which is a chart that identifies all documents for which they are asserting the privilege. Parties may also sometimes refuse to produce a certain type of document on the ground that it is not related to any of the issues of the case. The parties then exchange correspondence in which they cite to legal authority that supports their positions regarding the documents at issue.

If the correspondence does not lead to a resolution of the discovery dispute, the party seeking the documents may make a motion to the court to compel production of the disputed documents. Judges often look unfavorably on parties who cannot manage discovery by themselves, so the party seeking certain documents may pragmatically balance the value of receiving whatever documents it does not have against the concern that a motion to compel would irritate the judge.

E-discovery refers to electronic discovery, where documents are in electronic form. On one hand, it makes discovery more convenient in the sense that the parties do not need to produce paper copies of thousands of documents, but on the other hand, it causes problems in that businesses now create far more documents than ever before, particularly emails. Moreover, electronic documents frequently contain metadata, where parties can see earlier versions of the documents at issue. Indeed, document requests now often explicitly request metadata — all of the versions of the documents.

b. Requests for Admission

With requests for admission, one party presents the opposing party with a list of factual statements, such as "At the meeting of its Board of Directors on June 30, 2012, the Board of [Defendant] voted on [Defendant's] proposal to acquire [Plaintiff]. Admit or deny." The party that receives the requests to admit must admit or deny each statement; partially admit and partially deny it and then explain why; or state that it is without sufficient information to admit or deny the allegation, and therefore denies it (to preserve it as a factual issue for trial). Admissions are binding at trial; thus, the other party does not need to prove them. Well-drafted requests for admission include instructions and definitions that make the scope of the requests clearer and that reduce the chances for objections.

c. Interrogatories

Interrogatories are written questions that one party presents to the other. When a corporation is a party to the lawsuit, the interrogatories must be signed by a corporate official who has knowledge of the assertions. The Federal Rules of Civil Procedure currently provide a limit of only 25 written interrogatories, including subparts, unless otherwise stipulated or ordered by the court.[7] Interrogatories are not necessarily questions; they may say, for example, "Identify all persons who were present at the June 30, 2012 meeting of [Defendant's] Board of Directors." As with requests for admission, admissions are binding at trial; thus, the other party does not need to prove them. Also, as with document requests and requests for admission, well-drafted interrogatories include instructions and definitions that make the scope of the interrogatories clearer and that reduce the chances for objections.

d. Depositions

Perhaps the most well-known type of discovery, depositions tend to occur somewhat later in the discovery process, usually after the parties have produced documents to each other. At a deposition, a lawyer for one party asks a **deponent** (witness) from the other party (or perhaps a former employee of the other party) a series of questions under oath, in the presence of a court reporter who administers the oath and who writes a transcription of the deposition. A lawyer for the other party "defends" the deposition by stating objections for the record, but may only tell the deponent not to answer a question if doing so would disclose privileged information.

Lawyers use depositions for discovery purposes, and also for trial preparation. Lawyers depose the people who they will later cross-examine at trial, and ask them questions that they will later ask at trial. Because the deposition is taken under oath, if the witness changes his or her answer at trial, the lawyer can use the deposition to **impeach** the witness and damage his or her credibility.

2. Advantages and Disadvantages of the U.S. Discovery System

The unique discovery system that we use in the United States has powerful advantages and disadvantages when compared to the fact-investigation systems that are used in other legal systems.

Among the advantages, the open and extensive discovery system allows both parties to have more complete and comprehensive access to the facts and the evidence than they do elsewhere. This especially benefits plaintiffs, and this, combined with the American Rule, under which each side pays for its own attorneys no matter who wins or loses,[8] has greatly empowered plaintiffs, who believe that they have been wronged and are entitled to justice. Another advantage is that because the parties themselves control the discovery process, they do not need to rely on the court, which may or may

[7] Fed. R. Civ. P. 33(a)(1).

[8] There are a number of fee-shifting statutes under which a successful plaintiff can obtain attorney's fees, but these statutes are not common, and are typically designed to assist plaintiffs who might not otherwise have the funds to hire their own attorneys, such as ex-employees who bring discrimination suits.

not be as diligent in its factual investigation as the parties would be.

The great disadvantage of the U.S. discovery system is also directly related to the liberal scope of discovery: its cost. In major litigation between large companies, the parties can produce millions of pages of documents to each other, and attorneys need to review them.[9] Indeed, the cost of discovery is by far the largest part of litigation costs, and it can sometimes be disproportional to the amount of money at issue.

As a result, recent proposed amendments to the Federal Rules of Civil Procedure provide lower limits for the number of depositions and interrogatories and would limit the scope of discovery so that it is proportional to the size and needs of the case.[10] However, most trials occur in the state court systems. Many state court discovery rules do not provide as many discovery limitations as the Federal Rules of Civil Procedure do, and even if the proposed amendments to the federal rules become law, they do not affect the state courts.

D. PRE-TRIAL CASE RESOLUTION

The great majority of cases are settled or dismissed either before a trial begins, or before the jury reaches a verdict. In the federal court system, approximately only 2% of all cases are resolved by a trial.[11] In state courts, 92% of cases are resolved before trial, and fewer than 1% reach a jury.[12]

Parties often settle "on the courthouse steps" (shortly before a trial), or they settle after conducting a good amount of discovery. Although the reasons for parties to settle at this stage vary from party to party, they tend to include caution and cost. First, as the trial approaches, parties become more realistic (and more uncertain) about their chances of winning or losing. Second, parties settle to avoid the additional expenses of a trial, and to avoid any unfavorable publicity that might result from a trial.

If the parties have not resolved the dispute, judges in both the federal and state court systems typically arrange for a pre-trial conference shortly before the trial begins. At the conference, the parties stipulate as to certain factual issues that are no longer in dispute after the discovery process, and they stipulate as to which documents may be admitted into evidence without objection. By doing so, they narrow the issues for trial and decrease the number of objections that the parties would make during trial. The judge issues a pretrial order that will govern the proceedings at trial. He or

---

[9] To lessen the high cost of litigation for clients, law firms increasingly outsource large document reviews by hiring "contract attorneys" on a temporary basis at a much lower rate, by using sophisticated computer searches to eliminate many documents without direct human review, and by outsourcing document reviews to attorneys in other countries.

[10] Debra Cassens Weiss, *Will Federal Discovery Be Streamlined? Proposals Would Limit Depositions, Emphasize Proportionality*, ABA Journal, Apr. 23, 2013, www.abajournal.com/news/article/will_federal_discovery_be_streamlined_proposed_amendments_would_curtail_dep?utm_source=maestro&utm_medium=email&utm_campaign=tech_monthly.

[11] Mark Galanter, *The Vanishing Trial: An Examination of Trials and Related Matters in Federal and State Courts*, 1 J. Empirical Legal Stud. 459, 459 (2004).

[12] Brian J. Ostrom, Shauna Strickland & Paula Hannaford, *ExaminingTrial Trends in State Courts: 1976–2002*, 1 J. Empirical Legal Stud. 755, 768 (2004).

she also frequently makes a final attempt to encourage the parties to settle the dispute before trial.

E. THE TRIAL

1. Jury Trials and Bench Trials

In most civil cases, the parties have a constitutional right to a jury trial, but waive that right if they fail to demand a jury trial at the pleading stage. If either party demands a jury trial, there will be a jury of 6 to 12 citizens. The jury is called the "trier of fact" because it makes the factual determinations. The judge makes the legal determinations, such as what to admit into evidence and what to exclude, ruling on the attorneys' objections, and providing instructions to the jury at the close of the trial on what the relevant rules of law are. If the parties waive the right to a jury trial, the judge will decide all issues of law and fact in a bench trial.

2. Opening Statements and Examination of Witnesses

The trial begins with both parties making opening statements, beginning with the plaintiff. Then the plaintiff presents its case in chief, during which the plaintiff's attorney calls witnesses and conducts direct examinations of them. Direct examinations consist of open-ended questions that typically begin with "question words," such as, "Where did you go on June 30, 2012?"

After the plaintiff's attorney concludes the direct examination, the defense attorney cross-examines the witness with leading questions, which are basically statements that require only a "yes" or "no" response, such as, "It was dark that night, wasn't it?" If witnesses give a response that is different from what they previously gave in a deposition, the attorney impeaches the testimony and damages their credibility. Traditionally, judges and lawyers in common law countries see cross-examinations as one of the greatest tools in the law for finding the truth.

3. Objections

If an attorney makes an improper question or statement, opposing counsel must object immediately and state the reason for the objection. Even if the judge rules against the objecting attorney, the objection is generally necessary to preserve the issue for appeal. Although parties can later attempt to raise an issue on appeal where the attorney failed to object at trial by using the "plain error" doctrine, appeals courts are often reluctant to employ the doctrine. As a result, some attorneys object frequently in court. However, this strategy is also risky, because juries often dislike attorneys who frequently object, and this can hurt the lawyer's client. Thus, wise attorneys "choose their battles" and only object when necessary. Constantly having to determine whether or not to object adds to the stress that counsel already experience during trial.

4. Motions for JMOL and Closing Arguments

After introducing all of its testimony and evidence, the plaintiff rests its case. At this point, defense counsel may move for judgment as a matter of law ("JMOL") on the ground that as a matter of law, the plaintiff has failed to produce sufficient evidence to allow a reasonable finder of fact to find for the plaintiff.[13] If the judge grants the motion, he or she enters a judgment in favor of the defendant. Perhaps because this takes the matter out of the jury's hands in a jury trial and denies the jury the chance to reach a verdict, judges are often reluctant to grant a motion for JMOL in the middle or later portions of a trial.

If the court denies the defendant's JMOL motion, the defendant puts on its own case in chief, calling its own witnesses, which the plaintiff can then cross-examine. When the defendant's case ends, either party can move for a JMOL. If the motion is denied, the parties present their closing arguments.

5. The Decision

If it is a bench trial, the judge applies the relevant law to the facts which he or she has admitted into evidence and renders a decision. If it is a jury trial, the judge instructs the jury as to the relevant law for the case and what they should consider. The jury deliberates and ultimately reaches a verdict, which is its decision as to the issues in the case. The losing party may make a renewed motion for JMOL. The judge grants the motion if he or she finds that there was insufficient evidence to support the verdict, but judges rarely do so because they accord the verdict great deference, and frequent reversals of the verdict would undermine the legitimacy of the jury system. The judge may not substitute his or her own judgment for the jury's and must deny the motion if the verdict was reasonable.

F. APPEALS AND RES JUDICATA

1. The Appeals Process

After the verdict is entered, the losing party may move to the trial judge for a new trial, but such a motion is rarely granted. Typically, dissatisfied parties must rely on the appeals process. The losing party may appeal once as of right, as may a winning party that is not satisfied with the outcome. For example, if a plaintiff receives much less in damages than it was seeking, it may choose to appeal even though it "won" in the trial court. However, parties have a limited amount of time in which to file the appeal, generally within 30 days of the trial court's decision. The party who appeals is called the appellant and the party who responds is called the appellee. In the highest appellate courts, the parties are generally called the petitioner and the respondent.

In the federal and state court systems, the intermediate appellate court typically consists of a three-judge panel. Appeals are based on claims of specific error; they are

---

[13] Fed. R. Civ. P. 50(a)(1).

not based on a party's general desire that the panel review and reconsider the whole trial.

Procedurally, an appeal is quite different from a trial. Appellate courts do not generally accept new evidence, and they rely on the trial court record, which consists of the parties' filings, including briefs and motions; all trial and hearing transcripts; and the evidence. It is not a retrial, with witnesses giving testimony. Rather, the panel relies on the parties' appellate briefs. The panel may schedule oral arguments on the briefs, but they do not have to do so, and in many cases, panels schedule no oral arguments. In the arguments, counsel for each party has a short period of time (often 15 to 30 minutes) to state his or her client's arguments, while the members of the appellate panel interrupt and ask questions.

The appellate panel issues a written opinion that states its decision and the reasons for the decision. The appellate court may affirm the judgment, finding insufficient error to change the result;[14] it may reverse the decision and possibly remand it to the lower court, so that the lower court can make findings in light of its opinion; or it can vacate the decision and call for a new trial.

Each party has an appeal to the intermediate appellate court as of right. Appeals to the highest appellate courts, however, are not guaranteed;[15] rather, the party petitions to be heard, and petitions are rarely granted.

2. Res Judicata

After a case has been litigated, a final judgment has been entered, and the appeals process has been exhausted (either through failure to file an appeal within the given period of time or through the highest appellate court's disposition of the appeal), the doctrine of res judicata attaches and the parties can no longer litigate any issue that is related to the events that gave rise to the litigation.[16]

Even if any of the decisions — trial or appellate — that are part of the litigation are later reversed, it does not affect the parties to the original litigation. This is because "[t]he indulgence of a contrary view would result in creating elements of uncertainty and confusion and in undermining the conclusive character of judgments."[17] Res judicata thus prevents parties from attempting to re-litigate the old case to take advantage of a later change in the law.

QUESTIONS FOR DISCUSSION

1. Have you ever performed legal work that related in some way to a lawsuit in the

---

[14] For the appellate court to disturb the trial court's decision, the error must have been sufficiently important to affect the outcome of the case; anything that fails to meet that standard is called "harmless error."

[15] There are a very limited set of circumstances under which the highest appellate court is required to hear the appeal, often involving the death penalty in states where the death penalty exists.

[16] *Federated Dep't Stores, Inc. v. Moitie*, 452 U.S. 394, 398 (1981).

[17] *Id.*

United States? If so, did the work involve discovery practice, such as a document production or a deposition? Did the discovery procedures seem strange to you at the time?

2. Would you like to see your country's legal system adopt a similar style of discovery practice to that of the United States? Why or why not?

3. What do you think about the attempt to streamline the discovery rules in the Federal Rules of Civil Procedure so that discovery will be somewhat more limited? Do you think that it will discourage plaintiffs from suing because they will have more limited discovery opportunities, or will it encourage them because litigation may become more affordable?

Chapter Review

- When a potential plaintiff walks into a law office, the lawyer evaluates the potential case by interviewing the potential client to learn the background facts of the dispute, and by conducting legal research to clarify the types of claims that are available and to determine their likelihood of success;
- If the lawyer agrees to represent the client, he or she often attempts to settle the dispute before litigation begins;
- If the attempts fail, the plaintiff's lawyer determines which court to sue in and which jurisdiction's law applies, but the defendant has the ability to contest both the venue and choice of law after the suit has been filed;
- The plaintiff begins the suit by filing a complaint with the court, and by serving the complaint and a summons on all defendants;
- Defendants may answer the complaint or file a motion to dismiss it;
- If the motion fails, the defendant files an answer to the complaint, which may include affirmative defenses, counterclaims, and cross-claims;
- The discovery process in the United States is conducted by the parties, and it is liberal and extensive, with document productions, requests for admission, interrogatories, and depositions;
- The parties conduct discovery on their own, and the judge acts as a referee in the event of a discovery dispute;
- Parties often settle cases during discovery or before the trial begins, and judges schedule pre-trial conferences to limit the scope of disputed issues, determine the admissibility of much of the evidence, and make a final attempt to encourage the parties to settle the dispute before trial;
- The great majority of cases settle prior to trial;
- If the trial takes place, the lawyers for the parties do most of the work at trial, by giving opening and closing statements, conducting direct examinations and cross-examinations of witnesses, and objecting;
- In a jury trial, the judge makes legal rulings and instructs the jury as to what the relevant law is, and the jury determines the facts;
- In a bench trial, the judge determines the law and the facts;

- Parties who are dissatisfied with the decision typically have one appeal as of right, and further appeals by petition; and
- If a party fails to appeal within the given time period or exhausts its appeals, res judicata attaches and the parties may no longer litigate any issue that arises from the events that gave rise to the litigation, even if any of the decisions are reversed at a later time.

Chapter 9

DEDUCTIVE AND INDUCTIVE REASONING

Chapter Preview

This chapter describes the two major types of reasoning that lawyers in the United States legal system use to analyze and resolve their clients' legal problems: deductive and inductive reasoning. This chapter discusses:

- The syllogism;
- How deductive reasoning is rule-based, and how it progresses from the general to the specific;
- How deductive reasoning enables lawyers to apply the rules to the facts of the client's problem to predict the result;
- How inductive reasoning progresses from the specific to the general;
- How inductive reasoning enables lawyers to synthesize rules and to state what the law is; and
- How inductive reasoning works by analogy to compare legal problems to precedent, and enables lawyers to predict the result.

Lawyers throughout the world employ certain principles of logic and patterns of reasoning to analyze a client's legal problems, arrive at a conclusion, and persuade a court or opposing counsel of the strength of the client's position. In the United States legal system, attorneys regularly employ two different types of legal reasoning in their work: deductive and inductive reasoning. As we shall see, the two types of reasoning are in some ways mirror images of each other, but lawyers need to skillfully use both of them to represent their clients successfully.

A. DEDUCTIVE REASONING

Deductive reasoning, which is rule-based reasoning that moves from the general to the specific, is the most common type of reasoning that U.S. lawyers use. We use the process of deductive reasoning (1) to take the rules that apply to a legal issue, such as a statute, a regulation, a common-law rule, or a judge-made rule that interprets the statute or regulation, and (2) to apply them to the facts of the client's problem, in order to predict the likely outcome.

1. The Syllogism and the Movement from General to Specific

The syllogism is a classic pattern of deductive reasoning that was made famous by the ancient Greek philosopher Aristotle more than two thousand years ago.[1] Here is a classic syllogism, which you have very possibly studied before:

Major Premise:	All men are mortal.	(All x is y.)
Minor Premise:	Socrates is a man.	(Z is x.)
Conclusion:	Therefore, Socrates is mortal.	(Thus, z is y.)

As long as the major and minor premises are true — all men are mortal, and Socrates is a man — the conclusion is unavoidable. The key to the syllogism is the shared term that provides a link between the major premise and the minor premise; here it is "men"/"man." Because Socrates is a member of the category "man," and all members of that category are mortal, he must be mortal.

The major premise is a more general statement, and the minor premise is a more specific statement:

All of the books in my office are about law.	(general statement)
This is one of the books in my office.	(specific statement)
Therefore, it is about law.	(conclusion)

Applying the syllogism format to a simple legal issue:

---

[1] Ruggero J. Aldisert, *Logic for Lawyers: a Guide to Clear Legal Thinking* 46 (NITA 1997).

Issue:	Mary is 19 years old, and she is a U.S. citizen. Is she old enough to vote for the president of the United States in the election this year?
Major premise:	The federal government and state governments cannot prevent U.S. citizens who are 18 years old or older from voting because of their age. (legal rule)[2]
Minor premise:	Mary is a 19-year-old U.S. citizen. (the facts)
Conclusion:	Therefore, neither the federal government nor her state's government can prevent Mary from voting because of her age.

Although the syllogism might be called the "deep structure" or the "skeleton" upon which a deductive argument rests, lawyers need to state the rules and apply them to the facts more explicitly. Thus, the typical organization of legal analysis that uses deductive reasoning looks like this: **I**ssue, **R**ule, **A**pplication (of the rule to the facts), **C**onclusion. For short, lawyers use an acronym (a word that is formed with the first letter of each of these words) to remember this pattern of organization: IRAC.

When the legal rule that is stated in the "R" section of IRAC is somewhat ambiguous or unclear, or it needs further explanation, we add another section to IRAC. The new section illustrates the meaning of the rule, often by showing how courts have applied it in precedent. In that case, IRAC becomes IREAC, with the "E" standing for rule "**E**xplanation."

Different versions of this acronym exist. For example, in **T**REAC, the "T" stands for "Topic sentence" or "Thesis statement"; in **C**REAC, the first "C" stands for "Conclusion." But whether the first letter of the acronym is I, T, or C is unimportant. All three really refer to the same thing: the statement of the legal issue or topic that the analysis will cover. Sometimes, especially in persuasive briefs to the court, lawyers begin the analysis by expressing the issue or topic as a conclusion, which explains why one of the acronyms is "CREAC." We shall discuss the organization of legal analysis that uses deductive reasoning in more detail in Chapter 12.

2. Finding Weaknesses in an Opponent's Argument

If you have read Plato, you may know that a good way to question one of Socrates' arguments is to challenge the premise at the beginning of the argument, which may be of questionable validity. The same is often true with legal arguments. When you look at an IRAC (or IREAC, TREAC, or CREAC) analysis, look carefully at the "R" part — the statement of the legal rule.

In the issue above, the legal rule about the voting age comes from the Twenty-sixth Amendment. Look carefully at the language of the statement of the rule. The original language of Section 1 of the Twenty-sixth Amendment is as follows: "The right of citizens of the United States, who are eighteen years of age or older, to vote shall not

[2] U.S. Const. amend. XXVI, § 1.

be denied or abridged by the United States or by any State on account of age."[3] As we can see, the statement of that rule in the syllogism shown above is a **paraphrase** of the rule, not an exact quotation.

In the case of a constitutional or statutory rule such as this one from the U.S. Constitution, lawyers often quote the rule's original language, or at least any "terms of art," which are phrases or words that have an exact, specific meaning in a given area of the law. However, lawyers also frequently paraphrase a rule instead of quoting it, as shown above in the paraphrase of Section 1 of the Twenty-sixth Amendment. Indeed, when the rule comes from a case and/or is the product of rule synthesis (as we shall see in the next section), lawyers generally state the legal rule in their own words.[4]

Therefore, when you read legal analysis — particularly opposing counsel's writing — look carefully at how the writer stated the relevant legal rule. Is it inaccurate in some way? For example, is it too broad (too general)? Suppose that we had framed the major premise of the syllogism about voting as follows:

Major premise:	All U.S. citizens who are 18 years old or older can vote.

Is this an accurate statement of the rule? If we look at it quickly, it seems to be accurate. But let's think more carefully: Does Section 1 of the Twenty-sixth Amendment say that *all* U.S. citizens who are 18 years old or older can vote? Remember that the language of the Amendment states that the federal government, and the state governments, may not prevent a citizen who is 18 years old or older from voting "*on account of age*" (emphasis added).[5] Notice that the Amendment does not state that the federal government or the states can *never* prevent adult citizens from voting.

In fact, many states have "felon disenfranchisement" laws which state that adult U.S. citizens who have committed serious crimes known as felonies (crimes for which the possible penalty is one year or more in prison) lose their right to vote at least for a certain period of time if they are convicted of the felony.[6] Thus, it is not an accurate statement of the law to state that all U.S. citizens who are 18 years old or older can vote, because some convicted felons cannot vote. Thus, the "rule" that all U.S. citizens who are 18 years old or older can vote is not accurate because it is overly broad. Lawyers must be very careful to state the rules accurately: Inaccurate rule statements can harm clients, hurt a lawyer's credibility with the court, and thus damage the lawyer's career.

---

[3] *Id.*

[4] With rule synthesis, lawyers necessarily state the rule in their own words.

[5] *Id.*

[6] George Brooks, Comment, *Felon Disenfranchisement: Law, History, Policy, and Politics*, 32 Fordham Urb. L.J. 851, 872 (2005) ("Three states permanently disenfranchise felons, ten temporarily disenfranchise them, and thirty-six deny the vote to felons [who are on parole]. Even [the three] states that 'permanently' disenfranchise convicted felons provide a mechanism for restoration of those rights, however, usually by application to a board of the executive branch.")

B. INDUCTIVE REASONING

As we have seen, the most common pattern of legal reasoning in U.S. legal writing is deductive reasoning. With this pattern, we move from the general to the specific. For example, we take a legal rule that applies in many situations, and we apply it to one particular situation — our client's facts.

The legal rule is often from a statute, but it can also be a common-law rule from case law, or it can be a judge-made rule that interprets a statute, as we saw in the *Brennan's* case from Chapter 5. As you remember, in *Brennan's* the Second Circuit applied an 8-factor test to determine the "likelihood of confusion" under the Lanham Act, and that test was originally devised by Judge Friendly in the *Polaroid* case.[7]

1. The Movement from Specific to General

On the other hand, inductive reasoning follows the opposite pattern: it moves from the specific to the general. How does this work? Lawyers may need to "collect" legal rules from several different cases to make a complete summary of the law for that legal issue. This is necessary because of the evolutionary nature of case law.

Unlike statutes or constitutions, which do not change unless they are amended, repealed, or revised, case law constantly evolves. Each new case has unique facts; no two cases are exactly the same. Inevitably, over time, a new legal situation will occur. Lawyers call this a "case of first impression," meaning that no court in that jurisdiction has previously ruled on that particular legal issue. As new legal issues arise, courts rule on them, and due to stare decisis, these new holdings are precedent that later courts must follow. Thus, over time, the law changes and grows as it adapts to new circumstances.

Inductive reasoning often begins as a pre-writing stage of reasoning. For example, after you interview a prospective client, you look at the specific facts of the case, determine what the facts have in common or what larger issues they suggest, and move from the specific facts to how they relate to more general legal principles.

In another example of inductive reasoning, if you have to determine what law applies to a given legal issue, you must first determine what the current state of the law is for that issue. You may be fortunate and find a recent case that provides a comprehensive summary of all of the relevant legal rules for that issue. But you can't count on that, and even if you find a case that seems to comprehensively state the rules, you must confirm that by researching the case law and finding other relevant cases for that legal issue. Do any of them contain rules that were not mentioned in the recent case?

2. Rule Synthesis

Often, a single case will not set out every legal rule for a given area of the law, because some of the rules are not relevant to the issues of that particular decision. Therefore, to make a complete statement of the law that applies to a given legal issue,

---

[7] *Brennan's, Inc. v. Brennan's Restaurant, L.L.C.*, 360 F.3d 125, 130 (2d Cir. 2004).

lawyers employ a process called "rule synthesis." They take individual holdings and synthesize them into a single common-law rule, or they take more specific rules and synthesize them into a larger, more general rule.

If you come from a civil-law system, you might feel uncomfortable at first with this process. Although you might feel that engaging in rule synthesis is "inventing" law, that is not what you are doing. Rather, you are describing what the state of the law currently is by collecting all of the relevant rules of law and stating them in a way that is logical, efficient, and clear.

A second type of rule synthesis occurs within one case. Sometimes, an opinion does not directly state the legal rule (perhaps because the judge thinks that it is obvious), and moves directly to the application of the unstated (or indirectly-stated) rule to the facts of the case. In that event, a lawyer who is explaining the case in a memorandum or a brief must state the "unstated" rule that the court used.

Also, an opinion may state the court's holding without providing a statement that clearly and efficiently explains why it ruled as it did. In that situation, it is necessary to craft a rule statement for the case that not only explains the holding, but the reasons for the holding.[8]

Because case holdings apply general rules of law to the specific facts of the case, there is inevitably always some ambiguity as to how broad or how narrow the holding is when a later court faces a similar issue and wishes to apply the holding under the principle of stare decisis.[9] For example, let's consider the *Brennan's* case again. How should we form the rule statement for the holding from that case? How broad or how narrow should that statement be? Let's look at several alternatives, ranging from narrowest to broadest:

1. There is insufficient likelihood of consumer confusion between two different expensive restaurants, both bearing the common family name "Brennan's," where the allegedly infringing restaurant name also bears the name "Terrance" and the restaurants are in New York City and New Orleans.

This very narrow rule statement is so specific that it would have little if any precedential value. Would it only apply to future cases where the parties both have expensive restaurants, both are named Brennan, the defendant is Terrance Brennan, and the restaurants are in New York and New Orleans? That particular combination of facts will not likely ever occur again, and a later court would certainly not interpret the holding of *Brennan's* this narrowly. Thus, when attorneys craft rule statements, they generally remove proper nouns (names) such as Brennan, Terrance, New York City, and New Orleans, and replace them with more general nouns.

2. There is insufficient likelihood of consumer confusion between two different expensive restaurants, both bearing the same common family name, where the allegedly infringing restaurant name also bears the chef/owner's first name and the

[8] *See generally* Robin Wellford Slocum, *Legal Reasoning, Writing, and Other Lawyering Skills* 130–34 (3d ed., LexisNexis 2011).

[9] *Id.* at 131–33.

restaurants are in the Northeast and the South.

This statement is broader and more reasonable, but it still may be too narrow. For example, does the rule really only apply to expensive restaurants in the Northeast and the South? What about other parts of the United States, or other types of businesses? An attorney for a plaintiff in a later case (who wants there to be a likelihood of consumer confusion) might try to craft a narrow rule such as this one for *Brennan's*, to distinguish it from the client's case and to minimize its application.

3. There is insufficient likelihood of consumer confusion between two different businesses bearing the same common family name where the name of the allegedly infringing business also bears the owner's first name, both businesses offer expensive services, and the businesses are more than 1,000 miles apart from each other.

This rule statement is broader than the second one, and looks like a reasonable description of the *Brennan's* rule. It applies more generally to businesses with expensive services, not just restaurants. Remember that one of the 8 factors in the "likelihood of confusion" test involves the cost of the products or services, because people are more likely to be careful when spending more money. Counsel for a defendant who wants the rule to be read broadly might consider making "1,000 miles apart" somewhat more general.

4. There is insufficient likelihood of consumer confusion between two different businesses that bear the same family name in two different cities.

This rule statement is the broadest of all the statements, but it is likely too broad. Notice that there are few specifics here: "two different businesses" could include any kind of business, even where people spend little money. "The same family name" could even include a very rare family name. "Two different cities" could be any two cities, even two that are next to each other. This rule statement thus distorts the holding, and a judge would likely reject it.

In conclusion, although attorneys have some flexibility as to how narrowly or broadly to state a legal rule, courts are unlikely to accept either very narrow or very broad rule statements. Rather, they look for a "reasonable" rule statement. When you are advising the client as to what the law is, try to make an objective statement of the rule, whether that favors the client's position or not. Then, if the case goes to court, you may use your advocacy skills to state the rule a bit more narrowly or broadly, in the way that favors your client. Remember, however, that the rule statement must still be reasonable, or courts will reject it and you will lose credibility as counsel, which is a bad result for both the attorney and the client.

EXERCISE 9 A

The Skypoint Tower Condominium Association (SCTA) has a written list of rules and regulations that apply to all building residents.[10] The members of the SCTA Board of Directors sit as a panel to determine whether the residents have committed

[10] The idea for this exercise was adapted from an exercise by Prof. William Chamberlain.

violations of the rules and to assess them fines in accordance with the SCTA Rules and Regulations.

The Board has had to meet on five separate occasions to deal with the problematic residents of Unit 305. Read the summary of the facts for each case and the Board's decision, and then synthesize a rule that covers all five cases:

Case 1: The residents of Unit 305 played very loud music after 10 p.m. on a Tuesday night. The Board gave them a warning, but did not assess a penalty.

Case 2: Three months later, the residents of Unit 305 again played very loud music after 10 p.m. on a Thursday night. The Board gave them a second warning, but did not assess a penalty.

Case 3: Two months after the second warning, the residents of Unit 305 had a very loud party after midnight on a Saturday night. The Board fined them $100 for the third violation.

Case 4: Two months after the loud party, the residents of Unit 305 again played very loud music after 10 p.m. on a Sunday night. The Board fined them $200 for the fourth violation.

Case 5: Two weeks after the Board assessed the $200 violation, the residents of Unit 305 caused a loud disturbance after 10 p.m. on a Wednesday night. Upon further investigation, the Board determined that the visiting grandfather of one of the residents had suffered a heart attack, and the residents were trying to save his life. The Board found that the residents did not violate the SCTA Rules and Regulations, and they did not assess a fine.

1. Synthesize the rule:

   ____

   ____

   ____

   ____

   ____

2. Answer these questions:
   a. When do "quiet hours" begin on Friday night?
   b. What will the penalty be for the residents of Unit 305 if there is a fifth violation?
3. Can you use the rule that you synthesized to answer Questions 2a and 2b? Why or why not? If not, what do you think the Board will decide based on the policy values of the SCTA Rules and Regulations?
4. How would you describe the policy values of the SCTA Rules and Regulations?

EXERCISE 9 B

Read the excerpts from three Illinois cases below. The cases discuss a common law principle called "intra-family tort immunity." The page numbers are included to help you to discuss the cases with classmates and to help you to understand how the writers of casebooks heavily edit case excerpts.

After reading each case, write down the rule or rules from that case about intra-family tort immunity.

Then, after you have finished reading all three cases, synthesize the rules about intra-family tort immunity from all of the cases into one rule section. Remember, just as in the *Brennan's* case, rule sections may be several sentences long.

Case 1: Foley v. Foley, 61 Ill. App. 577 (2d Dist. 1895)

[578] Plaintiff in error, a minor, brought suit charging defendant in error, in the various counts of the declaration, with assault and battery; with wrongfully requiring plaintiff, as his servant, to use and drive a vicious horse, by which he was kicked and permanently injured; and with neglect to furnish medical attendance or surgical aid at the time of such injury.

It was proved at the trial that plaintiff, when a child of four years, was left, after the death of his father, with the defendant, his uncle, by his mother, who afterward went to Bloomington, Illinois. She was married to a man named Pemberton. Plaintiff lived with defendant about fourteen years . . . At the expiration of that time, defendant wrote to her to come and get her son . . . She went to Grundy county where defendant lived, and took plaintiff home with her. His right arm had been broken and dislocated some years before and he was crippled in that arm . . . [580] It is doubtless the law, that a child cannot maintain an action for damages on account of maltreatment against a parent, whether the relation is by blood or created by adoption, under the statute, followed by all the legal consequences and incidents of the natural relation.

The judgment will be reversed and the cause remanded.

1. This is the Illinois case that introduces the general rule of intra-family tort immunity.

State the rule here. Don't copy it as a quote, but paraphrase it:

____

____

____

____

Case 2: Schenk v. Schenk, 100 Ill. App. 2d 199 (4th Dist. 1968)

[200] This is a suit by a father against his seventeen-year-old, unemancipated daughter for injuries sustained when she negligently ran into him with an automobile while he was a pedestrian on the streets of Bloomington. Defendant's motion to dismiss was allowed, plaintiff elected to stand on his complaint, and the trial court entered a judgment in bar of the suit. The trial court's action was based on the proposition that absent any allegations of willful and wanton misconduct on the part of [201] the defendant, no cause of action is stated. . . .

[202] The doctrine of parental immunity was court created and may be court destroyed. The public policy involved is the interest of the State in maintaining harmony, avoiding strife, and insuring a proper atmosphere of cooperation, discipline and understanding in the family. The rule and the reason for it was again expressed in *Mroczynski v. McGrath*, 34 Ill. 2d 451, 216 N.E.2d 137. Enunciated as it is in those instances where it is the child suing a parent, we see no persuasive reason why a like policy is not equally involved in a parent's suit against the child for his tortious conduct. . . .

[206] We therefore conclude that there are no impelling reasons for eroding or emasculating the family immunity rule for conduct of either parent or child arising out of the family relationship and directly connected with the family purposes and objectives in those cases where it may be said that the carelessness, inadvertence, or negligence is but the product of the hazards incident to inter-family living and common to every family. In such instances the immunity doctrine is neither unjust, unreasonable nor without a sound and solid foundation. To hold otherwise is to inject into the courts a judicial supervision over everyday family conduct of parent and child, and invite endless litigation over what is or is not ordinary negligence in the operation of a household. The assumption of the role of paterfamilias by either the courts or State, except under most compelling circumstances, is foreign to our way of life. . . .

The statement of these principles, however, does not preclude a holding that the complaint in the case at bar states a cause of action. As stated in Cooley on Torts, 2d ed., p. 276: 'Where the child is injured in his own property or person redress has no necessary connection with the family relation.' The facts here charged occurred during the exercise by both the father and the child of his individual rights on the public streets and with no direct connection with the family relationship. It seems thus clear to us that reason and justice require that the immunity rule should not stand as an insuperable bar to redress for injuries occasioned by the exercise of those rights.

Accordingly, we hold that the complaint states a cause of action for tortious conduct having no direct family relationship and states a good cause of action. The judgment of the trial court is reversed and the cause remanded to that court with directions to vacate the judgment, deny the motion to dismiss, require the [207] defendant to answer, and for further proceedings in conformity with the views herein expressed.

Reversed and remanded.

State the rules here:

____

____

____

____

____

Case 3: Cates v. Cates, 156 Ill. 2d 76 (1993)

[77] On June 9, 1985, Heather Cates, aged 4 years, was a passenger in an automobile driven by her father, Timothy Cates. At the time, Cates was transporting

his girlfriend, her minor son and Heather to his home for the evening. As Cates' auto approached an intersection of two State highways, it collided with an automobile driven by Phillip Darwin. Heather was seriously injured as a result of the accident. At the time of the incident, Cates was exercising his visitation privileges as a noncustodial parent. . . .

[78] We must determine whether the trial court properly granted summary judgment for defendant. The parties raise two issues: whether this court has adopted the parent-child tort immunity doctrine; and whether that doctrine bars plaintiff's action which alleged the negligent operation of an automobile. . . .

[85] In sum, while this court has not rendered a decision holding that the parent-child tort immunity doctrines bars negligence actions, its recognition of the doctrine in this area of the common law and subsequent confirmations of that recognition have precedential effect. The appellate court misperceived the effect of those several pronouncements. We do not, however, reverse its decision. We must yet consider whether the parent-child tort immunity doctrine bars plaintiff's automobile negligence action. . . .

[91] . . . Illinois stands in that group of jurisdictions, a minority, which have partially abrogated the doctrine by carving out exceptions to it. . . . [92] where the doctrine's public policy [93] purposes do not appear to be served. In *Nudd*, this court "modif[ied]" the immunity doctrine by recognizing an exception in an automobile accident case where willful and wanton misconduct was alleged. (*Nudd*, 7 Ill. 2d at 619, 131 N.E.2d 525.) Illinois courts, however, have carved out additional exceptions to the immunity in the area of negligence. An exception to the immunity rule is now recognized where a child sues a deceased parent. (*Johnson v. Myers* (1972), 2 Ill. App. 3d 844, 277 N.E.2d 778 (when the family relationship is dissolved by death, the policy basis for the immunity doctrine ceases to exist as well) . . . Another exception allows children to sue grandparents. *Gulledge v. Gulledge* (1977), 51 Ill. App. 3d 972, 10 Ill. Dec. 41, 367 N.E.2d 429 (rationale behind immunity loses persuasive force when family relations more distant than parent-child are involved); see also *Busillo v. Hetzel* (1978), 58 Ill. App. 3d 682, 16 Ill. Dec. 315, 374 N.E.2d 1090.

[94] Illinois courts also reject application of the parent-child tort immunity doctrine as a bar to third-party contribution actions against allegedly negligent parents. (*Hartigan v. Beery* (1984), 128 Ill. App. 3d 195, 83 Ill. Dec. 445, 470 N.E.2d 571 . . . .

[103] We fully agree with *Schenk*'s attempt to limit application of the parent-child tort immunity doctrine to instances related to the parent-child relationship. . . . [104] Unfortunately, as previously stated, *Schenk* is less than clear about the standard which should be applied. Moreover, *Schenk*'s expansive language, focusing on such concepts as "purpose," has lent itself to judicial interpretations which miss the point of the underlying rationale. Given the interpretation problems associated with *Schenk* and its apparent similarity in rationale to the *Goller* standard, we believe a modification of its exception is appropriate. We wish to clarify the *Schenk* exception so that "purpose" and "objective" are not paramount. We also wish to tailor the exception to conform to standards utilized by jurisdictions which have limited parent-child negligence actions to a more discernible area. . . .

We believe the more appropriate inquiry, yet based on the *Schenk* rationale, would not concern whether "family purposes" were furthered by a parent's conduct, but whether the alleged conduct concerns parental discretion in discipline, supervision and care of the child. Looking to *Schenk, Cummings*, as well as the various foreign jurisdictions, which have grappled with the problem of creating a discernible standard (*Goller, Gibson* and *Holodook*), we conclude that the immunity should afford protection to conduct inherent to the parent-child relationship; such conduct constitutes an exercise of parental authority and supervision [105] over the child or an exercise of discretion in the provision of care to the child. These limited areas of conduct require the skills, knowledge, intuition, affection, wisdom, faith, humor, perspective, background, experience, and culture which only a parent and his or her child can bring to the situation; our legal system is ill-equipped to decide the reasonableness of such matters.

The standard we have thus developed focuses primarily on conduct inherent to the parent-child relationship, which conduct we describe by approximating the *Goller* standard without its enumerated duties. Such a standard is consistent with other jurisdictions which have abrogated the immunity in order to achieve greater clarity in the area of parent-child negligence. The standard we have created is not, however, as extreme because we do not fully abrogate the immunity, but rely on an exception. Our standard also allows a broader area of negligent conduct to remain immunized. Thus, under our standard, parental discretion in the provision of care includes maintenance of the family home, medical treatment, and supervision of the child. A child may attempt to sue a parent alleging that the child fell on a wet, freshly mopped floor in the home, but the immunity would bar such an action because the parent was exercising his discretion in providing and maintaining housing for the child. . . .

In this case, we are asked to consider whether the immunity doctrine bars plaintiff's action which alleged the negligent operation of an automobile by a parent. Applying [106] the standard we have created, we conclude that the negligent operation of an automobile is not conduct inherent to the parent-child relationship; such conduct does not represent a parent's decision-making in disciplining, supervising or caring for his child. (See *Schneider v. Coe* (Del. 1979), 405 A.2d 682; *Williams v. Williams* (Del. 1976), 369 A.2d 669 (impliedly adopting reasoning in *Schenk* as applied to automobile negligence cases).) The duty which Cates owed in operating his vehicle on State highways was owed to the general public and not to Heather as his child. The negligent operation of a vehicle even when exercising visitation privileges does not constitute conduct inherent to the parent-child relationship. The parent-child tort immunity doctrine cannot be applied to bar a negligence action, alleging such conduct.

[107] Accordingly, the judgment of the appellate court is affirmed.

State the rules here:

____

____

____

____

____

2. On a separate piece of paper, take the rules from each of these three cases and synthesize them in a rule section. Remember that the rule section can be a paragraph (or two) long — it does not have to be one sentence.

3. The first case was from 1895, the second case from 1968, and the third case from 1993. How did the style of writing change over the years?

4. Is the statement in *Cates v. Cates* that a child's suit against a parent for falling on a wet, freshly mopped floor would be barred by the intra-familial tort immunity doctrine part of the holding of that case? Why or why not?

Chapter Review

- Lawyers in the U.S. legal system use both deductive and inductive reasoning in their work;
- Deductive reasoning, the most common type of legal reasoning in the U.S. legal system, is related to the classical form of reasoning known as the syllogism. Deductive reasoning is rule-based, and progresses from the general to the specific;
- Deductive reasoning enables lawyers to apply the relevant legal rules to the facts of the client's problem to predict the result;
- On the other hand, inductive reasoning progresses from the specific to the general;
- Inductive reasoning enables lawyers to look at a client's facts and connect them to more general legal issues, or to synthesize rules and to state what the law is; and
- Rule synthesis is necessary because in the common law system, case law evolves to address new legal issues, and the law changes over time. Thus, lawyers thus must be able to collect legal rules from various cases, and to state what the law is at the present time.

Chapter 10

INTRODUCTION TO U.S. LEGAL RHETORIC

Chapter Preview

This chapter describes U.S. legal rhetoric, by which we mean the pattern, organization, and style of argument, persuasion, writing, and speaking that lawyers in the United States legal system use to analyze the law, communicate with their clients, persuade legal decision makers, memorialize agreements, conduct discovery, inform the public, and accomplish any other tasks that lawyers may be called upon to perform. This chapter discusses:

- The "writer-responsible" nature of U.S. legal writing;
- The goal of communicating clearly, precisely, and efficiently, with no wasted words or digressions; and
- Plain English, which avoids "legalese," redundant phrases, the overuse of passive voice, and long, confusing sentences that legal readers must reread several times to understand.

Good written and oral communication skills are essential for U.S. lawyers, and of course, for lawyers in all countries. You have learned how to become a good writer in your native language, and also how to become a good legal writer in your country's legal system, whether by practicing law or at least by obtaining a law degree there.

To study at a U.S. law school, you must also have already become a good (or at least competent) writer in English. What you need to do now is to learn how to become a good legal writer in the context of the U.S. legal system. As you remember from your own country, not all good writers are good *legal* writers, because legal writing is a specialized skill that is somewhat different from general writing.

It is natural to think that you will succeed by doing the same type of legal writing that you did in your country, but with English grammar, vocabulary, and legal terminology. Unfortunately, that is not likely to work well, because just as different languages have different grammar and vocabulary, different legal cultures have different ways of organizing and communicating legal analysis. In short, what is considered good legal writing in one country may not be considered good legal writing in a different country, and vice versa, because each language — and each legal culture — has its own preferences in legal rhetoric. In this chapter, we will introduce the preferred style of U.S. legal rhetoric.

A. THE DEVELOPMENT OF THE MODERN U.S. LEGAL WRITING STYLE

1. No Wasted Words: The Importance of Clear, Concise Legal Writing

According to a frequently-cited 1993 article from the then-President and Vice-President of the American Bar Foundation, practicing lawyers see good written and oral communication skills as the most important skills for young lawyers to have.[1] Indeed, for the past 30 years or more, judges and practicing attorneys have consistently complained about the poor writing skills of new attorneys.[2] What are they looking for? Clear, precise legal writing that states a party's arguments directly and efficiently, in plain English, with no wasted words or irrelevant digressions. It sounds easy, but writing in this style is difficult to do at first, and requires patience, persistence, and hard work.

---

[1] Bryan G. Garth, Joann Martin, *Law Schools and the Construction of Competence*, 43 J. Legal Educ. 469, 473–74 (1993) (describing a large study of hiring partners and young attorneys at Chicago law firms, and attorneys in smaller cities). *See also* Mark K. Osbeck, *What is "Good Legal Writing" and Why Does it Matter?*, 4 Drexel L.R. 417, 418–19 (2012) (discussing at length the reaction to the 1993 Garth and Martin study and the ongoing demand from legal employers for better communication and practical skills in the legal field).

[2] James Etienne Viator, *Legal Education's Perfect Storm: Law Students' Poor Writing and Legal Analysis Skills Collide with Dismal Employment Prospects, Creating the Urgent Need to Reconfigure the First-Year Curriculum*, 61 Cath. U. L.R. 735, 741 (2012) (noting that good legal writing is "clear, concise, and engaging," and that confusing legal writing tends to reflect confused thinking).

2. Traditional English Legal Rhetoric

For years, traditional legal English in the United States followed the old British style.[3] Long oral opinions were written down, still in the oral style, with digressions, unnecessary language, imprecise and changing definitions, legal vocabulary from Latin and medieval French, long sentences, and very long paragraphs.[4] The language was difficult or impossible for non-lawyers to understand.

Thomas Jefferson, who was the drafter of the Declaration of Independence in 1776, the third President of the United States, and a lawyer, complained that his fellow lawyers drafted statutes by "making every other word a 'said' or 'aforesaid' and saying everything over two or three times, so that nobody but we of the craft [lawyers] can untwist the diction and find out what it means . . . ."[5] In this quote, Jefferson was already complaining about the use of **legalese**, the specialized language of lawyers that annoys everyone from the general public to other lawyers.

3. Plain English and Modern U.S. Legal Rhetoric

Complaints such as Jefferson's from the public and even from within the legal profession led to the rise of the plain English movement in both U.S. and U.K. law more than 40 years ago. Indeed, in the United States, executive orders by Presidents Clinton and Obama require that federal government documents be drafted in plain English,[6] and judges have written opinions severely criticizing attorneys who waste their time by filing motions and briefs that are filled with legalese and unnecessary language.[7]

B. BASIC RULES OF GOOD U.S. LEGAL WRITING IN PLAIN ENGLISH

The following 10 rules contain well-established principles of good modern legal writing in the United States. Try to use all of these rules in all of your legal writing in English: when you write in a U.S. law school, if you have a law-related job in the United States, if you take a state bar examination such as the New York Bar Examination, and for all other legal writing that you do in English, including when you

---

[3] *See* Jill J. Ramsfield, *Culture to Culture: A Guide to U.S. Legal Writing* 147–49 (Carolina Academic Press 2005); Richard C. Wydick, *Plain English for Lawyers* 3 (5th ed., Carolina Academic Press 2005).

[4] *See* Ramsfield, *supra* note 3 at 147.

[5] Wydick, *supra* note 3 at 3 (quoting David Mellinkoff, *The Language of the Law* 23 (Little, Brown 1963)).

[6] Plain Language in Government Writing, Pres. Memo. of June 1, 1998, 63 Fed. Reg. 31,885 (June 10, 1998) (issued by President Clinton) (requiring that all federal government documents other than regulations be drafted in plain language); Improving Regulation and Regulatory Review, 76 Fed. Reg. 3821, (Jan. 18, 2011) (issued by President Obama) (extending plain language requirement to regulations).

[7] *See, e.g.*, Joseph Kimble, *A Federal Judge Takes on Legalese*, Mich. B.J. 48 (Jan. 2013) (printing an August 7, 2012 order from a district court judge in the Middle District of Florida containing editing marks that delete approximately 75% of the introduction to plaintiff's motion for containing legalese and unnecessary language).

are doing legal writing in English in your country for English-speaking clients.[8]

1. Consider Your Audience Before You Begin Writing

This rule holds true for all writing, including legal writing. Lawyers have many audiences: judges, arbitrators, mediators, partners and other more senior lawyers, lawyers with a similar level of seniority, junior associates, paralegals and other legal staff, in-house counsel, clients and potential clients with law degrees, opposing counsel (collectively, "legal readers"), non-lawyer clients and potential clients, and the general public (collectively, "non-legal readers").

Because it is the lawyer's purpose to inform and persuade the reader,[9] or to draft documents such as contracts that will be read and used by the reader, the legal writer must begin by considering the audience and the purpose of the document: How much legal knowledge do the readers have? What do they need to know? What is likely to persuade them? Also, realize that while you may be writing the document initially for one person, it may later be read by many others. For example, if you are drafting an office memorandum that analyzes a legal issue for a partner in your law firm who is very familiar with the case, remember that your memo may later be read by other lawyers who will be assigned to work on the case and who are not familiar with the facts and issues of the case.

2. View the Reader as More Important Than the Writer

Most East Asian and Middle Eastern languages are considered "reader-responsible" languages, meaning that the writer is considered the authority and the expert, and if the reader does not understand the writing, it is the fault of the reader, not the writer. The writing is sometimes indirect, and at times may suggest ideas rather than stating them explicitly. Readers do not expect to understand everything that they read quickly, and are not frustrated if they do not.[10]

English, on the other hand, is a "writer-responsible" language, meaning that the main responsibility for clear communication lies with the writer, not the reader.[11] The writing is expected to be clear, direct, and explicit, and any ambiguity is considered the writer's fault, not the reader's.

---

[8] U.S. lawyers are often frustrated and upset by English-language legal work product that they receive from foreign lawyers, and partners may ask junior lawyers, especially those who speak the foreign lawyer's native language, to write an executive summary of it or even to "translate" it into the style of U.S. legal writing.

[9] In one sense, all legal writing is persuasive. For example, even in the case of office memoranda, which are considered to be objective and not persuasive, the writer is trying to persuade the legal reader that his or her analysis is correct.

[10] Anne Enquist & Laurel Currie Oates, *Just Writing: Grammar, Punctuation, and Style for the Legal Writer* 284–85 (3d ed., Wolters Kluwer 2009) (citing John Hinds, *Reader versus Writer Responsibility: A New Typology* in *Writing Across Languages: Analysis of 2L Text* (Ulla Connor & Robert B. Kaplan eds., 1987)).

[11] *Id.*

This generalization is especially true for legal writing. Although readers of literature may have some tolerance for ambiguity, legal readers do not. Indirect, ambiguous, or unclear legal writing is considered poor legal writing. Indeed, this presumption is embodied in the principle of *contra proferentum* ("against the offeror"), under which courts interpret any ambiguities against the party who drafts the document (unless there is a clause in the contract stating that each of the parties bears equal responsibility for drafting the document and ambiguities should not be interpreted in a way that is unfavorable to one party).

In more practical terms, think of your legal audience as more important than you are. If you are an attorney in a law firm, your legal reader will often be a partner in your law firm, a judge, or a corporate client (either in-house counsel or corporate executives).

A senior partner in your law firm may control your work assignments and performance evaluations; a judge has the power to rule in favor of (or against) your client; and your corporate client has the power to continue to hire your firm, or to take its business to a different law firm. In each of these examples, the legal reader is highly likely to be a very busy person with many documents to read each day. As a result, the legal reader has little patience for long-winded legal writing with unnecessary language that takes too long to get to the point. He or she wants to know what the answer is, and how you arrived at that answer, quickly and without "interesting digressions" that waste his or her time.

3. Follow U.S. Rhetorical Patterns

U.S. legal writing typically progresses from general to specific, and from more important to less important. Writers generally follow the IRAC, TREAC, etc. pattern of organization, although this is not mechanical: It depends on variables such as what the substance of the issue is, how complex the issue is, and how much support the conclusion requires.

Get to the point quickly — state your conclusion at the beginning, generally in the thesis paragraph, and then show how you reached that conclusion. Help the legal reader by using several paragraphs per page, and including headings and sub-headings that introduce each step of the analysis (often as sentences that express conclusions). Work through the legal issues one at time, methodically finishing one point before moving onto the next one. Explicitly state conclusions, and the reasons for the conclusions.

4. Support All Assertions with In-Text Citations

The legal reader is looking for analysis that is supported by citations to legal authority. Lawyers are skeptical people, and have no reason to trust your conclusions unless they are supported by citations. Thus, all of your assertions should be supported by citations, preferably to primary legal authority, such as case law or statutes.

For practicing lawyers, citations to authority belong in the text, immediately following the assertion. They are punctuated separately, like sentences, and are actually called "citation sentences." Although academic legal writing (such as articles by law professors called "law review articles" or this book) may use footnotes, writing by practitioners requires in-text citations. Why? As we discussed, legal readers are busy people who do not want to waste time, and it is distracting and time-consuming to constantly look down from the text at footnotes. In the U.S. legal system, the authority is considered as important as the text, so we place them together in the text, not in footnotes.

5. Avoid Unnecessary Language and Legalese

Traditional legal writing is famous for being "(1) wordy, (2) unclear, (3) pompous, and (4) dull,"[12] with redundant sentences that "use eight words to say what could be said in two."[13] The language says: Look at me! I'm an educated, sophisticated lawyer. You should be impressed!

In well-drafted modern U.S. legal writing, unnecessary language has been deleted before the legal reader sees it. If it is not, the legal reader will not be impressed. Rather, he or she will be annoyed.

a. Unnecessary Introductory Comments

Here are some examples of unnecessary language to introduce an assertion:

- It is important to realize that . . .
- It is interesting to note that . . .
- The first thing that we must consider is . . .
- I am of the opinion that . . .
- After carefully researching the statutes and the case law, I have come to the conclusion that . . .
- It is necessary to consider . . .

What value does this language add? None — it is empty rhetoric. The legal reader already assumes that the writer is only saying what is necessary and important, so that language adds nothing. The legal reader also understands that you have carefully researched the law — that is the minimum obligation for all lawyers, and it will impress no one if you brag about having done your job adequately.

The legal reader is a very busy person who does not care about the writer's opinion of what is interesting. In fact, *he or she is not interested in the writer's opinion at all*, and is looking for analysis that is supported by the facts of the case and by citations to legal authority. Of course, your conclusion is really your opinion of what the answer is to a given legal question. Legal readers understand this, so it is not necessary to write "It is my opinion that . . .", "it is my conclusion that . . .", or "I believe that

---

12 Wydick, *supra* note 3 at 3 (quoting David Mellinkoff, *The Language of the Law* 23 (Little, Brown 1963).

13 *Id.*

. . . ." Instead, simply state your conclusion without the introductory language.

There are a limited number of situations where this language may be used, such as in a particular type of letter called an "opinion letter," or in an office memorandum that explicitly provides a law firm's opinion about a possible legal event, such as whether a governmental regulatory authority will impose a fine on a company (*see* the memo in Appendix B). In general, however, simply state your conclusion without introducing it as an opinion, and generally avoid using the first person ("I" or "we") or the second person ("you"), especially in a brief or motion to a court.

b. Wordy Phrases

Wordy phrases are phrases that contain unnecessary language. They were often used in traditional legal writing, and some lawyers may think that they sound "lawyerly." The majority of U.S. lawyers today, however, see them as what they are — wasteful and unnecessary — and edit them out.

This brief list (and the following lists) contains the problematic phrase on the left and a suggested alternative on the right:[14]

Wordy Phrase	**Good Alternative**
at this point in time	now
at that point in time	then
because of the fact that	because
during the course of	during
for the purpose of	to
in close proximity	near
in light of the fact that	because, given that
in the event that	if
owing to the fact that	because
with reference to	about, concerning

c. Pompous Language

Lawyers sometimes use pompous or archaic language because they think it sounds "lawyerly" and formal, or perhaps they want to sound sophisticated. In any case, your legal reader will be grateful if you avoid words such as these:

Pompous Language	**Good Alternative**
allocate	give, divide
ascertain	make sure
cease	stop
contiguous to	next to

---

[14] Many lists of unnecessary language exist. *See, e.g.*, Wydick, *supra* note 3, at 11, 13–14, 18; Enquist & Oates, *supra* note 3, at 116–20, 125–26; Eugene Volokh, *Writing a Student Article*, 48 J. Legal Educ. 247, 269 (June 1998).

Pompous Language	**Good Alternative**
cognizant of	aware of, knows
forthwith	immediately
notwithstanding	despite
numerous	many
subsequent to	after
substantiate	prove
utilize	use

d. Legalese

Also called "lawyerisms," legalese is the specialized, often archaic legal language that often confuses the public, and annoys many lawyers as well. Some lawyers defend legalese as traditional, accepted "lawyer language," and some assert that it is precise, when in fact it is often unclear and ambiguous.

Legalese is especially common in contracts, where many clients expect these words, and law firms often use models that still contain legalese, particularly in transactions between sophisticated commercial parties. Many legal writing experts currently state that it is a best practice today, however, to achieve clarity by reducing or avoiding legalese even in contracts.[15] This is especially true in contracts where one of the parties is a consumer (a member of the general public), such as insurance policies or loans. Indeed, some state statutes and regulations require consumer contracts to be drafted in plain English.

As shown below, many of these examples of legalese share common prefixes such as "here-", "there-", and "where-":

Examples of Legalese

aforementioned, aforesaid

behoove

hence, henceforth

hereby, herein, hereinafter, hereto, heretofore, hereupon, herewith, etc.

thereby, therein, thereof, thereon, thereto, thereunder, thereabout, etc.

whereby, wherein, whereupon

thence, thenceforth

"said" as an adjective ("the said contract," "the said accident," etc.)

---

[15] *See, e.g.*, Scott J. Burnham, *Drafting and Analyzing Contracts* 271–96 (3d ed. LexisNexis 2003); Tina Stark, *Drafting Contracts: How and Why Lawyers Do What They Do* 4–5 (Aspen 2007) (recommending "contemporary commercial drafting," which is similar to plain English, for commercial contracts that are not for consumers).

"same" as a pronoun ("Buyer shall sign the Agreement on or before June 30 and deliver same to Seller . . .")

"such" as a later reference to a previously-described noun ("He bought such car the next day . . .")

6. Keep Sentences a Reasonable Length

Sentences in traditional legal writing were often very long: six or more lines of writing, with 75, 100, 150, or even 200 words. The sentences often contained five or six clauses (phrases that contain a subject and a verb), and were difficult to understand unless you read them several times.

In modern legal writing, we consider a sentence to be poorly written if it must be read several times to be understood. Writing is far easier to understand if long, complicated sentences that contain multiple ideas are broken down into several sentences. In general, it's best to restrict a sentence to one or two ideas, and to keep your average sentence 25 words long or shorter. A good rule of thumb: no more than three lines of writing per sentence.

That said, sentence variety is important to make writing interesting, so make some sentences shorter and others longer, and vary the sentence structures somewhat. Although legal writing is not literature and its purpose is not to entertain the reader, it must accomplish its purpose of informing and persuading the reader. Boring writing is not effective because bored readers do not pay careful attention to the writing, and thus may fail to understand your arguments and analysis.

7. Keep Subjects and Verbs Together, and Avoid Interrupting Phrases

English is an S-V-O language, meaning that the typical sentence has the subject-verb-object structure. An example would be "The plaintiff sued the defendant." "The plaintiff" is the subject of the sentence, "sued" is the verb, and "the defendant" is the object. This pattern quickly and efficiently tells the reader who did what to whom, which is information that the legal reader wants and expects to know as soon as possible.

This example sentence is easy to understand because "The plaintiff sued the defendant" is short and has only one clause. Many longer sentences, however, may have two clauses or more. Some lawyers like to "interrupt" the normal S-V-O order of English to give extra information about the subject immediately after the subject and before the verb, but this is a bad habit. Resist the temptation to put a clause or phrase between the subject and verb of the main clause of the sentence. It is confusing and may require the reader to read the sentence two or three times to understand your point. For example:

"The lawyer, running late for court because she had gotten a flat tire and then gotten stuck in a traffic jam, and unable to phone the court's clerk to explain that she would be late for the hearing because her cell phone's battery was dead, missed the hearing and was fined $500 by the judge and cited for contempt of court."

Did you find this sentence to be confusing? A legal reader may have to read the sentence two or three times to completely understand it, because the subject of the main clause, "the lawyer," is separated from the main verb, "missed," by 42 words. Also, the language is weaker because the sentence uses passive voice. Moreover, the information that explains why she missed the hearing interrupts the main clause (we don't know the result of her missing the hearing until the very end), and this violates the normal logical order. Here is a possible revision that makes this passage clearer:

"The judge fined the lawyer $500 and cited her for contempt of court for missing the hearing. The lawyer was late for court because she had gotten a flat tire and then gotten stuck in traffic. Moreover, she was unable to phone the judge's clerk to explain that she would be late for the hearing because her cell phone's battery had died."

The revision took one overly-long sentence with passive voice and changed it to three sentences that are in active voice and have reasonable length. The revision also follows natural logical order by beginning with the most general and important information (the judge punished the lawyer for missing the hearing). Then it gave the main reason why (flat tire and traffic jam), and explained why she could not tell the court that she was late (her cell phone had died). This follows the general logical pattern requirement of the third rule: general before specific, more important before less important.

8. Use Active Voice in Most Sentences; Only Use Passive Voice if You Have a Specific Reason for Doing So

As we discussed above, English is an S-V-O language, in which the typical word order is subject-verb-object. The subject is the focus of the sentence, which gives information about him, her, or it. For example, in "Mary Johnson sued Ajax Corporation for sexual discrimination," the sentence is about Mary Johnson and what she did, making her the "doer." The object, Ajax Corporation, is the "receiver" of the action. Like most English sentences, this sentence is in the active voice, because we put the "doer," Mary Johnson, at the beginning of the sentence, and we put the "receiver," Ajax Corporation, after the verb.

Sentences that use passive voice flip this order, and put the active voice object at the beginning of the sentence. The active voice subject either (1) follows the verb in a prepositional phrase beginning with "by," or (2) completely disappears, so we no longer know who the "doer" is:

- Ajax Corporation was sued for sexual discrimination by Mary Johnson; or
- Ajax Corporation was sued for sexual discrimination.

We form the verb in the passive voice with "to be" plus the past participle of the verb, which is formed with "-ed" in a regular verb. We show the verb tense by changing "to be": "am/is/are" for the present tense, "was/were" for the past tense, "will be" for the future, "has/have been" for present perfect, "am/is/are being" for present progressive tense, etc.

Both types of passive voice sentences, with the "by" phrase and without it, can be problematic. In the first sentence, "Ajax Corporation was sued for sexual discrimination by Mary Johnson," we at least know who sued Ajax Corporation, but the sentence is longer and weaker, and we have to wait until the end of the sentence to find out who sued it. In the second sentence, "Ajax Corporation was sued for sexual discrimination," we do not know who sued the company at all. Depending upon the context, the sentence can be ambiguous and frustrating for the legal reader.

Does this mean that lawyers should never use passive voice? No — there are several situations where it can be useful. For example, we use passive voice when the active voice subject is either obvious or unknown, and we wish to focus on the active voice object. When we say "Spanish is spoken in Colombia," we are focusing on the language, not the speakers of the language. It is not necessary to use the "by" phrase and to say "by Colombians" or "by people" because it is obvious — only people speak human languages. Similarly, if we say "My bicycle was stolen," we are focusing on the bicycle, and we likely do not know who stole it (it would be silly to say "by someone").

For lawyers, passive voice is also useful when you want to distance your client as much as possible from an unfortunate event. For example, in a criminal case, you can say that "John Doe was killed" without stating that your client allegedly killed him. Even if it is undisputed that your client killed John Doe and your client's defense is that he killed Doe in self-defense, it may be useful to use the passive voice here to avoid emphasizing who killed Mr. Doe.

Lawyers in some countries frequently use this grammar pattern in their native languages. Do not use passive voice in legal English, however, unless you have a specific reason for doing so, such as distancing your client from an unfortunate event or focusing on the active voice object.

9. Avoid Nominalizations, Elegant Variation, and Sexist Language

a. Avoid Nominalizations

A nominalization is a noun that has been formed by adding a suffix such as "-tion" or "-sion" to a base verb form. For example, "decide" becomes "decision," "move" becomes "motion," "act" becomes "action," and "interpret" becomes "interpretation." Other common suffixes that can be used to form nominalizations include "-ment," ("state" becomes "statement"), "-ance" ("avoid" becomes "avoidance"), and "-al" ("acquit" becomes "acquittal").

When we use nominalizations, we must add other words such as "of" and "the," so the writing becomes more wordy. Even worse, writing that is full of nominalizations is the dead, dull language of bureaucrats and mediocre lawyers. For example, "[t]he court's decision, which gave recognition to the plaintiff's abandonment of its trademark, was a vindication of the defendant's strategy" contains four nominalizations and sounds weak. The sentence becomes more powerful and easier to understand when we write "the court decided that the plaintiff had abandoned its trademark, which vindicated the defendant's strategy."

b. Avoid Elegant Variation

In many languages, it is considered a sign of elegant writing to use many synonyms for a noun rather than repeating the same word, a technique that we call "elegant variation." For example, if we are writing about a car, instead of repeating the word "car" five or six times, the writer might refer to it as a vehicle, an automobile, and a sedan, and the writer may also refer to the make and model of the car.

In English, elegant variation is a good technique for journalists or literary authors, but not for lawyers. Why not? Because to lawyers, terms have precise meanings, and "vehicle" and "automobile" may have different legal definitions. That's why it's important to use terms consistently; don't worry about the style. This is especially true of terms of art, such as "reasonable measures." If a statute specifies that a party must take "reasonable measures" to prevent something, are "feasible measures" or "practical measures" the same? No, they are not, and they are not the words used in the statute. Therefore, avoid elegant variation.

c. Avoid Sexist Language

Unfortunately, English does not have a singular pronoun that could refer either to a man or a woman; instead, we just have "he" for men and "she" for women. The law applies equally to men and women, of course, so English can have a problem describing this in a non-sexist way. When we refer to individuals, English traditionally used "he" to refer to either a man or a woman. Today, that is considered sexist language, and it is no longer acceptable. So what should we do?

There are several choices, and none of them are perfect. In informal spoken English, we say "they" instead of the awkward "he or she." In legal writing, however, most lawyers would consider this unacceptable because "they" is plural, not singular. Some other options: some writers always use "she" (which seems unfair in the same way that always using "he" was), and others randomly alternate, using "she" sometimes and "he" at other times (which is definitely fair, but can sometimes be confusing).

One answer is to use several different approaches: (1) Avoid the need for pronouns entirely by writing the sentence differently; (2) make sentences plural where it is possible (e.g., saying "lawyers" and "they" instead of "a lawyer" and "he or she"); and (3) when nothing else works, use "he or she" or "she or he." Occasionally, you might even use the passive voice to solve the problem, but as we discussed, the passive voice carries its own problems, so do not do this often.

10. Use Action Verbs and Specific, Concrete Language

a. Use Action Verbs

As we discussed above, too many lawyers write boring, dull work product because they use too many nominalizations. This is even more true for international lawyers, because if English is your second language, you are likely to be more comfortable with nouns than with verbs. Thus, many international lawyers use only the most basic

English verbs such as "be," "do," "have," and "make," and then try to sound sophisticated by using many, many nominalizations. Instead, the writing sounds weak and lifeless.

The best way to give your writing in English added efficiency and power is by using action verbs. Instead of saying, "The committee made a decision . . . ." say "The committee decided . . . ." Instead of saying "The defendant made a motion to dismiss the case," say "The defendant moved to dismiss the case." This is how partners edit the work of junior associates in U.S. law firms, and if you can write this way, your writing will look more sophisticated and more like it was written by a U.S. lawyer.

If you feel less confident about your verb vocabulary, pay attention to the verbs that you read in your law school textbooks and cases and try to use them. Often, you can "discover" an action verb by removing the suffix that converts the verb into a nominalization, such as "- *ment*." For example, you can guess that if the noun is "attainment," the verb is probably "attain" (and it is). You should then use a dictionary to confirm that your guess is correct.

b. Use Specific, Concrete Language

Concrete words are words that are not abstract or categorical; rather, they are particular and specific. For example, "meal" is an abstraction, but "lunch" is somewhat more concrete, and "sandwich" is concrete. "Vehicle" is an abstraction, but "Toyota Camry" is concrete.

It is especially important to use specific, concrete language when you are working with facts. An abstraction often becomes a conclusion, which prevents another lawyer from checking your work.

For example, if you simply say that the defendant was "driving too fast," the legal reader will be frustrated because you have provided only a conclusion, and there is no way for the legal reader to decide whether or not she or he agrees with you. Because lawyers are skeptical people, this leads to frustration and even distrust of your work.

But if you say that the defendant received a ticket for driving 65 miles per hour when the speed limit was 35 miles per hour, you have given concrete facts that the legal reader will trust. Then legal readers can determine on their own that the defendant was driving too fast, and they also understand how fast the defendant was going. If the defendant were only going 39 miles per hour in a 35 mile per hour zone, for example, it would technically also violate the speed limit, but it would be considered a less serious violation than if the defendant were driving 65 miles per hour. Thus, remember to be specific and to use concrete facts instead of abstract conclusions.

Chapter Review

- Remember that what is considered good legal writing can vary from language to language and legal system to legal system. It will likely not be a successful method if you try to write like you do in your country, but with English vocabulary and grammar.

- Traditional U.S. legal writing involved long sentences, with unnecessary words and legalese, and some older or more traditional lawyers still write this way, especially when drafting complex commercial contracts.
- Today, however, the trend is to write in plain English, in a style that is easier for non-lawyers to understand, and clearer for other lawyers as well.
- U.S. legal writing is writer-responsible, meaning that the writer bears the responsibility for clear communication, and if the reader does not understand the material, it is considered the writer's fault, not the reader's.

Follow the 10 legal writing rules below to write well in the U.S. legal system:

- Consider your audience before you begin writing;
- View the reader as more important than the writer;
- Follow U.S. rhetorical patterns;
- Support all assertions with in-text citations;
- Avoid unnecessary language and legalese;
- Keep sentences a reasonable length;
- Keep subjects and verbs together, and avoid interrupting phrases;
- Use active voice in most sentences, and only use passive voice if you have a specific reason for doing so;
- Avoid nominalizations, elegant variation, and sexist language; and
- Use action verbs and specific, concrete language.

Chapter 11

CONTRASTS BETWEEN THE RHETORICAL STYLES OF ENGLISH AND OF OTHER LANGUAGES

Chapter Preview

This chapter looks at differences between the rhetorical style that U.S. legal readers prefer and the rhetorical styles that readers of many other languages prefer. The chapter discusses:

- The problem of first-language interference;
- The fact that rhetorical preferences can vary between languages, between different cultures that speak the same language, and even between different academic fields within the same culture and language;
- The rhetorical preferences of U.S. legal readers; and
- The rhetorical preferences of readers in many other languages.

As we discussed in the last chapter, different languages have different rhetoric: varying writing styles and preferences regarding patterns, organization, and types of logic, argument, and persuasion. The particular rhetorical style that your language uses may have been explicitly taught to you in school, but you likely learned much of it indirectly during your many years of education. This indirect learning involves not only years of reading throughout your academic career, but also years of listening to lawyers, professors, politicians, skilled public speakers, and anyone who has a talent for persuading others that his or her statements, analysis, and opinions are correct.

Those years of practicing law, studying, and listening have taught you the "proper way" to analyze, organize, and present information and arguments. There's a problem, however: *There is no universal "proper way."* What you learned was the proper rhetorical style for your language, culture, and legal system. Indeed, "proper" rhetorical style can mean something different in each language, each culture, and even each professional field within the same language and culture.

A. RHETORICAL DIFFERENCES ACROSS LANGUAGE, CULTURE, AND FIELD

Just as English rhetoric may be somewhat different from Chinese, Spanish, Japanese, Portuguese, Polish, Russian, Korean, French, or Arabic rhetoric, smaller differences in rhetoric may exist between cultures even when those cultures speak the same language. For example, Spanish is spoken in many countries, including Mexico, Colombia, Argentina, and Spain, yet each Spanish-speaking country may have differences in its preferred style of rhetoric. Moreover, there may be rhetorical differences between fields within one language and one culture, as a U.S. lawyer's brief to a court will have a somewhat different rhetorical style from a U.S. doctor's article in a medical journal or a U.S. historian's academic textbook on world history.

1. Interference Problems

We have been speaking our first language and developing rhetorical skill in it for many years. Over time, our minds become so familiar with the grammatical and rhetorical patterns of our native language that we unconsciously use them when we speak or write a second language that we have learned. We transfer the grammar and rhetoric of our first language into the second one in a phenomenon that linguists call "interference."[1]

a. Direct Interference Problems: Translating

Interference problems are most severe when students try to write in English by thinking first in their native languages, and then "translating" their thoughts into English. The resulting writing can be difficult or even impossible for a U.S. legal reader to understand.

[1] *See generally, e.g.*, Michael Swan & Bernard Smith, eds., *Learner English: A Teacher's Guide to Interference and Other Problems* xi (2d ed., Cambridge 2001) (interference problems exist in discourse structure as well as sentence-level grammar).

When you think first in your native language and then translate your thoughts into English, you mix the two languages together. The writing may have English vocabulary, and much of the grammar, word order, and rhetoric of your native language. You may have heard of names for this type of mixture: "Chinglish," "Spanglish," "Japlish," "Korenglish," "Hinglish," "Portuglish," "Arablish," etc.

You can avoid this problem by being mentally disciplined. Stop yourself when you think in your first language while writing, and make sure that you are thinking in English. Also, do not use bilingual translating dictionaries. Using them is bad because it keeps you thinking in your first language, and because bilingual dictionaries contain roughly similar words that are often inaccurate translations.

What do you do when you are thinking in your native language, you look up a word from your language that you do not know in English in your bilingual dictionary, and you see four or five different English words as possibilities? Which word will you choose? Many students choose randomly by guessing, and the resulting English sentences often make no sense. This leaves U.S. legal readers frustrated and unhappy. Instead, you should put away your bilingual electronic dictionaries and use English-English general dictionaries and legal dictionaries, such as *Ballantine's Legal Dictionary and Thesaurus* or *Black's Law Dictionary.*

If your writing in English shows interference problems at the sentence-structure level, you can fix the mistakes by going through the sentences one at a time and making sure that they follow English sentence patterns and grammar rules. You have studied English grammar for years, and so with practice you can look at your writing and check to make sure that it uses English grammar patterns: S-V-O word order, the correct verb tenses, sentences where the subjects and the verbs agree in number, articles, plural nouns, and the like.

But it can be far more difficult to notice when your writing bears the rhetorical style of your native language instead of English. First, you have likely studied English grammar more than rhetoric, and the rhetorical patterns of your first language may be "invisible" to you. Second, if you write in English but use the rhetorical style of your first language, it will probably look good to you because the rhetorical style *is* good in your native language.

b. Indirect Interference Problems

Even if you think in English as you write, it is still possible to write in a style that shows the influence of your first language, both in grammar and rhetorical style. We can think of this as an "indirect" interference problem, because you are directly thinking in and working with English, yet the influence of your first language may still be present like an echo.

To understand when you are using the rhetorical style of your first language instead of the rhetorical style of English, it is important to be aware of the rhetorical style of each language. Accordingly, this chapter presents a brief summary of the rhetorical styles of English, compared to those of some other languages. Hopefully, your first language is included here. If it isn't, please look at the description of a language with a rhetorical style that is similar to that of your first language as a basis to help you to compare.

Here are a few things to keep in mind as you read these comparative rhetoric summaries:

- Comparative rhetoric is a controversial subject area among linguists,[2] and the existing studies are not complete.
- Languages and writing styles are constantly evolving. For example, in the previous chapter we discussed how the style of U.S. legal writing has changed over the past 40 years or so.
- Consequently, you may disagree with the summary of your first language's rhetorical style, or you may believe that it was accurate in the past, but it is not so accurate today.
- You may also conclude that the summary describes a general rhetorical style for your language, but not the rhetorical style of legal writing.

Despite these potential issues, this chapter includes these contrastive rhetorical summaries to help you to gain an "outside" perspective on the rhetorical style of your first language, and to consider how that style is similar to and different from the rhetorical style of English. These generalizations are not intended to carry any value judgments about any language or culture. The rhetorical preferences of one language or culture are not better or worse than those of any other; they're just different.

If you are more aware of the rhetorical differences between English and your first language, it should help you to use the rhetorical style of U.S. legal writing more easily and confidently as you do your legal writing in English and in the context of the U.S. legal system.

B. RHETORICAL PREFERENCES OF ENGLISH AND OTHER LANGUAGES[3]

1. Author, Reader, and Purpose

As we discussed in the last chapter, languages tend to be either "writer responsible" or "reader responsible" in that they either place the burden of clear communication on the writer (as in the U.S. and much of the West), or the reader (as

---

[2] *See* Bradley Paul Benz, *"ESL Trouble Spots": Composition Handbooks, Ideology, and the Politics of ESL Writing and Global English*, at 71–83 (2001) (Ph.D. dissertation microformed on UMI Microform 3013929) (including the criticisms that the research does not sufficiently account for the stylistic differences between individual writers and stereotypes them); *see also* Bernard A. Mohan and Winnie Au-Yeung Lo, *Academic Writing and Chinese Students: Transfer and Developmental Factors* 515–34, TESOL Quarterly, Vol. 19, No. 3 (Sept. 1985) (asserting that Chinese organizational patterns are currently similar to U.S. patterns, and that organization skills develop late, so organizational mistakes might occur for Chinese students in both languages).

[3] The following summary of rhetorical preferences across languages draws from a large number of linguistic and legal scholarly sources, cited generally here: Laurel Currie Oates and Anne Enquist, *The Legal Writing Handbook: Analysis, Research, and Writing* 746–69 (5th ed., Wolters Kluwer 2010) (excellent

in much of Asia and the Middle East).

Because U.S. legal writers view the legal reader as more important than the writer (e.g., a more senior lawyer, an overburdened judge, or a client), writing is designed to be as concise and to-the-point as possible due to the legal reader's heavy workload and impatience. A writer is admired when he or she can analyze and explain a difficult legal issue quickly and clearly, in a way that is easy to understand and requires only one reading to be understood.

The purpose of the writing is pragmatic: the lawyer must communicate his or her analysis to the legal reader, persuade the legal reader that the analysis is correct, and perhaps persuade the legal reader to take an action, such as to rule in favor of the lawyer's client, or to act in accordance with the lawyer's recommendation.

Because of the nature of the common law system, the writer is an advocate who is taking, supporting, and defending a position. It is acceptable and often expected for the legal writer to criticize opposing viewpoints (although such criticism should never be personal). The originality of the writer's work is also valued. The lawyer "adds value" by applying the law to the unique facts of the client's case in a way that demonstrates the original thinking and insights of the lawyer. Thus, ideas are the intellectual property of the writer, and quotation marks and citations are needed when one lawyer uses another lawyer's words to avoid a charge of plagiarism.

In reader-responsible languages, on the other hand, direct and explicit writing is not greatly admired. There is more tolerance for ambiguity, and readers do not expect to understand everything that they read quickly. For example, Japanese readers assume that the writer might be hiding the meaning. Similarly, Chinese writers may provide concrete examples similar to how writers in English would, but they would be less likely to provide an explicit conclusion and might only indirectly suggest a conclusion, leaving it unstated.

Japanese writing is even more indirect, implying or suggesting points, and repeatedly returning to themes without explicitly stating them. Indirectness shows the writer's intelligence and sensitivity, and overly direct writing may be seen as impolite. Similarly, Korean writers may state criticisms indirectly in metaphors, believing that direct and explicit argumentation may upset readers and be counterproductive.

The indirect approach that is traditionally used in Japanese, Chinese, and Korean writing expects the educated reader to make the connections and to provide a conclusion by himself or herself. This approach shows the writer's respect for the

---

summary of contrastive rhetorical preferences); Ilona Leki, *Understanding ESL Writers: A Guide for Teachers* 88–104 (Boynton/Cook 1992) (same); Brett Cumming, *Literature Review of Japanese Contrastive Rhetoric*, Nov. 28, 2012, (Education Resources Information Center, available at http://www.eric.ed.gov/ERICWebPortal/search/detailmini.jsp?_nfpb=true&_&ERICExtSearch_Search Value_0=ED537439&ERICExtSearch_SearchType_0=no&accno=ED537439); Carolyn Matalene, *Contrastive Rhetoric: An American Writing Teacher in China* 789–808, College English, Vol. 47, No. 8 (Dec. 1985); Mohan and Lo, *supra* note 2, at 515–34; Robert T. Oliver, *Communication and Culture in Ancient India and China* 261–72 (Syracuse University Press 1971); Terry Prothro, *Arab-American Differences in the Judgment of Written Messages*, The Journal of Social Psychology 3–11 (Aug. 1955).

reader's intelligence, as the writer assumes that the reader can understand the writing on his or her own, without an explicit conclusion. It also promotes harmony by avoiding direct statements that might anger a powerful reader. Although there is some evidence that Chinese writing is currently moving toward the writer-responsible approach, current Chinese writing may show evidence of both approaches.

2. Citations and Support

U.S. legal readers are very skeptical, and place little or no value in legal assertions that are not specifically supported. Therefore, U.S. lawyers support their writing with concrete, specific facts from the case and with statistics and other factual information. They also support their legal assertions with citations to statutes, regulations, case law, and occasionally secondary sources. The lawyers for each party may describe both the law and facts in a way that puts their clients in the most favorable light, but they may not lie or distort either the law or the facts.

Writers from civil law systems are not used to focusing on the facts in such detail, and may feel that the U.S. lawyer's focus on facts is trivial. Spanish-language writers are valued for the ability to draw general statements from the facts and do not focus on specific facts as much as a U.S. lawyer does. A Spanish-speaking lawyer's personal, unsupported opinions are given more respect by Spanish-language legal readers than is true with U.S. writers and legal readers.

Writers from reader-responsible East Asian cultures refer more to historical events, literary references, metaphors, and authority from the past, and may use examples, analogies, traditionally-valued sayings, and familiar phrases in their writing. Rather than articulating an individual position, writers attempt to express the views of the group and announce the truth. Traditionally, originality is not valued, although this may be changing.

Polish writers often repeat and restate main points in slightly different ways. Citations to authority are not highly valued, given the historical distrust of authority in the culture. Arabic writers also repeat and restate points, often with warnings, rather than supporting positions with specific examples.

3. Structure and Organization

U.S. legal writers typically begin with an introduction that lets the legal reader know the parties, the key facts that pertain to the events at issue, and what the writing will analyze. Then, in the opening paragraph(s) of the Discussion section of a memorandum or brief, U.S. legal writers guide the legal reader by providing an overview of the legal issue, a "roadmap" that shows the organization and order of the analysis, and a conclusion that lets the reader know the ultimate answer to the issue from the beginning. Impatient U.S. legal readers do not want to wait in suspense for the conclusion until the end.

U.S. legal writing follows a linear organization model. Digressions are not appreciated; they are seen as irrelevant and annoying. Headings, sub-headings, and numerals show a hierarchical organization and approach. The reasoning is usually deductive, progressing from general to specific, and uses a tight logical structure, with issues and sub-issues covered in turn. There are several paragraphs per page, but few if any one-sentence paragraphs, and there are frequent transition words and phrases that explicitly make logical connections between one sentence and the next, and one paragraph and the next.

Conclusions in U.S. legal writing are explicit, and may be repeated, such as in the short answer section at the beginning of an office memorandum, at the end of the thesis paragraph of the Discussion, and in a separate final conclusion section at the end. All of these logical devices show the U.S. legal writer's respect for the legal reader by making the legal work product as clear as possible.

Other cultures show a variety of preferences for introductions. In Spanish, where elegance and beautiful writing are important in professional writing, introductions are often long, and begin with more general statements. Arabic writers also often begin with general statements. Chinese, Japanese, and Korean writers, on the other hand, tend to prefer an inductive writing style, moving from specific to general. A thesis statement may not exist in a predictable place; it is often indirect, and if it exists at all, it may do so near the end of the writing.

Spanish uses a linear organization model, but not as strict a model as English. Digressions to interesting related points are favored, and show the writer's intelligence and depth of knowledge. Similarly, French writing does not follow a strict linear pattern: writers often digress, consider related material, and then return to the main theme. French also often avoids explicit topic sentences, which are viewed as too obvious for educated readers.

Chinese writing is not linear; it has been described as following a circular pattern, beginning on the edge of the circle to outline the broad area of discussion and then moving toward the center of the circle as the writer eventually gets to the point.

Japanese writing tends to follow a four-part pattern that begins by stating the argument, then developing it, and then turning to a theme which bears a partial but indirect connection to the main theme. Finally, the writing brings it all together in a conclusion, which may be tentative, and which may even take a different viewpoint from the beginning of the argument. The Japanese writer may repeatedly return to a main theme which is never explicitly stated, which to a U.S. reader feels like a vague circling around the issue.

Unlike current U.S. legal writing, which is fairly extreme in its desire to be concise, Spanish, Portuguese, French, Russian, and Arabic are concerned with beautiful writing, and do not find beauty in concise writing. Spanish and French speakers often use long sentences with flowing, flowery vocabulary, particularly noun phrases and nominalizations. Russian writers show their education with intentionally long and complex sentences and paragraphs. Arabic speakers prefer coordination to subordination, and make long, parallel constructions using "and."

Conclusions also tend to vary, and are often not as explicit as U.S. legal writing conclusions. Chinese traditionally avoids conclusions, and Japanese also often avoids explicit conclusions, ending instead with conclusions that express some uncertainty or even include a question. As shown above, the final conclusion in Japanese writing may also be different from the earlier statements, surprising and confusing U.S. legal readers.

Arabic, on the other hand, tends to express opinions and conclusions so strongly that it causes confusion for U.S. legal readers, and vice versa: What seems neutral to a U.S. writer seems like an understatement to an Arabic-speaking reader, and what seems neutral to an Arabic-speaking writer seems like an overstatement to a U.S. legal reader.

French conclusions often introduce a new, similar topic, leaving the reader with additional "food for thought." With their low tolerance for digressions, U.S. legal readers look at this type of conclusion and find it irrelevant.

C. SUGGESTIONS FOR INTERNATIONAL LEGAL WRITERS

Hopefully, your first language has been described in the section above, or at least a language that is similar to yours has been described, and you can easily note differences between the rhetoric of your first language and English.

If the description above pertains to writing in your language in general, but not as much to legal writing, you should still assume that those rhetorical preferences may affect your writing in English. For example, if you speak an East Asian language such as Chinese, Korean, or Japanese, legal writing that seems direct to you may not seem direct to a U.S. legal reader.

Flexibility is an essential habit to develop at a U.S. law school. You are living in a different country and culture, and studying and writing in a new language and legal system. As a result, you are faced with new and unfamiliar things every day, from the food and the people, to the classes, books, legal system, and writing. At times, it is exhausting, and it is natural to try to do everything as you did back home. Unfortunately, that will not lead to success in a U.S. law school. Try to be flexible, and to adapt to a different way of working with the law and writing about it. It will seem foreign and strange to you at first, but you will become more comfortable with practice.

Specifically, try to approach legal writing with the attitude of a U.S. lawyer, rather than the attitude of a lawyer from your country. See your audience as an impatient, overburdened partner, judge, or client who wants you to write concisely and explicitly, in plain English. Follow the rhetorical preferences of U.S. legal readers, from the introduction to the conclusion. Think in English as you analyze the law, work with the facts at a detailed level, make sure that you have all of the relevant legal rules — which are your analytical tools — and apply those rules to the specific facts of the legal problem. Support your legal assertions with citations to statutes, regulations, and case law. If you follow this rhetorical style, you will have a happier legal reader, one who is more likely to believe your analysis.

Chapter Review

- There is no universal "proper way" to write; different languages have different rhetorical preferences. Even within the same language, there may be different preferences from country to country, or from field to field.

- Because we grow up within our own language and cultural community, it is easy to feel that its rhetorical preferences are correct, and that different preferences are incorrect, but this kind of attitude is not productive or useful.
- If we think in our first language when studying and writing in a second language, we will mix the languages and their rhetorical styles together in a phenomenon known as "interference." The result is very problematic.
- Even if we think well in the second language, our writing can still show signs of the grammar and rhetorical preferences of our first language, which is problematic.
- Thus, it is helpful to be aware of the differences in rhetorical style between your first language and English, to be sure that you are following the rhetorical preferences of U.S. legal readers when you are writing about U.S. law in English.
- Rhetorical differences include the level of directness, the organization, the sentence style and structure, citations and support, the use of facts, and conclusions.

Chapter 12

WRITING THE OFFICE MEMORANDUM: LARGE-SCALE AND SMALL-SCALE ORGANIZATION

Chapter Preview

This chapter introduces the office memorandum as a fundamental type of U.S. legal writing. The chapter discusses:

- The typical parts of an office memorandum (large-scale organization); and
- The structure of the analysis of one legal issue, often known by an acronym such as IRAC or TREAC (small-scale organization).

The office memorandum ("memo") is a common, foundational type of attorney work product. In the United States, young attorneys often write office memoranda when they are still law students. If J.D. students are able to obtain work with a law firm in the summer following their second year of law school (in "summer associate" positions), they typically write several office memos over the course of the summer. The quality of the memos plays a large role in determining whether the students are offered jobs with the law firms after graduation. After they become attorneys, many young associates (especially litigators) continue to write office memos for at least the first several years of their careers.

Office memos typically include all of the components of most legal writing, such as an introduction to the facts of the matter, a description of the legal issue(s), a statement of the law that pertains to the issue(s), and an analysis of the legal issue(s) in which the writer applies the law to the relevant facts and determines the likely outcome.[1] These basic components of legal writing exist in one form or another in most legal writing, from office memos to motions or briefs to the court, or even client letters. Therefore, an office memorandum is typically the first type of legal writing that U.S. law students learn.

A. THE PURPOSE OF AN OFFICE MEMORANDUM

An office memorandum is a tool that lawyers use in the decision-making process. We use the term "office" memorandum because most memos never leave the law office — they are designed for the internal use of the law firm or legal department. Sometimes clients ask for a copy of the memo, especially if they review their bills and see that a memo has been written. This is more likely to be true where the client is a corporation with a legal department, or at least a general counsel.[2] Most of the time, however, the memo is written for internal purposes.

More specifically, a memo is a written answer to a legal question that reflects the research and analysis of the writer. The assigning attorney has given the memo assignment because he or she is considering a legal strategy and wants to know whether it is well-grounded in the law, and/or what its chance of success is. Ultimately, this information will enable the partner to advise the client, and to help the client decide what to do in a given situation.

1. Rule 11 and the Need for Research and Analysis

Legal research is essential because under the Federal Rules of Civil Procedure and analogous state procedural rules, all representations to the court must be well-grounded.[3] That means that all claims, defenses, and other assertions about the law

---

[1] Of course, not all attorney work product contains all of these features. A contract, for example, may contain or refer to several of these components, such as the facts that lead to the deal, the provisions that constitute the deal, and the applicable law.

[2] Associates at law firms should always write memos with the understanding that they may be sent to the client, sometimes with little notice or time for revision.

[3] *See* Fed. R. Civ. P. 11(b).

are "warranted by existing law or by a nonfrivolous argument for extending, modifying, or reversing existing law or for establishing new law."[4] Similarly, factual assertions and denials must have evidentiary support and be warranted by the evidence, or be reasonably believed and likely to have factual support after conducting discovery.[5] Finally, none of the legal or factual assertions may be made for an improper purpose, such as increasing litigation costs, causing unnecessary delay, or harassing the other party.[6]

Rule 11 and the analogous state rules make the parties and legal counsel responsible for knowing the law and the facts of the case. Violations of the rule can hurt both the parties and their lawyers, damage an attorney's credibility and career, and even lead to disciplinary actions and legal malpractice suits. Thus, before lawyers recommend strategies to their clients, they need to be confident that the strategies are grounded in the law and have at least a reasonable chance of success.

Lawyers often concentrate their practice in a limited number of areas, and with years of experience, they become experts in those areas. Even so, U.S. law is constantly evolving: Statutes may be written, revised, or abrogated at any time, and new case law may bring significant changes in the law. Therefore, even experienced, expert lawyers need to research the law at issue, to ensure that their understanding is accurate, complete, and current. That's why they assign memos to their associates. Many assignments are about narrow, more specific legal issues, and partners want to receive the results in short email memos[7] or even orally. For the most important strategic decisions, however, they often still assign office memoranda.

2. Common Types of Office Memoranda

Office memos may be written by lawyers who practice any kind of law, whether criminal or civil, including transactional law, litigation, law that has a regulatory aspect such as environmental law or utilities law, and practice areas that combine aspects of both transactional and litigation practice, such as intellectual property or labor and employment law.

In environmental law, for example, a memo might analyze whether a client's proposed action would violate existing environmental regulations, or it might predict what the result might be of a client's regulatory violations.

The sample office memorandum in Appendix B analyzes what potential civil and criminal penalties a client faces for submitting inaccurate reports to a state's environmental protection division and for failing to properly inspect two leak detection systems at one of its factories.

In litigation, memos can be assigned and written at virtually any time during the litigation process, from before a complaint is filed until shortly before the appeals

[4] Fed. R. Civ. P. 11(b)(2).

[5] Fed. R. Civ. P. 11(b)(3), (4).

[6] Fed. R. Civ. P. 11(b)(1).

[7] Chapter 21 covers email memos.

process is exhausted. They are often assigned at or near the beginning of the litigation, to help counsel and client determine which strategies to choose.

For example, if a plaintiff files a complaint that contains several causes of action, the defendant needs to decide whether to file a motion to dismiss or an answer. A partner might assign a memo requiring the associate to analyze each cause of action, whether the plaintiff has sufficiently pled each element, and what the plaintiff's chances of prevailing on each cause of action are, given the alleged facts and in light of the most relevant case law.

Another example: If the defendant has to file an answer, it needs to consider which affirmative defenses to assert, if any. Because the defendant cannot file groundless affirmative defenses, a partner may assign a memo that analyzes whether several possible defenses are available.

The sample office memorandum in Appendix C analyzes whether four common law defenses (implied waiver, equitable estoppel, implied acquiescence, and laches) are available to the client under the Telephone Consumer Protection Act ("TCPA"),[8] a federal statute, or whether the client is limited to the one statutory defense enumerated in the statute. It also provides an analysis of the client's chance of establishing the four common law defenses, articulating theories under which the defenses could apply to bar the plaintiff's claims.

B. LARGE-SCALE ORGANIZATION — THE SECTIONS OF AN OFFICE MEMORANDUM

1. The Outline of an Office Memorandum

Office memoranda typically have the same three or four main sections, although they may use different names for the sections. They also have one of the two following sequences (listed below as "Option 1" and "Option 2"):[9]

Option 1:

1. Issue(s)/Question(s) Presented And Short Answer(s)	**OR**	Executive Summary
2. Background/Introduction/Statement of Facts		
3. Discussion		
4. Conclusion (optional)		

[8] 47 U.S.C. § 227 (2006).

[9] If the memo is based on the analysis of a statutory issue, there may also be an additional section called "Applicable Statute," which contains a direct quotation of the relevant statutory language. If a memo contains an Applicable Statute section, it is placed immediately before the Discussion section.

Option 2:

1. Background/Introduction/Statement of Facts 2. Issue(s)/Question(s) Presented And Short Answer(s) 3. Discussion 4. Conclusion (optional)	**OR**	Executive Summary

Using the order presented in Option 1, here is a short description of each section:

1. **Issue(s)/Question(s) Presented:** The statement of the legal issue(s) raised by the facts. The question can be written one of several ways: (1) as a question, often using the "under — does — when" format that we learned in Chapter 6 for case briefs; (2) as a clause beginning with "whether"; or (3) as a few sentences giving the most important facts, followed by a simple question. The more traditional name is "Question Presented," but some lawyers today prefer the term "Issue," which is less formal.

   Short Answer(s): Immediately following the question, a short summary of the answer to the question. It gives the author's conclusion(s) about the legal issue without citations. If the memo addresses more than one issue, there may be a Question Presented and a Short Answer for each issue.

   OR

   Executive Summary: A modern alternative to the Question Presented and Short Answer, the Executive Summary provides a short (usually two, three or four paragraphs long) summary of the legal issue(s) and the author's conclusion(s). Like a Short Answer, an Executive Summary usually does not have citations.

   The purposes of either format (Question Presented and Short Answer or Executive Summary) are (1) to provide a complete, stand-alone section that summarizes the entire memo for a busy partner or client who does not have time to read the entire memo, and (2) to provide a summary of the entire memo that the legal reader may quickly review before a meeting or telephone call.

2. **Background/Introduction/Statement of Facts:** An introduction to the topic of the memorandum that introduces the parties and the legal issue(s), and provides the facts that are relevant to the issue(s) that the memorandum will analyze. The more traditional name for this section is "Statement of Facts," but many lawyers today prefer the terms "Background" or "Introduction," which are both less formal and somewhat more general.

3. **Discussion:** This is the main section of the memorandum. It provides the attorney's analysis of the legal issue(s) in question, and contains citations. In more informal office memos, parts of the Discussion section (especially case summaries) are sometimes written in bullet-pointed paragraphs instead of

traditional paragraphs.[10]

4. **Conclusion:** Some office memoranda provide a stand-alone Conclusion section following the Discussion section. This is especially common in longer, more complex memos, or in memos where the conclusion is a prediction and contains more information.[11] Because the conclusion has already been stated in the Short Answer(s) or Executive Summary, and it has been repeated at the end of the thesis paragraph of the Discussion section, some lawyers choose not to include this section, especially in shorter or simpler memos.[12]

2. How to Organize the Discussion Section of a Memo

At its most general, the Discussion section begins with a thesis paragraph, which typically provides (1) an overview of the law at issue, (2) a "roadmap" that sets forth which issues or sub-issues will be analyzed,[13] and (3) a conclusion. After the thesis paragraph, the Discussion section analyzes the issues one at a time:

- Thesis paragraph
- Issue 1
  - Sub-issue 1 (if there is a sub-issue)
  - Sub-issue 2, etc.
- Issue 2 (if there is a second issue), etc.

Discussion sections are often organized around the type of legal rule(s) at issue. Certain rules contain **elements** (all of which the plaintiff must meet); others contain **factors** (some of which the plaintiff must meet). There may be one issue with several sub-issues (i.e., elements or factors), or there may be several separate issues.

In a rule that involves elements, all of the parts of the rule must be met. For example, to vote for President of the United States, the potential voter must be (1) 18 years of age or older; and (2) a U.S. citizen. This rule has two elements: the age requirement and the citizenship requirement. Voters must meet both requirements to vote.

Many statutory rules involve elements, as do some common law rules. For example, to prevail on a common-law claim of negligence under Illinois law, a plaintiff must establish that (1) the defendant owed a duty of care to the plaintiff; (2) the defendant breached that duty of care; and (3) that breach caused the plaintiff's injury.[14] The cause of action has three elements, and the plaintiff must establish all three of them

---

[10] *See* Appendix C for an example of a memo with bullet-pointed paragraphs.

[11] *See* the office memorandum in Appendix B.

[12] *See* the office memorandum in Appendix C.

[13] Some legal writers place the roadmap at the end of the Introduction/Background/Statement of Facts section, which allows for a shorter thesis paragraph that focuses only on the law and the conclusion. *See* Chapter 16.

[14] *Reed v. Galaxy Holdings, Inc.*, 394 Ill. App. 3d 39, 42 (1st Dist. 2009).

to prevail.[15]

With factors, on the other hand, not all of the parts of the rule must be met. In Chapter 6, we read the *Polaroid* rule developed by Judge Friendly of the Second Circuit to determine whether a "likelihood of confusion" exists under the Lanham Act (the federal trademark law). That rule has eight non-exclusive factors to analyze:

> (1) the strength of the mark, (2) the degree of similarity between the two marks, (3) the competitive proximity of the products, (4) actual confusion, (5) the likelihood the plaintiff will bridge the gap, (6) the defendant's good faith in adopting its mark, (7) the quality of the defendant's products, and (8) the sophistication of the purchasers.[16]

A plaintiff does not need to establish every factor to prevail.

When a plaintiff must establish every element of a rule of law, a memo will likely analyze each element separately, unless one element is not at issue.[17]

If we are analyzing a legal rule with several elements, the organization is as follows:

- Thesis paragraph
- Element 1
- Element 2, etc.

The organization of a memo that analyzes a legal rule with factors may depend upon the facts of the case. For example, a memo that analyzes whether a likelihood of confusion exists under the Lanham Act could analyze all eight factors of the test, but the partner that assigns the memo may ask the associate to focus only on four of the factors because she is confident that she already understands how the judge will rule on the last four factors.

C. SMALL-SCALE ORGANIZATION — THE IRAC OR TREAC STRUCTURE

United States legal readers expect legal analysis, whether it is expressed in an office memo, a brief to the court, or any other form, to follow a certain logical order. As we discussed in Chapter 9, the most basic and common description of that order is known as "IRAC," which stands for **I**ssue, **R**ule, **A**pplication, **C**onclusion. For example, your law school professors will expect your final examination writing to follow this structure.[18]

---

[15] In many states, the negligence rule has four elements: duty, breach, causation, and damages. Illinois case law describes the rule as having three elements by combining causation and the injury in one element.

[16] *Brennan's, Inc. v. Brennan's Restaurant, LLC*, 360 F.3d 125, 130 (2d Cir. 2004).

[17] If an element is not in dispute, the writer of an office memo may explain that fact in the "roadmap" section of the thesis paragraph or introduction, and mention that the memo will analyze the remaining elements that are at issue.

[18] Chapter 24 discusses writing law school final examinations.

As we also discussed in Chapter 9, a slightly expanded version of the basic IRAC format adds an **E**xplanation of the rule; depending on the term that you use for the statement of the issue, it is known as "IREAC," TREAC," "CREAC," or a similar acronym. As with IRAC, this format communicates the analysis of a single legal issue efficiently. It gives the legal reader the information the reader wants in the order that the legal reader expects and needs. If we want to add a counterargument, the structure expands further to "TREACC," which stands for:

Topic sentence (or thesis statement)

Rule section

Explanation of the rule

Application (analysis)

Counterargument (if any)

Conclusion

The TREACC pattern of organization is especially useful when your issue involves facts that you will compare to the facts from precedent. Legal memoranda do not contain any headings or sub-headings labeled "IRAC" or "TREACC" (or Rule, Explanation, etc.). Instead, the headings and sub-headings usually describe the substance of the analysis. Nevertheless, you should keep this "invisible" structure in mind for the small-scale structure of your legal writing, whether it is a short analysis of a legal issue in which the whole TREACC structure exists in one or two paragraphs, or a longer analysis stretched over several pages, where each section (T, R, E, etc.) is a paragraph or more.

If we are analyzing a statute section or a common law rule with several elements or factors, we often use the TREACC structure to analyze each element or factor separately, *e.g.*, Element 1 (TREACC), Element 2 (TREACC), etc.

Let's consider a case in which your law firm represents a supermarket chain. On a very wet, rainy day, a customer, Monica Jackson, slipped and fell[19] on the floor of one of the client's supermarkets in Chicago, about 10 feet (three meters) inside the store entrance. Ms. Jackson was injured in the fall, and has sued the supermarket for negligence, asserting that the store negligently failed to maintain a safe condition in the store. Your client, Wholesome Food Markets, Inc., has told you that none of its employees or other customers had spilled water or a liquid in the store, and no one had washed the floor. Rather, many customers entered the store with wet shoes, and tracked the water in with them.

A partner in your firm has asked you to write a memo in which you evaluate the likelihood of success of Ms. Jackson's negligence claim.[20]

---

[19] Lawyers call this a "slip-and-fall claim."

[20] The assignment would also expect you to review Illinois case law to determine if there have been any significant recent slip-and-fall decisions that have changed the law in any way, and to analyze whether Ms. Jackson properly alleged all of the elements of her negligence claim.

After an Introduction section that introduces the facts of the case and an Executive Summary that summarizes the results of your analysis,[21] the Discussion session of the memo should begin with a thesis paragraph that contains the following:

(1) It should set forth the legal claim (i.e., it should state that the issue is whether or not Ms. Jackson can prove that Wholesome Food Markets was negligent in maintaining the floor of the supermarket);

(2) It should provide an overview of the law by stating the elements of a negligence claim under Illinois law (duty of care, breach of the duty, causing damages);

(3) It should state the elements that it will not analyze and why (e.g., the parties agree that because she was a customer of Wholesome Food Markets, the business owed Ms. Jackson a general duty to keep the entrance to and exit from the business reasonably safe, so the memo will not analyze the first element); and

(4) It should conclude by briefly stating your conclusion on the probable result of the claim (i.e., Ms. Jackson will likely not be able to prove that Wholesome Food Markets breached its general duty of care to her, because under Illinois law, stores have no duty to constantly remove tracked-in rainwater.[22] Therefore, her claim is unlikely to succeed).

Then, after the thesis paragraph, we analyze the legal issue by providing a TREAC (or TREACC) analysis of the second and third elements of the claim, analyzing each element separately. In other words, we use the TREAC or TREACC structure to analyze the second element, we use the structure again to analyze the third element, and we follow it a third time to analyze the fourth element.

Here's how to organize your discussion of the second element (whether Wholesome Food Markets breached its duty of care to Ms. Jackson):

1. (T)TOPIC sentence stating the issue

A strong topic sentence introduces the issue, sub-issue, or element that you will analyze. It serves as a transition from what you discussed earlier, and it provides a roadmap of what you will discuss.

State the issue either as an issue or as a conclusion:

> The first issue is whether Wholesome Food Markets breached its duty of care to Ms. Jackson. (stated as an issue)

[21] As we discussed in Section B, if the partner, firm, or client has more traditional preferences, the sections may also be called the Statement of Facts, Issue or Question Presented, and Short Answer.

[22] *See Lohan v. Walgreens Co.*, 140 Ill. App. 3d 171, 173–75 (1st Dist. 1986).

Wholesome Food Markets did not breach its duty of care to Ms. Jackson. (stated as a conclusion)

2. (R)State the governing RULE(S)

State the applicable legal rule(s), which you have derived from statutes, cases, and any other authority, preferably from the relevant jurisdiction (Illinois, in this example). Think of this as a rule *section.* Often, you will write a paragraph that contains several rule sentences, not just one sentence.

Rule sections go from more general to more specific, e.g., a statement of the general rule, then a rule that defines how or where the rule is used, followed by an exception to the rule, and finally an exception to the exception. Generally, you should state the rule in your own words, not a quotation, as it may synthesize several different authorities. For example, the general rule comes from an old case. Then a more recent case adds to the rule. If so, a complete rule statement must include the rule(s) from both cases.

Always cite to the authority when giving a rule. For example, a rule section with four sentences should have four citations, one after each sentence. If the citation is to case law, a full citation provides the name of the case; the name, volume, and series of the reporter; the page that the case begins on; the page from which the rule is taken; the name of the court; and the year of the opinion.

> Under Illinois law, businesses owe their customers a general duty to keep the entrance to and exit from the business reasonably safe. *Reed v. Galaxy Holdings, Inc.*, 394 Ill. App. 3d 39, 42 (1st Dist. 2009) (internal citations omitted). Under the "natural accumulation rule," however, business operators and property owners have "no duty to remove natural accumulations of ice, snow, or water" from their properties. *Krywin v. Chicago Transit Auth.*, 238 Ill. 2d 215, 227 (2010); *Reed*, 394 Ill. App. 3d at 42. They also have no duty to continuously remove water that customers have tracked into the building from natural accumulations of water, snow or ice outside. *Lohan v. Walgreens Co.*, 140 Ill. App. 3d 171, 173–74 (1st Dist. 1986); *Reed*, 394 Ill. App. 3d at 42. Business operators may be liable if the injuries were caused by an unnatural accumulation of water or where the operator aggravated the natural condition, *Reed*, 394 Ill. App. 3d at 43, and they may be liable if the plaintiff establishes that the building is "particularly slippery and dangerous when wet." *Id.* (citing *Selby v. Danville Pepsi-Cola Bottling Co.*, 169 Ill. App. 3d 427, 436 (4th Dist. 1988); *Lohan*, 140 Ill. App. 3d at 173–74).

3. (E)EXPLANATION of how the rule applies from relevant precedent (talk about the facts, holding, and reasoning of the case(s))

Illustrate how the rules from the rule section work by examining precedent and showing how courts in those cases applied the rules to different facts. Discuss the facts, finding, and reasoning of each case. Begin with a quick one-clause or one-sentence summary of what the case is about to provide context for the legal reader. The holding and reasoning should explain the court's decision and how it reached its decision.

Don't give a long general summary of the case. Focus only on the facts relevant to the rule(s) from the Rule section, and remember that the purpose of the E section is to illustrate the rules and to show how courts apply them. Here is an example of a case summary from precedent:

> In *Lohan v. Walgreens Co.*, 140 Ill. App. 3d 171, 172 (1st Dist. 1986), a customer slipped and fell at the entrance to a Walgreens Pharmacy on a rainy day. The First District affirmed the dismissal of her complaint, holding that the company did not have a duty under Illinois law to continuously remove the rainwater that had accumulated at the entrance to the store. *Id.* at 175.

The Explanation section does not necessarily discuss case law. For example, if the Rule section discusses a regulation, the Explanation section might explain how the regulatory agency interprets and enforces the regulation.[23]

4. (A)APPLICATION of the rule to your facts by comparing your facts to the facts of the case precedent(s) and by applying the rule directly to your facts

This is really the most important part of TREACC — it's the part where you provide the analysis for the legal issue.

Analogize (show similarities) and distinguish (show differences) the facts of your case with the facts of the precedent case(s) described above in the E section. Begin the application part with a sentence that lets the reader know which way your analysis is leading:

> The facts in this matter are very similar to the facts in *Lohan*.

Should the result of the case brought by Ms. Jackson be similar to that of the precedent case(s) you described in the E section (*Lohan v. Walgreens Co.*), or different? Your purpose is to show why the court should reach either the same or a different result in our case than in the precedent. Do this by specifically comparing the facts of the case(s) in the E section to the facts of our case.

Tell the reader the similarities (draw analogies), and tell the reader the differences (draw distinctions). Make fact-to-fact comparisons:

> Like the defendant in *Lohan*, which did not continuously remove the water that the customers had tracked into the drugstore on a rainy day, Wholesome Foods Market did not continuously remove the water that the customers had tracked into the supermarket. (analogizing)

Or you can distinguish the precedent:

> Unlike the plaintiff in *Lohan*, who slipped at the entrance to the drugstore, Ms. Jackson slipped 10 feet inside the supermarket. (distinguishing)

---

[23] For an example of this, look at the Explanation section in Section II of the Discussion section, on page 5 of the office memorandum in Appendix B.

Don't be conclusory here. In other words, don't give the reader your conclusion without specifically describing the facts. You add value by showing detailed analysis of the issue. Remember, the legal reader has no use for unsupported conclusions — you must support your analysis by comparing the facts of those cases to the facts of your problem. If you simply compare holdings, such as saying "The court in *Lohan* affirmed the trial court's decision in favor of the defendant, Walgreens Co., and our court should find in favor of Wholesome Foods Market," you are not providing the legal reader with any reason to support your conclusion. This makes legal readers skeptical and frustrated.

5. (C)Identify and evaluate strong COUNTERARGUMENTS, if any exist

Remember that an office memorandum is objective, not persuasive. It's your job to analyze the law, and to evaluate how strong or weak the client's case is so that the partner can provide the client with realistic and accurate legal advice. Your memo might even tell the partner that the client has a weak case or will probably lose. Thus, in an objective memorandum, you need to show the legal reader that you have considered the arguments of both parties, and determined which party has the stronger arguments.

A counterargument is an argument that goes against your analysis of an issue, whatever that is (it does not necessarily go against your client's position — you might conclude that your client is unlikely to win the issue). In other words, you are playing the "devil's advocate" by showing the argument that is contrary to your conclusion, and then showing why that argument is weaker.

For example, if you conclude that your client has the stronger argument, the counterargument is an argument against your client's position (and then you rebut the counterargument by showing why it is weak and will probably lose). On the other hand, if your analysis leads you to believe that *your client* will probably lose on that issue, the counterargument will be your client's best argument, followed by a rebuttal that shows why that argument is unlikely to succeed. The rebuttal should be supported with a citation to legal authority, if possible.

In your analysis of the second element of Ms. Jackson's negligence claim, if you conclude that Ms. Jackson will likely not be able to prove that Wholesome Food Markets breached its general duty of care to her, the counterargument will be the strongest argument that Ms. Jackson can make.

Introduce the counterargument with language like: "Ms. Jackson might argue that . . . . However, this argument is unlikely to succeed because . . . .":

> Ms. Jackson might argue that, unlike the accident scene in *Lohan*, where the plaintiff had slipped and fallen in the wet entrance of the drugstore, she fell 10 feet inside the supermarket, which is not a location which she had

> expected to be wet. However, this argument is unlikely to succeed[24] because under Illinois law, owners have no duty to continuously remove water that customers have tracked inside the building. *Id.* at 174 (internal citations omitted).

Sometimes, there will be no strong counterargument against your analysis. If there is a strong counterargument, state what it is and then rebut it by showing how your analysis is correct and defeats the counterargument. However, if there is no strong counterargument, do not waste the reader's time by inventing a weak one. Thus, many issues or sub-issues may have "TREAC" analysis instead of "TREACC" because there is no strong counterargument.

6. (C) State your CONCLUSION on the issue

Your conclusion for the second element should be brief and objective. You can qualify your conclusion with words such as "likely" or "probably" because those words have a value that is more than 50%. However, you must provide a conclusion of some kind (i.e., a statement that something is more than 50% likely). Legal readers get very annoyed if you simply say something like "It's too close to call" and give no prediction. Also avoid words like "may," "might," "can," "could," and "possibly" because these words are vague and too weak to be of any predictive value; thus, they are not really conclusions either. Almost anything is possible; it is possible that you could win the lottery today or be hit by lightning! The legal reader wants you to take a position and to say what you think is *probable* (more than 50% likely to happen).

Repeat the same TREAC or TREACC structure for the third element. Then, at the end of the memo, provide a brief Conclusion section that sums up your overall analysis: why Ms. Jackson will probably not be able to prevail on her negligence claim.

Chapter Review

- Before lawyers can realistically and accurately advise their clients on the appropriate strategy for a lawsuit or any course of action, they must understand what law applies to a given issue, what the current state of the law is, and how the law applies to the facts of their clients' situations.
- This is not only a practical requirement; it is an ethical one as well. Rule 11 of the Federal Rules of Civil Procedure and analogous state procedural rules require that all legal claims and assertions that lawyers make be sufficiently well-grounded, both legally and factually.
- If they are discovered, violations of these rules harm the client's case and the lawyer's reputation. Violations can also lead to legal malpractice suits against the attorneys and their law firms, and possible disciplinary actions against

---

24 "[T]his argument is unlikely to succeed" is not necessary language and many lawyers would edit it out: "However, under Illinois law, owners have no duty. . . ." We have included it here to help you to understand the meaning and the reasoning of a rebuttal.

the lawyers by the state bars that license them.

- Accordingly, lawyers must know (and research) the law and analyze how it applies to the facts of any matter. Often, they give associates assignments to research and analyze a particular legal issue or issues, and to write up their analysis in a document called an office memorandum.
- An office memorandum provides an objective analysis of the law and how it applies to the facts of the client's problem. It helps attorneys to understand the strengths and weaknesses of the client's position, and is used as a basis for advising the client.
- For a narrower, more specific issue, or for a smaller matter where the client has a smaller budget, the associate may report orally or write an email memo to the partner. For a larger, more complex matter, the associate may write a traditional office memorandum.
- The memo begins with a section that states the legal issue that it will analyze and provides a short summary of the writer's conclusion. This part acts as a stand-alone summary of the whole memo, and busy legal readers can use it to refresh their memories of the memo's contents. This part comes in two forms: either (1) as a question called the "Question Presented" (or "Issue"), followed by the "Short Answer," or (2) as a short summary of the legal question and answer that is two or three paragraphs long, and called the Executive Summary.
- The memo then introduces the facts that pertain to the legal issue. It is usually called the "Background," "Introduction," or "Statement of Facts."
- Some lawyers, law firms, or clients prefer for the Background/Introduction/Statement of Facts section to be at the beginning of the memo, before the Question Presented and Short Answer or Executive Summary.
- The next and most important part of the memo is called the Discussion section. The Discussion section describes the relevant law and analyzes the issue(s).
- The Discussion section begins with a thesis paragraph that states the legal issue; usually provides an overview of the applicable law; gives a roadmap of what the section will discuss (and what it will not); and states the answer to the legal issue.
- After the thesis paragraph, the discussion section analyzes the issues one at a time, with a structure that we describe with acronyms such as IRAC and TREAC.

A TREACC analysis includes an Explanation section and a Counterargument section, as follows:

- (T) **T**opic sentence stating the legal issue;
- (R) **R**ule section stating the governing rule(s);
- (E) **E**xplanation from relevant precedent of how the rule applies (discussing the facts, holding, and reasoning of the case(s), or explaining how courts or

administrative agencies or bodies interpret a statute or regulation);

- (A) **A**pplication of the governing rule(s) to your facts by comparing your facts to the facts of the case precedent(s) and by applying the rule(s) directly to your facts;
- (C) Identify and evaluate strong **C**ounterarguments, if any exist; and
- (C) State your **C**onclusion on the issue.
- This structure repeats itself for each issue and may be followed by a separate section that provides the overall conclusion, especially if the memorandum is longer and has multiple issues and/or sub-issues.

Chapter 13

THE HEART OF LEGAL REASONING

Chapter Preview

This chapter takes a further look at the key substantive sections of written legal analysis: the Rule, Explanation, and Application sections of IRAC and TREAC. The chapter discusses and gives examples of:

- Rule sections, whether the rules come from statutes or case law;
- Whether and when to use Explanation sections;
- Explanation sections that illustrate how courts, administrative bodies, or other legal decision makers interpret the rules; and
- Application sections that apply the legal rules directly to the facts and/or that analogize or distinguish precedent with fact-to-fact comparisons between the precedent and the current matter.

In Chapter 12, we learned that an office memorandum contains several parts: (1) the summary of the memo's contents, which may be expressed either as a Question Presented and Short Answer, or as an Executive Summary; (2) the Introduction/Background/Statement of Facts; (3) the Discussion section; and often (4) a separate Conclusion after the Discussion.

All of these sections are useful, because:

- We need to know the background facts that we will use in analyzing the memorandum's legal issue.
- Also, it is helpful to have a summary of the whole memo for review purposes, or for lawyers who must enter a meeting or advise a client without having had sufficient time to carefully read the entire memo.
- Moreover, it is often helpful to have a separate conclusion after the Discussion section that collects the various "partial conclusions" in the Discussion and summarizes all of the author's conclusions in one or two comprehensive paragraphs. This solidifies the conclusions from the Discussion section in the legal reader's mind.

Without doubt, however, the most important part of a memorandum is the Discussion section. That is where the legal writer provides the legal analysis that he or she was asked to produce. The Discussion section is broken down into one or more IRAC or TREAC analytical structures, each of which states the legal issue (T), describes the legal rules that govern the issue (R), and analyzes the issue by applying those rules to the facts of the matter (A).

Because the legal writer was assigned the legal issue, it is not difficult to state what it is. Rather, the heart of the legal writer's work is to determine and to state the relevant legal rules accurately, clearly, and comprehensively (R); to determine whether to write an Explanation section that shows how the relevant legal decision maker[1] interprets the legal rules (E) (and to provide it if necessary); and to apply the legal rules to the facts of the matter to analyze the legal issue (A). The Application section may also compare the facts of the matter to the facts of relevant precedent to predict what a legal decision maker is likely to do in the matter being analyzed.

In other words, the legal writer needs to decide how to organize and structure the various sections and sub-sections of the Discussion section. The writer can use the R and A sections of IRAC (Rules + Application), the R, E, and A sections of TREAC (Rules + Explanation + Application), a combination of the two (some IRAC sections and some TREAC sections), or possibly another structure, if he or she chooses.

There are no mechanical "rules" that tell the legal writer what to do. It is the writer's job to determine the clearest way to describe the results of his or her research and analysis. Ultimately, the structure depends upon the substance of the issue, and may vary somewhat from memo to memo. That said, however, legal readers have definite expectations, such as Rules + Application or Rules + Explanation +

---

[1] Here and throughout the book, we use the term "legal decision maker" to refer to the person or body that is responsible for rendering a decision in a legal controversy. It could be a judge, or a panel of judges; an administrative judge or panel; a government agency; an arbitrator or arbitration panel; or a mediator.

Application. When the writer violates those expectations too much, the legal reader is irritated and may also be confused.

A. ISSUES THAT ARE NOT IN DISPUTE

In a legal dispute, not all of the issues or facts are disputed. When an issue is not in dispute, a motion or brief to the court can typically dispose of the issue in a few sentences by stating the rule, providing a citation for the rule, and then providing the facts in a way that shows that the facts fit within the meaning of the rule.

EXERCISE 13 A

The following material deals with the first element of the common law negligence claim in the slip and fall case from Chapter 12.

Both parties agree that because the plaintiff, Ms. Jackson, was a customer at Wholesome Foods Market, the store owed her a general duty to keep the entrance to the store and the exit from the store reasonably safe. Thus, there is no need to write an entire IRAC or TREAC analysis of the first element of the negligence claim: whether the store owed a duty of care to her.

1. When the issue is not in dispute, the writer can dispose of it quickly in one of several possible ways. Three different examples are shown below, listed (a), (b), and (c). Below each example, write what writer did and whether you think it is effective:

> (a) Under Illinois law, businesses owe their customers a general duty to keep the entrance to and exit from the business reasonably safe. *Reed v. Galaxy Holdings, Inc.*, 394 Ill. App. 3d 39, 42 (1st Dist. 2009) (internal citations omitted). Because Ms. Jackson was a customer of Wholesome Food Markets, it owed her a general duty of care.

What did the writer do?

Is it effective?

> (b) Wholesome Food Markets owed Ms. Jackson a general duty to keep the entrance to and exit from the business reasonably safe. *Reed v. Galaxy Holdings, Inc.*, 394 Ill. App. 3d 39, 42 (1st Dist. 2009) (holding that business owners owe invitees a general duty of care to keep entrances to and exits from businesses reasonably safe).

What did the writer do?

Is it effective?

> (c) (*In the thesis paragraph*): The parties agree that because Ms. Jackson was a customer of Wholesome Food Markets, the store owed her a general duty of care to keep the entrance to and exit from the business reasonably safe, so this memorandum will not analyze the first element.

What did the writer do?

Is it effective?

2. The three options listed above, (a), (b), and (c), are all valid, but legal writers may choose to use them in different situations.

When might a writer choose option (a)?

When might a writer choose option (b)?

When might a writer choose option (c)?

B. THE DIRECT APPLICATION OF RULES TO FACTS (WITH NO EXPLANATION SECTION)

Sometimes, the legal writer may decide that the legal rules are clear and straightforward, and the analysis can go directly from stating the rules to applying them to the facts. If a case explanation will not help the legal reader to understand the rules, or to understand how a court is likely to apply the rules, there is no need to write one.

EXERCISE 13 B

The following material includes the Rules and Application sections for the first issue of an email memo. The complete memo is in Appendix D. In the memo, the writer has been asked to analyze some of the possible defenses that a trucking company (the client) may have if an insurance company sues it for breach of contract. The alleged breach of contract related to the trucking company's alleged non-payments for the insurance company's services in connection with the claim servicing agreements between the parties.

The email memo discusses the possibility of a statute of limitations defense.[2]

1. In the right margin, write down the names of the two sections (Rules and Application) and where they begin:

---

[2] A statute of limitations specifies the amount of time that a plaintiff has to bring a lawsuit. For example, in many U.S. states, a plaintiff must bring a tort claim within two years and a breach of contract claim within five years, although such periods may vary from state to state.

The statute of limitations for breach of contract actions in Texas is four years. *Continental Casualty Co. v. Dr. Pepper Bottling Co. of Texas, Inc.*, 416 F. Supp. 2d 497, 506 (N.D. Tex. 2006). Texas law is clear that "where a demand is a condition precedent to suit, the plaintiff may not, by failing or refusing to perform the condition, toll the running of the statute and reserve to himself the right to sue within the statutory period from such time as he decides to make a demand." *United States v. First City Capital Corp.*, 53 F.3d 112, 115 (5th Cir. 1995). The general rule in cases in which a demand for payment is a condition precedent to a suit is that "[a] demand must be made within a reasonable time after it may lawfully be made." *Id.* The reasonableness of any delay is typically a question of fact, but "the law will ordinarily consider a reasonable time as being coincident with the running of the statute[.]" *Stevens v. State Farm Fire and Cas. Co.*, 929 S.W.2d 665, 671 (Tex. App. 1996). Thus, in Texas, a party has four years as of the date the right to payment accrues to demand it. "[A]n action will be barred if a demand is not made within that period." *Id.*

In this case, Truck Co. can assert that Insurance Co. has failed to make a demand for payment for the Year 1 and Year 2 claim servicing agreements within a "reasonable time." The Year 2 agreement (and presumably the Year 1 agreement, which I have not seen) put the onus on Insurance Co. to bill Truck Co. At the top of the Fee Schedule, there is a clause stating that "[t]he following fee schedule [is] [*sic*] to be billed to you by Insurance Co. Risk Management." This agreement was in effect until the end of Year 2. At that point in time, Insurance Co. could demand payment from Truck Co. for the claim servicing arising from the term of the Year 2 agreement. Insurance Co. had until the end of Year 6 to make that demand for payment. Because Insurance Co. failed to do so, the Texas statute of limitations would bar Insurance Co. from seeking recovery under the Year 2 claim servicing agreement.

In Arkansas, however, the statute of limitations for breach of contract actions arising from written contracts is five years. *Zufari v. Architecture Plus*, 323 Ark. 411, 419 (Ark. 1996). Thus, if Arkansas law applies to this case, Truck Co. will probably be unable to invoke the statute of limitations as a defense to any claim arising from the Year 2 agreement. The statute of limitations defense may still apply to the Year 1 agreement, however, because even the five-year statute of limitations has run for any claim based on that agreement.

2. Look at the rule sentences that comprise the Rule section. How would you characterize the rules? How did the legal writer decide upon the proper order of the rules in this section?

3. How is the Application section organized? Do you think that the organization is effective? Can you think of a different way to organize it?

C. THE WHOLE PACKAGE: RULES, EXPLANATION, AND APPLICATION SECTIONS

Sometimes, the legal writer decides that a legal rule is not especially clear. Perhaps the language of a statute section is intentionally vague, so that a court has flexibility in interpreting the rule. For example, what are "reasonable efforts" or "reasonable measures"? How do courts assess whether a "likelihood of confusion" exists under the Lanham Act?

Courts often develop tests to help judges to apply vague rules such as these to the facts of their cases. We have seen the example of the Second Circuit's eight-factor *Polaroid* test, which helps judges to determine whether a likelihood of confusion exists under the Lanham Act. In that situation, the writer adds the judge-made rule to the rule section, after the general rule with the vague language.

Even then, however, it can be very useful to examine how legal decision makers such as courts or government agencies have used the legal rule in cases with similar facts as a way to understand better what a court is likely to do when given the facts of our case. No two cases have identical facts, but if the facts are very similar, lawyers can understand what the legal decision maker is likely to do in the current case by comparing the facts of the new case to the facts of the previous case.

If the facts of the precedent and the current case are very similar, the result should be similar due to stare decisis. If the holding of factually-similar precedent favors our client's position, we can **analogize** our case to it by showing the similarities. Hopefully it is binding. Even if the holding is merely persuasive, it can still be very useful. At the least, the precedent may illustrate how our court is likely to analyze the issue. Perhaps we will be able to use the case in persuasive writing to the court, to persuade the judge(s) to adopt our client's position.

On the other hand, if the holding of factually-similar precedent is contrary to our client's position, we can **distinguish** it from our case by showing any important differences between the facts of the precedent and our case's facts. When we distinguish a case, we argue that the facts are different, so the result should be different, or at least that the result from precedent does not control our case because the facts are sufficiently different that the precedent is not relevant.

EXERCISE 13 C

The following material includes the Rules, Explanation, and Application sections that a legal writer might draft for the second element of the common law negligence claim in the slip and fall case from Chapter 12 (whether or not Wholesome Foods Market breached its duty of care to the plaintiff, Ms. Jackson).

1. In the right margin, write down the names of the three sections (Rules, Explanation, and Application) and where they begin:

Under Illinois law, businesses owe their customers a general duty to keep the entrance to and exit from the business reasonably safe. *Reed v. Galaxy Holdings, Inc.*, 394 Ill. App. 3d 39, 42 (1st Dist. 2009) (internal citations omitted). Under the "natural accumulation rule," however, business operators and property owners have "no duty to remove natural accumulations of ice, snow, or water" from their properties. *Krywin v. Chicago Transit Auth.*, 238 Ill. 2d 215, 227 (2010); *Reed*, 394 Ill. App. 3d at 42. They also have no duty to continuously remove water that customers have tracked into the building from natural accumulations of water, snow or ice outside. *Lohan v. Walgreens Co.*, 140 Ill. App. 3d 171, 173–74 (1st Dist. 1986); *Reed*, 394 Ill. App. 3d at 42. Business operators may be liable if the injuries were caused by an unnatural accumulation of water or where the operator aggravated the natural condition, *Reed*, 394 Ill. App. 3d at 43, and they may be liable if the plaintiff establishes that the building is "particularly slippery and dangerous when wet." *Id.* (citing *Selby v. Danville Pepsi-Cola Bottling Co.*, 169 Ill. App. 3d 427, 436 (4th Dist. 1988); *Lohan*, 140 Ill. App. 3d at 173–74).

In *Reed v. Galaxy Holdings*, plaintiff Oletha Reed slipped and fell on a puddle of water that was between the inner and outer doors of the defendant's business, Laundry World Laundromat, while she was doing her laundry on a rainy day. 394 Ill App. 3d at 40–41. Reed sued the laundromat for common law negligence, and the trial court granted summary judgment to the defendant. *Id.* at 42. The appellate court affirmed, holding that the business had no duty to remove the water that the customers had tracked into the store and that had naturally accumulated between the doors, and that the plaintiff had provided no evidence that the water accumulation was unnatural. *Id.* at 46–48. *See also Lohan*, 140 Ill. App. 3d at 175 (holding that store owners had no duty to remove tracked-in rainwater at the entrance of a drugstore).

Reed v. Galaxy Holdings and *Lohan v. Walgreen Co.* are both on point.[3] Like the plaintiffs in *Reed* and *Lohan*, who slipped on accumulations of water in the entrances of a laundromat and a drugstore on rainy days, Ms. Monica Jackson slipped and fell on an accumulation of water on the floor of Wholesome Food Markets just inside the store entrance on a rainy day. Like the *Reed* and *Lohan* plaintiffs, Ms. Jackson has not alleged that the accumulation of water was unnatural, or that there was anything special about the floor of the supermarket that made it especially slippery or dangerous when wet.

Thus, Ms. Jackson has alleged nothing that could challenge our client's position that she slipped on a natural accumulation of water that customers had tracked into the store. The natural accumulation rule should bar her claim because it applies both to the entrances of businesses and to the interiors of businesses. Wholesome Food Markets did not breach its duty of care to Ms. Jackson because, under the natural accumulation rule, it had no duty to remove the water from the floor.

[3] "On point" means directly relevant, because the facts and the legal issues are both very similar.

2. Look at the rule sentences that comprise the Rule section. How would you characterize the rules? How did the legal writer decide upon the proper order of the rules in this section?

3. Look at the order of the sentences in the case explanation. How would you characterize these sentences? How did the legal writer decide upon the proper order of the sentences in the case explanation?

4. Look at the order of the sentences in the Application section. What is the purpose of the first sentence in this section? What types of sentences follow the first sentence?

The Explanation section of TREAC is not restricted to case explanations. A Rule section where the rules are statutory can be followed by an Explanation section where the legal writer describes how administrative agencies, administrative bodies, or courts apply the statutes or regulations.

EXERCISE 13 D

The following material includes the Rules, Explanation, and Application sections for the second issue in an office memo on environmental law issues. The complete memo is in Appendix B.

In the second issue of the memorandum, the writer analyzes what civil and criminal penalties his or her client ("Company") potentially faces for submitting inaccurate Discharge Monitoring Reports ("DMRs") to the State-X Environmental Protection Division ("SXEPD") ("EPA" stands for the Environmental Protection Agency, an agency that is part of the federal government). The State-X Environmental Protection Division is State X's version of the federal EPA.

1. In the right margin, write down the names of the three sections (Rules, Explanation, and Application) and where they begin:

Under the laws of State-X, "[a] person who knowingly makes a false representation in a report required by a permit under these laws . . . shall be punished by a fine of not more than $30,000[.]" Stat. § 820.[4] The Clean Water Act contains nearly identical language and provides for a maximum fine of $10,000. 26 U.S.C. § 1319(c)(4).[5]

Additionally, the federal False Statements Statute, 18 U.S.C. § 1001, provides that a corporation that, in any matter within the jurisdiction of the executive, legislative, or judicial branch of the Government of the United States, knowingly and willfully falsifies a material fact, makes any materially

[4] Under the State-X statute, an individual can also be imprisoned for up to two years. Stat. § 820(b).

[5] Under the federal statute, an individual can also be imprisoned for up to two years. 33 U.S.C. § 1319(c)(4). A person previously convicted of a knowing violation faces double the fine and maximum prison term. *Id.*

false statement or representation, or makes any false writing knowing it to contain any materially false statement, shall be fined up to $500,000 or imprisoned not more than five years, or both. 18 U.S.C. §§ 1001, 3571(c). Courts broadly interpret "Government of the United States" to include state agencies where a program is either federally funded or the federal government has delegated authority to the states to enforce federal law. *See, e.g., United States v. White*, 270 F.3d 356 (6th Cir. 2001) (false statements made to state water agency came within jurisdiction of EPA for purposes of prosecution under 18 U.S.C. § 1001, since EPA retained authority to enforce its regulations and actively ensure state compliance with national safe water standards); *United States v. Wright*, 988 F.2d 1036 (10th Cir. 1993) (false water quality data reports which water treatment plant manager filed with state health department were within jurisdiction of EPA, even though EPA had granted primary authority for safe drinking water standards to state, since such grant was not exclusive, EPA having retained authority to enforce its regulations). Here, the EPA has delegated primary enforcement of the Clean Water Act to the SXEPD, but it has retained its authority to enforce its own regulations, including violations of permits issued by state agencies. Therefore, Company could be convicted under 18 U.S.C. § 1001 if it knowingly and willfully submitted a false DMR to the SXEPD.[6] Each DMR is arguably a separate violation of 18 U.S.C. § 1001.

Based on our current knowledge, we do not believe that Company knowingly or intentionally submitted a false DMR. However, if further investigation changes these conclusions, Company could face up to $300,000 in fines under State-X law ($30,000 times 10 false DMRs) and $5,100,000 in fines under federal law ($10,000 times 10 false DMRs violating the Clean Water Act plus $500,000 times 10 false DMRs violating the False Statements Statute).

2. Where did you say that the Explanation and the Application sections begin? Was it more difficult to decide in this memo excerpt than it was in the slip-and-fall problem? Why or why not?

EXERCISE 13 E

The following material involves an office memo with a different format from that of the environmental memo. This memo includes the Rules, Explanation, and Application sections for the first of four possible common law affirmative defenses, implied waiver, to a statutory claim under the Telephone Consumer Protection Act ("TCPA"), a federal statute. The complete memo is in Appendix C.

In the lawsuit related to the memo, the plaintiff ("Small Corp") allegedly received nine unsolicited faxes over two years, and then waited over five years to sue the defendant ("Big Corp"). Below, the memo considers whether the common law defense of implied waiver may bar Small Corp.'s claim for damages under the TCPA.

---

[6] In fact, the DMR itself acknowledges that submitting false information could be a violation of the False Statements Statute.

1. In the right margin, write down the names of the three sections (Rules, Explanation, and Application) and where they begin:

A. Implied Waiver

1. Case Law

Waiver is the most firmly entrenched common-law defense to statutory rights. *See, e.g., Ebling v. United States Dept. of Justice*, 2011 WL 2678935 (D.D.C. 2011). It is well established that "[w]aiver, as defined by federal common law, requires an 'intentional relinquishment of a known right,' " — i.e., that "the parties were aware of their rights and made the conscious choice, for whatever reason, to waive them." *New York Tel.*, 930 F.2d at 1011 (waiver under Maritime law); *Apponi v. Sunshine Biscuits, Inc.*, 809 F.2d 1210, 1217 (6th Cir. 1987) (waiver under Labor Management Relations Act); *Gonyea v. John Hancock Mut. Life Ins. Co.*, 812 F. Supp. 445, 450 (D. Vt. 1993) (waiver under ERISA).

Although most cases involve waiver by express agreement, waiver of a right may also be implied from the conduct, acts, or words of a party. *Delta Consulting Group, Inc. v. R. Randle Const., Inc.*, 554 F.3d 1133 (7th Cir. 2009) (applying Illinois law); *see also Am. Airlines, Inc. v. United States*, 77 Fed. Cl. 672, 681 (2007) ("A waiver need not be express, but may be inferred from a pattern of conduct."). Implied waiver arises "where a person against whom the waiver is asserted has pursued such a course of conduct as to sufficiently evidence an intention to waive a right or where his conduct is inconsistent with any other intention than to waive it." *Delta Consulting Group, Inc.*, 554 F.3d at 1140 (emphasis added); *see also PPM Finance, Inc., v. Norandal USA, Inc.*, 392 F.3d 889, 895 (7th Cir. 2004) (waiver implied when a party's conduct is inconsistent with an intention to assert that right). Inaction or silence can be the basis for implied waiver where that inaction or silence is inconsistent with an intent to claim a right. *Patrons Mut. Ins. Ass'n v. Union Gas System, Inc.*, 250 Kan. 722 (Kan. 1992). However, implied waiver is disfavored, and courts usually require that the act relied on to constitute the waiver must be clear. 31 C.J.S. Estoppel and Waiver § 88.

The circumstances under which courts have concluded that a course of conduct constituted an implied waiver of a right are varied. For example:

• **Passage of Time:** In *Hidalgo Properties, Inc. v. Wachovia Mortgage Co.*, the Tenth Circuit considered a defense of implied waiver in the context of a breach of contract claim. 617 F.2d 196, 199–200 (10th Cir. 1980). Wachovia had entered into a standby loan commitment with Hidalgo that required Hidalgo to complete certain conditions prior to disbursement of the loan upon completion of Hidalgo's construction project. One condition was provision of a "foundation completion certificate." *Id.* at 199. Hidalgo never provided the required certification, and Wachovia refused to release the funds at the agreed time. However, evidence showed that Wachovia representatives had viewed the project at various stages of completion and there was no dispute "that Wachovia knew the foundations had been completed." *Id.* According to the court, Wachovia's "[failure] to demand performance when it knew the time for performance had arrived and passed created . . . waiver [issues] for the jury." *Id.*

• **Failure to Object to Prior Violations:** In *Schuster v. Dragone Classic Motor Cars, Inc.*, an S.D.N.Y. court considered a claim of implied waiver of a statutory right arising under New York law. 98 F. Supp. 2d 441, 448–49 (S.D.N.Y. 2000) (applying NY waiver law). Schuster had obtained automobile repair work from Dragone Classic on 15 occasions, with each repair done under an oral agreement. When a dispute arose over the cost of four repairs, Dragone Classic sued for breach of contract. *Id.* at 445. As a defense, Schuster argued that Dragone had failed to comply with a New York statute requiring the issuance of a written estimate prior to the repair work and moved for summary judgment. *Id.* at 448. The court denied the motion: "Defendants' allegations regarding the parties' prior course of dealing [suggests] that plaintiff, in failing to object to the lack of a written authorization or record of his consent to the estimates in the prior eight transactions, waived his right to both the authorization and the record of his consent." *Id.* at 449.

Waiver cases are highly fact specific and ultimately turn on the intent of the party alleged to have waived its right. Although no court appears to have addressed a claim of waiver of a statutory right under circumstances identical to Small Corp, cases like *Hidalgo* and *Schuster* suggest that a waiver theory could be successful.

2. Theory

Small Corp was well aware that its statutory rights were being violated when it received faxes from Big Corp. Small Corp nevertheless chose not to object to Big Corp's conduct, instead choosing to accept the benefits of Big Corp's faxing and to enter into business with Big Corp on the basis of those faxes. Accepting this trade off shows an intent on the part of Small Corp not to enforce its statutory rights.[7] That Small Corp waited years to enforce its rights — and, indeed, even let some of its claims lapse — shows that Small Corp's delay cannot be explained by anything other than an intent to relinquish its claims.[8] Small Corp cannot now change its mind.

2. This memorandum has a different style from the previous memorandum. What do you notice that is different about the style?

---

[7] Small Corp's likely response will be to point to its collection and preservation of faxes as evidence of its continuing intent to stand on its rights under the TCPA. Research has not identified a clear response to this argument.

[8] An implied waiver argument could be strengthened by evidence that Small Corp only sued after Big Corp stopped sending its faxes; such evidence would support an inference that Small Corp re-evaluated its decision not to sue once it stopped receiving the benefits conferred on it by Big Corp's faxing.

3. By looking at the style of this memo, do you think that it is intended for internal law firm use only? Why or why not?

Chapter Review

- Although all of the main parts of an office memorandum are useful, the most important part is the Discussion section, because that is the "main part" of the memo where the lawyer states what the relevant rules of law are to the legal issue or issues, and then applies the rules of law to the facts of the matter.
- In the small-scale organization patterns that we called IRAC and TREAC, the most important sections are the R + A sections of IRAC, and the R + E + A sections of TREAC.
- Every full analysis of a legal issue requires at least the R + A sections, because the writer must always state what the relevant legal rules are, and then apply them to the facts of the client's case.
- If the writer determines that it is useful, he or she should also include an Explanation section that explains the legal rules. This section could take different forms. For example, it could be the summary of a case that illustrates how the court applied the legal rules that are contained in the Rule section. It could also be language describing how courts or agencies apply a statute section.
- There is no one required analytical format that all lawyers must use. Instead, each lawyer must determine for himself or herself the clearest, most logical way to analyze an issue and then communicate that analysis in writing. For example, if a memo contains two issues, one issue might follow the IRAC pattern, and the other might follow the TREAC pattern, or perhaps the writer does not completely follow either pattern.
- If an issue is undisputed, a full IRAC/TREAC treatment is unnecessary. The legal writer can state a rule, provide a citation, and show how the facts fit within the scope of the rule in two or three sentences. The writer can also mention that the issue will not be analyzed in the thesis paragraph, if the assigning lawyer said that it was not necessary to analyze the issue.
- Legal writers choose a Rule + Application pattern if the rules are clear and explanation would not be helpful. They choose a Rule + Explanation + Application pattern if it would be helpful to show how legal decision makers apply the rules. Often, this is done with a case description that shows how a court applied the rule(s) to the facts of the case.
- Then, the Application section may be a combination of analysis that directly applies the rules to the facts, and analysis that analogizes or distinguishes the facts of the precedent from the E section to the current facts.
- The writing style may vary somewhat, depending upon the preferences of the assigning lawyer, the writer, the client (if the client will see the memo), and the amount of time that the writer is allowed to spend on the memo. For example, memos typically have substantive headings, but may have more

generic ones, or they may describe case law in paragraph form or in bullet-pointed paragraphs.

Chapter 14

CITATIONS TO AUTHORITY

Chapter Preview

This chapter introduces citations, which are an essential part of U.S. legal writing. The chapter discusses:

- How important citations are in U.S. legal writing and why we must use them;
- How to write citations;
- Where we use them;
- How and when we use quotations; and
- How to make parenthetical citations.

Citations are an essential part of U.S. legal writing. Used well, they support a writer's arguments, build the writer's credibility, and help the legal reader to accept the writer's conclusions. Used poorly, they cause distrust and lead the legal reader to assume that the writer is careless, lazy, or incompetent.

It goes without saying that you want the legal reader to see you as a careful, skilled legal writer whose arguments are well-grounded in the law, and you do *not* want the legal reader to view you as careless, lazy, or incompetent. Thus, it is well worth your time for you to learn how to cite to U.S. legal authority correctly, and for you to spend the time and effort when you edit to make sure that your citations are correct.

A. WHY WE USE CITATIONS

1. To Demonstrate That the Writer's Arguments Are Grounded in the Law

Lawyers are skeptics. There is no reason for any legal reader to trust a writer's assertion of what the law is if the writer does not offer proof. What is the proof? It is provided in the form of a citation that shows the source of the legal rule. By using the citation, the legal reader can check the source for himself or herself and see if the writer stated the law accurately.

In many civil law legal systems, citations are considered somewhat less important or they are used less frequently than they are in the United States because the main source of primary law is the code, and legal experts are presumed to be familiar with the code in their area of expertise.

In the United States, however, no lawyer can be expected to know all of the law even in his or her area of expertise because the volume of law in this country is immense. There is federal law, state law (for each of the 50 states), and local law. There are constitutions, statutes, regulations, and millions of cases. All of these are sources of law, and all of them require citations.

If a writer fails to provide a citation after a legal assertion, a skeptical legal reader thinks, "What is this? Is this the writer's *opinion* of what the law is? Why should I care about that?"

2. To Help the Legal Reader to Understand the Weight of Authority

As we discussed in Chapter 4, legal readers cannot understand what the legal rules truly are for a given dispute until they understand the status of those rules: Are they binding legal authority for the case, or are they merely persuasive? Writers give legal readers this information in citations because the citation states the source of law.

For example, an Illinois statute binds an Illinois court, but a Wisconsin statute would only be persuasive. It's not enough for the legal writer to merely quote statutory language; the writer must also provide a citation for the statute that tells the reader which jurisdiction the statute is from.

The same is true for case law. If there is a brief or an office memorandum that relates to a case that is pending in the Northern District of Illinois, the legal reader must know if the precedent that the writer is describing is from the United States Supreme Court, the Seventh Circuit, or another court. Cases from the United States Supreme Court and the Seventh Circuit are binding on a Northern District of Illinois court if the legal issues and facts are sufficiently similar. However, if the precedent is from the Second Circuit, the Central District of California, or even the Northern District of Illinois, it would only be persuasive (although the case from the Northern District would be highly persuasive).

Also, the legal reader also needs to know if the precedent is recent or old. Old cases generally carry less weight, as the law tends to change over time. Case citations provide the name of the court that issued the opinion, and the date of the opinion. Simply by reading the citation, the legal reader can determine whether or not the case is potentially binding, or just persuasive, as well as how recent it is.

3. To Give the Reader a Way to Find the Law

Basically, a citation is a formula (a name followed by a series of numbers and letters, really) that allows the reader to locate a particular legal source. If you type the citation into a search box on an online legal research website such as LexisNexis, Westlaw, or Bloomberg Law, it will permit you to retrieve the item, whether it is an article of a constitution, a statute section, a regulation, a case, or a secondary source such as an entry in a legal encyclopedia or a law review article.

Lawyers use the term "citation" either to refer to both the name of the item and the numerical part, or just the numerical part itself. When doing online legal research, you just need to type in the numerical part of the citation. You can generally also obtain the item by typing in just the name, although it is more efficient to use the numerical part of the citation.

Before lawyers did research online, legal authority was found only in books. A citation served the same purpose (and still does), telling the lawyer where to find the legal item: which source, which book volume, and which page.

As discussed above, this is essential because lawyers are highly skeptical people. Legal readers often pull every legal source by using the citations. Then they check to see if the writer has accurately stated the law. In a motion or brief to the court, the parties should assume that the court will pull every legal authority that is cited and check for accuracy. Without citations, this would not be practical.

4. To Build Credibility with the Legal Reader

Citations are important, so legal readers look at them carefully. Most lawyers view missing citations, or citations that have incorrect form, as being similar to mistakes in spelling, grammar, or punctuation.

All around the world, lawyers are exacting people who expect legal writing to be polished work product, with no spelling mistakes, grammatical errors, or punctuation mistakes. Legal writers who have problems with their citations, just like legal writers who have problems with spelling, with grammar, or with punctuation, are seen as careless or even incompetent.

Careless or incompetent lawyers lose their credibility, and with that, they lose the ability to persuade the legal reader that their analysis — or their client's position — is correct. On the other hand, careful lawyers gain credibility with well-reasoned, well-supported, logical arguments, and with accurate citations, spelling, grammar, and punctuation. If the legal reader sees that your work is careful, he or she is more likely to trust your conclusions and to be persuaded by them.

In short, accurate citations build your credibility, and poor citations damage your credibility. It is worth taking the time to learn how to make accurate citations because you cannot afford to lose credibility with your legal reader.

5. To Avoid Charges of Plagiarism

Different cultures have different ideas regarding how to learn, and that includes whether it is acceptable for a student to imitate or copy the work of another. In some cultures, this is a traditional and acceptable way to learn.

In the United States, a writer's words are considered his or her own intellectual property, and when one writer copies the work of another without using quotation marks and citations, it is considered plagiarism. Plagiarism is academic dishonesty, and it may also be a violation of copyright law.

Plagiarism can cause a law student to get into serious trouble, such as getting a failing grade on a plagiarized paper or examination, which may cause a failing grade for the course. The guilty student may be required to leave the law school. Students who are allowed to graduate but who have been found guilty of plagiarism must report the violation on the character and fitness documents that they submit before they can take a state bar examination.

With law firms, the rules are different. Lawyers may not plagiarize the writing of a lawyer outside the firm, but they are free to use or copy the work of other attorneys within the firm, because the work product is seen as the intellectual property of the law firm, not the individual.

The rules are also different for judges. If a judge particularly likes the language in one party's brief, he or she may use some of the language in the judicial opinion without quotation marks or citations. In that case, the writer is very pleased, because it likely means that the judge is ruling in favor of the writer's client and is impressed with the quality of the writer's brief!

B. HOW WE WRITE CITATIONS

There are many detailed rules for citations. In fact, to learn how to use citations, and to have a reference book for future citation questions, U.S. lawyers typically rely on one of two citation manuals: either *The Bluebook*[1] ("Bluebook") or *The ALWD*

---

1 *The Bluebook: A Uniform System of Citation* (Columbia Law Review Ass'n et al. eds., 19th ed. 2010).

Citation Manual[2] ("ALWD"). The rules given in the two large citation manuals are almost identical. Each book is very long because of the large number of specific rules and examples, and because the books contain appendixes giving specific rules for each U.S. jurisdiction.

Your legal writing professor has likely required you to buy one of these two books. This chapter will cover the most general, important citation principles, and you can look at your citation manual for the detailed rules.

In general, there are three kinds of citations:

- Full citations, which you use the first time that you cite to a legal source;
- "*Id.*," which you use when you cite to the same source two or more times in a row; and
- Intermediate short citations, which you use when you have already cited to the source, but you cannot use *id.*, because the previous citation was to a different source.

We will look at the rules for each of these kinds of citations in turn.

1. Full Citations

The first time that you cite to a document, you must use a full (complete) citation. In the boxes below, there are examples of federal and state citations for cases, statutes, and constitutions, and there are also citation forms for certain books and other secondary sources.

a. Cases

As we learned in Chapter 5, a case citation for a case includes the name of the case, followed by the volume number of the reporter, an abbreviation for the reporter, the series number if there is more than one series, the page the case that begins on, information about the jurisdiction, and the year of the decision.

Federal

U.S. Supreme Court:

Citizens United v. Fed. Elections Comm'n, 558 U.S. 310, 365 (2010).

The name of the case contains only the name of the first party on each side of the "v." If the party is an individual, use only the last name (family name). In a federal criminal case, the first party is the U.S. government, which we shorten to "U.S." (e.g., "*U.S. v. Smith*").

---

[2] ALWD & Darby Dickerson, *ALWD Citation Manual* (4th ed., Aspen Publishers 2010).

In the name, certain common terms are abbreviated, such as "commission" (*see* citation above).[3] The abbreviations are listed on pages 430–34 of the Bluebook, and pages 532–37 of ALWD. Although the abbreviations are almost all the same in the two citation manuals, the Bluebook occasionally uses an apostrophe where ALWD uses a period, so "Commission" is abbreviated as "Comm'n" in the Bluebook and "Commn." in ALWD.

Most lawyers today write case names, *id.*, and signals such as "*see*" in italics, although it is also correct to underline them: Citizens United v. Fed. Elections Comm'n, id., and see. Underlining was the only option when we wrote on typewriters, before the era of personal computers, and some older or more traditional lawyers still prefer underlining.

As for the numerical part of the citation for *Citizens United*, this case is found in volume 558 of the U.S. Reports ("U.S."), and the case begins on page 310 (which is why the citation is written as 558 U.S. 310). The number after 310 is called the "pinpoint cite." This means that the writer is quoting language or taking ideas or information from page 365. U.S. Reports only contains cases from the United States Supreme Court, so there is no need to put the name of the court in parentheses with the year.

U.S. Circuit Court (intermediate appellate court):

> *Brennan's, Inc. v. Brennan's Rest., L.L.C.*, 360 F.3d 125, 130 (2d Cir. 2004).

All case citations that come from reporters put the volume number before the name of the reporter, the first page of the case after the reporter, and the pinpoint citation after that. When you see "2d" or "3d" after the name of the reporter, it refers to the series, which typically consists of 1,000 volumes.[4] Thus, the *Brennan's* case is found in volume 360 of the third series of the Federal Reporter ("F."). The Federal Reporter is only for Circuit Court cases. The pinpoint cite is 130, which means that the writer is quoting language or taking ideas or information from page 130.

Because the reporter only lets us know the general type of court (a circuit court), we need to put the specific court's name in the parentheses with the year. Here, the case was decided by the Second Circuit in 2004, so we write "(2d Cir. 2004)." We write "2d," not "2nd," and "3d," not "3rd." Never use superscript (i.e., keep the "d" in "3d" the normal size).

U.S. District Court (trial court):

---

[3] "Federal Elections Commission" is abbreviated as "Fed. Elections Comm'n."

[4] Each volume is approximately 2,000 pages long and may contain hundreds of cases.

Schuster v. Dragone Classic Motor Cars, Inc., 98 F. Supp. 2d 441, 448–49 (S.D.N.Y. 2000).

This case is found in volume 98 of the second series of the Federal Supplement ("F. Supp."), which is the reporter for federal district court cases. The case begins on page 441, and the writer is quoting language or taking ideas or information from pages 448 and 449. When you take information from two pages in a row, use a dash, and either repeat every number (e.g., 448–449), or repeat only the last two numbers (448–49). If you take information from two pages that are not consecutive, put a comma between them. For example, if you took information from pages 449 and 452, you would write the pinpoint pages as "449, 452": *Schuster v. Dragone Classic Motor Cars, Inc.*, 98 F. Supp. 2d 441, 449, 452 (S.D.N.Y. 2000).

States with small populations have only one federal district, so the District of Delaware would be written as "D. Del." States with larger populations have more than one federal district, divided geographically: "N.D. Ill." is the Northern District of Illinois, "C.D. Cal." is the Central District of California, and "S.D.N.Y." is the Southern District of New York.

Notice that when one-letter abbreviations are next to each other, there is no space between them: with the Northern District of Illinois, "N" and "D" have no space between them because each is a one-letter abbreviation, but there is a space between "D" and "Ill." because "Ill." has three letters: "N.D. Ill." In the case of the Southern District of New York, each of the four abbreviations has only one letter, so there are no spaces between them: "S.D.N.Y."

Cases that are only available online may be cited to the LexisNexis, Westlaw, or Bloomberg Law citation, as follows:

Bates v. City of Chicago, No. 5 C 1564, 2012 U.S. Dist. LEXIS 11429, at *6 (N.D. Ill. Jan. 21, 2012).

Bates v. City of Chicago, No. 5 C 1564, 2012 WL 280664, at *6 (N.D. Ill. Jan. 21, 2012).

The LexisNexis citation includes some information about the level of the court in the citation ("U.S. Dist. LEXIS 11429"), while the Westlaw citation does not ("WL 280664"). Under the Bluebook rule, you should include the docket number of the case ("No. 5 C 1564"), but under the ALWD rule, it is optional. To show the pinpoint citation with an online case, write "at" and an asterisk before the page number ("at *6" means "at page 6"). The name of the court and the specific date of the decision (not just the year) are included in the parentheses.

State

Like with the federal reporters, most states have official reporters for each appellate level of the court system (remember that state trial court decisions are not published).

As we described in Chapter 5, certain state appellate court decisions are also reported in regional reporters such as "N.E." for North Eastern Reporter, or "A." for Atlantic Reporter. Those reporters contain decisions of intermediate appellate courts and supreme courts for the states in that region.

We will look at Illinois cases as an example of state court citations:

Illinois Supreme Court:

Krywin v. Chicago Transit Auth., 238 Ill. 2d 215, 227 (2010).

The *Krywin* case appeared in volume 238 of the second series of Illinois Reports. The case begins on page 215, and the writer is quoting language or taking ideas or information from page 227. Because Illinois Reports only contains Illinois Supreme Court cases, we can write (2010) for the year without adding the name of the court. This system works for the highest appellate court of every state.[5]

If the case appears in both the official state reporter and the regional reporter, many jurisdictions currently want you to cite only to the official state reporter.[6] In the past, you would have also had to cite to the regional reporter. *Krywin* also bears the citation 908 N.E.2d 887, meaning that it is also found in volume 908 of the second series of the Northeastern Reporter, and the case begins on page 887.

Often, when you read a judicial opinion, you will see citations to two or even three reporters for one case. These are called "parallel citations." These citations are rarely used today. Unless you are in one of the few jurisdictions that still require parallel citations, cite to the official state reporter only, or to the regional reporter if the local rules prefer that.

Illinois Appellate Courts:

Lohan v. Walgreens Co., 140 Ill. App. 3d 171, 173–74 (1st Dist. 1986).

The *Lohan* case is found in volume 140 of the third series of Illinois Appellate Court Reports, and begins on page 171. The writer is quoting language or taking ideas or

---

[5] For example, if you see 892 Minn. 234 (2006), you know that the case was decided by the Minnesota Supreme Court in 2006. If you see a reporter name that you do not know, you cannot recognize the name of the state from the abbreviation, and you want to know which state the decision is from, go to Table 1 in the Bluebook, pages 215–77, or Appendix 1 in ALWD, pages 405–64.

[6] Each state has its own local court rules for citations; attorneys who file documents to the court must know those rules, which are on pages 30–51 of the Bluebook in a short form, and pages 465–526 of ALWD in a more complete form. They are also online on the various state judicial websites.

information from pages 173 and 174, and the information in parentheses mentions the particular appellate court district (the First District, which is in Chicago) as well as the year of the decision.

b. Statutes and Regulations

Statutes:

Sarbanes-Oxley Act of 2002, 15 U.S.C. § 7201 *et seq.* (2006).

(Also cited as: Pub. L. No. 107-204, 116 Stat. 745).

The Sarbanes-Oxley Act of 2002, subtitled "An Act to protect investors by improving the accuracy and reliability of corporate disclosures made pursuant to the securities laws, and for other purposes," is found beginning in Title 15 of the United States Code ("U.S.C."), and it begins with Section ("§") 7201. The term "*et seq.*" means "*et sequentia*" ("and following"), and it is used to show that the statute has more than one section.

The official U.S. Code citation is to the book form, which is published every six years, most recently in 2006. It takes another two years or more to publish the new edition of the Code, so the 2012 publication will likely come out in 2014 or 2015.

If you are quoting two or more sections of a statute, use the section symbol twice: "§§ 7201–03" would refer to Sections 7201, 7202, and 7203; "§§ 7202, 7204" refers to Sections 7202 and 7204.

The official Bluebook and ALWD rules say to cite to the most recent publication of the U.S. Code in book form (i.e., 2006), but many practicing lawyers ignore the rule and do not use a date. They get the statute online, and the online sources are very current. Accordingly, most practicing lawyers would simply write: Sarbanes-Oxley Act of 2002, 15 U.S.C. § 7201 *et seq.*[7] The name of the statute is not a required part of the citation — you could simply write: 15 U.S.C. § 7201 *et seq.* (2006).

As for the other citation forms for this law, "Pub. L. No. 107-204" is the "session law" format, which states that this was the 204th public law passed by the 107th Congress (each session of Congress meets for two years). The new session laws are compiled in softcover form, and at the end of the year are compiled in an official hardcover form, called the "Statutes at Large," abbreviated "Stat." "116 Stat. 745" means that this law is found in the 116th volume of the Statutes at Large, beginning on page 745.

Then, the law is placed in scattered sections into the United States Code. For example, sections of the Sarbanes-Oxley Act are found in Title 15 and Title 18. Because

---

[7] Instead of the official publication date, you can refer to the online date by clicking on "currentness," and writing: "Current through P.L. [number] approved [date]."

the codified law is scattered throughout the relevant titles and sections of the Code, it is sometimes useful to click on the Statutes at Large citation, where you can see the entire law in one place.

> Del. Code Ann. 6 § 17-301 (2005).
>
> 210 Ill. Comp. Stat. Ann. § 5/1 (2008).
>
> Ind. Code Ann. § 9-23-3-7 (2005).

State statutes are written with citations that are similar to those of the U.S. Code, but each state has its own slightly different system. Here are examples of statutes from Delaware, Illinois, and Indiana. All three of these are taken from sets of annotated codes, which are often used by practicing attorneys in that state. An annotated code is a book of statutes where short summaries of cases called "annotations" are placed after each relevant code section. For Illinois, "Comp. Stat." refers to "Compiled Statutes"; some states such as Delaware and Indiana use the term "code"; and others might refer to "Rev. Stat.," which refers to "Revised Statutes." As with the U.S. Code, the date of publication shown is the date of publication of the code in book form.

Regulations:

> 17 C.F.R. § 240.10b-5 (2012).

This regulation is from Title 17 of the Code of Federal Regulations ("C.F.R."), which is published at least once per year.

Before they are codified, federal regulations are published in the Federal Register:

> Plain Language in Government Writing, Pres. Memo. of June 1, 1998, 63 Fed. Reg. 31,885 (June 10, 1998).

Not all new regulations are codified, so the only citation may be to the Federal Register.

With cases, statutes, and regulations, the online research websites and the courts sometimes use their own citation forms, which may not correspond to the Bluebook and ALWD forms. For example, "FR" refers to the Federal Register ("Fed. Reg."). For courts, "CCA 9" means "Circuit Court of Appeal 9" — in other words, the Ninth Circuit ("9th Cir."). When the online form or the form in a judicial opinion does not follow the Bluebook or ALWD rules, *do not use that form.* Instead, rewrite the citation in the proper Bluebook or ALWD form. It's your responsibility as a writer to use the correct citation form!

c. Constitutions

There is the United States Constitution, and there are state constitutions for each of the 50 states. The citation forms are similar for all of them. When a lawyer writes "the Constitution," the capital letter generally refers to the U.S. Constitution. When we refer to state constitutions in general, the letter "c" is not capitalized (although it is capitalized when we name a particular state constitution, such as the California Constitution).

The U.S. Constitution is divided into articles, and articles are divided into sections. The abbreviations for article ("art.") and amendment ("amend.") are not capitalized. Numbered subsections are called "clauses." The Constitution has 27 amendments as of 2013. Articles and amendments are written with Roman numerals, and sections and clauses take Arabic numerals:

U.S. Const. art. I, § 10, cl. 2.

U.S. Const. amend. XX, § 2.

Ill. Const. art. I, § 2.

Cal. Const. art. III, § 1.

When the constitutional provision to which you are citing is currently in force, do not use a date. If it is no longer in force, however, state in a parenthetical when it was repealed and explain what replaced it, if it was replaced:

U.S. Const. amend. XVIII (repealed 1933 by U.S. Const. amend. XXI).

d. Books, Periodicals, and Other Secondary Sources

There are a very wide range of secondary sources, including books, law review articles, legal encyclopedias, treatises, periodicals such as magazines and newspapers, online sources, etc. One difference between the Bluebook and ALWD rules is that ALWD requires the name of the publisher, where the Bluebook only does so for older material published before 1900:

Books:

Marc I. Steinberg, *Securities Regulation* 85 (5th ed., LexisNexis 2009).

Helene S. Shapo, Marilyn R. Walter, and Elizabeth Fajans, *Writing and Analysis in the Law* 201 (6th ed., Foundation Press 2013).

Or

Shapo et al., *Writing and Analysis in the Law* 201 (6th ed., Foundation Press 2013).

For the first citation, the writer is referring to information found on page 85 of Marc Steinberg's book. If there are two authors, give the names and use both authors. If there are three or more authors, either list the first author and "et al." for the others, or list each name if there is a particular reason that the names are important.

Law review articles:

> Richard Marcus, *Bomb Throwing, Democratic Theory, and Basic Values — A New Path to Procedural Harmonization?*, 107 Nw. U.L. Rev. 475, 491 (2013).

This is an article from the Northwestern University Law Review. Appendix 5 in ALWD and Table 13 in the Bluebook give the abbreviations for each law review and legal journal.

Legal encyclopedias:

> 69 Am. Jur. 2d *Securities Regulation* § 268 (2008).

American Jurisprudence ("Am. Jur.") is a very large legal encyclopedia that is an excellent place to gain background knowledge and key terms of art when you begin to research an issue. This citation refers to Section 268 of the entry on securities regulation, which is found in volume 69 of the second series.

Treatises:

> Dennis J. Horan & George W. Spellmire, Jr., *Attorney Malpractice: Prevention and Defense*, 10–19 (Garland Law Publishing 1986).

Treatises are one-volume works or multi-volume sets that focus on a particular area of law, and are used heavily by practicing attorneys. This treatise has an unusual system of numbering pages: the pinpoint cite refers to page 19 of chapter 10, not pages 10 through 19.

Annotations:

> Milton Roberts, *Pendent Jurisdiction of Federal Courts in Actions Based on Diversity of Citizenship*, 71 A.L.R. Fed. 117, 122 (1985).

American Law Reports ("A.L.R.") is a useful secondary source that contains articles on specific areas of the law, followed by annotations, which are lists of short case summaries of cases that are relevant to the topic of the article. There are six series of American Law Reports for state law issues, and one series for federal law issues ("A.L.R. Fed."). The article referenced in the citation begins on page 117 of volume 71, and the material being referenced is found on page 122.

Newspapers:

> Editorial, *What Makes the D.C. Circuit Different?*, N.Y. Times, June 12, 2013, at A16.

As newspapers are available online as well as in paper versions, citations to online articles should contain the URL (the web address of the article).

EXERCISE 14 A

Write the citations below:

1. Mary Smith sued Hogarth Hams Corporation in the Southern District of New York. The opinion was published in 2011, in volume 810 of the second series of the Federal Supplement. The opinion begins on page 774, and you want to cite to material found on pages 779 and 780. Write the citation:

2. In a criminal matter, the federal government prosecuted Ms. Sarah Jones in the Northern District of Illinois. The opinion was published in 2012, in volume 824 of the second series of the Federal Supplement. The opinion begins on page 1315, and you want to cite to material found on pages 1324 and 1326. Write the citation:

3. Mary Smith appealed the decision in her case to the Second Circuit. The opinion was published in 2012, in volume 537 of the third series of the Federal Reporter. The opinion begins on page 198, and you want to cite to material found on page 201. Write the citation:

4. You want to cite to a statute which has been codified in Title 37 of the United States Code, as section 290. The most recent publication of the United States Code is 2006.

5. You want to cite to a law review article. It was written by Charles Weems for the 104th year of the Northwestern University Law Review, which was published in 2010. The article begins on page 685, and you want to cite to pages 692 and 693. The article is called "K Street Parade: The Profusion of Corporate Lobbying in the Wake of Citizens United."

EXERCISE 14 B

Look at the citations below. Correct any mistakes, and count how many mistakes there are per citation.

1. U.S. Const. Amend. 14, § 3 (1868).

2. *Edward Robinson & Samuel Skinner v. William Johnson*, 390 A.2d 871, 869 (Dist. Del. 2009).

3. 210 Ill. Code Ann. § 5/1 (2008).

4. *United States Government v. Tad Hendrickson*, 534 U.S. 321, 329 (U.S. 2008).

5. 47 U.S.C. § 1292 (2013).

---

2. *Id.*

> *Id.* at 139.
>
> *Id.*
>
> *See id.* at 139.

"*Id.*" is short for "*idem*" (meaning "the same"). *Id.* serves the same purpose as "ibid." in non-legal documents. If you make two, three, or more citations in a row to the same source, use the full citation the first time that you cite to the source, and use "*id.*" for the citations to that source immediately following it.

For example, if your full citation is to *U.S. v. Smith*, 125 F. Supp. 2d 123, 131 (E.D.N.Y. 2009),[8] and then you continue to discuss *Smith* and cite to it twice more, the citations would be, for example, "*Id.* at 139." and "*Id.*" The full citation referred to information on page 131. If the second citation referred to information on page 139, the citation would be "*Id.* at 139." If the third citation also referred to information on page 139, the citation would be simply "*Id.*" without a page number. If you then cite to a different case, and return to *U.S. v. Smith* after that, do not use *id.* for *U.S. v. Smith*, because the preceding citation was to a different case. In that situation, use the intermediate citation form.

Because citations usually exist in their own separate "citation sentence," a citation sentence that begins with "*id.*" has a capital letter, and the citation sentence ends with a period.[9] If the citation sentence begins with a signal such as "*see*," then "*id.*" would not be capitalized: "*See id.* at 139."

Id. may be used with any type of legal source: cases, statutes, constitutions, regulations, and secondary sources. With every source, it tells the reader to look to the preceding citation for information about the source. If you use "*id.*" with a section symbol or a paragraph symbol instead of a page number, do not use "at": "*Id.* § 5/1." or "*Id.*¶ 5."

---

[8] This is a hypothetical case.

[9] Occasionally we put citations in the middle of a sentence, set off by commas: "Xxxxxxx, *id.* at 139, xxxxxxxxxx." In this case, "*id.*" would begin with a small letter because it does not begin a sentence. In this example, the citation would only refer to the part of the sentence before it.

3. Intermediate Short Citations

> *Smith,* 125 F. Supp. 2d at 131.
>
> *In Smith,* the court considered whether the defendant had been entrapped by undercover federal agents. 125 F. Supp. 2d at 131.
>
> 15 U.S.C. § 7201.
>
> § 7201.

With a case, the intermediate short form consists of one party's name, a comma, the volume number and name of the reporter, the word "at," and a pinpoint citation to the page on which the cited material appears. Usually, the name of the first party is used, unless it is a name that appears in many cases, such as "*U.S.*" in a federal criminal case. In that situation, use the second party's name.

- Do ***not*** include the page number for the first page of the case after the name of the reporter.
- If the case name is already part of the sentence, you can omit it from the citation at the end of the sentence: "In *Smith*, ... 125 F. Supp. 2d at 131."

Here are the short citation rules for sources other than cases:

- **Constitutions:** *Id.* is the only acceptable short form; there are no intermediate short forms.
- **Statutes:** Either use the citation for the statute without a date, or just use the section number ("15 U.S.C. § 7201" or "§ 7201").
- **Regulations:** Same as statutes.
- **Secondary sources:** In a citation that a practicing lawyer would use for a court, etc., use the author's name, a short form of the title, and the pinpoint cite: "Roberts, *Pendent Jurisdiction*, at 129." In a law review article, use "*supra*" and the number of the footnote that gave the full citation:
- "Roberts, *supra* note 10, at 129." If the article refers to two different works by the same author (or another author with the same family name), also use a short form of the title.

C. WHERE WE USE CITATIONS

The general rule is that you should use a citation after every sentence, or portion of a sentence, that contains information from a source other than yourself. In other words, if the idea is not your own, use a citation.

Always cite when you are directly quoting from a source (and also use quotation marks). You should also cite to a paraphrase — when you take another writer's idea, but put it in your own words. Finally, you should cite even where you take a general idea from the source. In other words: *When in doubt, use a citation!*

This general rule becomes clearer with citation advice for the various sections of TREAC:

- **Rule section:** Have a citation after each sentence in the rule section. Each rule sentence should have a citation.
- **Explanation section:** According to the Bluebook, cite to every sentence — when you describe the facts, holding, and reasoning of precedent. However, in practice, lawyers often do not do this, and the ALWD rule, which is a bit more relaxed, reflects practice: Within the E section, if you refer to information from the same page, section or other subdivision of the same source, you may cite the source once at the beginning of the paragraph and once at the end (and not after every sentence). Do not use this convention if the Explanation cites information from different pages, sections or sub-divisions of the source.
- **Application section:** In general, do not cite in this section. It contains your own analysis and your own thoughts, so citations are not usually needed in a memorandum. In a trial brief, however, the Application section of a TREAC might cite to relevant documents, such as a contract or letter between the parties. Also, there is no need to cite when you do fact-to-fact comparisons between precedent and the facts of the matter that you are analyzing, because you have already cited to the precedent in the Explanation section.
- **Counterargument:** If you are writing a counterargument, which you then rebut with legal authority, provide a citation for the legal authority.

EXERCISE 14 C

Below are the Rules, Explanation, and Application sections from Chapter 13 for the second element of the common law negligence claim in the slip and fall case (whether or not Wholesome Foods Market breached its duty of care to the plaintiff, Ms. Jackson).

1. There is a blank line after each sentence. Without going back to look at Chapter 13, put a check mark ("√") after every sentence that needs a citation.

Under Illinois law, businesses owe their customers a general duty to keep the entrance to and exit from the business reasonably safe. ___. Under the "natural accumulation rule," however, business operators and property owners have "no duty to remove natural accumulations of ice, snow, or water" from their properties. ___. They also have no duty to continuously remove water that customers have tracked into the building from natural accumulations of water, snow or ice outside. ___. Business operators may be liable if the injuries were caused by an unnatural accumulation of water or where the operator aggravated the natural condition, ___, and they may be liable if the plaintiff establishes that the building is "particularly slippery and dangerous when wet." ___.

> In *Reed v. Galaxy Holdings*, plaintiff Oletha Reed slipped and fell on a puddle of water that was between the inner and outer doors of the defendant's business, Laundry World Laundromat, while she was doing her laundry on a rainy day. ___. Reed sued the laundromat for common law negligence, and the trial court granted summary judgment to the defendant. ___. The appellate court affirmed, holding that the business had no duty to remove the water that the customers had tracked into the store and that had naturally accumulated between the doors, and that the plaintiff had provided no evidence that the water accumulation was unnatural. ___.
>
> *Reed v. Galaxy Holdings* and *Lohan v. Walgreen Co.* are both on point.___. Like the plaintiffs in *Reed* and *Lohan*, who slipped on accumulations of water in the entrances of a laundromat and a drugstore on rainy days, Ms. Monica Jackson slipped and fell on an accumulation of water on the floor of Wholesome Food Markets just inside the store entrance on a rainy day. ___. Like the *Reed* and *Lohan* plaintiffs, Ms. Jackson has not alleged that the accumulation of water was unnatural, or that there was anything special about the floor of the supermarket that made it especially slippery or dangerous when wet. ___.
>
> Thus, Ms. Jackson has alleged nothing that could challenge our client's position that she slipped on a natural accumulation of water that customers had tracked into the store. ___. The natural accumulation rule should bar her claim because it applies both to the entrances of businesses and to the interiors of businesses. ___. Wholesome Food Markets did not breach its duty of care to Ms. Jackson because, under the natural accumulation rule, it had no duty to remove the water from the floor.

2. Go back to Exercise C in Chapter 13 and compare your check marks to where you see the citations. Did you make the check marks in the correct places?

D. WHEN AND HOW WE USE QUOTATIONS

1. When to Quote

In this chapter, we have been discussing the importance of supporting your assertions about the law by using citations. Many U.S. law students, whether J.D.s or international LL.M.s, believe that it is logical to support those assertions by quoting frequently from legal authority. Perhaps they think that statutes or judicial opinions state the law better than they can, so it makes sense to quote frequently.

Whatever the reason, they are incorrect. It is considered poor legal writing style to quote frequently. Legal readers draw two conclusions when they see legal writing that is filled with quotations: (1) the writer is lazy, and is cutting and pasting instead of thinking; or (2) the writer does not understand what he or she is writing about, and hopes that the frequent quotations will answer whatever questions the legal reader may have. These are very bad ideas for a legal reader to have about your work!

Lawyers add value by providing in-depth legal analysis, and that includes how writers state the relevant rules of law. Do not quote every legal rule, because many are written in a context that is not directly relevant to your legal issue, and some are poorly written. Instead, good legal writers need to engage in rule synthesis, as we discussed in Chapter 9. While rule statements must be accurate, most should be in your own words, especially the narrower, more specific rules.

That said, sometimes it makes good sense to quote from legal authority. When should you quote?

- Quote language from a statute, especially when it is the main rule that applies to an issue (e.g., in a thesis paragraph);
- Consider quoting the main rule of an issue from case law as well (such as the judge-made 8-factor test for "likelihood of confusion" under the Lanham Act);
- Quote key terms of art in rules (e.g., "reasonable measures");
- Consider quoting key language in a court's holding and reasoning, *but not if you can paraphrase it more clearly or efficiently*; and
- Consider quoting "great" language from precedent, meaning language that especially favors your client's position.

2. When Not to Quote

It's hard to give a comprehensive set of rules for when not to use quotations. Perhaps the most important idea is to figure out what you really should quote and then to keep the rest of your quoting to a bare minimum. Some suggestions:

- Look at the context. Do not use a large amount of quotations in any one area, even a rule section. If you notice that the last half of a page that you have written is largely quotations, you need to go back and revise it. Turn many of those quotations into paraphrases.
- Do little quoting in the Explanation section. Do not quote facts from a court's opinion — they are not important enough to require quotations. Paraphrase them.
- Generally do not quote when drawing analogies/distinctions in TREAC sections "A" or "C."

3. How to Quote

When you quote language from a source, you need to do two things: (1) use quotation marks (". . ."); and (2) use a citation after the quotation. Periods and commas should be inside the quotation marks, even if they are not part of the original quotation.

Different languages have different types of quotation marks. You need to use the quotation marks that we use in English when writing in English. Make sure that you do all of your writing on a U.S. version of Word. If you use one that is set for Spanish, Portuguese, French, or another language that has different quotation marks (or if your U.S. Word is set to use a language other than English), it will insert the other language's quotation marks, which are not acceptable in English.

a. Avoiding Plagiarism

The general rule for when you **must** use quotation marks is called "the five-word rule": If you copy five or more words in a row, you must use ***both*** quotation marks and a citation. It may be a good idea to use quotation marks for single words or phrases of fewer than five words if you want to show that you are using a term of art or other key language, such as "likelihood of confusion" or "reasonable efforts." With repeated key language, you only need to use the quotation marks the first time. Thus, if you use the phrase "reasonable efforts" three or four times on a page, you only need to use quotation marks and a citation the first time, to show that it is the actual language used in the legal rule.

In law school especially, and even at times in law practice (except for when you are using work product from inside your own law firm or company, or when you are using a standard form document), if you fail to use the five-word rule, you are committing plagiarism. This rule is so important that it bears repeating: *if you quote five words or more without using* ***both*** *quotation marks and a citation, you are committing plagiarism.*

Why is this true? If we used quotation marks but did not provide a citation, we would be telling the legal reader that these are not our words, but we would *not* be telling the reader whose words they are, or what the legal authority is for this assertion. Equally bad, and arguably even worse, if we provided a citation but did not use quotation marks, we would be telling the legal reader that this is not my idea, but these *are* my words, which would be untrue. Thus, to avoid charges of plagiarism, always remember to follow the five-word rule, and to use quotation marks and a citation after the quote.

b. Altering Quotations

If you only change the language of a quotation slightly, it is improper to call it a paraphrase. Rather, you should treat it as a quotation, and show where you made the changes by placing the change in square brackets: "[ ]." There is one exception, however: when you remove words, use the ellipsis, which is three spaced periods: ". . .". If you remove the end of a sentence, use an ellipsis with four periods instead of three: ". . . ." Do not put square brackets around the ellipsis.

To show other alterations, use the square brackets. For example, you can edit writing by changing a pronoun such as "he," "she," or "it" to the noun that it represents. Other common alterations include changing verb tenses or endings: "watch[ed]." Even small changes must be shown, such as changing a small letter to a capital letter or vice versa.

c. Block Quotations

As we have discussed, it is best to quote sparingly. When we do quote, it is best to keep most of the quotations short. However, when you quote a statute section or a multi-factor test, the quote may be fairly long. If the quote is at least 50 words, use a special format that is called a block quotation. With this form, indent both sides of the quotation from the normal margins; single-space the quote with full justification (even if the memo or brief is double-spaced); and do not use quotation marks, because the block format tells the legal reader that the language is a long quotation. Finally, place the citation after the block quotation, on the regular left margin. For example, here is the 8-factor rule for the likelihood of confusion under the Lanham Act:

> (1) the strength of the mark, (2) the degree of similarity between the two marks, (3) the competitive proximity of the products, (4) actual confusion, (5) the likelihood the plaintiff will bridge the gap, (6) the defendant's good faith in adopting its mark, (7) the quality of the defendant's products, and (8) the sophistication of the purchasers.

Brennan's, Inc. v. Brennan's Restaurant, LLC, 360 F.3d 125, 130 (2d Cir. 2004). Notice that the citation comes after the block quotation, and returns to the normal margins.

d. Internal Citations and Quoting Quotations

As we discussed, when you are stating a rule that comes from a case, you must provide a citation to that case. However, that case often cites to an older case for the same rule. For example, if you are taking a rule from Case X (2009), Case X is likely taking that rule from an older case, such as Case Y (2003). How do you show this in your citation? You have two main choices:

1. You provide a citation to the earlier case in parentheses following your citation. This is called an "internal citation." Inside the parentheses, you write "citing" and then provide a full citation for the older case, unless you have already cited to the older case before:

Cat v. Mouse, 532 F. Supp. 2d 123, 125 (S.D.N.Y. 2009) (citing *Fox v. Hound*, 359 F.3d 456, 459 (2d Cir. 2003)).

2. You do not provide a citation to the older case. Then you write "internal citation(s) omitted"[10] in parentheses following your citation:

Cat v. Mouse, 532 F. Supp. 2d 123, 125 (S.D.N.Y. 2009) (internal citation omitted).

As the writer, you may choose whether to provide the internal citation or to write "(internal citation omitted)." If the older case is a well-known case, or a case from a higher court in the relevant jurisdiction than the court to which you are citing, it is often a good idea to provide the internal citation.

However, if you are quoting from a case, and that case is also quoting from an older case, you must give the internal citation. Write "quoting" instead of "citing" in parentheses:

---

[10] If Case X cites to Case Y and Case Z, you would write "internal citations omitted."

It is "simply natural and instinctual" for cats to chase mice. *Cat v. Mouse*, 532 F. Supp. 2d 123, 129 (S.D.N.Y. 2009) (quoting *Dog v. Cat*, 345 U.S. 211, 261 (1968)).

E. HOW WE WRITE PARENTHETICALS

At times it is useful to write a citation with an explanatory parenthetical, which is a short explanation that shows why the authority is being cited.

Immediately after the citation, and thus still within the citation sentence, the explanatory parenthetical appears in parentheses. Often, the comment is not a complete sentence. Rather, it is a phrase that often begins with a gerund (a form of a noun that ends in -ing). Introduce the citation with a signal such as "*see*," "*see also*," or "*see, e.g.*,".

The purpose of a parenthetical is to show that additional legal authority exists to support your assertion, but it is either not sufficiently important to give a full explanation of the case in the E section because it does not add anything material to the analysis, or the parenthetical saves space.

If a case is important, however, it should be fully addressed in the text of your writing (in the E section), not in a parenthetical. Readers will assume that cases with parenthetical explanations are less important that the cases you discuss in the text.

Although your parenthetical must relate to the assertion for which you are citing the authority in support, it should not simply repeat the assertion. For example, the parenthetical written below adds no new information and does not explain the reasoning behind the holding (i.e., it states that the statements came within the jurisdiction of the EPA, but does not explain why). Thus, it is not very helpful:

Courts broadly interpret "Government of the United States" to include state agencies where a program is either federally funded or the federal government has delegated authority to the states to enforce federal law. *See, e.g., United States v. White*, 270 F.3d 356 (6th Cir. 2001) (false statements made to state water agency came within jurisdiction of EPA).[11]

The author of the memo in Appendix B wrote a more complete parenthetical than this, however. In the actual parenthetical, the writer not only explains the holding, but the reasoning for the holding:

Courts broadly interpret "Government of the United States" to include state agencies where a program is either federally funded or the federal government has delegated authority to the states to enforce federal law. *See, e.g., United States v. White*, 270 F.3d 356 (6th Cir. 2001) (false statements made to state water agency came within jurisdiction of EPA for purposes of prosecution under 18 U.S.C. § 1001, since EPA retained authority to enforce its regulations and actively ensure state compliance with national safe water standards).[12]

---

[11] This shortened parenthetical, which is taken from the memo in Appendix B, is not what the author actually wrote.

[12] This is the complete parenthetical from the memo in Appendix B.

In short, parentheticals are similar to quotations: they can be effective when used properly, but they should not be used frequently.

Chapter Review

- Citations are an essential part of U.S. legal writing. They are so important that practicing lawyers in the U.S. place citations directly in the text, not in footnotes. We use footnotes for the following reasons:
- Citations demonstrate that the writer's analysis is grounded in the law;
- Citations provide the legal reader with a way to check the writer's assertions by looking at the legal authority listed in the citations;
- Citations help legal readers in the U.S. to understand the weight of the authority that supports the arguments;
- Well-written, careful citations tell the legal reader that the writer is careful and competent, and they build the writer's credibility; and
- Citations help the writer to avoid charges of plagiarism.
- There are three kinds of citations: a full citation, which is used the first time the writer refers to the source; *id.*, the short form that is used when one refers to the same source several times in a row; and intermediate short citations, which are used when *id.* is not possible, but the source has already been cited.
- Legal writers use citations whenever they use a quotation or a paraphrase, or simply state an idea that they have seen in another source.
- Use citations after each rule statement, in Explanation sections, and when rebutting counterarguments with legal authority.
- Legal writers generally do not use citations in Application sections because they are providing their own analysis, and/or they are comparing facts from precedent that they have previously cited in the E section to the facts in their present matters.
- When citing to a rule from Case X, which provides a citation to an older case for that rule, you may write an "internal citation," which is a citation that is followed by a citation to the older case in parentheses.
- Legal writers may choose to provide the internal citation or to write "internal citation(s) omitted" in parentheses. If the older case is well-known or from a higher court in the relevant jurisdiction, it is a good idea to provide the internal citation.
- Do not use quotations often; save them for the main rules, key terms of art, and especially helpful language from precedent.
- Remember "the five-word rule": if you are quoting five words in a row or more, you *must* use quotation marks and provide a citation. Failing to do this may expose you to plagiarism charges.
- When you alter quotations, show the changes with square brackets and/or ellipsis.

- If the quotation to which you are citing is itself a quotation from an older case, you must provide the internal citation, but write "quoting" instead of "citing" in the parentheses, followed by the internal citation.
- Do not use parentheticals often. They can be useful when you want to save space and the case is not significant enough for a full summary.

Chapter 15

THE QUESTION PRESENTED, THE SHORT ANSWER, AND EXECUTIVE SUMMARIES

Chapter Preview

This chapter looks at the parts of an office memorandum that serve as a stand-alone summary of the contents of the memo: the Question Presented and the Short Answer, or in a more recent alternative form, the Executive Summary. The chapter discusses:

- How to write a Question Presented;
- The various uses of this question form;
- How to write a Short Answer; and
- How to write an Executive Summary.

When we introduced the large-scale organization of an office memorandum at the beginning of Chapter 12, we said that the traditional office memorandum consists of several main parts:

- a stand-alone section that summarizes the memorandum, either in a Question Presented and Short Answer or an Executive Summary;
- an Introduction section (also called the Background or the Statement of Facts), which describes the background facts that are relevant to the legal issue;
- the Discussion section, which states the relevant legal rules and applies those rules to the relevant facts to arrive at a reasoned conclusion; and
- a short Conclusion section, which summarizes the conclusions for each sub-section and the reasons for each conclusion.

Following that, Chapters 13 and 14 covered the Discussion section in more detail, and described the forms of citations and quotations that we use in discussing and referring to legal authority.

This chapter and the following chapter return us to the introductory sections of an office memorandum: the stand-alone summary of the memo and the introduction of the relevant background facts. As we learned in Chapter 12, there is no universally-accepted pattern of organization: some attorneys prefer to begin with the background facts, and others with the summary of the issues and analysis.

The trend seems to be to begin with the summary, likely because impatient legal readers want to see the issue and the answer immediately. Still, it might be a good idea to ask your assigning attorney which style of organization he or she would prefer,[1] or to ask a senior associate whether that attorney has a preference, and if so, what it is. Also, look at the memos that other attorneys in your department or group have written: is there a standard style, or does the order vary?

If the partner is too busy to be bothered or says "you decide," and if other junior attorneys do not give you a definite answer, you will need to decide what to do yourself. In any case, it is best not to assume that one format is always better than another.

If the issue is straightforward or not very fact-intensive, it may make sense to begin with the summary of the memo, as we see in the office memorandum in Appendix B. On the other hand, if the issue involves a more complex set of facts or has a complicated procedural history, it may be better to begin with the factual background first, and then proceed to the summary. We see this pattern in the office memorandum in Appendix C.

---

[1] Some senior attorneys do not mind answering non-substantive questions such as these, but many others are annoyed by them. If you have never worked with the assigning attorney before, it's a good idea to ask other attorneys with a similar level of seniority to you for advice as to the assigning attorney's personality and work preferences before you meet with the assigning attorney, if that's possible. If not, get a sense of the attorney from the assignment meeting and consider whether or not it would be prudent to ask such a question.

A. THE PURPOSE OF THE STAND-ALONE SUMMARY

As we discussed at the beginning of Chapter 12, attorneys write office memoranda to memorialize their answer to a legal issue that concerns their client. Attorneys need to have a realistic understanding of the strengths and weaknesses of their clients' situations to competently advise the clients.

Thus, a senior attorney provides a junior attorney with the factual background to the client's situation, describes the legal issue to be researched and analyzed, and sends the junior attorney off (1) to determine what the relevant jurisdiction's law is for that legal issue, (2) to apply that law to the client's facts, and (3) to determine what the likely outcome will be. If the issue is narrow and the case small, the answer could be oral, or expressed in an email. If the case is larger and the issue is more complicated or important, the junior attorney memorializes the answer in an office memorandum.

The office memorandum serves both short-term and longer-term purposes. In the short term, it tells the assigning partner what the answer is to the legal question, and provides the answer in writing so that the senior attorney can check the accuracy of the junior lawyer's work, and review the answer before talking to the client. In the longer term, depending on the case, the memo may be used and re-used for the next several years with multiple audiences: attorneys who may be even more senior than the assigning partner, perhaps, or other senior attorneys; other junior attorneys who are working on the case at that time or a later time; and perhaps even the client.

Any of these potential legal readers may be facing time pressure to keep their billable hours for the case at a reasonable level, and they are certainly under pressure to read and understand the memo as quickly as possible. As a result, the legal reader is somewhat stressed, and he or she wants to be reminded at the beginning of the memo as to what the legal issue is, and what the answer is. The legal reader also wants to either learn or be reminded of which background facts are relevant to the legal issue. Armed with this knowledge — the issue, the answer, and the relevant facts — the legal reader now feels comfortable and prepared to look at the detailed legal analysis that is contained in the Discussion.

There is another reason why this stand-alone summary of the memo is so important: the legal reader may pick up this memorandum again six months later or two years later, and wants to be able to review its contents quickly, in a minute or two. Indeed, a busy partner may not even have enough time to read the entire memo before the client calls, looking for the partner's guidance. When that happens, the senior attorney must completely rely upon the summary of the memo to advise the client. This happens more often than you might think!

As stated in Chapter 12, that stand-alone summary of the memo's contents may take one of two forms: (1) either it states the legal issue in a question called the "Question Presented" (or "Issue") and briefly answers the question in the "Short Answer" (or "Brief Answer,") or (2) it states both the legal issue and answer in a two- or three-paragraph section called the Executive Summary. We will look at both forms.

B. THE QUESTION PRESENTED AND SHORT ANSWER

1. The Question Presented

Simply put, the Question Presented states the legal issue that the memo will analyze in the form of a question. If the memo covers two or more separate legal issues, each legal issue receives its own Question Presented and Short Answer. In that situation, keep the Questions Presented and Short Answers together (Question Presented 1, Ahort Answer 1; Question Presented 2, Short Answer 2).

Although there is no universally-accepted format for the Question Presented, it traditionally states the legal issue, the relevant law or jurisdiction, and the most relevant facts that are used in answering the question.[2]

a. Various Uses of the Question Presented

Practicing attorneys typically use Questions Presented in two places: in office memoranda, and in appellate briefs. As we saw in Chapter 6, law students also write them when drafting a case brief, when they state the legal issue as a question.

Because an office memorandum is supposed to be objective, the Question Presented for an office memorandum should describe the relevant facts in a "neutral" way, not favoring either party.

EXERCISE 15 A

When an appellate brief includes a Question Presented, the brief is a piece of persuasive advocacy where a lawyer tries to win on behalf of his or her client. Thus, unlike a Question Presented in an office memorandum, the facts are often described in a way that puts a positive "spin" in the client's favor. Sometimes appellate Questions Presented are not written as a question. Instead, they begin with "Whether" and end with a period rather than a question mark:

> Whether a medical supplies company's covenant not to compete that prevents a medical supplies salesman from selling medical supplies to any existing or new customer within a 50-mile radius of his former employer for a period of three years is an unreasonable restraint of trade that is impermissibly overbroad under Illinois law.

1. Is this language really neutral, or does it put a slight "spin" on the issue?
2. If so, who do you think drafted this Question Presented — the attorney for the company, or the attorney for the former salesman?

---

[2] Instead of using the traditional term "Question Presented," some lawyers use "Issue," or even "Issue Presented."

3. What language supports your conclusion?

b. The "Under-Does-When" Format

As we discussed in Chapter 6, we may draft a Question Presented by applying the "under-does-when" format for Questions Presented:

- Under [insert the law (statute, common law principle, jurisdiction, etc.)],
- does/is/can/will, etc. [state the legal issue],
- when [insert legally relevant facts]?

For the "under" part of the Question Presented, the reference to the law may be very general or very specific. It could simply refer to the type of law or jurisdiction ("under federal law," or "under Illinois law,"), it could refer more specifically to a statute or type of law ("under the Lanham Act" or "under the Illinois Commercial Code"), or it could refer specifically to the citation for the statute ("under 810 Ill. Comp. Stat. 5/2-207").

The legal issue is stated simply, with an auxiliary verb in the question such as "do/does," "can/could," "is/are," etc.

For the facts, state only the legally relevant facts. This means the facts that are necessary to determine the answer to the legal issue. If the legal issue has several factors or elements, include the most important facts for each factor or element in the question.

Traditionally, the Question Presented does not identify the parties by name, but by role: e.g., "a trucking company" and "a truck driver" instead of "Johnson Trucking Co." and "Mr. Rodriguez." In modern internal office memoranda, writers may identify the parties by name, but in appellate briefs, it is still common to refer to the parties by their roles.

When writing Questions Presented for an office memorandum, make sure that the questions are neutral and objective. One way to do this is by generally avoiding adjectives and adverbs (e.g., "reckless" or "negligently"), because these words often contain conclusions. Even words like "large," "tall," or "expensive" contain conclusions.

Make sure that the question does not contain any conclusions of law or of fact if they are at issue. For example, if the memo will analyze whether a client made "reasonable efforts" within the meaning of a certain statute, do not state that the defendant made reasonable efforts in the Question Presented. A question must not contain its own answer!

> Under Illinois law, is a medical supplies company's covenant not to compete overbroad when it prevents a medical supplies salesman from selling medical supplies to any existing or new customer within a 50-mile radius of his former employer for a period of three years?

c. Alternatives to the "Under-Does-When" Format

Keep in mind that the "under-does-when" format is not required, but is just a possibility. Also, you could keep all of those parts, but change the order, such as "does (issue) under (law) when (facts)." Sometimes, especially if the context makes it clear, the "under" part is suggested without using the word "under."

For example, the Question Presented for the office memorandum in Appendix C states:

> What civil and criminal penalties does Company potentially face for submitting inaccurate Discharge Monitoring Reports to the State-X Environmental Protection Division and failing to properly inspect two leak detection systems at the Company Plant located in Town-X of State-X?

By referring generally to "civil and criminal penalties" having to do with environmental violations, the U.S. legal reader understands that the writer will discuss penalties under both the law of State X and applicable federal environmental law.

Also, it is not a problem here for the Question Presented to refer to "submitting inaccurate Discharge Monitoring Reports" or "failing to properly inspect two leak detection systems." These are not improper conclusions because these statements are not at issue. As the Introduction section of the memo makes clear, those violations are not in dispute. Rather, the memo analyzes the potential civil and criminal penalties that the client faces for the violations.

d. When There Are Many Legally Relevant Facts

It is important for the Question Presented to contain the legally relevant facts for determining the legal issue. Where the legal issue is based on the law, such as the duty of care that a store owed to a customer, there may not be that many key facts, which makes the Question Presented somewhat easier to write. On the other hand, if the legal issue is based on the fact pattern, there may be many important facts. This can lead to a long Question Presented that is difficult to read.

In that case, some attorneys write two or three sentences that state the facts, and then present the legal issue in a short, simple question.[3] Let's consider the *Brennan's Restaurant* case from Chapter 5. The case analyzed whether a likelihood of confusion existed between two different restaurants with similar names. Among the relevant facts:

- Both restaurant owner/chefs were successful.
- Both restaurants were expensive.
- Both restaurants shared the same family name (Brennan's).

[3] *See, e.g.*, Bryan Garner, *The Redbook: A Manual on Legal Style* 344, 347 (2d ed., Thomson West 2006).

- The family name is common in the United States.
- One restaurant was in New York City, and the other was in New Orleans, Louisiana.

Let us imagine that we are an attorney working on the *Brennan's* case, and we have been asked to write a memo analyzing the likelihood of confusion. Here is a possible Question Presented that uses the "under-does-when" format:

> Under the Lanham Act, does a likelihood of confusion exist where two expensive restaurants that use the same common family name as part of the restaurant's name operate in cities that are more than a thousand miles apart from each other?

Here is a possible Question Presented under the alternate method, with three sentences followed by a simple question:

> The owner of a well-known, expensive New Orleans restaurant sues a prominent New York City chef who opened a new restaurant in Manhattan under his own name. Both restaurants contain the same common family name, Brennan's, and both restaurants are expensive. The restaurants are more than 1,000 miles apart from each other. Is the owner of the New Orleans restaurant likely to establish that there is a likelihood of confusion between the names of the two restaurants?

Notice that in the first example, the Question Presented follows the more traditional Question Presented model of only identifying the parties by their roles and not their names, while in the second example, the writer uses the name Brennan's. Which Question Presented is easier to understand?

EXERCISE 15 B

Let's return to the slip-and-fall case that we have been discussing in recent chapters. Some key facts include the following:

- It was a wet, rainy day in Chicago.
- Monica Jackson was a shopper at the Wholesome Food Markets, Inc. store that day.
- Because it was a rainy day, many customers tracked the rain into the store on their shoes.
- According to the client, none of its employees or other customers had spilled water or a liquid in the store, and no one had washed the floor recently.

- Monica Jackson slipped and fell about 10 feet (three meters) inside the store entrance, and was injured.
- She sued the store for negligence, asserting that it breached the duty of care that it owed to her.

1. Take these facts, and draft a Question Presented using the "under-does-when" style.

2. Draft a Question Presented that states the facts in a few sentences and then asks a simple question.

2. The Short Answer

After the Question Presented, the writer answers the legal issue that the question poses in the Short Answer (an alternate name is the "Brief Answer"). Short Answers are often very short — a few sentences long — or they may be slightly longer, perhaps as much as two paragraphs.

Here are the steps to follow in drafting your Short Answer:

1. Consider beginning the Short Answer by answering the Question Presented directly with "Yes" or "No," or perhaps qualifying the answer somewhat ("Probably" or "Probably not"). If the answer is less definite, give a reason for why the question is close or the answer is uncertain.
2. That being said, be sure that you have given a definite answer. Do not say "may," "could," "can," "might," "possibly," etc. The legal reader expects an answer to the Question Presented, and words like "may" or "maybe" do not provide an answer. Instead, they mean something like "50-50; it's possible; I don't know." An annoyed partner might respond, "*Anything's* possible. I'm paying you to give me an answer!"
3. After the yes/no answer, the Short Answer typically summarizes the analysis from the Discussion by referring to the main rule(s), giving the main points of the analysis, and concluding. It should be quite short, perhaps one paragraph long (two to six sentences).
4. After the yes/no answer, you may refer to the main rule by name and/or generally describe it, but do not quote the rule or cite to a statute or any cases. For example, in a Short Answer that addresses the "likelihood of confusion" test for trademark infringement, you might mention that there is an 8-factor test that is originally from the *Polaroid* case, and you might mention the key factors that you will evaluate in the Discussion section, but don't quote the whole 8-factor test, and don't provide a citation.[4]
5. An exception to the "no citation" rule for Short Answers: If you find one case that "perfectly" answers the Question Presented because it is on point and

[4] Occasionally, where the rules or regulations are specific and there are no factual disputes, the Short Answer may not describe the relevant rule. *See* the memo in Appendix B, which evaluates the client's potential liability for certain undisputed violations of environmental regulations. The Short Answer is divided into two one-paragraph sections, for potential civil and criminal penalties.

binding, you might mention the case by name and cite to it in the Short Answer. This is unusual, however.

6. Remember that the Question(s) Presented and Short Answer(s) stand alone as a summary of your memo. Unless the memorandum is very short, you should probably still include a separate paragraph after the Discussion that provides a conclusion for each of the issues and the whole memo overall.[5]

C. THE EXECUTIVE SUMMARY

The Executive Summary is a newer style of summarizing the contents of the Discussion section of the memorandum. It replaces both the Question Presented and the Short Answer.

As the name implies, Executive Summaries were originally designed to summarize documents for business executives, not senior lawyers, but since then, they have also become popular in legal office memoranda. If the office memorandum begins with an Executive Summary, it summarizes the legal issue that the writer will analyze, and then provides a summary of the analysis and conclusion in several paragraphs.

If the memorandum begins with an Introduction (Background/Statement of Facts) section, however, the legal issue that the memo will analyze is often stated at the end of the Introduction. In that case, the Executive Summary that follows will most likely focus on the answer to the legal question that is posed at the end of the Introduction, although its opening sentence might include the issue as a transition between the Introduction and the Executive Summary.

For an example of an Executive Summary, see the memorandum in Appendix C about whether non-statutory common law defenses will bar a claim arising under the Telephone Consumer Protection Act (TCPA).[6]

Chapter Review

- Office memoranda need to provide a stand-alone summary of the legal issue and the answer to the legal issue.
- This is necessary for several reasons: busy legal readers want to know the answer immediately; they might not have time to read the entire memo carefully before they advise the client; or they may want to review the contents of the memo at a later time.
- The summary can be written two ways: as a Question Presented (or "Issue") and a Short Answer, or as an Executive Summary.

---

[5] Thank you to Professors Grace Dodier, Brian Silbernagel, Susan Provenzano, Kathleen Dillon Narko, Elizabeth Inglehart, Martha Kanter, Dana Hill, and any other current and former members of the Communication and Legal Reasoning faculty at Northwestern University School of Law whose ideas may be reflected in this list.

[6] The Executive Summary in Appendix C begins with an Introduction whose last paragraph states the issue that the memorandum will analyze. Then it restates the legal issue in the opening sentence of the Executive Summary as a transition from the Introduction: "Few if any courts have specifically considered the extent to which non-statutory common law defenses will bar a claim arising under the TCPA."

- The Question Presented usually states the legal issue; the relevant law, statute, type of law, or jurisdiction; and the legally relevant facts.
- In an office memorandum, the Question Presented is objective and neutral. In an appellate brief, it is persuasive, and often begins with "Whether . . ." and ends with a period, not a question mark.
- The Question Presented may use the "under-does-when" format: "under (law) + does (legal issue) + when (legally relevant facts)?"
- Traditionally, the parties are referred to by their roles and not by their names, but modern office memos often use the client's name.
- If there are many legally relevant facts, it is often clearer to write the facts in two or three sentences, followed by a simple question that states the legal issue.
- The Short Answer is short (usually 2 to 6 sentences). It usually refers to the main legal rule, but doesn't quote it or use citations. Then it summarizes the reasoning.
- An Executive Summary contains both the statement of the legal issue and the answer, and it is usually two or three paragraphs long.
- If the memorandum begins with an Introduction that states the legal issue at the end, the Executive Summary may begin with the answer, or it may include the issue in the first sentence as a transition between the two sections.

Chapter 16

THE INTRODUCTION, OR STATEMENT OF FACTS

Chapter Preview

This chapter looks at the part of an office memorandum that introduces the facts that are relevant to the legal issue(s). Traditionally called the "Statement of Facts," many legal writers now call this section the "Introduction" or "Background." The chapter discusses:

- The contents of an Introduction section;
- The organization of an Introduction section; and
- Whether or not the section contains citations to the case documents.

Whether we use the more traditional name "Statement of Facts," or the more modern names "Introduction" or "Background,"[1] this section plays an important role in a formal office memorandum. It introduces the legal reader to: (1) the client and the other party; (2) what the client wants the lawyers to do; (3) the facts of the matter that are relevant to the issue that the memorandum discusses; and (4) what the memorandum will analyze. All of this information is necessary to provide a context and a background for the legal analysis that occurs in the Discussion section.

A. LARGE-SCALE ORGANIZATION: WHICH SECTION SHOULD COME FIRST?

As we discussed in Chapters 12 and 15, the Introduction may either precede or follow the Question(s) Presented and the Short Answer(s) in a formal office memorandum. Unless the legal reader is known to prefer one style, the writer may choose the order that seems more appropriate for the assignment.

The choice may depend upon who the legal reader is expected to be: if he or she is already very familiar with the case, then the Question Presented and Short Answer (or Executive Summary) should probably come first. On the other hand, if the writer knows that the memorandum will be read by many legal readers over time, some of whom are not familiar with the facts of the case, it would likely make more sense to put the Introduction section first.

B. WHY IS THE INTRODUCTION SECTION NECESSARY?

The Introduction section is important because the memorandum may be read and used by many people on a litigation team or deal team to become familiar with the facts of a matter. Even the assigning partner, who is likely already familiar with all of those facts and many others as well, is working on many matters at the same time and may need to review the most important facts of a case or deal.

The legal reader is also looking for the writer to provide focus as well as background. Even if the reader is familiar with the matter, he or she would appreciate an Introduction that focuses on only the facts that are relevant to the issue that the memorandum analyzes. Matters may contain thousands of facts, and not all of them are relevant to the legal issue that the memo analyzes. Therefore, it is the writer's responsibility to be a good editor: to identify the facts that are necessary for analyzing the issue, to let the legal reader know what those facts are, and to avoid mentioning irrelevant facts.

C. SMALL-SCALE ORGANIZATION: THE PARTS OF THE INTRODUCTION

Here are some important ideas to remember when writing an Introduction section:

---

[1] For the rest of the chapter, we will refer to this section as the "Introduction."

1. The length of the Introduction section varies, depending upon how fact-intensive the legal issue is (i.e., how many facts you need to introduce to the legal reader). Typically, in a seven- to twelve-page memo, it will be somewhere between half a page and one and a half pages long.
2. The Introduction section typically begins by introducing the client and the client's problem, and what the client wants our legal team to do. As we mentioned, although the first legal reader will likely be the assigning attorney, many other legal readers may read the memo, and they want to know this information immediately.
3. The Introduction section often describes the relevant facts by organizing them as a story, in chronological order, but it may also organize the facts by the issue, such as by providing the facts that are most relevant to analyzing whether the client meets certain legal requirements.
4. Remember to provide only the background facts that the legal reader needs to know to understand the issue that you are analyzing.
5. That being said, the Introduction section should include *all* of the relevant facts that you will use in analyzing the issue. In other words, it should state every fact that you will discuss in the Application sections of the TREACs that are in the Discussion section. If the legal reader is surprised by a "new" fact that appears for the first time in one of the Application sections, the writer has made a mistake.
6. Include all of the relevant facts whether they are good or bad for your client. Remember that the purpose of the office memorandum is generally to help the senior attorney decide what the proper strategy is so that he or she can best advise the client. For that reason, the legal reader needs a complete assessment of the facts, whether they help or hurt the client's case.
7. The Introduction typically ends by introducing the legal issue that you will analyze in the Discussion section of the memorandum. Do not use "I" or "we," but begin by saying "This memorandum analyzes . . . ."

   There are two options: either (1) the writer states the issue in one sentence, and then provides a "roadmap" that outlines the Discussion section in the thesis paragraph of the Discussion; or (2) the Introduction ends with a one-paragraph statement of the legal issue that includes a roadmap of the organization of the Discussion section.

If the writer chooses the second option, the thesis paragraph of the Discussion section can go directly into a statement of the applicable law, without needing to include a roadmap.

The memorandum about the environmental issue in Appendix B provides an example of the one-sentence issue statement at the end of the Introduction:

> This memorandum provides a preliminary assessment of Company's potential liability.

The fourth and final paragraph of the Introduction section in the memo about the Telephone Consumer Protection Act in Appendix C gives a one-paragraph statement of the legal issue along with a roadmap as to the structure of the Discussion section:

> This memorandum analyzes the availability of common law defenses to a TCPA action. This memorandum begins by surveying the existing case law on common law defenses under the TCPA and identifying common law defenses that could theoretically bar Small Corp's claims. Because the availability of common law defenses to TCPA actions is an open question, this memorandum continues by setting out a framework for arguing for the recognition of various non-statutory common law defenses. This memorandum concludes by explaining the content of potentially applicable common law defenses and articulating theories under which those defenses could apply to bar Small Corp's claims.

Because the writer of the TCPA memorandum has provided a roadmap to the Discussion section at the end of the Introduction, it is unnecessary to do so again in the thesis paragraph of the Discussion section.

D. CITATIONS IN THE INTRODUCTION SECTION

Like the Executive Summary or Short Answer, the Introduction section does not usually provide citations to legal authority, and the reason is fairly obvious: the main purpose of the section is to introduce the case facts or deal facts, not the governing law. The Introduction may provide citations to other important documents, however, depending upon the facts of the matter, the purpose of the memorandum, and the timing of the litigation, investigation, or transaction.

Many office memoranda are written shortly after the law firm or legal department has begun to work on the matter, when the parties are trying to determine what their strategy will be. When the memorandum is written at this stage, there are not usually any citations to important client documents in the Introduction. For example, the memoranda in Appendix B and Appendix C are written at this early stage, and they contain no citations to key documents.

Office memoranda may also be written at a later stage of the litigation, investigation, or transaction. For example, they may be written during the middle of the discovery process, after the parties have already exchanged thousands or even millions of pages of documents, or after the parties have begun to take depositions. In that event, it may be useful to provide citations to key documents, such as contracts, deposition transcripts, discovery documents, court documents, etc. The Bluebook and the AWLD Citation Manual both provide rules for citing to these types of documents.

Here are some examples of citations to documents, followed by explanations of each citation in parentheses:

> Johnson Aff. 3. (Johnson affidavit, page 3)
>
> Pl.'s Resp. to Def.'s Interrog. No. 7. (Plaintiff's response to Defendant's interrogatory number 7)
>
> Smith Dep. 3:11–4:6, Aug. 11, 2013 (Smith deposition of August 11, 2013, from page 3, line 11 to page 4, line 6)
>
> Compl. ¶ 32. (Complaint, paragraph 32)

If you learned facts about the matter from an assignment memo or email from the senior lawyer who assigned the work to you, do not provide a citation for any facts that you take from the assignment memo or email.

EXERCISE 16 A[2]

This exercise contains three possible Introduction sections for the slip-and-fall problem.

1. First, rank the Introductions: "1" for the best one, "2" for the second-best, and "3" for the worst one. Then decide what, if anything, is "wrong" with each Introduction.

Introduction A

> Monica Jackson, 54, was shopping at the Wholesome Food Markets, Inc. store on Halsted Avenue in Chicago on April 23, 2013, which was a wet, rainy day. She had just finished work for the day, and perhaps she was tired and less careful than usual when she entered the store.
>
> Ten feet inside the main entrance to the store, Ms. Jackson slipped on the floor and fell. The floor was wet because it had been raining all day, and the customers were tracking the rainwater into the store on their shoes. According to an interview with the client's store manager who was on duty at the time of the accident, none of its employees or other customers had spilled water or a liquid in the store, and no one had washed the floor recently. The manager

[2] The idea for this exercise was adapted from Helene F. Shapo, Marilyn R. Walter, and Elizabeth Fajans, *Writing and Analysis in the Law* 178–79 (5th ed., Thomson West 2008).

concluded that the floor was not wet because of an employee's mopping it, but because of the other customers carrying it in on their shoes.

Monica Jackson broke her hip in the fall, dislocated her right knee badly, and tore the anterior cruciate ligament in her right leg. She is currently in a wheelchair while her hip heals, and her doctor believes that she might need to walk with a cane for the rest of her life. She is suing the store for $500,000 in damages, alleging that Wholesome Food Markets, Inc. negligently breached its duty of care to her by allowing the floor to remain wet inside the store.

Rank: ___________

Problems: ____

____

____

____

Introduction B

Our client, Wholesome Food Markets, Inc., is facing a negligence claim in a slip-and-fall case in Chicago, and it has asked our firm to analyze its potential liability to determine how to respond to the complaint.

The plaintiff, Ms. Monica Jackson, 54, was shopping at the Wholesome Food Markets, Inc. store on Halsted Avenue in Chicago on April 23, 2013 when she slipped and fell on a wet part of the floor 10 feet inside the main entrance to the store.

It had been raining throughout the day, and some water had accumulated near the entrance to the store and between the inside and outside entrance doors. As they entered the store, customers were tracking the rainwater into the store on their shoes. Ms. Jackson slipped on the water and fell. The manager who was on duty at the time said that none of the store's customers or employees had spilled water or any other liquid in the store, and no one had washed the floor recently. He stated that any water on the floor thus must have come from customers tracking the rainwater in on their shoes.

As a result of her fall, Ms. Jackson broke her hip, dislocated her right knee, and tore the anterior cruciate ligament in her right leg. At this time, she is in a wheelchair until her hip heals, and her doctor told her that she may need to walk with a cane for the rest of her life. She is suing for $500,000 in damages. Jackson's complaint alleges that Wholesome Food Markets negligently breached its duty of care to her by allowing the floor to be wet 10 feet inside the store entrance.

This memorandum analyzes whether Wholesome Food Markets, Inc. negligently breached its duty of care to Ms. Jackson.

Rank: ____________

Problems: ____

____

____

____

Introduction C

Ms. Monica Jackson, 54 years old and overweight, is a regular shopper at the Wholesome Food Markets, Inc. store on Halsted Avenue in Chicago. She has been shopping there for years and never had a problem until April 23, 2013, when she slipped on the floor of the store.

It was a wet, rainy day, and Jackson had just finished work at the day care center where she had been working for the past two weeks. It was her third different job in the past two years. It had been raining all day, and the parking lot and entrance area were quite wet due to the heavy rain. Jackson entered the store and slipped and fell on a wet area of the floor about 10 feet inside the entrance door.

The on-duty manager of the store said that no store employee had washed the floor before the accident, and no employee or other customer had spilled anything on the floor. This means that the water was carried in on the shoes of the other customers.

Jackson broke her hip when she fell. She also dislocated her right knee badly and tore the anterior cruciate ligament in her right leg. Her added weight may have made her injuries worse. Jackson is currently in a wheelchair until her hip heals, and her doctor apparently told her that she may need to use a cane for the rest of her life. Perhaps he is sympathetic to her, and is exaggerating her injuries so that she can win a higher damages award.

Ms. Jackson is suing our client for $500,000. She alleges that the client negligently breached its duty of care to her by leaving the floor wet.

Rank: ____________

Problems: ____

____

____

____

2. Look again at each Introduction. Are they organized chronologically or according to the legal issue? Write your answer below.

Introduction A:

Introduction B:

Introduction C:

Chapter Review

- The Introduction section may be called "Introduction," "Statement of Facts," or "Background."
- It may be the very first section of an office memorandum, or it may follow the Question Presented and Short Answer or their modern equivalent, the Executive Summary.
- The main purpose of the Introduction is to introduce the legal issue and the facts of the matter that the writer will use to analyze the legal issue.
- The Introduction generally begins by introducing the client and the client's legal problem, or what the client wants the lawyers to do.
- The Introduction section may organize the facts in chronological order or by the legal issue.
- It should only contain the relevant facts that the legal reader needs to know to understand the legal issue that you are analyzing.
- The Introduction should include all of the relevant facts that you will use in analyzing the issue, whether they are good or bad for the client.
- The Introduction section typically does not contain citations to legal authority. If it is early in the litigation or deal, and the lawyers are determining their initial strategy, there will probably not be any citations to documents. If it is later in the litigation or deal, there may be citations to relevant documents, such as contracts, letters, affidavits, deposition transcripts, pleadings, motions, or briefs.
- The Introduction typically ends by introducing the legal issue that you will analyze in the Discussion section of the memorandum: "This memorandum analyzes . . . ."
- The writer may introduce the legal issue in one sentence, and then provide a "roadmap" to the Discussion section in the thesis paragraph of the Discussion.
- Instead, the writer may choose to end the Introduction with a one-paragraph statement of the legal issue that includes a roadmap of the organization of the Discussion section. In that case, there is no need to repeat the roadmap in the thesis paragraph of the Discussion section.

Chapter 17

WRITING AND EDITING THE WORK: VERB TENSES, ARTICLES, PLURALS, AND PUNCTUATION

Chapter Preview

This chapter looks at areas in which lawyers who speak English as a second language are likely to make mistakes when writing in English. These problem areas include:

- Correctly choosing the appropriate verb tense;
- Having subject-verb agreement;
- Using articles (*a*, *an*, and *the*);
- Making nouns plural; and
- Using proper punctuation for U.S. legal writing.

It is difficult enough for lawyers to write well in their native languages. As we all know, it is even more difficult to write well in a second language. The standard is very high: legal writing in English is expected to be accurate, clear, and grammatically correct, whether English is your native language or not. Writing that is filled with mistakes such as incorrect verb tenses, missing articles and plurals, and inaccurate punctuation looks unprofessional. Worse than that, it looks incompetent, and leads to a loss of credibility.

Legal readers read such writing and think to themselves, "Why should I trust this writer? Why should I believe in the accuracy of the analysis if he or she cannot even write correctly?" Whether these thoughts are fair or not is irrelevant — it's reality, and as practicing attorneys, we must deal with reality.

When you learned English in your country, the focus was likely on reception (reading, listening, and understanding) rather than production (writing, speaking, and communicating your thoughts). The teachers were probably not native speakers of English, and likely made mistakes when they spoke or wrote in English.

Here, the focus is quite different, because much more is expected of you. It's true that you must have good receptive skills to do well in a U.S. law school. You will do a great deal of reading, and must listen to and understand the professors' lectures and questions. But that's not enough.

You must also have strong productive skills to do well. You must be able to answer if you are asked a question in class, and your grades are based on how well you do on written final examinations, which are usually essays. You must speak well enough to ask questions when you do not understand the material: in class, after class, and at the professor's office. You also will take classes together with J.D. students from the United States, and may be required to work with them in class or outside of class.

Although attending law school in the United States will challenge your English skills, the standard increases again if you take a state bar examination or work for a year at a U.S. law firm, or if you return to your country and work with U.S. lawyer colleagues, counterparts, or clients in English. You will be expected to have native — level proficiency.

The bottom line: excellent, native-like legal writing is expected and required. Make sure that your writing is accurate, polished, and professional — it will help your career greatly!

A. CHOOSING THE APPROPRIATE VERB TENSE

Let's begin with a review of the English verb tenses, what they mean, and how they are used:

1. The Simple Tenses

Form: past: *-ed* (or irregular verb)

present: (simple verb), with *-s* or *-es* for *he/she/it*

future: will + (simple verb)

Past	Sharp Trucking Co. **signed** the agreement yesterday.
Present	The prosecution **intends** to call another witness. Most intermediate appellate courts **have** three-judge panels. The trial **begins** tomorrow.
Future	The court will rule on the motion tomorrow.

Meaning: The simple tenses show simple time relationships in the past, present, and future.

The Past Tense

- The past tense refers to an action that occurred at a time in the past, and has finished by the time that the writer is describing it.
- When you describe an event in the past tense, you should usually give a specific time in the past (yesterday, last night, in 2011, etc.).
- **Caution:** when you use the past tense without giving a specific past time, it may suggest that something was true in the past, but is no longer true. "He **was** a good manager" could mean that he is not the manager now (or that the writer is not working there now), but if he is still the manager, it would imply that he is not a good manager now! The context is very important. Similarly, "Bob **was** a good judge" could mean that Bob is not a judge now, but it could also imply that Bob is dead, or that he is not a good judge now. Avoid this problem by describing the past time specifically, or by using sentences like these in a context that explains the meaning, such as "Bob **was** a judge until he retired last year. He **was** a good judge."
- In legal writing, use the past tense when describing precedent, such as in the E or A sections of TREAC. This makes sense because the case has already been published. Precedent is, by its nature, an older case than the case that you are working on, and the decision is final. If you forget to use the past tense when describing precedent, the legal reader will be very confused.

The Present Tense

- In legal writing, the present tense often refers to an action that is occurring at the time that the writer is describing it: "We **move** to dismiss, Your Honor," or "Ajax Co. **asks** this Court to award it two million dollars in damages."[1] This use of the present tense sounds formal and serious.

- The present tense is used very often to make general statements, and to describe facts or habits: "The defendant **lives** in Chicago," "The United States Supreme Court **has** nine justices," or "I **study** every night until 1 a.m."
- The present tense can also be used with a time in the future to express the future. It is often used in this way to describe plans: "We **have** a meeting tomorrow morning at 9 a.m.," or "My flight to New York **leaves** in three hours."
- Most important of all, perhaps, the present tense is used when stating rules of law: "Conversion is an intentional interference with the plaintiff's possession or ownership of property that is so substantial that the defendant should pay the property's full value."

The Future Tense

The future tense with "will" expresses the future: "The defense **will begin** its case in chief next week."

2. The Perfect Tenses

Form: *to have* + past participle[2]

Past Perfect	A spokesperson for the company stated that it **had decided** not to appeal the decision.
Present Perfect	The company **has fired** many of its top executives. Mr. Williams **has been** the CEO of the company for three years. Mr. Williams **has been** the CEO of the company since 2011.
Future Perfect	By the time the court issues an arrest warrant, he will **have left** the country.

Meaning: The perfect tenses show a relationship between two times. Either one action was completed before a second time in the past or present, it continues until the second time, or it will be completed before a future time.

The Past Perfect Tense

- The past perfect tense shows that one action occurred before another one in the past. In "A spokesperson for the company stated that it **had decided** not to appeal the decision," the spokesperson was speaking in the past, and the company made the decision not to appeal before he or she spoke.

---

[1] In everyday speech, people use the present progressive tense to describe something that is happening now: "I'm watching TV," not "I watch TV."

[2] The past participle is formed with *-ed* in regular verbs. For irregular verbs, it is the "third form." For example, the past participle of "*to go*" is "*gone*" ("*go/went/gone*").

The Present Perfect Tense

- The present perfect tense is used to state that an action has been completed before a given time. Do not use a specific past time with the present perfect tense. For example, in "The company **has fired** many of its top executives," the company fired the executives before the writer made that statement, but the writer did not say when. If the writer had given a specific time like "last year," the sentence would use the past tense: "The company fired many of its top executives last year."
- When the present perfect is used in this way, it tells the legal reader that although the action occurred in the past, exactly when it occurred is not important. Also, the action is relevant to the present, and perhaps it may continue. For example, "I **have appeared** in court twice for this case" implies that the case is still ongoing and the writer may appear in court again. Sometimes the writer makes this meaning more explicit by adding "so far." If the case has concluded, the writer should use the past tense: "I went to court three times for that case."[3]
- The present perfect tense is also used to describe a continuing activity that began in the past and continues to this day. It is used with "*for*" and "*since*" in this way.
- "*For*" describes the length of time: "Mr. Williams **has been** the CEO of the company for three years" means that he became CEO three years ago, has continuously been the CEO, and is still the CEO at present.
- "Since" introduces the beginning time: "Mr. Williams **has been** the CEO of the company since 2011" means that he became the CEO in 2011 and is still the CEO now.

3. The Progressive Tenses[4]

Form: *to be* + present participle[5]

Past Progressive	We **were having** a board meeting when the telephone rang.
Present Progressive	The jury **is deliberating**, but we hope that it will reach a verdict soon. She **is deposing** the witness tomorrow morning.
Future Progressive	The President **will be meeting** with members of Congress all day.

Meaning: The progressive tenses show that an action is occurring and continuing at a given point in time.

---

[3] The demonstratives "*this*" and "*that*" also help to make the meaning clear. "*This*" suggests that something is near in time or space, and "*that*" indicates that something is distant in time or space.

[4] Some ESL/EFL instructors, grammar books and ESL textbooks refer to the progressive tenses as the "continuous" tenses.

[5] The present participle is formed with *-ing* ("*having*," "*deliberating*").

The Past Progressive Tense

- The past progressive tense shows that an action was occurring at a given time in the past. For example, "We **were having** a board meeting when the telephone rang" means that the board meeting was interrupted by the phone call — it had not finished yet.

The Present Progressive Tense

- The present progressive tense shows that an action is occurring at the present moment, and it has not concluded yet. For example, "The jury **is deliberating**, but we hope that it will reach a verdict soon" means that at the present moment, the members are discussing the case during their deliberations, and they have not reached a verdict yet.
- In spoken English, the present progressive tense is the most common way to describe something that is occurring at this moment.
- In legal writing and in spoken language to a court, lawyers often use the simple present tense in this situation. It sounds more formal.
- The present progressive tense is also used with a future time to discuss the future: "She **is deposing** the witness tomorrow morning."

The Future Progressive Tense

- The future progressive tense has the same meaning as the present progressive tense when it is used with a future time. "She **will be** deposing the witness tomorrow morning" largely means the same thing as "She **is deposing** the witness tomorrow morning," although the future progressive tense emphasizes that this will take place in the future.

4. The Perfect Progressive Tenses

Form: *to have* + past participle + present participle

Past Perfect Progressive	By the time Big Co. acquired them, New Tech Co. **had been developing** the new microchip for two years.
Present Perfect Progressive	Mary **has been studying** for her final examination in her Business Associations class since 7 o'clock this morning (it's now 11 p.m.).
Future Perfect Progressive	Let me think — at the end of this year, I **will have been practicing** law for more than 20 years!

Meaning: The perfect tenses show a continuing relationship between two times. They are not used very often, but it is important to understand them, and to be able to use them when necessary.

Past Perfect Progressive

- Past perfect progressive tense describes an earlier event that happened continuously until a second event occurred. For example, "By the time Big Co. acquired them, New Tech Co. **had been developing** the new microchip for two years" means that New Tech Co. began developing a new microchip two years before Big Co. acquired them, and it continued to develop the microchip until the time that it was acquired.

Present Perfect Progressive

- Present perfect progressive tense describes an earlier event that has happened continuously until the present. For example, "She **has been studying** for her final examination in her Business Associations class since 7 o'clock this morning (it's now 11 p.m.)" means that she began studying 16 hours ago, at 7 a.m., and she is still studying now at 11 p.m.
- Present perfect progressive tense has the same meaning as present perfect tense does when the present perfect action has continued until now (i.e., "She **has studied** . . . since 7 o'clock this morning" means the same thing). Adding the progressive feature places extra emphasis on the continuing activity. In this example, 16 hours of continuous studying is a very long time, and using present perfect progressive tense emphasizes the length of time.

Future Perfect Progressive

- Future perfect progressive tense looks at a time in the future, and measures the amount of continuous time from the beginning of an action in the past until the future time. For example, if I will have my twentieth anniversary of practicing law on September 5 of this year (i.e., in the future), I can state that "at the end of this year, I **will have been practicing** law for more than twenty years."

EXERCISE 17 A

In the writing samples below, some of the verb tenses are correct, and others are not. Edit the sentences by fixing the incorrect verb tenses.

1. The members of the jury were standing when the judge enters the courtroom.

2. In *Jackson*, the defendant murdered a convenience store clerk while he is on parole after serving seven years for armed robbery.

3. By the end of this year, he will have been the president for six years.

4. In *Wingo*, the plaintiff accuses her former employer of racial discrimination.

5. The general rule is that landowners owed no duty of care to trespassers.

B. FORMING THE APPROPRIATE VERB TENSE

After choosing the appropriate verb tense, you must still form it accurately. Many types of mistakes are possible. This section will focus on two common problems for legal writers who speak English as a second language: (1) using auxiliary verbs correctly; and (2) having subject-verb agreement.

1. Using Auxiliary Verbs Correctly

Auxiliary verbs (e.g., "*be*," "*have*," "*do*," and "*will*") work together with the main verb of the sentence in many English sentences. As we saw in the previous section, "*be*" is the auxiliary verb for the progressive tenses and "*have*" is the auxiliary verb for the perfect tenses. The progressive and perfect tenses require auxiliary verbs in affirmative sentences, negative sentences, and interrogative sentences (questions). We will look at two progressive tenses and two perfect tenses as examples:

Present Progressive Tense

Affirmative	The jury **is deliberating.**
Negative	The jury **is not deliberating.**
Interrogative	**Is** the jury **deliberating?**

Past Progressive Tense

Affirmative	We **were having** a board meeting when the telephone rang.
Negative	We **were not having** a board meeting when the telephone rang.
Interrogative	**Were** you **having** a board meeting when the telephone rang?

Present Perfect Tense

Affirmative	The company **has fired** many of its top executives.
Negative	The company **has not fired** many of its top executives.
Interrogative	**Has** the company **fired** many of its top executives?

Past Perfect Tense

Affirmative	A spokesperson for the company stated that it **had decided** not to appeal the decision.
Negative	A spokesperson for the company stated that it **had not decided** whether to appeal the decision.
Interrogative	**Had** the company **decided** whether to appeal the decision before it was acquired?

Note about word order: The negative word "not" is placed between the auxiliary verb and the main verb in a negative sentence, and the auxiliary verb is moved before the subject in a question.

Second-language writers are much more likely to make mistakes with auxiliary verbs in the simple present and past tenses, which are less regular.

The simple present and past tenses use *"to do"* as the auxiliary verb, but only in negative sentences and in questions:

The Present Tense

Affirmative	Most intermediate appellate courts **have** three-judge panels. The trial **begins** tomorrow.
Negative	Most intermediate appellate courts **do not have** three-judge panels. The trial **does not begin** tomorrow.
Interrogative	**Do** most intermediate appellate courts **have** three-judge panels? **Does** the trial **begin** tomorrow?

Note: When you make the third-person singular form (*"he/she/it"*) negative, remove the *"-s"* or *"-es"* from the main verb (i.e., *"begins"*), and use *"does not"*: ***"does not begin."***

Common mistakes: "do not begins" (*incorrect*) and "does not begins." (*incorrect*)

The Past Tense

Affirmative	Sharp Trucking Co. **signed** the agreement yesterday.
Negative	Sharp Trucking Co. **did not sign** the agreement yesterday.
Interrogative	**Did** Sharp Trucking Co. **sign** the agreement yesterday?

Note: When you make the past tense negative, remove the *"-ed"* from the main verb (i.e., *"signed"*), and use *"did not"*: ***"did not sign."***

Common mistakes: "do not signed" (*incorrect*) and "did not signed" (*incorrect*).

The future tense uses "will" in affirmative sentences, negative sentences, and questions:

The Future Tense

Affirmative	The court **will rule** on the motion tomorrow.
Negative	The court **will not rule** on the motion tomorrow.
Interrogative	**Will** the court **rule** on the motion tomorrow?

If you are thinking in your native language as you write in English, it is easy to use your native language's grammar, e.g., "he no have" (*incorrect*) instead of "he does not have," or to get the word order wrong with questions, e.g., "The court will rule on the motion tomorrow?" (*incorrect*) instead of "Will the court rule on the motion tomorrow?" Even if you are thinking in English, this problem may still occur, so watch out for it as you write!

EXERCISE 17 B

In the sentences below, fix the incorrect questions or negative statements.

1. Mr. McGee did not worked after he had the accident in 2013.
2. What he expects to achieve by suing a poor defendant?
3. She no passed the New York Bar examination last year.
4. You were working in New York when the accident occurred?
5. Did Mr. Smith signed the agreement yesterday?

2. Having Subject-Verb Agreement

The basic concept is not difficult: subjects and verbs must agree with each other in form. Singular subjects require singular verbs, and plural subjects require plural verbs. You have likely studied these rules for years, and they are not generally very difficult. Yet legal writers who speak English as a second language make this mistake very frequently. Partly it is because they are not being careful; partly it is because they may be thinking in their native language, or unconsciously using the grammar patterns of their native language; and partly it is because there are several grammar patterns that are tricky.

After a brief introduction, we will review some of the more difficult patterns, which you have likely studied when preparing for the TOEFL, IELTS, or a similar test. Unlike when you take a standardized test, however, it is not enough to recognize the correct answer on a multiple-choice test. Here, you must use the correct form in your own writing.

a. Singular Subjects Require Singular Verbs; Plural Subjects Require Plural Verbs

Before we choose the correct singular verb, we need to recognize when the subject is singular. "*I*" is singular; "*he/she/it*" is singular; and "*you*" may be either singular or plural, because it can refer to an audience of one person ("singular *you*"), or more than one ("plural *you*").

Part of what makes subject-verb agreement challenging in English is the nature of the language. Most European languages are heavily inflected; each person ("*I-you-he-she-it-we-you-they*") requires a different verb ending. The major East Asian languages, on the other hand, are uninflected (there are no word endings). English is somewhere in the middle — although it has lost many of its word endings over the centuries, a few remain and must be used, such as third-person singular ("*he/she/it*"), which requires a present tense verb to end in "*-s*" or "*-es*": "The trial **begins** tomorrow."

- When you see "*-s*" or "*-es*" on a noun, it is plural: "The **regulations require** . . . ."
- When you see "*-s*" or "*-es*" on a present-tense verb, however, it is singular: "The **regulation requires** . . . ."

Suggestion: Analyzing subject-verb agreement is easier with pronouns than with nouns, so when you see a noun, ask yourself which pronoun it would take. For example, "*the trial*" would take the pronoun "*it*," so the verb should be "*begins*" because we say "*it begins*." When you are proofreading your work, mentally substitute a pronoun for each subject to check for subject-verb agreement problems.

b. Be Careful With Certain Nouns and Certain Structures

It is not always easy to determine which subjects take singular verbs and which take plural verbs. Here are some categories of words that can be problematic: (i) uncountable nouns; (ii) many indefinite pronouns; (iii) certain other words used as pronouns; (iv) certain words and expressions; (v) certain compound subject structures; and (vi) certain verbs that express advice.

(i) Uncountable Nouns

Most English nouns are countable. This simply means that the noun can be counted and takes the plural ending:

one case, two cases	one court, two courts
one statute, two statutes	one rule, two rules
one judge, two judges	one contract, two contracts

Some nouns, however, are uncountable, such as:

- items that are too small and numerous to be counted (like rice, sand, grass, dirt, soil, or hair);
- liquids (like gasoline, oil, water, coffee, tea, beer, or soda);[6]
- some types of food (like beef, pork, chicken, or fruit);
- some substances or materials (like metal, wood, steel, or plastic);
- some general categories of items (like furniture, money, stationery, baggage, or clothing); or
- certain abstract ideas (like peace, harmony, hope, wisdom, democracy, socialism, or information).

There are quite a few uncountable legal nouns, including:[7]

---

[6] With drinks, people may say "two coffees," two beers," etc., as a short way to say "two cups of coffee," "two glasses of beer," etc.

[7] Laurel Currie Oates & Anne Enquist, *The Legal Writing Handbook* 723 (5th ed., Aspen Publishers 2010).

abandonment	depreciation	insurance
access	discretion	intent
arson	duress	land
authentication	evidence	malice
capital (money/property)	extortion	negligence
commerce	harassment	privacy
conduct	insolvency	real estate

Remember that because uncountable nouns cannot be counted, they cannot take a plural form. They take singular verbs:

> The **evidence is** overwhelming.

There are also some words that may be either countable or uncountable, depending upon the meaning. For example, "*law*" is uncountable when we are speaking generally and abstractly, but we can also say "*laws*" to refer to individual statutes.

(ii) Indefinite Pronouns

Many of the indefinite pronouns in this list seem plural in meaning, but all of them take singular verbs:

anybody	either	everything	nothing
anyone	every	neither	somebody
anything	everybody	nobody	someone
each	everyone	no one	something

> **Everyone is waiting for** the ruling, which is expected tomorrow.
> **Each defendant has** his own lawyer.
> **Every motion** that the defendant filed **was denied.**

(iii) Certain Other Words Used as Pronouns

These words always take plural verbs when they are used as pronouns:

both	few	many	several

> Most of the sections in this chapter of the state code are old, but **several were passed** recently.

(iv) Certain Other Nouns and Expressions

Gerunds are words ending in "*-ing*" that function as nouns. Gerunds that function as subjects always take singular verbs, even when followed by other plural words:

> **Swimming is** excellent exercise.
>
> **Filing** several dispositive motions **is** expensive.

In these sentences, "*swimming*" and "*filing*" are gerunds that function as subjects. In the second sentence, the plural word "*motions*" is not the subject of the sentence — "*filing*" is.

Certain words that describe categories or academic subjects that end in "*-s*" may look plural, but are singular:

torts	contracts	ethics	news	mathematics	physics	economics

> **Torts is** a core first-year course for law students, as **is contracts.**
>
> **Economics is** a challenging subject for most students.
>
> **The news** of the deaths **is** devastating.

In a sentence like "**The news** of the deaths **is** devastating," do not be tricked by the prepositional phrase that comes between the subject and the verb ("of the deaths"). "*Deaths*" is the object of the preposition "*of.*" Therefore, it is not the subject of the sentence — "*the news*" is.

(v) Certain Compound Subject Structures

There are three common structures that we use with compound subjects:

either . . . or	neither . . . nor	not only . . . but also

The pattern is really "either X or Y (verb)," "neither X nor Y (verb)," and "not only X but also Y (verb)." In all three patterns, the compound subjects are X and Y. For all three of these structures, the verb follows the closer subject to it, which is Y (the second subject):

Neither the **Simpson children** nor **Mark Johnson is** an adult.
(plural) (singular)
Neither **Mark Johnson** nor the **Simpson children are** adults.
(singular) (plural)

(vi) Certain Verbs That Express Advice

As counselors, lawyers frequently give clients advice, and they make requests or demands on behalf of their clients. As a result, a common sentence pattern for lawyers involves the following 10 verbs:

ask	insist	propose	request	suggest
demand	prefer	recommend	require	urge

In the pattern, one of these 10 verbs is followed by a noun clause ("*that*" + subject + verb). The verb always takes the base form (no endings), even if the subject is third person singular:

The Company **requires that he sign** the agreement by January 31, or the offer will no longer be valid.

Several of these 10 verbs, including "*ask*," "*require*," "*urge*," and "*recommend*," also often take an object and an infinitive or another phrase that begins with "*to*:"

I **asked them to be** quiet.

The regulation **requires your factory to be inspected** every year.

He **urged her to reconsider**.

She **recommended you to me**.

EXERCISE 17 C

Some of the sentences below are correct, while others have subject-verb agreement problems. Write "OK" if the sentences are correct, and fix the subject-verb agreement problems where they exist.

1. Everybody are convinced that the defendant will be convicted.
2. The new edition of the casebook sell for $90.
3. I advise that he sign the contract tomorrow, not next week.
4. The evidence support the jury's verdict.
5. Neither the plaintiff nor the defendants were satisfied with the verdict.

C. USING ARTICLES CORRECTLY

Articles ("*a*," "*an*," and "*the*") are difficult to use correctly: there are many rules, and many exceptions to those rules. There are a few important main rules, however, that will allow you to use articles correctly most of the time, provided you use them.

We learned with word endings that many European languages use them for every person, many East Asian languages do not use them, and English falls somewhere in between, using them sometimes.

The same is true with articles. Many European languages always use articles with nouns; many East Asian languages never use them; and English uses them sometimes but not always, which can be confusing. As a result, speakers of many European languages overuse articles in English, especially "*the*." On the other hand, speakers of many East Asian languages (and certain other languages such as Polish) underuse them, which is likely a worse problem. These words are among the very most commonly-used words in English, and if you are missing many or even several articles on each page, U.S. legal readers find it distracting and unpleasant to read. Worse, the legal reader may have to guess what you mean at times, because these articles can provide important information.

1. The Three Articles

The three articles have different meanings and different uses. "*A*" and "*an*" are called indefinite articles, and "the" is called the definite article. In this case, "*definite*" means specific, and "*indefinite*" means not specific, or general.

The grammar is different:

- "*A*" and "*an*" are used with singular, countable nouns only.

  They cannot be used with uncountable nouns or plural nouns.

- "*The*" may be used with any kind of noun: singular or plural, countable or uncountable.

Tip: Be sure to remember that singular, countable nouns always take an article (*"a,""an,"* or *"the"*).

The meaning is also different:

- As indefinite articles, *"a"* and *"an"* are general in meaning. This means that the reader (or listener) does not know which one the writer is talking about, or that something is being described generally as a member of a group:

He bought **a car**.

She is **a partner** in **a large law firm**.

You, the reader, do not know which car he bought, nor do you know which large law firm she works at. This is what we mean by *"indefinite."*

When we say that she is **a partner**, we are saying that she is a member of a general group or category: the category of lawyers known as "partners." If we write "She is **a professor**," or "She owns **a cat**," she is a member of the general category *"professor,"* and her pet is a member of the general category *"cat."*

- As the definite article, *"the"* is specific in meaning. This means that the reader (or listener) *does* know which one the writer is talking about. It is knowledge that the writer and the reader share.
- This knowledge may be common to everyone (e.g., we all know what "the sun" is) or just to the writer and the reader or listener (e.g., both of us know which book is on my desk because both of us are sitting in my office).
- Often, this common knowledge is provided by the context of the writing or speaking, as in the example above.

Context may be provided by referring to the noun a second time:

Mark filed **a motion. The motion** asked the court to dismiss the case with prejudice.

In the first sentence, we do not know which motion Mark filed — it could be any motion. In the second sentence, however, we now have some context. Because of the first sentence, we know that we are talking about one specific motion — the motion that Mark filed.

Another way to make nouns specific is to use a phrase that restricts or limits the meaning of the noun. We often use a prepositional phrase beginning with "*of*" for this purpose:

> **the owner** of the vehicle
> **the president** of the condominium association
> **the corner** of the building

Here, prepositional phrases beginning with "*of*" restrict or limit the meaning of the noun. They help us to know "which one" we are talking about:

> Which owner? (the owner of the vehicle)
> Which president? (the president of the condominium association)
> Which corner? (the corner of Michigan Avenue and Ontario Street)

These restrictive phrases can often (but not always) be written as possessives:

> the vehicle's owner
> the condominium association's president
> **Note:** "the streets' corner" sounds unnatural.

Many writers prefer to use the possessive form for people (e.g., "John's case"), and the "*of*" form with things, places, or ideas (e.g., "the beginning of the trial").

Not all phrases that begin with "*of*" restrict or limit the meaning of the noun, however. Instead, they are often used with "counters," which are countable nouns that help to measure or define uncountable nouns. Commonly, these "counters" are words that refer to an amount or a part of something uncountable. When we use one of these phrases, we use "*a*" or "*an*":

a liter of water	**a kilogram** of sand	**an act** of violence
a piece of evidence	**a cup** of coffee	**a pound** of rice

We can also use restrictive dependent clauses beginning with "*that*" to make a noun specific:

the motion that Mark filed	**the contract** that you signed

In these examples, the restrictive clause "that Mark filed" tells the reader which motion we are discussing, and the restrictive clause "that you signed" tells the reader which contract we are discussing. Because the reader knows which motion and which contract are being discussed, those nouns are specific, and take "*the*."

2. The Difference Between "A" and "An"

You have probably learned years ago that we use "*an*" with nouns that begin with vowels (*a, e, i, o, u*) and "*a*" with nouns that begin with consonants (the other letters of the alphabet). Then you probably learned that there are exceptions involving the letters "*u*" and "*h*," depending on how those letters are pronounced.

Here's a simpler way to state the rule, which eliminates the exceptions:

- We use "*a*" before words than begin with consonant sounds and "*an*" before words that begin with vowel sounds.

Most of the time, the sound is the same as the spelling, but not in the cases of "*u*" and "*h*":

- "*U*" can be pronounced as a vowel (the "ə" sound, pronounced "*uh*"), as in "*ultimatum*," or "*underwriter*." Words that begin with this sound take "*an*":

an ultimatum	an underwriter

- "*U*" can also be pronounced as a consonant (the "*yoo*" sound, which begins with the consonant "*y*"), as in "*university*" or "*unit*." Words that begin with this sound take "*a*":

a university	a unit

- "*H*" can be silent. This means that the first sound of the word is pronounced as a vowel because the "*h*" is followed by a vowel sound, as in "*honor*" or "*heir*." Words that begin with this sound take "*an*":

an honor	an heir

- "H" can also be pronounced as a consonant (simply by being pronounced), as in "*hazard*" or "*heart*."Words that begin with this sound take "*a*":

a hazard	a heart

3. Proper Nouns (Names) and "The"

The general rule is that proper nouns (names) do not take articles. We say, "My name is John Smith," not "the John Smith" (*incorrect*). There are, unfortunately, many exceptions to the rule. While a complete review would take too long, here are some common examples:

- Use "*the*" before plural family names, and many plural proper nouns, such as island chains or mountain ranges:

the Thorntons	the Hawaiian Islands	the Himalayas
the Joneses	the Canaries	the Alps

- Use "*the*" before longer names of countries, universities, etc., that contain "*of*" in the title, but usually not in the short name:

the People's Republic of China, but China
the Federal Republic of Germany, but Germany
the University of Notre Dame, but Notre Dame
the University of California at Los Angeles, but UCLA

- With countries, use "*the*" when the country's name includes certain political terms such as "*United*," "*Union*," "*Kingdom*," or "*Republic*":

the United States	the Dominican Republic
the United Kingdom	the European Union

4. Questions to Ask When Deciding Which Article to Use, If Any

As we have recently discussed, sometimes we use the articles "*a*," "*an*," and "*the*," and sometimes we do not. Also, the articles have specialized meanings: "*a*" and "*an*" are used with singular, countable nouns that are general in meaning, whereas "*the*" is always specific in meaning. Unlike "*a*" and "*an*," however, "*the*" can be used with any type of noun — countable or uncountable, singular or plural.

Thus, whether you speak a language that always uses articles with nouns, or a language that has no articles at all, the English article system can be difficult and challenging. Because frequent article mistakes are annoying and potentially confusing for legal readers, it is important to do the best you can to use articles accurately. The best way to do this, especially when you are proofreading, is to ask yourself a series of three questions for each noun that you have written.

Here are the three questions that you should ask yourself:

1. Is the noun countable or uncountable?
2. Is it general or specific?
3. Is it singular or plural?

If the noun is countable:

- Is it general or specific?

If it's specific, use "*the*":

The car that he bought is used.

The cars that they bought are used.

(In these sentences, "the car" and "the cars" are specific because the restrictive clauses "that he bought" and "that they bought" tell the reader which car we are discussing.)

- If it's general, is it singular or plural?

If it is singular, use "*a*" or "*an*":

I bought **a book**.

(In this sentence, "*book*" is singular and countable, so it requires an article. It is general because the reader does not know which book I bought. Therefore, use "*a*.")

If it is plural, do not use an article:

I like **books.**

(In this sentence, "*books*" is plural and countable. It is general because the meaning is very general: I like books generally, and am not talking about a specific book.)

If the noun is uncountable:

- Is it general or specific?

If it is general, do not use an article:

Violence is a major problem in our society.

(In this sentence, "*violence*" is general and uncountable. It is general because the meaning is very general: Violence is a major problem generally, and I am not talking about a specific act of violence.)

If it is specific, use "*the*":

The violence after they announced the verdict was shocking.

(In this sentence, "*violence*" is specific and uncountable. It is specific because the restrictive clause "after they announced the verdict" tells the reader which acts of violence we are discussing.)

EXERCISE 17 D

The following passage is excerpted from an assignment memo to an associate at a law firm. The assignment memo introduces the facts of the case to the associates and asks the associate to research a legal issue.

The plaintiffs in the case are the Rileys, a married couple from the United States who went on a safari vacation in Africa, were badly injured while on safari, and sued the safari operator and its parent company.

The passage is missing articles. Fill in the blank with "a," "an," "the," or "X" (no article).

___ Rileys, who had always dreamed of visiting _____ Africa and going on ___ safari, saw ___ attached advertisement promoting ____ Wyatt Kilimanjaro Safari Lodge and its safari adventures, and they decided to fulfill ____ lifelong dream and to book ____ safari vacation in Tanzania in March 2012. In particular, ____ Rileys wanted to take ___ spectacular safari in Ngorongoro Crater, ____ world's largest intact inactive volcanic caldera, to see its amazing wildlife.

___ Rileys booked the vacation. Everything was fine until they took ____ tour of Ngorongoro Crater. There is only one winding narrow one-lane dirt trail that goes down from ____ rim of ___ Crater to its floor, and another one-lane dirt road that goes back up for ____ vehicles that are leaving ____ Crater. In their complaint, ____ Rileys allege that it was raining that day, leaving ____ dirt trail muddy and slippery, and ____ driver was driving dangerously fast down ____ narrow dirt trail. ____ Rileys were involved in ____ accident near ____ bottom of ____ trail that goes down to ____ Crater floor. Sean Riley broke both of his legs and now walks with ____ cane, and Sarah Riley injured her spine and is now ____ paraplegic. She is in ___ wheelchair, and ____ doctors believe that she will never walk again. Among other allegations, ____ Rileys assert that ____ tour guide and driver never told them to wear their seatbelts while they were driving down to ____ bottom of ____ crater.

D. PROBLEMS WITH PLURALS

There are two types of mistakes that attorneys who speak English as a second language commonly make with the plural forms of nouns:

forgetting to add the plural ending where it is necessary, and incorrectly making uncountable nouns plural.

1. Watch for Missing Plural Endings with Countable Nouns

As you know, English requires plural nouns to have plural noun endings. Typically, it's formed by adding "-*s*" to a noun:

book, books	jurisdiction, jurisdictions	contract, contracts

There are, of course, exceptions to the general rule:

- If the noun ends in *s, ss, x, z, ch*, or *sh*, we form the plural with "-*es*":

box, boxes	class, classes	wish, wishes

- If the noun ends in *y* and is preceded by a consonant, *y* changes to *i* and we add "-*es*":

lady, ladies	country, countries	fallacy, fallacies

- If one-syllable nouns end in *f* or *fe*, the *f* is changed to *v* and we add "-*es*":

knife, knives	thief, thieves	wife, wives	life, lives

- There are certain irregular plurals:

child, children	man, men	woman, women	tooth, teeth

- Nouns that are derived from other languages such as Latin often take the original plural form of that language, although some of them are changing over time to regular English plurals:

-*us* becomes -*i* (alumnus, alumni; stimulus, stimuli; syllabus, syllabi)
-*um* becomes -*a* (datum, data; memorandum, memoranda; forum, fora)

-is becomes *-es* (crisis, crises; parenthesis, parentheses; thesis, theses)

-on becomes *-a* (criterion, criteria; phenomenon, phenomena)

-ex, *-ix* becomes *-ices* (index, indices; appendix, appendices)

Some attorneys now use English plural forms for several of these words:

memorandums	forums	indexes	appendixes

Tip: When you use a word before the noun that indicates that the meaning is plural, such as *"three," "many," "both,"* or *"several,"* make sure that the noun has the proper plural form:

both jurisdictions	many objections	several motions

Tip: When you make a general statement, you are not speaking about one person, place, thing, or idea, but about many of them. Therefore, make sure that the countable nouns are plural:

Defendant should not make statement to the media. (*incorrect, incorrect*)

The correct answer:

Defendants should not make statements to the media.

2. Do Not Make Uncountable Nouns Plural

As we discussed above, uncountable nouns cannot be plural because they cannot be counted. In order to count them, we need to use "counters." Make counters plural, not uncountable nouns:

The police collected many evidences during their search. (*incorrect*)

The correct answer:

The police collected **many pieces** of evidence during their search.

EXERCISE 17 E

Some of the sentences below are correct, while others have errors with singular-plural forms. Write "OK" if the sentences are correct, and fix the singular-plural problems where they exist.

1. Many lawyer make too many objection while defending deposition.

2. The migrant workers harvested tomato pursuant to an agreement with the grower.

3. Their advices were very useful for us.

4. All of the evidence that the plaintiffs presented was consistent with the testimony of Bill and Mary.

5. Both crisis occurred during the President's first term.

E. WATCH FOR BASIC PUNCTUATION ERRORS

While there are many types of punctuation errors that legal writers can make, this section will focus on common types of errors that lawyers who speak English as a second language often make. These errors involve problems in understanding what a sentence is.

1. Sentence Fragments

As you likely know, a sentence must contain a subject and a verb, and it must express a complete idea. Although we call English a "subject-verb-object" language because that is the most common sentence structure, a sentence may contain as few as two words:

He died.

This sentence has a subject ("he"), a verb ("died"), and it expresses a complete idea. However, this is not a sentence:

Because he died. (*incorrect*)

This is not a sentence (even though it is longer than the first sentence) because the word "*because*" makes the idea incomplete. This incorrect sentence is called a "fragment" because it only expresses part of an idea.

"*Because*" makes this a dependent (subordinate) clause. A clause is a group of words with a subject and a verb. The independent (main) clause contains a subject, a verb, and a complete idea, so it may function independently as a sentence. A dependent clause, on the other hand, cannot function as a sentence because it must be connected to an independent clause. Words like "*because*" are called subordinating conjunctions, because they turn clauses into dependent (subordinate) clauses.

Here is a list of common subordinate conjunctions:

although	who	before
because	which	while
unless	whose	after
if	that	when
though	where	since
even though	why	whenever
	how	as soon as
		until
		ever since[8]

Watch out for sentence fragments. If you begin a sentence with a subordinating conjunction like "although" or "because," be sure to write a sentence with two clauses: the dependent clause beginning with that word, and the independent clause that completes the idea:

> **Although** he did not want to sign the contract, Mr. Smith believed that he had no choice.

2. Comma Splices and Run-On Sentences

Unlike a sentence fragment, in which a part of a sentence is punctuated as a complete sentence, comma splices and run-on sentences are two different sentences that are improperly punctuated as one sentence:

> He is an attorney, he lives in Chicago. (*incorrect*) (comma splice)
>
> He is an attorney he lives in Chicago. (*incorrect*) (run-on sentence)

- A comma splice occurs when two independent clauses (i.e., two sentences) are joined together with a comma, but without a conjunction.
- A run-on sentence occurs when two independent clauses (i.e., two sentences) are joined together without any punctuation or conjunction between them.

There are several ways to fix these problems. One way is to add a coordinating conjunction:

[8] Allen Ascher, *Think About Editing: A Grammar Editing Guide for ESL Writers* 244 (Heinle & Heinle Publishers 1993).

and	but	or	yet	nor

He is an attorney, **and** he lives in Chicago.

A second way to fix the problem is to use a semi-colon instead of a comma:

He is an attorney; he lives in Chicago.

A third way to fix the problem is to simply write the two independent clauses as two sentences:

He is an attorney. He lives in Chicago.

EXERCISE 17 F

Some of the sentences below are correct, while others have punctuation errors — they may be fragments, comma splices, or run-on sentences. Write "OK" if the sentences are correct, and add the proper punctuation or rewrite the sentences if they are not.

1. Although the plaintiff had a famous lawyer. The defendant won.

2. The defendant made a motion for judgment as a matter of law, the judge denied the motion.

3. If you want to meet Bob, who is the district attorney.

4. I think you should know that Ms. Jenkins, who has been your attorney for this matter, no longer works with Fayre Dinkum & Goode LLP.

5. You should ask Mary she worked on that case last year.

Chapter Review

- Checking your grammar as you write, and proofreading it throughout the writing process, is essential for all lawyers, and this is even more true when English is your second language.
- Work product that is filled with mistakes is unprofessional and leads to a loss of credibility.

- English has many verb tenses that show a precise focus on time and time relationships. We have the simple tenses (past, present, and future), the perfect tenses (past, present, and future), the progressive tenses (past, present, and future), and the perfect progressive tenses (past, present, and future).
- The simple past tense refers to a finished action that occurred in the past, and is typically used with a past time.
- We use the simple past tense when describing precedent (i.e., cases that are finished), and when describing completed events with a past time marker such as "last week." We also use the past tense to describe completed events in an ongoing case (e.g., "The Defendant breached the contract when it refused to deliver the goods at the price that the parties had agreed on.")
- The simple present tense refers to an action that is occurring, in formal court language ("We move to dismiss, Your Honor"); to make general statements of fact; to describe habits; and with a future time to indicate a plan ("The train leaves at 9 p.m. tomorrow").
- We use the simple present tense for all of these purposes, and for stating rules of law.
- The simple future tense expresses the future. We use the future tense to discuss and/or to predict future events, such as how a court will likely rule.
- The perfect tenses show a relationship between two times, such as one time before another time in the past (past perfect); a completed past action with no given past time and the present (present perfect); and an action that began in the past and continues until the present (present perfect).
- The progressive tenses show that an action was in the middle of occurring at a given point in time in the past (past progressive); is in the middle of occurring now (present progressive); and will be in the middle of occurring at a given time in the future (future progressive).
- The perfect progressive tenses show a continuing relationship between two events, whether in the past, the present, or the future.
- Be careful with forming the negative and interrogative (question) forms of each verb tense. When we use an auxiliary verb with a negative, the time and person changes are made on the auxiliary verb, not the main verb (e.g., "did not study," *not* "did not studied" (incorrect)).
- Check for subject-verb agreement problems, especially with third-person singular subjects.
- Uncountable nouns require singular verbs, as do many indefinite pronouns such as "*anybody*," "*everyone*," and gerunds (nouns that use "*-ing*," such as "*swimming*.")

- Certain verbs that express advice (such as "*recommend*") take a special form involving "*that*" + subject + base verb (no endings).
- English uses the articles "*a*," "*an*," and "*the*" in most but not all situations.
- "*A*" and "*an*" are always used with singular, countable nouns that are general in meaning. By "*general*," we mean that the reader does not know which person, place, thing, or idea the writer is discussing.
- "*The*" is used with any kind of noun — singular or plural, countable or uncountable — but it is always specific in meaning. This means that the reader knows which noun the writer is discussing.
- The reader knows which noun the writer is discussing because it is a universally-known object, the context makes it clear, or a phrase or a clause identifies which noun is being discussed.
- We count uncountable nouns with words called "counters."
- When checking to see if you have used the correct article, ask whether the noun is countable or uncountable, general or specific, and singular or plural.
- Make sure that plural countable nouns have the correct plural form, especially in general statements.
- Check to be sure than uncountable nouns do not have a plural ending, although they may be preceded by a plural "counter."
- All sentences must have a subject and a verb, and they must express a complete idea. Check for sentence fragments, which are incomplete because they do not have all three of these.
- Check for comma splices, which place just a comma between two different sentences, and run-on sentences, which have no punctuation between them.
- Comma splices and run-on sentences can be fixed with a semi-colon, a period, or a comma and a coordinating conjunction such as "*and*."

Chapter 18

EDITING UNNECESSARY LANGUAGE AND CHECKING FOR PROPER LEGAL VOCABULARY, ACTIVE VOICE, AND ACTION VERBS

Chapter Preview

This chapter continues to discuss editing skills that help international lawyers to improve their legal writing in English. The chapter focuses on two areas where lawyers from civil law systems and from other legal cultures frequently have difficulty. These problem areas include:

- removing unnecessary phrases and language;
- removing wordy and pompous language;
- removing legalese; and
- checking to make sure that we are using the proper verbs to describe the actions of parties, trial courts, and appellate courts.

In Chapter 10, we discussed the rhetorical style of U.S. legal writing. In that chapter, we learned about the "writer-responsible" nature of U.S. legal writing. We saw that the responsibility for clear communication rests with the writer, and that the writer should write with the belief that the legal reader is "more important" than he or she is, because the legal reader is often likely to be a more senior lawyer, a judge, or a client.

We described how the writer shows respect for the legal reader by communicating clearly, precisely, and efficiently, with subject-verb-object sentences, action verbs, and concrete vocabulary instead of passive voice and abstract words. The writer also shows respect for the legal reader by writing in plain English. This means avoiding legalese, frequent nominalizations, and long, confusing sentences that legal readers must reread several times to understand.

In this chapter on editing your writing, we will revisit these ideas in more detail, and give you practice in editing your writing so that it follows this style better. We will also discuss editing your writing to make sure that you are using the appropriate vocabulary for the U.S. legal system, and especially the court system.

A. AVOIDING UNNECESSARY LANGUAGE

As a profession, lawyers have a reputation for loving the sound of our own voices. The general public often accuses us of being long-winded, and speaking in overly long and complex sentences that they cannot understand. In particular, they complain about the vocabulary that we use — abstract language, Latin phrases, legalese such as "*herein*," and vocabulary that they do not understand.

If we're honest with ourselves, we must admit that there is some truth in those criticisms. The traditional language of lawyers *is* incomprehensible to the average citizen. We have rationalized that the complex language is needed for precision, but that's often untrue. Lawyers have traditionally used such language partly because that is what we learned to do, and partly because it makes us sound sophisticated and highly educated. Many lawyers seem to think that if we speak in a way that most people cannot, they will know that they need to hire us, and they will be impressed by us.

Over the past 40 years or so, lawyers in the United States have tried to address these issues by adjusting how we speak and write — thus, the plain English movement. We also work to make writing as brief and efficient as possible. There are several reasons for this. It is not only a way to show respect for the legal reader by getting to the point quickly. It is also because clients do not want to pay for documents that are longer than necessary, and because courts in the United States often have strict page or word limits that require lawyers to be very economical with their language. Try to persuade the court that your client is right about three different legal issues in 15 double-spaced pages! It is very difficult, and requires you to eliminate every unnecessary word.

1. Avoiding Unnecessary Introductions and Commentary

Different languages and legal systems have different rhetorical styles. Lawyers from many countries often begin their writing with long introductions, and use frequent phrases that provide commentary on their ideas:

> It is worth mentioning that
>
> What must be considered is that . . .
>
> It goes without saying that . . .
>
> It is interesting to note that . . .
>
> It is worthwhile for us to consider . . .
>
> It is important to remember that . . .
>
> It must be concluded that . . .
>
> It is important to understand that . . .
>
> The first thing that that we must consider is . . .
>
> I am of the opinion that . . .
>
> After carefully researching the statutes and the case law, I have come to the conclusion that . . .
>
> It is necessary to consider . . .

These phrases may occasionally be acceptable in U.S. legal writing, but are generally unnecessary and ill-advised. It's best to avoid them because legal readers generally consider these introductory phrases to be unnecessary padding. They do not care what you think is "interesting" or "worth mentioning." They assume that *everything* the writer tells them is important and necessary — otherwise, why would the writer waste their time?

Lawyers from civil law countries also frequently make the mistake of introducing legal rules that come from case law with commentary: "In *Smith v. Jones*, a landmark Second Circuit case, the court devised the following test for . . . ." It's usually better to simply state the rule without commentary. There's no need to tell the legal reader in the text whether a rule comes from a statute or case law because the citations do that for you. There is also no need to comment upon the level of the court — the legal reader sees that instantly when he or she reads the citation.

If you frequently use these introductory phrases or comments in your legal system and language — especially if you have been doing so for several years or longer — it can be hard to change this habit. That's OK. Just remember to look for them when you proofread your writing, and remove them.

2. Avoiding Pompous Language and Legalese

Also, look to edit out pompous, stuffy "lawyerly" vocabulary:

Pompous Words	**Better Alternatives**
allocate	give, divide
ascertain	make sure
cease	stop
contiguous to	next to
cognizant of	aware of, knows
forthwith	immediately
notwithstanding	despite
numerous	many
subsequent to	after
substantiate	prove
utilize	use

Many of these words are used mostly by lawyers, particularly lawyers who want to impress people with their vocabulary. This kind of pompous, stuffy language annoys judges and other legal readers, and it may confuse juries or clients who are not lawyers, so it's wise to edit it out of your writing and speaking.

Another type of pompous language is wordy phrases that use three to six words to say what can be said perfectly well in one or two words:

Wordy Phrases	**Better Alternatives**
at this point in time	now
at that point in time	then
because of the fact that	because
during the course of	during
for the purpose of	to
in close proximity	near
in light of the fact that	because, given that
in the event that	if
owing to the fact that	because
with reference to	about, concerning

Here's a good rule to remember: one word is better than two words, and four words are better than eight words. In other words, if you have a choice between using fewer words or more words, *fewer words is better.*

A third type of pompous, stuffy lawyer language is used almost exclusively by lawyers, and has earned the pejorative label of "legalese":

Legalese

aforementioned, aforesaid

behoove

hence, henceforth

hereby, herein, hereinafter, hereto, heretofore, hereupon, herewith, etc.

thereby, therein, thereof, thereon, thereto, thereunder, thereabout, etc.

whereby, wherein, whereupon

thence, thenceforth

"said" as an adjective ("the said contract," "the said accident," etc.)

"same" as a pronoun ("Buyer shall sign the Agreement on or before June 30 and deliver same to Seller . . .")

"such," referring to a previously-described noun ("He bought such car the next day . . .")

The trend seems to be for lawyers to use less legalese these days, but many lawyers continue to use it, particularly in contracts, where the continued use of older contracts as models for new ones tends to keep these words in use. As we shall see in the chapter on contract drafting, there is a wide variety of practice in many types of contracts, but contracts where consumers are parties now must be written in plain English.

My advice: avoid legalese in most legal writing, such as in memos, briefs to the court, or letters to clients. When drafting contracts, limit the use of legalese unless you are working for a lawyer who uses it extensively. In that case, wise associates understand that their key "client" is really the partner that they are working for!

When editing and proofreading your work, make sure that your sentences follow the plain English format. Make your average sentence 25 words or less; use active voice and action verbs; follow the subject-verb-object pattern in most of your sentences; and avoid unnecessary phrases, wordy and pompous language, and legalese.

3. Limiting Passive Voice and Non-Action Verbs

As we discussed in Chapter 10, lawyers in many countries are very fond of passive voice. In legal English, however, we prefer the active voice, because it is shorter, more direct, and it clearly states who does what to whom. Passive voice can be useful, such as when you want to distance your client from a negative event ("Mistakes were made"); when the active voice subject is either unknown or very obvious; or when you wish to focus attention on the word that would be in the object position in an active voice sentence.

That said, it's best to avoid passive voice in legal English unless you have a specific reason for using it, such as the ones listed above. Do not let yourself use the passive voice habitually. If you find it in your writing and cannot explain to yourself why you are using it, remove it.

Finally, look at your verbs as you proofread. In addition to checking for the proper verb tense and subject-verb agreement, look at the verb you have chosen. Is it a specific, concrete action verb or is it a weak verb like "*to be*," "*to do*," "*to have*," or "*to make*"? If it is, try to rewrite the sentence with an action verb. For example, write "The defendant moved to dismiss the case" instead of "The defendant made a motion to dismiss the case."

EXERCISE 18 A

Revise and edit these sentences to remove unnecessary language, including introductory commentary, wordy and pompous phrases, legalese, passive voice, and non-action verbs.

1. It is important to point out that under the Worker's Compensation Act, the term "employee" shall be liberally construed.

2. A lack of supervision may be inferred by the nonexistence of directions from the supervisor for whom the service was rendered.

3. Also, the driver was instructed by the company as to the hour in which he had to depart to the customer's location and deliver the products.

4. The said contract, entered into by the parties for a term of 10 years, was signed by the CEOs of each party.

5. The defendant's motion to dismiss was denied by the court.

6. At this point in time, it is necessary to consider the issue and to reach a decision.

7. After carefully researching the statutes and the case law, I have come to the conclusion that the chances of success for the defendant's motion for summary judgment are small.

8. Subsequent to the hearing, the attorney informed her client of the court's decision to grant the injunction.

9. It must be concluded that Ace Technologies will likely be found to have been negligent.

10. In light of the fact that the case was dismissed with prejudice, we should ponder as to whether an appeal would be appropriate.

B. CHECKING FOR PROPER U.S. LEGAL VOCABULARY

Incorrect U.S. legal vocabulary, especially relating to the courts, is another problem that you should look for when proofreading. Your first approach may be to think of the words that you use to describe courts and what judges do in your first language, and to translate that into English. As we've said before, that approach leads to trouble.

When you think first in your native language and then translate, you tend to write with the rhetorical style, vocabulary choices, word order, and even grammar of your native language, but with English words. The problem: that is not really English! Linguists use the term "interlanguage" to describe this kind of output. People sometimes colloquially refer to the result as Spanglish, Chinglish, Japlish, Korenglish, Hinglish, etc. — a mix of the two languages that leaves you in the middle of the ocean, rather than on the ground in your law school in the United States.

Civil law systems around the world tend to use vocabulary for judicial rulings that is quite different from what the U.S. legal system does. Even other common law systems sometimes use different vocabulary to describe what judges and parties do. Thus, if you use vocabulary imported from your language when referring to the actions of judges in federal or state courts in the United States, it will often be confusing and inappropriate, and it will make little or no sense to U.S. lawyers. Thus, the time to find and fix the problem is during the proofreading stage, before the legal reader ever sees it.

The following verbs are appropriate to describe what the courts and the parties do. Note that many verbs apply only to the parties or to one type of court (either a trial court or an appellate court), while some verbs apply to both trial courts and appellate courts:

Only parties:

allege	**prove**
assert	**demonstrate**
claim	**show**
argue	**move**

Only trial courts:

find facts

dismiss motions or complaints

grant motions or summary judgment

Only appellate courts:

affirm or **reverse** factual findings, decisions, judgments, verdicts, the granting of motions or summary judgment

remand cases to the trial courts or lower appellate courts

Both trial courts and appellate courts:

hold, rule, conclude, reason, explain

You may sometimes see other verbs used to describe what the courts or the parties do, but these are commonly-used, important verbs that are safe to use once you understand what they mean.

As we discussed earlier, do not worry about repeating the same verbs — lawyers need to be precise, and do not care about "elegant variation." Learn how to use these verbs accurately, and stick with them.

EXERCISE 18 B

In the sentences below, the verbs that describe what the courts and parties do are sometimes used correctly and sometimes used incorrectly. If they are used correctly, write "OK," and if they are used incorrectly, substitute an appropriate verb.

1. The court argued that the defendant had been negligent in its hiring practices.

2. The Northern District of Illinois judge affirmed that the defendant had infringed the plaintiff's trademark.

3. The Second Circuit remanded the case to the trial court.

4. The judge alleged that the defendant had run the red light.[1]
5. The plaintiff held that the law was unconstitutional.

Chapter Review

- Proofreading should go beyond looking for mechanical errors such as grammar problems, punctuation errors, or spelling mistakes. It should also include improving the quality of your writing by making sure that your work has the appropriate style for U.S. legal readers.
- Avoid the following inappropriate writing features:
  - Unnecessary introductory phrases such as "The first thing that must be considered is . . ." ;
  - Unnecessary introductory phrases that introduce rules that come from case law;
  - Frequent use of long sentences of more than 25 words;
  - Frequent use of abstract language;
  - Pompous vocabulary;
  - Wordy phrases;
  - Legalese;
  - Habitual, predominant use of non-action verbs; and
  - Passive voice.
- Use the following writing features:
  - Plain English;
  - Sentences that are usually 25 words long or less;
  - Active voice;
  - Action verbs; and
  - Concrete language.
- Make sure that you use the appropriate verbs when describing the actions of:
  - Parties;
  - Trial courts; and
  - Appellate courts.

[1] To "run" a red light is an idiom that means to drive through the intersection illegally while the light is red.

Chapter 19

OVERVIEW OF LEGAL RESEARCH

Chapter Preview

This chapter provides an overview of how to conduct legal research in the U.S. legal system. The chapter focuses on:

- getting the "big picture" before you begin to research an issue;
- pulling a source and using it to find other sources if you already have a citation;
- beginning your research with secondary sources;
- deciding when to do online research and when to use books;
- using free online legal resources;
- running searches to research primary authority; and
- understanding and using citators.

Legal research is a fundamental skill that every lawyer in the United States must possess. It is often taught in U.S. law schools by a combination of law librarians, research attorneys from the main online legal research providers (LexisNexis, Westlaw, and Bloomberg Law), and the legal writing professor, and many entire books have been written on the subject. Therefore, this chapter is not intended to cover legal research in depth. Rather, it provides a broad overview of the topic, which should give you some background and help you to prepare for the more specific legal research classes that you will have in law school.

As an international LL.M. student, you will likely not need to develop your U.S. legal research skills as completely as a J.D. student would. Nevertheless, you will still need to do some legal research while you are a law student at a U.S. law school. For example, you may want to "pull" (get) some cases or statutes that you have read in an edited form in your textbooks or heard about in your classes, and to read the complete case or statute for yourself. You may also decide to take a seminar class, where you write a paper that requires significant legal research instead of taking a final examination.

Some of you may sit for a state bar exam and practice law in the United States for a year (or even longer). Thus, you need to know how to do legal research in the United States. Indeed, it is difficult, if not impossible, to gain a complete picture of the U.S. legal system until you have learned how to do legal research and gained some experience doing it.

A. GETTING THE BIG PICTURE

Before you research U.S. law, it is important to understand what we call the "big picture." This has several factors: understanding the size of the body of U.S. legal authority; understanding the end use of the particular legal research; determining the type(s) of law and the jurisdiction(s) involved; and understanding both the amount of time that you have in which to do the research and the depth of the research that the supervising lawyer expects.

1. Understanding the Size of the Body of U.S. Law

Until you have begun to research it, it is difficult to understand just how huge the body of primary authority is in the United States. There are several reasons for this:

- First, the country has the world's third largest population, and by far the largest number of lawyers in the world.
- Second, Americans are the world's most litigious people. We frequently sue each other when people in most other countries would not.
- Third, we have well-developed bodies of both federal law and law for each of the 50 states, as well for as other territories such as Washington, D.C. and Puerto Rico.
- Fourth, unlike civil law countries, our body of primary authority is not restricted to a constitution, a statutory code, regulations, and treaties. We

also count case law as primary authority, and usually must review it when we conduct legal research.

- Fifth, the sheer volume of law in each of these areas is immense. For example, the Code of Federal Regulations fills many bookshelves, and there have been millions of state and federal cases.
- Sixth, due to the nature of the common law, the law in any given area is constantly evolving, and attorneys must check to be sure that the law has not changed recently. This is true of statutes as well as case law. Unlike many civil law systems, which update their codes at regular, predictable intervals, state legislatures and the U.S. Congress may amend existing statutes without a set schedule. For example, one statute may be amended several times within a relatively short time span, while another may not be amended for a long period of time.

As a result of all of this, conducting legal research in the United States is quite challenging and time-consuming. According to a recent independent survey that the Research Intelligence Group conducted, new associates spend an average of 14.5 hours per week on legal research, which constitutes about 31% of their time (and associates in practice for less than two years spend even more time on legal research — about 35% of their time).[1] They divide that time as follows: 7.7 hours of research online with the major online research providers, 4.5 hours of free or low-cost online research, and 2.1 hours of research using books or other printed materials.[2] We will address all three types of legal research later in the chapter.

2. Understanding the End Use of the Research

Legal research is used for many different purposes, and at many different stages of litigation or a transaction. For example, research often occurs at the beginning of the representation to help attorneys to understand the strengths and weaknesses of their clients' position, and to plan strategy. Such research may either be broad-based or narrowly tailored to consider a specific issue. In either case, the research is used to evaluate the client's case and to plan strategy. The substantive law that the researcher finds may not be used immediately, and it may never be used, if the attorneys conclude that a contemplated strategy is unlikely to succeed.

Research that is conducted at a later stage of litigation or a deal may be used immediately in a motion, brief, trial, appeal, contract, or negotiation. The research is often narrower and more targeted, and the results may be needed more quickly.

3. Determining the Law and the Jurisdiction(s) Involved

Clients come to attorneys with legal problems and certain facts, and it is the attorney's responsibility to determine which legal issues are involved, whether federal and/or state law is involved, and which jurisdictions are involved. If a transaction

---

[1] Steven A. Lastres, *Rebooting Legal Research in a Digital Age* 3 (Aug. 10, 2013), available at http://www.llrx.com/authors/1225.

[2] *Id.*

occurred between parties from different states, for example, which state's law applies, and where should the lawsuit be filed?

If a partner is giving a research assignment to an associate, the partner will likely explain much of this information, but not all of it. For example, the partner might state that the case involves a breach of contract claim or a negligence claim, but he or she will probably not provide all of the relevant terms of art that apply to that particular area of the law, and that assist the associate in his or her research. It will be the associate's responsibility to determine what the relevant terms of art are, and to use those terms in the research.

4. Understanding the Scope (Time and Depth of Research)

Before beginning research, the associate must know the scope of the research assignment. How soon does the partner want the answer — by the end of the day, or by the end of the week? Should the associate provide an oral answer, write an email memorandum, or write a formal office memorandum? Does the attorney want a "quick and dirty" answer, a "scorched earth" search where the associate researches exhaustively and at length, or somewhere in between those two extremes? Approximately how many hours should the associate spend on the research? Associates must have answers to these questions before they begin their research.

B. BEGINNING THE RESEARCH

As we discussed earlier, there are two major ways to research: (1) pulling a case, statute, secondary source, etc. by using a citation that you already have, and (2) conducting legal research without having a source with which to begin.

1. Pulling a Source by Using a Citation

Often, when partners give an assignment, they mention the name of a case or a statute that they know, and associates use that as a starting place for their research. Let's return to our hypothetical problem from Chapter 7, in which your law professor (or the partner, if you are practicing law) has assigned you to do legal research for a legal problem where two similar products have similar names (in fact, as in the *Brennan's* case, the parties share the same family name). Is there a likelihood of confusion under the Lanham Act between the first product and the allegedly infringing product? The professor or partner may mention Section 43(a) of the Lanham Act, which is codified at 15 U.S.C. § 1125, or he or she may give you the name and perhaps the citation for the *Brennan's* case. How can we use these to begin our research?

First, we can enter the source's citation into the search box. These days, Lexis Advance™, Westlaw Next™,[3] and Bloomberg Law® all have search boxes that

---

[3] Lexis Advance™ and Westlaw Next™ are the new generation of search platforms by LexisNexis and Westlaw. Their older platforms, Lexis.com and Westlaw Classic, are still currently functioning, but are being phased out and are expected to function only for another few years.

resemble the Google® search box. All searches begin with the search box, whether you have a citation or not.

You do not need a complete, full citation in the Bluebook or ALWD citation format. For the *Brennan's* case, all you need to write is 360 F.3d 125 (in Lexis Advance™ and Westlaw Next™, you can even write it without proper capitalization, punctuation, or spaces as "360f3d125"). If you only have the name of the case, you can search for it that way as well, but it's easier to use the citation if you have it. Similarly, for the Lanham Act section, you would only need to write 15 USC 1125 (the periods in U.S.C. and the symbol for "section" are not necessary).

Lexis Advance™ and Westlaw Next™ have headnotes; Bloomberg Law® does not. You can find a relevant headnote, such as the headnote that includes the eight-factor *Polaroid* test for the likelihood of confusion, and click on it.

Because both *Brennan's* and *Polaroid* are Second Circuit cases, you can click on a link and find all cases within the Second Circuit that show that particular headnote (Lexis Advance™ shows 34 cases and Westlaw Next™ shows 35). You can also change the jurisdiction, and find opinions from other federal circuits that contain the same headnote.

You can also use a statute section as a way to find cases. If you go to 15 U.S.C. § 1125 on any of the three online search providers, you will find case **annotations,** which are summaries of cases that interpret that statute section.[4] Hopefully, at least one of the annotations is a case from the jurisdiction that you are researching.

Another way to use a known source is to look through the cases that have cited to it, which we will discuss in more detail later in the chapter.

2. Researching Without a Particular Source

Often, you will not have the luxury of beginning with a relevant source. In that case, you will need to frame and to design a search, and to decide whether to research online or to use books. All of these issues are covered in more detail below.

C. BEGINNING YOUR RESEARCH WITH SECONDARY SOURCES

When you are experienced in an area of U.S. law, it often makes sense to begin searching primary law immediately — cases, statutes, etc. Experienced lawyers know the relevant terms of art that apply to that area of the law. If you are researching an area of the law with which you are unfamiliar, however, it makes more sense to begin with a secondary source. If you are an international LL.M. student who is learning about the U.S. legal system, you should always begin with secondary sources!

---

[4] As of October 2013, Lexis Advance and Westlaw Next have annotations for all types of state and federal statutes. Bloomberg Law currently has annotations for securities, tax, and intellectual property statutes, and it is in the process of providing annotations for other statutes.

Even if you are reasonably familiar with a certain area of the law, it is still a good idea to begin by using secondary sources if you are having trouble thinking of relevant terms of art for your search. Secondary sources are a great way to gain background information about an area of the law. Depending upon the type of secondary source, there may also be case annotations. Even if there are no annotations, the background information may provide you with several terms of art that you can use to craft a better search.

There are many types of secondary sources, with varying levels of sophistication. In general, it is much better to cite to primary sources of law than to any secondary source, even the most sophisticated. However, certain types of secondary sources may be cited, particularly when you cannot find a primary source for the same proposition. These secondary sources include Restatements, uniform or model statutes, and highly respected treatises.

Restatements provide descriptions of what the law is or should be, according to a panel of experts in that area of the law. Restatement provisions are not considered primary authority unless courts adopt them or legislatures codify them.

Uniform or model statutes are similar. They are often adopted wholly or with minor revisions by the states. For example, the Uniform Commercial Code ("U.C.C.") has been adopted either exactly or with minor revisions by 49 out of 50 states. Although model or uniform statutes are primary sources of law in the jurisdictions where they have been adopted, practicing lawyers in that jurisdiction should then cite to them with the citation that they have acquired after their adoption.

A treatise is a multi-volume series of books that provides a sophisticated summary of a given area of the law, such as *Corbin on Contracts*, *Collier on Bankruptcy*, *Cyclopedia of the Law of Private Corporations*, *Wigmore on Evidence*, *Moore's Federal Practice*, or *Couch on Insurance*. Treatises also contain case annotations.

American Law Reports ("A.L.R.") and law review articles provide very useful background information and may be cited if no other source can be found. Other types of secondary sources, such as legal encyclopedias, hornbooks, nutshells, and information from websites may provide valuable background information, but should generally not be cited.

A.L.R. articles exist for both federal law and state law, and the topics are quite specific. The articles provide annotations to many different jurisdictions, and they are very useful if you can find one that is **on point** (directly relevant to your legal issue).

Law review articles are long articles about a specific legal topic that are filled with footnotes, many of which contain citations to primary authority. The articles are typically written by law professors and practicing attorneys, although law students sometimes write short articles called Notes or Comments.

American Jurisprudence 2d (usually called "Am Jur") and *Corpus Juris Secundum* (usually called "C.J.S.") are both massive multi-volume legal encyclopedias that provide comprehensive coverage of state and federal law with case annotations. Although they are a very useful way to gain information about an area of law, to learn terms of art that will help in a search, and to find annotations, they should not be cited.

Many states also have their own state-specific legal encyclopedias.

Hornbooks and Nutshells are one-volume summaries of an area of law that are frequently used by law students. They typically do not have annotations and may not be cited.

D. DECIDING WHEN TO DO ONLINE RESEARCH AND WHEN TO USE BOOKS

Most of the secondary sources listed above (except hornbooks and Nutshells) are available on the major online research providers. Given this fact, and given their preference for computers and the internet, many law students and some young lawyers do all of their legal research online, ignoring books and other printed materials. This is a mistake for several reasons.

First, if the law firm or law school already has the books and other printed materials in its library, they are a free legal resource. Although law students have free access to the major online research providers, law firms do not. For firms, using books and other printed materials is a way to keep down legal research costs.

Second, books and other printed materials can sometimes be easier to use, and equally efficient or even more efficient. For example, if you are researching in a broad area of the law such as contract law, the book form of *American Jurisprudence 2d* has an entire volume devoted to contract law. You can go to the contract law volume's index, and quickly turn to any of hundreds of sections. You can also browse through the book, possibly finding relevant material that would not fit the language of any searches that you might design.

When reviewing *American Jurisprudence 2d* online, however, a typical search may yield only one or two sections, and you are not able to see the other sections, which may potentially be more relevant than the one(s) your search has located, unless you run a new search. This principle holds true equally with treatises.

There is a way around this problem, however. The largest online providers have table of contents sections which enable you to see and find all of the sections — you just need to know how to find them. For example, you can find the table of contents for *American Jurisprudence 2d* in Lexis Advance by clicking on "Browse Sources," going to "Search Sources," typing in "American Jurisprudence 2d," and finding a link to the table of contents. You can do the same thing on Westlaw Next by clicking on "Secondary Sources," then "Texts & Treatises," then American Jurisprudence 2d," and that will bring you to the table of contents.

The online table of contents for *American Jurisprudence 2d* is similar to the table of contents for the United States Code: it shows the major parts of the topic, and then you can click on them, and it will break that down until you see the names of the individual sections. Similarly, the online table of contents for the United States Code first shows the 51 titles of the code, which are separate legal topics. The titles break down into chapters and then into sections and sub-sections. The same general principle applies to the statutes of each of the 50 states, and you can do table of contents searches for them online as well.

Given all of that, many experienced attorneys find it easier and quicker to reach for a volume of an encyclopedia, treatise, or annotated code in book form. Remember what we said earlier in the chapter: according to the survey, the average new associate still spends slightly over two hours per week researching in books and other printed materials. It is reasonable to believe that associates who use books more often than their peers will have happy assigning partners, as partners frequently complain about how young associates neglect books these days, thus missing on-point cases, and waste firm resources with excessive online research spending.

E. USING FREE ONLINE LEGAL RESOURCES

There are many free online legal research resources. Usually, they tend to be less comprehensive and easy to use than the commercial online legal research resources. Nevertheless, they are free or relatively inexpensive. Accordingly, as we saw earlier in the survey, young associates spend an average of 4.5 hours per week using free or low-cost online research resources to keep research costs down. This is especially likely on smaller matters, with highly cost-sensitive clients, or for law firms which "eat" the expense of online legal research as an overhead cost and do not bill the client.

If you are an international lawyer studying in the United States, these free websites will become very useful to you when you return home to your country and no longer have free access to commercial online legal research resources such as LexisNexis, Westlaw, and Bloomberg Law.

Free and low-cost online research resources include LexisOne, Findlaw, Google Scholar, Open Jurist, the Legal Information Institute at Cornell, the Library of Congress, Thomas (a government website that gives access to statutes and bills from the past 40 years), and many government websites such as state and local government websites, state and federal court websites, and administrative agency websites.

Lawyers also sometimes begin their legal research by running searches on Google to see if they can find any free background information or terms of art that are relevant to their research topic. Then they move on to the commercial services.

Although the internet has many free sources of legal information available, they are of varying quality and not all are accurate. For example, law firms often place articles about a legal topic on their firm websites as a way to attract clients, and that information is likely to be accurate. However, certain people (often non-lawyers) who are passionate about a legal topic may spread a great deal of misinformation. There is no quality control on the internet, so lawyers who do Google searches need to think carefully before trusting what they find there. Generally, Google searches should be used only as a quick and low-cost tool before one begins to use trusted legal content providers such as LexisNexis, Westlaw, and Bloomberg Law.

F. RUNNING SEARCHES TO RESEARCH PRIMARY AUTHORITY

As we said before, if we do not have the name or citation for a case or statute to begin with, we need to frame and run a search.

In general, it is important to use as many legal terms of art as possible — trying to run a search where the language is filled with facts but not legal terms often leads to disappointing results, with many irrelevant search results and few if any relevant ones. Thus, as stated above, if we do not have many terms of art, it is best to run a search first that looks for secondary sources, to hopefully obtain more terms of art.

1. Running a Broad Search, Then Filtering

How do we do this? As we discussed above, Lexis Advance™ and Westlaw Next™ both now have search boxes that look similar to Google search boxes. The search always starts there. In earlier versions, you would specify the jurisdiction that you were searching, but today the default pattern is to run a broad search that covers virtually all of the provider's databases, including primary and secondary sources.

Then, after obtaining an overly-broad result, often with thousands of results or more, it is easy to "filter" the search through a series of steps. For law firms, each "filtering" step is free. For example, if the search results include cases, statutes, and secondary sources, you can click on one of them, such as secondary sources. You can filter it again to look for only one kind of secondary source, such as certain treatises or legal encyclopedias.

Research typically relates primarily to one jurisdiction. For example, if our trademark problem is set in New York City, we can filter the results to include only cases, and then only federal appellate cases, and then only Second Circuit cases (because Second Circuit precedent is binding for the Southern District of New York, the federal trial court in New York City where a trademark infringement claim would likely be brought).

Other ways to filter searches include by date. Lawyers often filter a search to include only results for the most recent two or three years, for example. Lexis Advance™ offers an interesting feature called "timeline." It provides a graph that shows periods of greater and lesser activity with a given legal issue. You can click on the graph to filter the results according to the busiest period of time, when the most cases were decided.[5]

2. Natural Language Searches and Boolean Searches

With all of the online research providers, legal researchers can run two kinds of searches: natural language searches and Boolean searches.

a. Natural Language Searches

A natural language search sounds like what it is: the researcher writes the search in regular English. There are several ways to do this: the researcher can write the search as a question, as a sentence, or as phrases. In the past, this led to broader and

[5] The number of cases that deal with a particular legal issue often increases greatly for several years after a major change in the law caused by a new or amended statute, or by a landmark decision that changes the law. Then, after the law becomes settled again, the number of cases declines.

less reliable searches, because the computer could not "understand" the meaning of the language and would just look for the occurrence of those individual words. In other words, the computer would see "word OR word," etc. If you wanted the computer to "read" a group of words as a phrase, you would put the phrase in quotation marks, such as "likelihood of confusion."

Today, Lexis Advance™ and Westlaw Next™ are more sophisticated, and better able today to read certain phrases without quotation marks, particularly legal terms of art such as "likelihood of confusion." They also have more sophisticated algorithms that increase the likelihood that the results listed first are actually the most relevant results. That said, it is still prudent to use quotation marks for phrases, to make sure that they will be read correctly. Also, it is not necessary to use articles (*a, an, the*).

For our legal issue, here are some possible natural language searches:

1. Is there "likelihood of confusion" under "Lanham Act" when 2 marks have similar names but products are not identical?

   Results with Lexis Advance™: 8,437,359 results, 2,940,922 federal cases

   Results with Westlaw Next™: 51,459 results, 425 cases

2. "likelihood of confusion" "lanham act" similar name product different

   Results with Lexis Advance™: 4,074,411 results, 1,546,594 federal cases

   Results with Westlaw Next™: 47,226 results, 378 cases

3. Trademark Polaroid "family name" logo

   Results with Lexis Advance™: 71,608 results, 51,459 federal cases

   Results with Westlaw Next™: 25,137 results, 75 cases

The numbers here look very different, but the approaches are likely less different. Lexis Advance™ shows its complete results (thus, numbers in the millions in the first two searches), and Westlaw Next™ shows a more filtered result. In both cases, the most relevant results are featured first. No one will look at millions, thousands, or even hundreds of documents, so we would then begin the filtering process to reach more targeted results. Where the results numbers are very high, it may make sense to revise the search terms to make it more specific even before beginning to filter the results.

As for the three natural language search queries, the first one is closest to pure natural language, but it eliminates articles and the question mark, and it puts "likelihood of confusion" and "Lanham Act" in quotation marks to be sure that the search engine will read them as phrases. The second one is similar, but just uses phrases.

The third query takes a different approach. It uses "Polaroid" as a search term because the relevant eight-factor test for the likelihood of confusion comes from the landmark *Polaroid* case. It also gets a bit more specific with the facts, adding "family name" because in our problem, the parties share the same family name. Perhaps it is not surprising that this search yields the most targeted results.

b. Boolean Searches

A Boolean search is different from a natural language search in that it uses symbols to tell the search engine what to do. For example, an exclamation mark at the end of a word is called a root expander, and it tells the search engine to look for all forms of that word. "Similar!" would include "similarly," "similarity," and "similarities." A slash mark and a letter or number tells the search engine to look for a term within a certain distance of another term: "/s" means "within the same sentence"; "/p" means "within the same paragraph"; and "/3" would mean "within three words." As in mathematics, when terms are inside of parentheses, they should be used together, and first.

Unfortunately, although most of the terms are similar, there are some differences of "search grammar" between Lexis Advance™ and Westlaw Next.™ For example, Westlaw Next™ reads a space between words as "or," whereas Lexis Advance™ requires you to write "or." Similarly, where Westlaw Next™ uses the ampersand (the "&" symbol), Lexis Advance™ requires you to write "and."

Here are examples of Boolean searches for our problem:

1. "likelihood of confusion" /p mark /15 identical and "lanham act"

   Results with Lexis Advance™: 4,074,411 results, 1,546,594 federal cases

   Results with Westlaw Next™: 47,226 results, 378 cases

2. Lexis Advance™: "likelihood of confusion" and "lanham act" and (similar! or same or identical /3 name) /25 (item or product /6 different! or (no or "not" /5 same or similar! or identical))

   Westlaw Next™: adv: "likelihood of confusion" & "lanham act" & (similar! same identical /3 name) /p (item product /6 different! (no not +5 same similar! identical))

   Results with Lexis Advance™: 64 results, 27 cases

   Results with Westlaw Next™: 381 results, 91 cases

Again, as with the natural language search, the most relevant results are featured first for both research systems. No one will look at millions, thousands, or even hundreds of documents, so we would then begin the filtering process to reach more targeted results.

Of the two Boolean searches, the second one is more targeted and provides much lower numbers, so it would be wise to start with those results. However, it would also make sense to review the first several results of the broader search to see if the results are different. Did the first search find cases that the narrower one did not?

Overall, although natural language searching has improved greatly in recent years, it still makes sense to use the narrower, more targeted approach that Boolean searching can provide, particularly when you have more legal terms and search terms to work with. Natural language searches may make more sense when you have few terms of art to use.

G. UNDERSTANDING AND USING CITATORS

A **citator** is a key feature of the three large commercial search providers. It tells the researcher whether the primary authority that the researcher is viewing is still **good law**: whether, if the primary authority is a case, it has been reversed or overruled, or if it is a statute, it has been held unconstitutional, superseded, repealed, or amended.

When a lawyer supports an assertion with legal authority, he or she is telling the judge that the case or statute is still good law. If a lawyer knowingly cites to a source that is no longer good law, it is an ethical violation that can get the lawyer in serious trouble, leading to a fine or perhaps a suspension.

1. Shepardizing, KeyCiting, and BCiting

All primary authority on LexisNexis, Westlaw, or Bloomberg Law contains a citator symbol. That is, the document contains a symbol that provides a summary of how it has been treated in subsequent cases or other legal authority. If you click on the symbol, you can go to the listing of the cases or other legal authority that comments upon the case or statute.

The first citator was called Shepard's, and it provided this information in a large set of books. Although no one uses the books anymore, lawyers often still refer to the process of checking on the status of a case or statute as "Shepardizing." Today, LexisNexis owns the rights to Shepard's, and to the term "Shepardizing." Westlaw calls their version "KeyCite," and Bloomberg Law calls theirs "BCite."

The only symbols to really worry about are the red ones: Shepard's has a red stop sign, KeyCite has a red flag, and BCite has a red square with a negative sign in the middle. These symbols tell the legal reader that the case or other legal authority that they are viewing is no longer good law for at least one part of the document. For example, if the document is a case, it could mean that the entire case has been overruled, but it often means that just one holding of the case has been overruled, and the other holdings are still valid.

If you are looking at a case that has a red symbol on it, telling you that it is no longer good law, you must determine why it is no longer good law, and to what extent. If the holding that you want to cite to is still good law, you may use the source in a citation, but you must follow the citation with a parenthetical explanation that cites to the case that partially overruled it, e.g., "(partially overruled on other grounds by CITE)." In general, most lawyers would prefer to avoid a "tainted" case like this entirely, but they will cite to it if they cannot find another case to support the assertion.

You should also look to see if a case has been distinguished, and if so, why. The symbols are yellow for Shepard's and KeyCite, but BCite has a blue square with a check. Check to see if the case has been distinguished by a higher court in the same jurisdiction, which may have the effect of narrowing the scope of the opinion. If the case is distinguished by a court in a different jurisdiction, it is less important.

2. Using Citators to Find New Cases

As we have learned, when you Shepardize a case, you are looking at what later cases have said about it. Presumably the more recent cases have dealt with similar issues (although perhaps not the issue that interests you). Therefore, they may be relevant to your issue. If you find a case that is relevant, check the cases that cite to it and check to see if they are also relevant.

Look especially at the symbols for depth of treatment, which refers to how much time the later case spent discussing the earlier case. The symbols range from four bars for an extended discussion, to one bar for just a citation. The more bars, the more discussion there is.

Chapter Review

- Legal research is difficult and challenging in the United States because there is such a massive volume of law: federal law, law for each of the 50 states and certain territories, enacted law, and case law. With millions and millions of cases, it can be quite challenging to thoroughly research the law.
- Before you begin to research, understand the end product that the research is designed to help (advice to a client? Case strategy? Legal authority to support our client's position in a brief?).
- Make sure that you understand the issue that you are supposed to research, and what the relevant jurisdiction is.
- Also understand when the work is due, and what form your answer should take (oral summary? Email memo? Traditional office memorandum?).
- Finally, understand how deep they expect the research to be (quick and dirty; exhaustive, "scorched earth" research; or something in between?), and how many hours the research and writing should take.
- If you have the name and/or citation for a case, or the name and/or citation for a statute, begin there. Pull the case or statute. If it is a case, use the headnotes and citator to find other cases. If it's a statute, use the case annotations after the statute.
- As an international LL.M. who is still learning about the U.S. legal system, begin your legal research with secondary sources such as legal encyclopedias, treatises, or A.L.R. For treatises and legal encyclopedias, consider using the book rather than the online resources. This is especially true when you practice law, as existing books are free.
- Free online legal resources are a way for lawyers to keep legal research costs down, but they are generally not as complete or convenient as the major online legal research providers such as LexisNexis, Westlaw, or Bloomberg Law. They will be useful for you when you return home, as you will no longer have free subscriptions to LexisNexis, Westlaw, or Bloomberg Law.
- When you run a search on these providers, begin with a broad search through all of their databases, and then narrow your search results by using filters, which can narrow the jurisdiction, the type of source, the date, etc.

- The main types of searches are natural language searches and Boolean searches. Although natural language searching has improved in Lexis Advance™ and Westlaw Next™, it still usually yields broader results. It often works best as a first search when you have few terms of art.
- Boolean searches involve special symbols that tell the search engine what to do, such as "/s" or "/5." They often yield more targeted searches with better results.
- Be sure to Shepardize your research. In other words, check the citator to make sure that your case or statute is still good law.
- You can also use citing references from the citator to find more cases.

Chapter 20

WORKING IN U.S. LAW FIRMS

Chapter Preview

This chapter describes life in U.S. law firms and provides advice on how to communicate with partners, associates, staff, and clients. The chapter discusses the following:

- a brief history of U.S. legal employers;
- the structure of U.S. law firms;
- the culture of U.S. legal employers;
- communicating with partners;
- communicating with associates, paralegals, project assistants, other staff members, and your assistant;
- communicating with clients;
- work assignments; and
- billing time.

This chapter discusses legal practice settings in the United States, especially in law firms and in-house positions with the legal departments of corporations. It is important for all international LL.M. students at U.S. law schools to know about the culture and practices of U.S. lawyers and their work settings, regardless of your exact future plans.

Many of you may take a state bar examination, in New York or in other states, and hope to find a position as an international intern with a U.S. law firm in New York or another major city. Some of you may take the bar examination and then practice permanently in the United States, or for a longer period of time. For either of these groups, learning about legal practice in the United States is essential.

Others may work in your country at an international office of a U.S.- or U.K.-based law firm. Still others may work at a law firm in your country as local counsel for a U.S.- or U.K.-based law firm on an international business transaction, or you may work with a U.S.- or U.K.-based law firm that serves as local counsel for your law firm on an international business transaction. Finally, a U.S.- or U.K.-based law firm may work with your law firm as co-counsel or as opposing counsel on an international transaction.

In any case, part of the power of your international LL.M. from a U.S. law school is that you can add value as someone who is a "U.S. expert." This expertise can be far broader than just knowing U.S. law. It also involves understanding U.S. legal and business cultures and practices. In short, you can save deals that might be in danger of collapsing due to cross-cultural misunderstanding or mistrust because you can understand how and why U.S. lawyers or business people act the way they act.

This chapter provides information about U.S. law firms and in-house legal departments. Second, it talks about the work environments there. Third, it gives you advice on how to meet and exceed expectations if you work there.

A. A BRIEF HISTORY OF U.S. LEGAL EMPLOYERS

As we learned, the United States began as a British colony that used the common law system, and lawyers worked alone in solo practices. Solo practices continued after the U.S. won its independence. Law firms — practices with two or more lawyers working together as partners — began in the United States around the middle of the 19th century, and then spread to England.

Similarly, large law firms began in the United States in the late 19th century.[1] Regulations kept British firms at fewer than 20 lawyers until 1967, and they began to grow greatly in the 1980s after a loosening of the regulations restricting U.K. law firms, which has resulted in four of the five "Magic Circle" firms becoming huge.[2]

---

[1] Eli Wald, *Smart Growth: The Large Law Firm in the Twenty-First Century*, 80 Fordham L. Rev. 2867, 2868–69 (2012).

[2] Bruce E. Aronson, *Elite Law Firm Mergers and Reputational Competition: Is Bigger Really Better? An International Comparison*, 40 Vand. J. Transnat'l L. 763, 792–93 (2007).

1. Size of the Legal Market

The United States is the world's largest legal market. According to the American Bar Association, the U.S. has most lawyers of any country: there were 1,268,011 lawyers in 2012.[3]

The United States also has the highest number of large law firms. In 2008, about 700 U.S. law firms employed 50 or more lawyers, 23 firms had more than 1,000 lawyers, and the average number of lawyers for the 250 largest law firms was 535.[4] The number of U.S. law schools has doubled in the last 50 years to approximately 200, and the number of lawyers, the number of large law firms, and the size of large law firms has exploded during that time.

2. Law Firm Growth

Large law firms have greatly increased in size due to (1) national and transnational law firm mergers, and (2) internal growth. For example, DLA Piper, the world's largest law firm, had over 4,200 lawyers as of October 2013.[5]

An extensive series of law firm mergers, first at the national level and then at the international level, led to the formation of DLA Piper. The current form of the firm was formed in 2005 by a merger between three firms: San Diego-based Gray Cary Ware & Freidenrich LLP, Chicago-based Piper Rudnick LLP, and London-based DLA LLP.[6]

The world's second-largest firm, Chicago-based Baker & McKenzie, was the world's first international law mega-firm. It used the internal-growth model, growing by opening new offices instead of by merging with other firms. Baker & McKenzie had more than 4,100 qualified lawyers as of October 2013, in 74 offices that are in 46 countries.[7]

Baker & McKenzie now has about 3,800 attorneys in 70 offices in 42 countries. Two of the three most recent Chairs of the Executive Committee have been international lawyers: Christine Lagarde (now head of the International Monetary Fund) and Eduardo Leite.[8]

Even large U.S. firms that have not merged or gone international have grown greatly in size. For example, Jenner & Block, LLP, a national law firm headquartered in Chicago and with offices in New York, Washington, D.C., and Los Angeles, went

---

[3] ABA Lawyer Demographics, 2013, *available at* http://www.americanbar.org/content/dam/aba/migrated/marketresearch/PublicDocuments/lawyer_demographics_2013.authcheckdam.pdf.

[4] Bernard A. Burk & David McGowan, *Big but Brittle: Economic Perspectives on the Future of the Law Firm in the New Economy*, 2011 Colum. Bus. L. Rev. 1, 12 (2011).

[5] DLA Piper Global Home, http://www.dlapiper.com/home.aspx (last visited Oct. 7, 2013).

[6] Dash, Eric, *Two Law Firms to Join Forces*, N.Y. Times, Oct. 19, 2004, available at http://www.nytimes.com/2004/10/19/business/19law.html?_r=0.

[7] Baker & McKenzie Firm Facts, http://www.bakermckenzie.com/firmfacts/ (last visited Oct. 7, 2013).

[8] *See id.*

from about 35 lawyers in Chicago in the early 1970s to over 500 lawyers across the U.S. today.[9]

3. In-House Counsel

The growth in the number of in-house counsel at corporations did not equal that of law firms until recently. Corporations generally kept their legal departments small and gave most of their legal work to outside counsel (i.e., law firms).

Since the economic contraction caused by the financial crisis of 2008, however, the situation has reversed: while law firms have either grown very little or even shrunk, in-house legal departments have grown more significantly, as corporations have sought to decrease their legal bills by using less expensive in-house counsel to do work that was formerly done by outside counsel. Many experienced lawyers who have been laid off by their law firms since 2008 have found work as in-house counsel.

4. Changes in Legal Practice

In the past several decades, the diversity of the legal profession has greatly increased in terms of sex, race, and ethnicity. For example, 50 years ago, there were very few female law students; today, approximately 50% of law students are women.[10] Although the number of practicing women lawyers has increased, it is still not 50% yet.[11]

As the money has increased, the workload has increased, as has law firm productivity, due in part to computers and online legal research. Also, the competition for clients has greatly increased, as many corporations are no longer loyal to one law firm, or a small number of them. Today, corporations may have law firms compete to represent them in major litigation, and they also may use large law firms only for the most expensive matters, while using smaller and more inexpensive counsel for smaller matters.

Many have said that law has become more of a business and less of a profession. This is supported by changes in legal employment: In the past, lawyers often stayed with one firm for their entire careers. That is rarely true today. Because of the high turnover at large law firms, with associates frequently leaving after two to three years, firms are becoming more reluctant to train young lawyers and then see them leave. This is bad for associates, who have less mentoring and training at the firms, and are more on their own. New associates are expected to "hit the ground running," which is not completely realistic.

In short, young lawyers today should not trust that their law firms will continue to provide them with ongoing training and to continue to give them good work. You need to find and develop mentors on your own, and find the type of legal work that you

---

[9] *See* Jenner & Block Firm History, available at http://www.jenner.com (last visited Oct. 7, 2013).

[10] ABA Lawyer Demographics, 2013, *available at* http://www.americanbar.org/content/dam/aba/migrated/marketresearch/PublicDocuments/lawyer_demographics_2013.authcheckdam.pdf.

[11] *See id.*

want to do. Take charge of your own career!

B. THE STRUCTURE OF U.S. LAW FIRMS

U.S. law firms, like law firms in many countries, are very hierarchical organizations. Although seniority is important, the most powerful partners are the ones with "the biggest books of business" — the partners who are responsible for generating the most revenue by bringing in the most lucrative clients.

In the past, firms usually had one partnership "track" — all partners were "equity partners." In other words, they owned a share of the partnership, and shared in the firm's profits and losses. Now, most large U.S. firms now have two partnership tracks. The partners with the biggest books of business are equity partners who share firm profits. Newer partners, who generally have fewer clients but are expected to develop more business, are called "income partners." These partners are paid a salary and do not have a share of the firm's profits and losses.

Different firms have different types of income partners, and different relationships between equity partners and income partners. For example, at some firms, all newly-made partners are initially income partners. They are given a certain amount of time to develop business, and then are either promoted to equity partner or fired.

At other firms, lawyers may remain income partners for the rest of their careers at the firm. Also, equity partners who no longer bring in sufficient business to justify their ownership share may be "de-equitized." If this occurs, they either accept the demotion to income partner or leave the firm. In some cases, they may not be able to remain at the firm as income partners.

These changes are partly driven by the profit per partner statistic, which is published and which lawyers with large books of business find quite interesting. Law firms are worried that they will lose their partners with the most clients to other firms that offer higher profits per partner. As a result, they need to do what they can to maximize their own profit per partner. This results in a "thinning of the herd," as attorney salaries are typically a law firm's largest expense. Law firms can increase their profit per partner by firing associates and under-performing partners. The associates may have lower evaluations than their peers, or they may be in a department that is less busy.

1. Partners and Partner Pay

Although income partners have regular salaries and do not share firm profits, their salaries are typically higher than even senior associate salaries. Equity partners have different-sized shares in the firm according to the size of their book of business. As a result, the highest-paid partners make many times as much money as the lowest-paid partners.

According to the American Lawyer, for the 100 largest law firms in the United States in 2013, the highest-paid partners earned on average 10.5 times as much as the lowest-paid partners.[12] This business model has been called "eat what you kill," but no partners are going hungry. The average income of equity partners is over one million dollars per year in many large firms, and several million dollars at the most elite firms.

When lawyers become equity partners, they typically must invest money in the firm (becoming "stakeholders"), like making a down payment on a house. Many firms help them to finance the capital contribution.

2. Of Counsel

Senior lawyers who are not partners are called "of counsel." The term may be used in a wide variety of ways by different law firms. Some of them are similar to independent contractors, and they have their own clients. Others have few or no clients, and are considered worth keeping but not worthy to make partner. Those lawyers are dependent on other partners for business, much as associates are. Still others are semi-retired partners who stay on in a part-time or reduced capacity.

As a result, when you meet firm lawyers who are "of counsel," it can be somewhat difficult to understand their place in the hierarchy.

3. Staff Attorneys and Outsourcing

Traditionally, associates who did not make partner at a law firm after 7 to 9 years as an associate were fired, although a small number might become "of counsel." This system is referred to as "up or out," and some law firms still use it.

Recently some firms have retained useful attorneys whom they do not consider "partner material" by creating a new class of counsel called "staff attorneys." These attorneys do discovery work, legal research, and simple motions and briefs for low salaries — often significantly less than the salaries of first-year associates.

Firms also outsource document reviews to "contract attorneys," who are independent contractors who work for one project, for $30 to $40 per hour or less, often for only three or four weeks. Document reviews are also done by computers that are programmed to look for certain terms, or they are outsourced to other countries where the labor costs are much lower.

In recent years, disappointed by the quality of work that has been outsourced to other countries, some large American law firms have created "back offices" of lower-paid attorneys in smaller U.S. cities with lower costs of living. Since large document reviews tend to be electronic these days, it is irrelevant where the reviewers live.

---

[12] Debra Cassens Weiss, *These Big Law Firms Had the Highest Spreads in Partner Compensation*, ABA Journal Weekly Newsletter (June 19, 2013), http://www.abajournal.com/news/article/these_biglaw_firms_had_the_highest_spreads_in_partner_compensation/.

C. THE CULTURE OF U.S. LAW FIRMS AND IN-HOUSE DEPARTMENTS

Although each law firm or in-house department has its own unique culture, some general observations apply to most U.S. legal employers. If you work for a large legal employer in your country, you will probably be happy to hear that the culture in law offices here and the culture in law offices at home may be similar, but that does not mean that it is the same — relatively small differences can be important.

1. Law Firm Hierarchy

In the United States, as in many other countries, law firms are very hierarchical organizations, with many levels of management and authority:

- a chairman / chairwoman / chairperson / chair;
- an executive committee, typically comprised of the most powerful partners, including the managing partner;
- partners on other key committees;
- other corner-office partners;
- mid-level partners;
- junior partners;
- "of counsel" attorneys, whose rank in the hierarchy may vary somewhat from individual to individual and from firm to firm;
- senior associates;
- mid-level associates;
- junior associates; and
- staff attorneys.

In a sense, no two lawyers at a firm share the exact same rank in the hierarchy. Partner power varies according to factors such as the size of the book of business, the level of control over key clients (exclusive or partial), the number of hours billed in a year, and relationships with the most powerful partners, as well as the other partners in the partnership. Associate ranking depends on factors such as seniority, the number of hours billed in a year, the quality of the yearly evaluations, and the quality and depth of the relationships with powerful partners and the partnership in general.

It's relatively easy to learn about large differences in power, such as whether a lawyer is a department head, a committee member, a corner-office partner, a mid-level partner, or a junior partner; or perhaps an equity partner or an income partner; or a senior associate, a mid-level associate, or a junior associate.

It's more difficult to learn about smaller differences in rank, but it is worth the effort that it takes to do so. It is important to your future to learn who the "key players" are and to pay attention to the details and the etiquette of the hierarchy. For example, when sending an email to several lawyers in the firm, it is important to list their names in order of hierarchical rank.

Hierarchy in U.S. law offices is generally shown by the architectural floor plan: The most powerful and senior attorneys have corner offices (and are thus called "corner-office partners"). Mid-level partners may have bigger offices than junior partners. All partners generally have bigger offices than associates. Except perhaps in New York City, most associates have offices with windows.

Assistants (formerly called "secretaries") usually have desks in the hallways, unless they are executive assistants for the most senior partners. In that case, they may sit in the senior partner's outer office, if there is one. Paralegals and project assistants have small interior offices without windows and/or may share offices.

Compared to other countries, relationships between senior and junior attorneys may seem more egalitarian in the United States. Many international LL.M. students have said that they are surprised by how much and how easily associates here speak with partners; how there are few if any obvious physical signs of deference, such as bowing to the more senior attorney or keeping one's eyes down; and by how attorneys here call each other by their first names, including the chairperson of the firm.

Do not be fooled, however: everyone here knows what the hierarchy is, and junior lawyers are deferential to more senior lawyers. Although it may *appear* as if partners and associates talk together like equals, looks can be deceiving!

2. Firm Culture: Tips for Success

Most law offices in the U.S. now have a "business casual" dress code every day, not just on Fridays. Wear "business attire" (i.e., suits) on your first day of work, or if you are meeting clients or other non-firm people at a conference or another type of meeting. Litigators wear suits in court, for depositions, or when meeting clients. It's a good idea to keep an "emergency suit" hanging in your office in case you need to have business attire on short notice.

If you are not meeting with people from outside of the firm or going to court, you can — and should — dress in business casual clothing. That said, do not be overly casual. Clothes should look professional, and the attorney should be well-groomed. Associates should not wear flip-flops, sneakers, or other unprofessional shoes, and women should dress fairly conservatively.

You can ask associates at the firm for advice about clothing or just observe others. In general, regarding clothing and all forms of behavior, watch what successful associates actually do — it's even more important than what they *say* they do.

Depending upon your culture, you may need to make some adjustments in your physical behavior. For example, we do not show respect by looking down or keeping our heads down in the United States. If there is no eye contact, a speaker in the United States will likely feel uncomfortable and perhaps even disrespected. He or she might misinterpret your behavior, thinking that you are painfully shy and lacking in self-confidence, or perhaps even bored.

Look and sound confident when you talk to more senior attorneys. If you look like you have no confidence in yourself, they will have no confidence in you. That said, don't look arrogant or cocky — be respectfully, quietly confident.

Men and women do not have obviously different "gender roles" in a law firm. Treat men and women the same, with equal respect, and without different behavior due to gender.

A key aspect of respect is timeliness. Being on time is an essential, fundamental part of being a professional in the United States. Americans are very conscious of time, and are annoyed and perhaps even insulted if you are late. *Always* be early or on time. Never be late for a meeting, and respond to telephone calls and emails quickly.

If you have been invited to a partner's house for dinner, what do you bring, and when do you arrive? The answer may depend on whether it is a catered event for a large group of associates and interns, (perhaps all new associates and international interns have been invited), or a more personal invitation (perhaps just yourself and the firm's other new international intern have been invited, along with your partners[13]). Ask other associates and staff about the nature of the event, and what is expected.

If it's a catered firm event, be on time. You do not need to bring anything. If it's more personal, consider bringing flowers and/or a bottle of wine. Do not arrive early, but do not be late for a dinner party. If you are approximately 10–20 minutes late, it is called "politely late"; more than that isn't polite.

D. COMMUNICATING WITH PARTNERS

In the United States, as in all countries, efficient attorney communication is an essential part of successful legal practice. The general rules are likely to be similar everywhere, but details may be different.

1. Obvious Rules

The first rule for all lawyers (especially junior lawyers) is that you must be available and respond quickly. **Always** be early or on time, for everything and anything. Always submit your work assignments early or on time, and if an "emergency" assignment from another partner may cause your work for the first partner to fall behind schedule, make sure that both partners are aware of the situation. It may be best for the partners to work the schedule out between themselves.

At meetings, set your smart phone to vibrate when you receive an email, and respond quickly when possible (chimes annoy partners during meetings). Check your phone frequently for messages and pay attention to deadlines. Partners have been known to send non-essential emails Saturday evening to test your response time. If you respond quickly, they are pleased, and may say that the matter can wait until Monday.

---

[13] In this context, "partners" refers to romantic partners, such as husbands, wives, boyfriends, or girlfriends.

When you leave the office even for a day, set up "out of office" email and voicemail messages.

2. Less Obvious Rules

Sometimes, what partners say and what they mean are two different things. For example, during new attorney orientation, you may hear "we don't believe in 'face time' here. If you're not busy, you don't have to sit in your office all day."

Do not believe this! Even if you're not busy, you should generally be at work during "business hours," e.g., 8 a.m. to 6 p.m. (the hours will vary slightly from firm to firm and depending on the partner you work with the most). If a partner wants to talk to you and you're not in the office, that's not good for you, especially during business hours. They may learn not to trust you, and they may be less likely to call you again for future work.

Talk to other associates and find out when you are expected to arrive at the office and leave for home, how late you are expected to respond to communications (e.g., until 11 p.m.?), and how they want you to let them know when you're sick. For example, is it enough to tell your assistant that you are not feeling well and will work from home, so that he or she will tell the partners that you are working with, or should you directly inform them by email yourself? Keep in mind that different junior attorneys may have wildly varying styles and approaches — some may arrive later and leave later, and others may arrive earlier and leave earlier. Choose whom to ask wisely, and model yourself more after the associates that the partners like and trust.

These little "unwritten rules" may vary somewhat from firm to firm, and even from practice group to practice group within a large law firm. Often, different practice groups have different "group personalities." For example, the litigators may be more aggressive, and the employment law attorneys may be more easygoing.

3. Be Proactive

In your country, partners and associates may communicate less frequently than they do here. You need to be proactive with communication to serve both the partner and the client well. Do not always wait to hear from partners when you need to communicate with them.

If you do not understand what the partner wants you to do, ask questions to clarify the meaning. This is essential! Do not assume that the problem is language-related. Partners are often very busy and in a hurry, with many issues on their minds. They often think less about how to speak to associates than they do about how to speak to clients, judges, or opposing counsel.

Watch associates who were born in the United States. They often ask for clarification. If you misunderstand and do the "wrong" work or something that they do not want, that's a problem, so it's better to ask when you are not sure. If you do inappropriate work, partners have to "write off" your time, which can affect their compensation. They are not happy if you cost them money!

That being said, it is important to find a balance, because partners find it annoying when associates ask "too many" questions and want the partners to "hold their hand." Learn to determine which questions are directly related to the assignment and must be answered by the partner. Find others to answer the smaller or more procedural questions: senior associates or other associates working on that deal or matter; senior staff, such as experienced paralegals; or your assistant. Depending upon the question, all of these people may be able to provide the answer that you need without your bothering the partner.

E. COMMUNICATING WITH ASSOCIATES, PARALEGALS, PROJECT ASSISTANTS, OTHER STAFF MEMBERS, AND YOUR ASSISTANT

1. Communicating with Other Associates

Other associates are a valuable resource to help you to "learn the ropes" at a new legal job. Ask them how to get things done when you do not know how to do something.

Especially, ask them about the partners that you work for. Each partner has his or her own likes and dislikes, and they can be extreme, so it is important to learn them quickly. Find out about their work styles, expectations, and personalities. Ask how that partner likes to communicate, how to work with him or her, and what not to do. Watch what experienced, successful associates do and act accordingly.

2. Communicating with Paralegals, Project Assistants, and Other Staff Members

Large law firms and legal departments have large staffs: paralegals, project assistants, assistants (secretaries), etc., and they are essential to working efficiently on a time-sensitive matter. Paralegals manage the documents needed by both transactional lawyers and litigators, and may perform certain legal research or assist with drafting simple contracts at some firms. Project assistants help paralegals; they make copies, prepare document binders, run last minute filings to the clerk's office for filing if the court system does not allow electronic filing, etc.

Always treat staff as respectfully as other professionals on the same team — if you do not, the senior lawyers will notice, and judge you negatively. Do not "boss them around" — make them your friends. Also, do not model the behavior of senior partners because *you are not one*.

Staff members are knowledgeable professionals who can help your career and make you look good if you have a good relationship with them. Remember — they probably know the firm better than you do, and may know many aspects of practicing law that you do not, so consider them a valuable resource to be respected. They can also make your life very unpleasant and indirectly hurt your career if they feel that you do not respect them.

3. Communicating with Your Assistant

Your assistant is no longer called a "secretary." He or she can help you with many things, such as billing your time, making photocopies, and answering your phone for you. He or she may also be able to help to edit or proofread your letters, and even do electronic filing with the court. A good assistant also has a wealth of knowledge of the people and practices of the law firm or legal department. Be sure to take advantage of that. Don't worry about "asking stupid questions." The assistant knows that you are new and is there to assist you.

He or she is likely to work for at least three or four lawyers — often a partner, a senior associate, and a junior associate — and perhaps more. During the difficult economic conditions that law firms have faced since 2008, many large law firms have fired numerous assistants, forcing the ones who remain to work for more attorneys. As a foreign lawyer intern or a new associate, remember that the partner's work is the assistant's priority, not your work, so be considerate of your assistant's time and consider their workload when giving them work. Understand that they cannot always do your work instantly.

F. COMMUNICATING WITH CLIENTS

As a foreign lawyer intern or new associate, you will be seen as a junior lawyer on matters. Do junior lawyers speak directly to clients in your country? If so, under what circumstances?

1. Talking to the Client or the Client's Employees

Here, you must understand the partner's wishes before communicating with a client. The partner is in charge of the representation, and may want to be the only lawyer who speaks to the client. Or he or she may be happy for you to call or email the client's staff when needed. The answer may depend upon the partner, and even with the same partner, it may depend upon the nature of the client and the representation.

Find out when and under what circumstances you may speak to the client (or the client's employees). Do you need approval before doing so, or can you do it on your own? Typically, partners are more comfortable when you talk with the client's employees than the client or the client's officers.

2. Speaking at Telephone Conferences and Meetings

Find out what the partner expects from you at telephone conferences and meetings. Should you speak only if they ask you a question, or may you volunteer your opinion?

For telephone conferences, arrive at the conference room early, before the partner. Always bring the client's phone number and dial-in information to a conference call. Assume that it is your job to make the call and to ensure that the technology works smoothly. That way, you will be prepared to do so if necessary.

For meetings, the client may already be waiting in the conference room. In that case, you will likely meet the client together with the partner.

G. WORK ASSIGNMENTS

Most international LL.M. students who work at U.S. law firms are transactional lawyers. As transactional attorneys, the nature of your assignments will depend upon the type of work that you will be doing, such as mergers and acquisitions, securities law, capital markets, and project finance.

1. Common Types of Assignments for International Transactional Associates

International LL.M. graduates who obtain internships with U.S. law firms may receive work assignments such as the following:

Drafting documents (always or almost always in English, and based on firm forms), including:

- agreements;
- offerings (debt offerings, equity offerings, IPOs, private placements);
- SEC filings and regulatory compliance documents (e.g., 10-Ks);
- prospectuses;
- underwriting agreements;
- indenture agreements;
- offering memoranda;
- legal opinions to accompany a deal; and
- office memoranda.

Other work assignments may include:

- document reviews and due diligence, often involving documents in your native language;
- translating such documents into good English;
- researching certain business opportunities in international markets, perhaps in your native language;
- writing client letters or letters to opposing counsel, either in English or your native language;
- participation in telephone conferences or calls involving your native language; and
- Occasional work to help the litigation department if you are not busy (such as research memos, a motion for summary judgment that would not be used directly but would be used to help a senior associate or partner's motion).

2. Work Assignment Tips

When drafting a larger assignment, make steady progress — don't wait until the day before it's due. Leave sufficient time to edit and proofread. Continually edit and revise as you work, and always do a final proofreading before you submit any work.

If it's a longer project, touch base periodically with senior attorneys and let them know where you are with the work, and ask if you have any questions.

Ask for input and comments. Remember that a first draft is not an excuse for poor work. Even a first draft should look like finished work product and be the best that you can do. Of course, later drafts will be better because of partner comments, but the first draft should be your best work at that time.

3. Editing Tips

Although you may use a "redline" program such as Microsoft Track Changes when you edit others' work, it's also a good idea to know traditional proofreading symbols. If the firm where you are working still uses traditional proofreading symbols, they will give you a key to the symbols when you begin working there. Learn them. Even today, lawyers at large firms sometimes make edits by hand using proofreading symbols, and then send PDFs of the handmade edits. Why? There are two important reasons:

First, it is confusing if there are many different versions of the document on the system. This could lead to multiple lawyers making edits to the wrong version of the document, which leads to chaos. Accordingly, firms often designate a "keeper of the document" who has the "master copy."

Second, track changes and comments, even if accepted or deleted, may still exist as metadata and thus be discoverable. Partners may not want their opponents to have the opportunity to understand their strategic thinking by being able to view the changes made to the document over time.

H. BILLING TIME

1. Billable Hours and Flat-Fee Representations

In-house lawyers typically do not bill their time. If you work for a law firm, however, it's a key part of the job, even with a one-year internship.

Traditionally, U.S. law firms have charged their clients for their work by the hour, known as the "billable hour." Until fairly recently, lawyers billed their time in "quarters," or 15-minute increments. Then, as corporate clients pushed back against high legal fees, they began to demand that firms bill in "tenths," or six-minute increments. Billing in tenths began in bankruptcy court, but it has now become the standard, perhaps because clients were unhappy about paying for 15 minutes of attorney time for a telephone call that lasted for only five or six minutes.

Cost-sensitive corporate clients are also increasingly asking counsel to charge them a flat fee for each representation, especially for smaller matters. Large law firms have been reluctant to do this, partially because they may feel that they do not have a sufficiently accurate way to predict how many hours of work a case is likely to require. They worry that if they "underquote" in order to win the representation, they then have the difficult choices of either working too many hours for too little pay, or perhaps "cutting corners" and doing slightly less careful work in order to be more efficient. Nevertheless, there are many competent attorneys who need the work, so there has been some movement in this direction. This trend will likely continue, particularly as large firms become better at predicting what they are likely to earn by mining data from past representations to determine historical averages for different types of representation.

2. Billable Hour Requirements at Large Law Firms

Over the past several decades, as associate salaries increased, large firms gradually increased their billable hour requirements, from 1,800 hours, to 1,900 hours, and then to 2,000 or even 2,100 hours. To receive a bonus, associates often have to work 100 or 150 hours more than the requirement.

If you do not count hours in a similar fashion in your country, this may not sound so hard — after all, 2,000 hours is "only" 40 hours per week times 50 weeks per year. However, if you have practiced law, you know that in order to *bill* eight hours of work in a day, you may have to be at the office for 10 to 11 hours. Certain conversations with colleagues, timekeeping, mealtimes, reading firm administrative emails or attending firm training activities, trips to the bathroom: none of these are billable.

Moreover, legal work tends to not be as steady as we would prefer. There are months where you are extremely busy, and other months where you may not have as much work to do. It can be frustrating to sit in your office without billable work to do; hence the old saying, "the only thing worse than too much work is not enough work."

3. Tips for Billing Time

Many large U.S. law firms bill international interns' work at the rate for first-year associates. The firm will train you how to bill your time according to their style. Pay careful attention to the training, because poorly-written time may have to be written off (not billed), leaving an unhappy partner.

As you likely do at home in your country, note down the time as you work and try to do your time at the end of each day. Some firms now have timekeeping software that assists you in keeping and entering the time as you work on a matter. Your firm might require that you submit time every Friday, or perhaps at the end of each month, but it's a good idea to spend 15 minutes per day or so writing down that day's time.

Try to break up the time into smaller, more narrowly-described activities, and be sure to use action verbs that show how you add value. For example, instead of using a verb like "read" or even "reviewed," use "analyzed." If you write "Drafted complaint.

9.5 hours," clients may say that it shouldn't have taken so long to draft the complaint, and demand a fee reduction. Break the work up into smaller pieces — it's harder for clients to fight.

Chapter Review

- The United States has the world's largest legal market, the most lawyers, and the most large law firms.
- Over the past 40 years, the market has grown greatly in size, and law firms have grown much larger. Over the same period of time diversity has greatly increased, as there are now many more women attorneys, and attorneys from different racial and ethnic backgrounds.
- Law firm equity partners earn income based on the size of their books of business, in a system called "eat what you kill." On average, a large law firm's most highly paid partner earns about 10 times what its lowest-paid partner does, although that ratio may vary greatly from firm to firm.
- At many of the largest firms, the average profit per partner is over a million dollars per year, and at the most successful firms, it is several million dollars per year.
- U.S. law firms are highly hierarchical, with the hierarchy ranging from the firm's chairperson, to the senior partners on the executive committee and other high-ranking committees, to other corner-office partners, mid-level partners, and junior partners. The firm may also have income partners, who are paid a large salary but do not own a stake in the firm or share in firm profits.
- Below the partnership rank, there are "of counsel" attorneys, who are senior lawyers who are not partners for various reasons, including that they have too little business, or they are semi-retired. Below the "of counsel" attorneys, there are associates, who range from senior associates, to mid-level associates, to junior associates. Some law firms have a new class of lower-paid attorneys called "staff attorneys."
- Lawyers who have practiced in other countries are surprised at how egalitarian the U.S. law firm culture feels. Attorneys call each other by their first names: even junior associates typically call the firm chairperson by his or her first name. Nevertheless, everyone understands what the hierarchy is, and associates show deference to partners.
- Associates should respond quickly to emails from partners; submit work early or at least on time; let partners know their progress on larger projects; ask for clarification when they are unsure of what to do; and be available during business hours.
- To avoid annoying partners with procedural questions or smaller questions, associates should speak to more senior associates, paralegals and project assistants, and their assistants, who can often answer these types of questions. It is essential to treat staff respectfully and well.

- Associates should find out when they may speak to clients. Typically, they speak to the employees of corporate clients, but less so with corporate executives.
- International interns who are transactional attorneys may draft a wide variety of documents in English. At times, they may also sit in on meetings where they can translate, and they may be expected to translate documents. They may also at times work on document reviews, and help the litigation department if they are not busy.
- Law firm attorneys typically bill their time in six-minute increments, although flat-fee billing is becoming more popular.
- Bill your time each day. Break up long tasks into shorter descriptions, and use action verbs that show you are adding value.

Chapter 21

WRITING EMAILS AND THE EMAIL MEMORANDUM

Chapter Preview

This chapter describes writing emails and email memoranda. The chapter focuses on:

- writing internal office emails;
- writing emails to clients;
- the risks of writing emails, including:
  - writing unprofessional emails and accidentally hitting "reply all";
  - writing angry or annoyed emails to difficult clients;
  - having no expectation of privacy in emails or website viewing when at work;
  - inadvertently waiving attorney-client privilege; and
  - memorializing sensitive information in a potentially discoverable format.
- writing email memoranda, including:
  - using the email memo format to memorialize legal research and analysis in a quicker and more cost-effective fashion; and
  - retaining most of the basic parts of the office memorandum, but in a shorter, more relaxed format.

In the United States, emails have become the main form of communication between attorneys at the same firm, between attorneys representing different parties, and between attorneys and their clients. Although telephone calls are still important, especially for speaking to attorneys for the other party or the client, email is dominant. Often, attorneys send an email to the lawyer in the office next door, even if it is quicker to walk there and to speak to each other.

Lawyers may read 100 or more emails every day and write 10 or 20 emails. We look at our computers and smart phones constantly, and may feel anxious if there is a service outage or we are unable to receive emails on airplanes.

Emails are wonderfully convenient, but they carry several potential risks, ranging from: emails containing confidential information that the recipient may forward to others unwisely, possibly waving attorney-client privilege and disclosing confidential information; to poorly-considered, overly emotional emails that could inflame your relationship with opposing counsel or endanger your relationship with your client; to the potentially-discoverable memorialization of sensitive information that should only be spoken.

This chapter will discuss the appropriate form for professional emails, as well as the risks involved, and it will discuss how to write email memoranda.

A. WRITING EMAILS

Emails may have different levels of formality, depending on the audience, but you should consider every email that you write as an attorney as a professional communication. In other words, while an email may be somewhat more informal than a formal, traditional letter to a client, it should always remain professional.

Avoid slang (no emails should begin with greetings like "yo John!!"), informal acronyms such as "LOL," and shorthand spelling such as "r u ready 4 this?" It is also wise to avoid the cartoon-like symbols known as "emoticons" or "emoji" (e.g., "☺").

Emails should use plain English and avoid legalese. They may at first feel informal to you, if you are used to more formal communication in your country. They are most effective with shorter communication, such as an email that can fit on one computer screen. If the email will be much longer than that, consider sending it as an attachment, and if it is confidential, it is prudent to consider whether to send the message by express mail.

1. Writing Successful Internal Firm Emails

Keep internal firm emails short and to the point.

In the Subject: line, follow firm practice as to whether to include the client name and matter number. Be sure to include a title that explains what the email is about, and provides information about what action needs to be taken, and what the time frame for that action is (e.g., "MTD[1] to be filed by 10/7").

[1] "MTD" stands for "motion to dismiss."

This is essential because busy attorneys often prioritize when to read emails — if they understand from the Subject: line that the email can be answered later in the day, they will often do so. If you give them no clue as to the matter, the client, or the message (which may force them to read it quickly to determine the importance of the message), they will likely be annoyed.

When you write the salutation, use just the first name of the recipient (e.g., "Bob"). Although you might consider beginning with "Dear" if you have never written to that attorney before, he or she is older, and/or he or she has a reputation for being formal, U.S. attorneys typically just use the first name when addressing colleagues.

Do not consider using "Hi" (too informal) unless the other attorney has used it first, or calling the attorney "Mr. Smith" or "Ms. Jones" (too formal). Never use "Mr." or "Ms." with a first name only (i.e., do not write "Mr. Bob" or "Ms. Marie").

We often close the email with "Thanks," followed by our first name, instead of "Best Regards" or "Sincerely."

Do not use legalese or similarly stuffy business jargon. For example, do not write "attached please find" when sending an attachment. Today, large firm lawyers are more likely to write "I'm attaching" or "I'm enclosing" instead.

Proofread every email before you hit "send." Make sure that your grammar and spelling are accurate, because colleagues will notice if they are not. You are being judged even more because English is your second language. If you make basic grammar and spelling mistakes, it will make them judge your carefulness and your competence. On the other hand, with each accurate and grammatically correct email that you send them, you are confirming that your English is good enough for you to do the work, and they did not make a mistake in hiring you.

Partners may write you quick emails with typos and other mistakes, but please remember the hierarchy: *you are not a partner* and you are being judged on the quality of your work — emails included. Partners see mistakes as unprofessional, even if they are on internal firm emails. Lawyers are held to a high standard of care and accuracy. Show them they hired the right person!

EXERCISE 21 A

You are working with a more senior attorney in your firm named Bob Smith. You want to send him a short email with an attachment. You would like him to review the attachment and to give you comments.

Write the email below:

2. Writing Successful Emails to the Client

As an international intern or new associate, you will not likely write many emails directly to the client, unless a partner asks you to write the first draft of an opinion letter or another email providing legal advice that he or she will then revise. You may, however, frequently write emails to employees of the client, such as emails that ask for certain documents that are relevant to the services that your firm is providing.

On a smaller matter or a pro bono matter, you may find that you have more discretion to write emails to the client. Use that discretion carefully. For example, do not allow a difficult client who sends you many emails per day to pressure you into "shooting from the hip," i.e., providing advice based on intuition or a quick judgment rather than on careful research and reasoning.

Also, do not allow overly-frequent, annoying correspondence from the client to provoke you into writing an angry or annoyed email that damages the attorney-client relationship. Although being an attorney is a high-status job, never lose sight of the fact that attorneys are service providers, and there is no shortage of attorneys in the United States.

Emails to the client are more formal than internal firm emails. In fact, it is wise to think of them as similar in nature to traditional letters to clients, which we will discuss in the next chapter. Extra formality is unnecessary with colleagues, and may not always be necessary with clients, but it is better to err on the side of caution. Politeness is always appreciated, especially by the people who pay your fees!

B. THE POTENTIAL RISKS OF EMAILS

The law does not treat emails in the same way that it treats letters. They have a diminished expectation of privacy, and this has repercussions both in the emails that you send as an employee of a law firm or legal department, and the emails that you send your client.

1. Lack of Privacy for Employees

As an international intern or an associate attorney, or as in-house counsel in the legal department of a corporation, you are an employee of that law firm or that corporation. Keep in mind that, as a general rule, employees have no legitimate expectation of privacy in the data that is contained on their workplace computers.[2]

---

[2] 48 N.J. Prac., N.J. Arrest, Search & Seizure Review § 8:7 (2012 ed.) (collecting *United States v. Angevine*, 281 F.3d 1130, 1133–35 (10th Cir.) (no reasonable expectation of privacy in contents of workplace computer which was part of employer's network), *cert. denied*, 537 U.S. 845 (2002); *United States v. Simons*, 206 F.3d 392, 398 (4th Cir. 2000) (no legitimate expectation of privacy in contents of workplace computer where the employer had notified its employees that their computer activities could be monitored); *United States v. Bailey*, 272 F. Supp. 2d 822, 830–32, 836–37 (D. Neb. 2003) (no reasonable expectation of privacy in the contents of workplace computer where employee did not own it, and was provided passwords to access the employee's network and company data)).

If you work for a law firm or corporation, you should assume that the firm may be monitoring your emails and even the websites that you access. Thus, if you are writing an email only for one attorney or friend, and it would be embarrassing if others see the message, do not send that email. The same is true with the internet. Don't view embarrassing or unprofessional websites. For example, employees have been fired throughout the United States for viewing pornography on their work computers during business hours.

Call or meet your friend or colleague if you feel the need to give them a potentially embarrassing or unprofessional message, or better yet, consider not giving the message in the first place. There are well-known stories at large law firms of attorneys who sent nasty comments to a friend and accidently hit "reply all," so that more than 1,000 employees of the firm received the email! Such mistakes damage reputations and careers. Make sure that you are not the kind of person who lets one moment of carelessness or immaturity damage or destroy the good reputation that you have been working hard to build for many years.

2. Possible Waiver of Attorney-Client Privilege

Emails from attorneys to their clients that contain privileged information that is protected by the attorney-client privilege do not lose that privilege simply by being sent in an email. However, the privilege may be inadvertently waived in a number of ways.

For example, if the attorney includes or cc:'s certain third parties in an email to a client, or if the client forwards the privileged email on to certain third parties or even to a low-level employee, the privilege may be waived.

Another potential problem is when an attorney has frequent email correspondence with opposing counsel to set up depositions or to conduct discovery, and accidently sends an email containing privileged information to opposing counsel instead of to the client. Many jurisdictions impose an ethical obligation on counsel who have inadvertently received privileged material to delete it and inform opposing counsel of the mistake, but not all jurisdictions do. Even if counsel deletes the message, we say that "the bell cannot be unrung," meaning that opposing counsel still knows that information.

To prevent inadvertent disclosure and waiver of the attorney-client privilege, most law firms protect their outgoing emails in several ways. First, they require their attorneys to put a standard disclaimer on the bottom of the email that contains language similar to the following:

This email message is intended for the sole use of the intended recipient(s) and may contain confidential or privileged information. Any unauthorized review, use, disclosure or distribution is prohibited. If you are not the intended recipient, please contact the sender by reply email and destroy and delete all copies of the original message.

The purpose of this language is to put any accidental recipients on notice that they should delete all copies of the email and tell the sender that they mistakenly received the email. It is unclear how often accidental recipients actually do this, however.

Second, on emails from counsel to their clients, the emails frequently state in bolded, allcap words at the top:

PRIVILEGED AND CONFIDENTIAL

ATTORNEY-CLIENT PRIVILEGE

Third, some firms take the extra step of encrypting privileged emails.

3. Memorializing Potentially Discoverable Information

A third major danger with emails is that they "memorialize" communications by writing them down and preserving them electronically. Servers may archive emails for years, and they may be discoverable years later in litigation. With forensic recovery programs, even deleted emails may still exist and be recovered. If any internal firm emails or attorney-client communications are determined not to be privileged, or if the sender or receiver is determined to have waived that privilege somehow, that information could prove highly damaging in a trial. Indeed, for the past 20 years, emails have frequently provided the "smoking gun" evidence that has determined cases.

Thus, if you are speaking to colleagues or to your client about a highly sensitive issue, it is prudent to meet privately or to discuss the issue on the telephone instead of corresponding by email. Do not expose yourself, your firm, or your client to potential liability by writing or forwarding an email that could get you, the firm, or the client in trouble if someone else were to see it!

C. WRITING EMAIL MEMOS

As we discussed briefly in the chapters on writing the formal office memorandum, law firms and legal departments have gradually been moving away from the formal, traditional office memorandum, for several reasons.

First, email, electronic communications, and online legal research have all increased the speed at which attorneys operate, and they have also increased the frequency with which clients contact attorneys. Clients want answers to their questions, and these days, they expect the answers quickly. Accordingly, attorneys want to respond to their clients' needs and to provide answers in a timely fashion, but they still must ensure that the answers to the client's questions (1) describe the governing law accurately, and (2) apply the law to the client's facts carefully and accurately.

Second, given clients' resistance to what they see as excessive legal fees, attorneys need to provide their analysis in a more cost-effective fashion. One way to do that is to loosen the format of the traditional office memorandum by allowing written analysis that looks more like a letter. Thus, we have email memos.

With email memos, associates can write short answers to specific legal questions more quickly and more efficiently, and without all of the various sections of the office memorandum. Nevertheless, they can still provide partners reassurance that the answer to the client's question is sufficiently grounded in the law and in good legal reasoning.

1. Structure of the Email Memo

Unlike the office memorandum, which has existed for a long time and which tends to follow one of several possible variations of a standard structure, email memoranda have no set structure.

That being said, email memoranda do tend to follow a certain general structure:

- First, they state the legal issue that the associate has been asked to analyze, such as analyzing whether the client may bring a fraud claim given certain facts, or determining what possible defenses the client might have to a certain claim that a would-be plaintiff has threatened to bring, and end the issue statement with a quick conclusion.
- Second, they provide whatever factual background is necessary to provide the context for the analysis.
- Third, they state the relevant law for the general issue.
- Fourth, they analyze the legal issue.
- Fifth, they provide a conclusion for the analysis, and end the email memo in letter form, by asking the more senior attorney follow up questions, such as whether the partner would like them to continue to research the issue.

There are many similarities with the traditional memorandum: just like office memoranda, email memos begin by stating the issue and providing a quick answer; by stating necessary background facts; by providing rules followed by analysis; and by ending with a conclusion.

Unlike office memoranda, each of these sections may be covered in a sentence or two, without any particular format such as an "under-does-where" question.

The language in an email memo is also more conversational. Because the memo is written in the form of an email (which is nothing more than an electronic letter), it often begins with language such as the following:

"Dan,

You asked me to analyze whether . . ."

Or it can begin with more memo-like language:

"Dan,

This memo addresses whether [our client] . . ."

Email memos often summarize basic research that the associate has just undertaken. For example, the assignment may ask the associate to find some cases in Jurisdiction X that support whether the client is able to raise certain defenses given the facts of the matter (*see* Appendix D).

In summarizing the research results, the associate may use the first person in a conversational manner: "I have found several Texas cases that could help our client to assert that . . ."

2. The Length of an Email Memo

There are two basic types of email memo. The first one is one narrow, discrete issue, which the memo can often address in approximately one to two computer screens worth of writing (for example, whether the client may bring a fraud claim given certain facts) (*see* Appendix E).

The second type of research issue is a bit broader, and may at first seem more appropriate for an office memo (such as determining what possible defenses the client might have to a certain claim that a would-be plaintiff has threatened to bring) (*see* Appendix D). If there are four or five possible defenses, the email memo may have four or five screens of writing.

With the longer email memo, the partner may have assigned it as an email memo because the partner was not sure how many possible defenses there might be, so he or she might have thought that the answer might be short. More likely, the partner was well aware that there would be four or five possible defenses, but still preferred an email memo because it would be quicker to write and less expensive than a traditional office memorandum.

3. Headings and Sub-Headings

An email memo is a strange animal, something like the legal version of a duck-billed platypus. On one hand, it is an email, in the form of a letter. On the other hand, it is a legal analysis in the form of a memorandum.

Because the format is a hybrid of the two, and because attorneys have discretion in the format they choose, they can either make it look like an email, with no headings or sub-headings, or they can make it look like a memo, with headings and sub-headings.

While there is no correct answer, the goal is always to make the work clear and easy to understand. Thus, a good rule of thumb is to make an email memo look more like an email — without headings — when it is one or two pages long or it addresses one issue, such as the email memo in Appendix E. However, if the memo has four or five parts, such as the email memo that analyzes four or five possible defenses to a potential claim in Appendix D, it is better to use headings for each defense.

Because there is no set format for email memos, the headings may be numbered, or use letters, or be underlined, or not underlined. In general, however, the headings should be bolded. Many partners prefer for the headings to be written as a conclusion, rather than as a topic.

Chapter Review

- Emails have become the dominant form of attorney communication, whether between attorneys at the same firm or workplace, opposing counsel, or attorneys and their clients.

- Although emails are somewhat less formal than traditional letters, treat them as professional communication. While they should use plain English and avoid legalese, they should not be informal, like an email or instant message to a friend.
- Professional emails should not contain slang, current day abbreviations and acronyms such as "LOL" or "4 u" (instead of "for you"), or cartoon-like emoticons.
- With emails to colleagues in the same workplace, emails should contain a subject line with the topic and any key dates or requested actions.
- Generally, the salutation simply begins with the addressee's first name, (e.g., "Bob,"), and the closing ends with "Thanks" (e.g., "Thanks, John" or "Thanks. John").
- Emails to clients are somewhat more formal and polite than internal firm emails. Although emails are by nature less formal than traditional letters, emails to clients should still be professional, polite, and somewhat formal.
- As an employee of a law firm or law department in the United States, you have no expectation of privacy for materials stored on your computer. This extends to the emails that you write and the websites that you visit, both of which might be monitored by your employer.
- Although emails sent from attorneys to their clients that provide legal advice or discuss the client's legal issues are protected by the attorney-client privilege, that privilege is not absolute and may be waived in certain ways.
- Privilege may be waived when the attorney includes certain third parties on the email, or if the client forwards the attorney's email to certain third parties or low-level employees. It may also be waived in certain jurisdictions when an email is inadvertently misdirected.
- Accordingly, legal employers attempt to preserve the confidentiality of emails by containing language demanding that inadvertent recipients delete emails and inform the sender if they were received. They also boldly label emails to clients "PRIVILEGED AND CONFIDENTIAL ATTORNEY-CLIENT PRIVILEGE," and may encrypt their emails.
- Emails may also be discoverable, so consider delivering sensitive information in person or by telephone.
- Email memos have become increasingly common at law firms and in-house legal departments because they are quicker to write and thus less costly than traditional office memoranda.
- Email memos have salutations and closings like regular emails, but use a more streamlined, informal memo form in the middle: they state the legal issue and a quick conclusion; provide necessary background information; state the relevant legal rules; analyze the legal issues; and provide a conclusion.
- The writing style is somewhat more informal than that of an office memorandum and may include first-person pronouns.

- Some email memos use headings, but not all do. In general, email memos often have no headings if they are short, but generally do if they are longer or contain more issues. The goal is clarity: use headings if they make the memo easier to read.

Chapter 22

WRITING CLIENT LETTERS AND LETTERS TO OPPOSING COUNSEL

Chapter Preview

This chapter describes writing various kinds of letters, both to clients and to opposing counsel. The chapter focuses on:

- client letters:
  - informational letters,
  - opinion letters, and
  - advisory letters.
- letters to opposing counsel:
  - case- or transaction-management letters,
  - demand letters, and
  - settlement letters.

Letter writing, whether in a traditional letter or in an email, is likely the most common type of writing for any practicing attorney, whether the attorney is a litigator or a transactional lawyer. Lawyers write emails and/or traditional letters to their clients, to opposing counsel, and to third parties on a frequent (if not daily) basis. Because the potential universe of third parties is virtually limitless (e.g., courts, government agencies, police, lenders, insurance companies, title companies, hospitals, businesses of all kinds, former employees of parties, witnesses, investigators, accountants, expert witnesses, etc.), this chapter will focus on two common recipients of attorney letters: clients and opposing counsel.

What do lawyers write on a regular basis? Litigators are more likely to write briefs or motions to the court, and office memoranda or email memos (although transactional lawyers may sometimes write memoranda as well). Transactional lawyers are more likely to draft contracts, agreements, wills, and similar documents (although litigators may draft certain agreements as well, such as settlement agreements or separation agreements for departing executives).

Everyone writes letters. Ethical rules in every U.S. jurisdiction require attorneys to stay in contact with their clients, and to keep them informed as to the status of their matters and their strategic options. Thus, lawyers write their clients letters to provide and request information, to express opinions as to the legal validity of a potential action by the client, and to advise clients about the law affecting their matter, the lawyer's analysis of how the law is likely to affect their matter, and their options.

A. WRITING CLIENT LETTERS

Unlike legal memoranda, which are largely consistent in form, typically written for an audience of practicing lawyers, and which generally have the purpose of analyzing a legal issue and predicting the outcome or determining the best response, letters can vary enormously. They may vary greatly in terms of the audience and in terms of the purpose of the letter.

For example, the client could be a huge multi-national corporation with a large legal department or a small start-up company without a general counsel; a wealthy, highly educated individual or a poor one without much formal schooling; a young adult, a middle-aged person, or a senior citizen.

There could also be multiple audiences for the letter, including lawyers and non-lawyers, such as in-house counsel and executives, teenagers and their guardians, or the elderly and their caretakers. If the audience includes a lawyer, does the lawyer practice in the area of law in which you are providing counsel, or is he or she likely only to have general knowledge about it?

What is the emotional state of the audience? Is the client in great emotional distress because of a tragedy, or is this a business matter where the client is not as likely to have a strong emotional reaction? If the client is a company, are the client's decision makers angry at the actions of another party, or are they hopeful to conclude a deal with the other party?

Lawyers should carefully think about all of these considerations before they begin to write a letter to a client. Unlike an office memorandum, which is intended to be objective and typically has little emotional content, a client letter is a communication between the attorney and the client as human beings, not just as players of legal roles. Lawyers need to establish a connection with their clients in their letters, and to show the client, where it is appropriate, that they are understanding and empathetic in addition to being legal counselors. After all, this aspect of lawyering is included in the name "counselor."

In addition to the wide range of possible audiences, the purpose of the letter could vary greatly as well, from providing or requesting information, to expressing opinions as to the legal validity of a potential action by the client, to advising clients of their options so that the clients can make informed decisions as to strategy.

After carefully determining the type of client, the attitude of the client, and the purpose of the letter, attorneys then have the rhetorical framework with which to work: i.e., what to say, and how best to say it.

1. Writing Informational Letters

Informational letters, likely the most common type of client letter or email in sheer numbers, do not contain legal analysis or advice. Rather, they perform a range of basic functions that are necessary to keep the matter progressing and the client informed.

For example, informational letters summarize the status of the case or transaction by describing recent events and developments; they propose or confirm dates for client meetings, or for depositions or hearings; they summarize the contents of a previous in-person meeting or telephone call with the client so that the attorney can confirm that he or she understands the facts accurately and has all relevant information; they transmit many kinds of documents to the client, whether transactional or related to litigation; or they ask the client for documents that are relevant to the matter.

These letters can vary in length, according to the purpose. For example, cover letters that accompany documents may be just a few paragraphs or even sentences long. Even short and simple letters should be carefully thought-out, however. The attorney should make sure that the letter identifies all of the documents that accompany the letter, and tells the reader what the attorney would like the reader to do with the documents: read them, sign them, and return them; file them away for safekeeping; etc.

Informational letters are often emails, but they may also be sent in the U.S. mail, or by express mail, depending on the nature of the letter and the types of documents that may accompany it. They should not be filled with legalese ("Enclosed please find said motion"), but they should also not be too casual. Instead, these letters should be careful, controlled, specific, and professional in tone.

2. Writing Opinion Letters

Opinion letters provide a legal opinion about an issue that concerns the client. More specifically, they provide the law firm's opinion as to whether the action that the client is contemplating is legal.

Businesses that are concerned about the legality of a certain contemplated action can point to an opinion letter from a law firm as a form of "insurance." In other words, if a government regulator accuses the company of proceeding fraudulently or in bad faith, the client can point to the opinion letter as a form of due diligence: "We were not acting fraudulently or in bad faith, but prudently and out of an abundance of caution. We sought and received an opinion letter from counsel stating that our proposed action was legal. We acted reasonably and in good faith, in reliance on counsel's opinion."

If the opinion is incorrect and exposes the client to liability, the client might then sue the law firm that provided the opinion letter for legal malpractice. Thus, law firms are cautious about providing opinion letters. They might permit only a limited number of partners who have expertise and considerable experience in that area of the law to write these letters, and/or they might require the opinion letter to be reviewed and approved by a second partner, such as firm counsel.[1]

Opinion letters begin by identifying the topic and when the client asked for the opinion. Then they provide the opinion, and support the opinion by reviewing the facts and the applicable law.

The letter very carefully states the facts that the law firm considered in reaching its conclusion. After stating the facts, some firms add disclaimers stating that the legal opinion is based only upon the law of the relevant jurisdiction at the time that the letter was written, and on the facts stated in the letter, known as of the time that the firm drafted the letter; that the firm is not aware of other facts; and that if the facts are different from the facts described in the letter, that it might change the firm's opinion. The letter states the facts and disclaimer partly to ensure that the client has provided it with complete and accurate information, and partly to protect the firm in case it is sued for legal malpractice.

Everyone states the opinion in the opening paragraph (or perhaps in the second paragraph, but near the beginning of the letter) if the opinion is what the client wants to hear. If the conclusion will make the client unhappy, however, some firms hide the opinion until near the end, hoping that the body of the opinion letter will prepare the client to receive the bad news in a calmer fashion after having been prepared for it. Other firms take a more direct approach, stating the opinion at the beginning even if it is negative. This approach seems to be the more popular approach at present — good or bad, clients want to know the answer, and they do not want to wait for it.

---

[1] Firm counsel is in some ways analogous to the general counsel of a corporation. Although the firm counsel is typically not the chairperson of a large law firm, he or she has the law firm as his or her client, and advises it about issues where the firm may face potential liability or other negative consequences.

If you are an international associate for a large U.S. law firm with significant experience in a given area of law, a partner may assign you to draft an opinion letter for that partner's signature.

3. Writing Advisory Letters

Unlike opinion letters, which are a narrow and specialized type of attorney letters, advisory letters are very common, and all types of attorneys write them to their clients. By writing advisory letters, lawyers meet their ethical obligations to keep clients informed of the status of the matter and to provide clients with sufficient information for the clients to make informed decisions.

Although advisory letters do not carry as much obvious potential risk as opinion letters, unhappy clients may sue their lawyers for malpractice if they are very dissatisfied with the result, and their attorneys may use a carelessly-worded and conclusory advisory letter to support an argument that the attorney failed to meet standards of diligent and competent representation.

Therefore, prudent attorneys write advisory letters carefully, not only to provide their clients with excellent advice, but also to protect themselves against potential liability if the representation does not go well.

Advisory letters contain the following parts:

- the opening paragraph;
- the relevant facts;
- the legal analysis of the issue;
- the client's options and the attorney's recommendations; and
- the closing paragraph.

We will look at each of these parts in more detail.

a. The Opening Paragraph

A good opening paragraph provides a preview of the entire advisory letter. It is personal, and it gets right to the point. It states the legal issue, provides the attorney's conclusion, and then the attorney's recommendation.

The recommendation can be specific, such as whether the client should or should not file a motion for summary judgment. It could also state that the client has several options (if that is true) and that those options will be discussed later in the letter. The opening paragraph may end there, or it may conclude by suggesting the next step, such as meeting to discuss the issue and the client's options in more depth. It could either save the suggestion for the closing paragraph, or introduce it briefly in the opening paragraph and repeat it in more detail in the closing paragraph.

As with contracts, where law firms often use an older contract as a model for a new one, some law firms may have model advisory letters with standard language that they use as a basis for new advisory letters. This is usually a mistake for two reasons.

First, a letter that begins with standard, formal "attorney language" may make the client feel that the attorney does not care about them personally, and is simply "going through the motions" and treating the client as just another person standing in line. The attorney fails to connect with the client, which may hurt their relationship going forward. In order to represent your client excellently, you need to establish a good working relationship, with a clear line of communication. Disengaged, unhappy clients are less likely to provide all of the information that you need to represent them well.

Second, too many standard or traditional advisory letters contain a great deal of introductory language early in the opening paragraph. Perhaps they provide the roadmap for the letter before the writer has even stated the conclusion. This is likely to make the reader impatient and annoyed. An annoyed client is more likely to scrutinize the monthly bill carefully and to ask why that advisory letter was so expensive! While a roadmap is important, consider placing it after the conclusion or in the second paragraph — in other words, after you've already stated what the client wants to know.

When you write the salutation, use the name for the client that you have been using since the beginning of the representation. Although an advisory letter is somewhat more formal than a quick informational email, writers should consider using the same terms of address that they have been using on client emails.

For example, if the client is relatively new, you may call her "Ms. Jones." However, if you know the client well, or if you have already written many emails to her that begin with "Dear Mary," she may feel insulted by the more formal and distant "Ms. Jones," and she may even read the advisory letter suspiciously, thinking that you want to distance yourself from her, when you do not mean that at all.

The first sentence should be specific as to what the attorney and the client discussed, when they discussed it, and why the attorney is providing the advisory letter (typically at the client's request):

> When we spoke on the phone last Friday, you asked me to analyze whether a motion for summary judgment would be likely to succeed. I have concluded that although the motion would have a fair chance of success, the plaintiff is disputing enough facts that although the court may not see any one of them as definitely material, it will likely choose to err on the side of caution and be unwilling to deny the plaintiff its day in court. At this point in the litigation, your options include filing the motion for summary judgment, deciding not to file the motion and proceeding with discovery, and offering to settle the dispute. After reviewing the facts of your case and the governing law, I will discuss the advantages and disadvantages of each option in more detail below.

A specific opening sentence such as the one above personalizes the letter by mentioning the conversation with the client and what the client asked the attorney to do. Equally importantly, it protects the firm by providing a "paper trail" that reminds the client why the attorney has written the advisory letter. This may help the firm to avoid a future collections problem with a client that might dispute the fee for the advisory letter.

b. The Relevant Facts

Most advice letters then contain a summary of the facts that are relevant to the legal issue raised in the opening paragraph. This section is often the longest part of the advisory letter. It should be objective, similar to the Statement of Facts section of an office memorandum. The fact section serves two main purposes.

First, it tells the client the facts as the lawyer understands them, and asks for client input if the author is either missing facts or if any facts are inaccurate. Second, it protects the lawyer and the law firm by providing a disclaimer which states that the analysis is based upon the facts that are described in the letter, and that if any new material facts come to light, they might change the advice.

c. The Legal Analysis

The legal analysis section combines two parts of TREAC (or IRAC): the Rule section and the Application section. It states the governing rules of law for the issue, and then it applies the rules to the facts of the case that were mentioned above in the fact section.

The audience of the letter will affect this section greatly. If the readers of the letter include lawyers, such as the general counsel and the legal department of a corporation, the writer should strongly consider adding citations for the rules, especially if the letter is addressed to a lawyer. On the other hand, if the clients are not lawyers (e.g., the owner of a business without a general counsel, or an individual), the writer should just state the rules in language that non-lawyers will understand, and avoid citations.

d. The Client's Options and the Attorney's Recommendations

As the sample opening paragraph above stated, the client often has several options. If the client is a potential plaintiff, options include whether to file a lawsuit or to attempt to negotiate a settlement; if the client is a potential defendant, options include whether to file a motion to dismiss or answer a complaint.

In this example, the options included filing a motion for summary judgment, deciding not to file the motion and proceeding with discovery, and making a settlement offer. In other matters, recommendations could include a list of possible defenses that might be available to a client that has been sued (e.g., an advisory letter that would be related to subject of the office memorandum in Appendix C), seeking forums for alternative dispute resolution such as binding arbitration or mediation, ways to structure an acquisition so that the tax consequences are favorable, or suggestions for which procedures and formalities a corporate board of directors should follow to avoid liability.

The section should describe the options one at a time, setting out the advantages and disadvantages of each option. Should you provide your own opinion as to what the client should do? That would depend in part on whether the client has asked for an explicit recommendation. Although you might provide advice as to which option is preferable, remember that the client controls strategic decisions, not the attorney. Therefore, do not try to intimidate the client with overly strong language. Indeed, you might prefer to set out all of the options without stating which one you prefer in the letter. You might suggest that after the client has read the letter and thought about each option, both of you should meet to discuss the client's options in more detail.

The approach you take will depend upon your prior communications with the client and what the client may have asked for. It may also depend in part upon your style as an attorney, and your sense of what the client would prefer, if the client has not expressed a preference. Some clients may prefer to make their own decision first, and then to ask the attorney for the attorney's advice. Others might want to know immediately what the attorney would do. These types of considerations show why counseling clients is an art, not a science!

e. The Closing Paragraph

After finishing the "business part" of the letter, the closing paragraph returns to the personal level. This is where you would make your suggestions to meet with the client to discuss your analysis, and show that you are committed to serving the client. If there are any deadlines coming up or things that must be done within a certain time frame, mention it here.

For the closing, lawyers in the United States typically write "Very truly yours" (very formal) or "Sincerely" (formal). In this context — providing legal advice in a traditional letter format — it makes sense to stick with a more formal closing.

B. WRITING LETTERS TO OPPOSING COUNSEL

Unlike clients, who may be educated or uneducated, rich or poor, opposing counsel are a not a very diverse group in one sense — after all, they are all lawyers. Thus, we know that they are familiar with legal arguments and reasoning, and how to apply rules of law to the facts of the case. We know that we may use citations with them to support our assertions of law, and assume that they will understand our arguments, even if they do not agree with them.

That said, lawyers must still consider who their audience is, and do a bit of research to understand their opposing counsel. For example, is he or she an experienced lawyer, or a young one? Is he or she a partner at a large law firm, a solo practitioner with his or her own law office, or the general counsel of a corporation? Does the attorney have a good or bad reputation in the legal community? What about his or her personality? Is opposing counsel aggressive or cautious, combative or polite? The answers to these questions will affect and shape letters between counsel, much as client characteristics affect and shape letters to clients.

1. The Tone of Adversarial Letters

One of the major differences between client letters and letters to opposing counsel is in the tone of the letter. While letters to the client demonstrate the attorney's concern and desire to serve the client's needs, opposing counsel are interested in advancing their own clients' interests, not the opponent's. Thus, the tone should be respectful yet firm.

Some lawyers make the mistake of trying so hard to look fair and reasonable that they appear weak and apologetic, and they may fail to fully assert their clients' interests, "leaving dollars on the table." Other lawyers make the opposite mistake by seeing themselves as warriors defending their clients, and they attempt to intimidate, threaten, and bully the "enemy."

Such theatrics may impress certain clients, who are proud that they have hired a "pit bull" for an attorney, but they are likely to alienate the other party and actually reduce the chances for a settlement. When counsel argue over every little detail of a case, even over such non-substantive details as scheduling depositions, it is deeply counter-productive. Unnecessary hostility drives up the cost of litigation needlessly and often leads the opposing parties to harden their positions instead of compromising.

Indeed, although not much empirical research exists yet on the issue, some suggest that because demand letters (hopefully) initiate negotiation, their tone should increase the chances for a successful resolution by including certain negotiation techniques, such as focusing on collaboration rather than competition; avoiding the "fixed pie," zero-sum mindset; and thinking of creative solutions that could create a "win-win" result.[2]

The idea is attractive and sensible, but it is unclear how it would square with the format of a demand letter, which requires the writer to state a specific demand. Pointing out that the party writing the demand letter is flexible may tend to undercut that demand.

Perhaps this approach would work best in the context of a settlement letter, which has the flexibility of allowing the writer to choose one of several approaches: offering to pay a specific amount, making more comprehensive offers that include the possibility of non-monetary compensation, or inviting new demands and suggesting that the parties meet to settle the dispute.

Most skillful lawyers state their clients' positions forcefully, but treat opposing counsel respectfully because they need to work together to advance the process. Moreover, wise lawyers know that gratuitous nastiness reflects poorly on themselves, their law firms, and their clients.

Even very large legal markets such as New York, Chicago, Los Angeles, and Washington, D.C. have surprisingly "small" legal communities. Word of a lawyer's bad behavior can spread quickly throughout the legal community, particularly in the age

---

[2] *See* Carrie Sperling, *Priming Legal Negotiations Through Written Demands*, 60 Cath. U. L. Rev. 107, 140-42 (Fall 2010).

of the internet, where extreme, angry correspondence can quickly go viral and spread from law firm to law firm. Needless to say, the lawyer whose angry letter or email goes viral is not serving his or her client well!

2. Writing Letters About Case or Transaction Management

In the U.S. legal system, opposing counsel for each of the parties in litigation, as well as counsel for the parties to many transactions, are in frequent contact with each other. Lawyers from civil law systems are not surprised that counsel for parties to a deal need to communicate, and they are familiar with these sorts of communication. They are often surprised, however, by the frequent communication that opposing counsel have with each other in litigation.

If we remember what we discussed in Chapter 8 about the civil litigation process in the United States, this should not be so surprising. Courts stay out of the discovery process as much as they can, and let counsel for the parties conduct discovery among themselves, getting involved only where the parties cannot resolve a dispute.

Consequently, counsel write letters to each other before litigation begins in the form of demand letters and settlement letters, and they may also write settlement letters at any time throughout the course of the litigation. If the parties cannot resolve their dispute and the matter proceeds to court, counsel for the plaintiff asks opposing counsel if the defendant is willing to waive service. Later, during discovery, opposing counsel communicate with each other frequently by promulgating and responding to document requests, interrogatories, and requests for admission. They also must communicate to set dates for depositions, and to narrow evidentiary and factual disputes prior to a trial. Although some of these interactions may occur by phone, most of them occur in writing, by letter or by email.

Some of these letters, such as demand letters and settlement letters, are persuasive and substantive, as are letters that deal with discovery disputes. Many of these case management or deal management letters, however, simply involve administrative or procedural issues, not substantive ones. Opposing counsel use email for many of these communications, but are likely to use letters for the more formal or important requests and communications.

In general, the style of these letters is not all that different from the informational letters that attorneys send their clients. Letters to opposing counsel should also be respectful, careful, precise and unambiguous. It is unprofessional for opposing counsel to fight needlessly about unimportant matters; as discussed above, this wastes the clients' money and diminishes the chance for settlement.

3. Writing Demand or Settlement Letters

Lawyers write demand letters and settlement letters to attempt to resolve a dispute, or to comply with certain rules that impose a duty on the parties to attempt to settle disputes before bringing lawsuits. The rules might arise from a contract between the parties, or from certain laws. For example, several states have statutes requiring parties to send demand letters before they can sue, particularly in consumer actions and actions to collect a debt.[3]

Typically, in a demand letter, a plaintiff demands that the defendant pay a certain amount of money, or stop doing something that disturbs the plaintiff, or the plaintiff will sue. On the other hand, settlement letters offer or accept a lower sum of money that reflects a compromise, or they propose that the plaintiff make a new demand. For example, after receiving a demand letter from the plaintiff, the defendant could counter with a settlement letter that proposes a lower counter-offer in response to the demand letter.

A settlement offer can also be made by either party at any time during litigation, including during the appeals process. In the settlement letter in Appendix H, the appellants ask the appellees to provide a settlement term sheet that contains the appellees' terms and conditions for resolving the matter.

a. The Length of the Letter

Demand letters and settlement letters may be very short, or they may be longer and contain more assertions of fact or law. It is difficult to generalize when the letters are short, and when they are longer. It depends on such factors as the nature of the dispute, the stage when the letter is written, the strategy of the parties, and the personalities of the parties and their counsel.

Often, demand letters are short (*see* the short demand letter in Appendix F). Prior to litigation, the plaintiff may not know all of the facts that it will later learn through the discovery process, or it may not want to disclose all of its case to the defendant, or it may want to draft a short demand letter to comply with contractual obligations or with any statutes that may require the parties to try to settle the dispute before filing a lawsuit.

Perhaps most simply, a demand letter is short where the demand is basic and easy to support, such as when one party fails to pay according to the terms of an agreement between the parties. The drafter simply needs to state the terms of the agreement, note that the other party has failed to comply with those terms, and demand payment by a date certain (*see* Appendix F).

Similarly, a defendant may draft a short settlement letter offering a certain amount to compromise the case or seeking a new demand from the plaintiff (*see* the short settlement letter in Appendix H).

On the other hand, the plaintiff may draft a longer demand letter that attempts to convince the defendant that the plaintiff's case is so strong that it makes sense not to go to trial. This could happen either before or during discovery, or it could happen before trial if the plaintiff is convinced that it has a strong case (*see* the long demand letter in Appendix G).

Either party can draft a longer settlement letter that integrates the facts and the law to tell its story persuasively. This may increase the chances for settlement,

---

[3] *Id.* at n.11, n.178 (citing Cal. Civ. Code § 1782(a)(2) (West 2009)); Mass. Gen. Laws Ann. Ch. 93A, § 9(3) (West 2006); Tex. Bus. & Com. Code Ann. § 17.505(a) (West 2002)).

particularly as the focused nature of discovery may not permit parties to tell their stories by integrating the facts and the law again until the trial.[4]

b. The Contents of the Letter

Demand letters and settlement letters are similar documents in several ways. Like client advisory letters, demand letters and settlement letters get to the point quickly. Both types of letters begin with an introductory paragraph that:

- identifies the writer as the legal representative of the client; and
- states the client's position for avoiding litigation (usually, a demand for X dollars or an offer to pay Y dollars).
- If a demand letter requires the defendant to pay a certain amount of money by a certain date to resolve the case, or a settlement letter offers to pay the plaintiff a certain amount of money to compromise the case, the letter should state that the demand or settlement offer is confidential pursuant to Rule 408 of the Federal Rules of Evidence and the relevant state jurisdiction's analogous rule of evidence.
- Typically, the letter only allows the demand or settlement offer to remain open for a limited amount of time, perhaps two weeks or less.

The statement about confidentiality is crucial because otherwise, the other party might attempt to introduce it into evidence during trial. Rule 408 and the analogous state rules of evidence are designed to encourage the parties to resolve disputes by keeping demands and offers to compromise confidential.

After the opening paragraph, the demand letter or settlement letter provides factual and legal support for the client's position. In collection letters, this may simply state that the parties entered into an agreement on X date which obligated the defendant to pay a certain amount by Y date, and the defendant breached that agreement by failing to pay by that date.

In more complex situations, the party making the demand may want to tell its story persuasively, describing the defendant's actions and how they have violated the law, or an agreement between the parties.

In the longer demand letter in Appendix G, counsel for Green Co. carefully set out the facts to show that Blue Co. breached and terminated the agreement between the parties, and that Blue Co.'s actions significantly harmed Green Co. Unlike a collection action (where the defendant is likely well aware that it has not paid its debt), a party that has allegedly breached a contract may not be aware of the alleged breach, or of the harm that the breach has allegedly caused the opposing party. Thus, a powerfully written demand letter will make the potential defendant aware of the situation, and may make it more likely that the parties will resolve the dispute before a lawsuit occurs.

---

[4] *See id.* at 125–27.

The concluding paragraph restates the demand. Depending upon the strategy of the party making the demand, it will likely include some (and perhaps all) of the following items:

- a time limit on how long the demand or offer remains open;
- the consequences if the other party fails to respond by the deadline; and
- an offer to meet for settlement talks.

The consequences frequently involve filing a lawsuit. Because a lawyer cannot afford to lose credibility, a demand letter should never make an empty threat — it should only threaten litigation if the party is willing to file a lawsuit.

Chapter Review

- Letters and emails are likely the most common type of writing for practicing attorneys.
- Lawyers need to write letters to clients to fulfill their ethical obligations to keep clients informed on the status of their matters, and to provide clients with enough information for clients to make informed decisions.
- Lawyers write letters to a wide variety of people, but two of their most important audiences are their clients and opposing counsel.
- Before writing letters, lawyers must consider the audience and the purpose of the letter. Clients can be a wide range of people, from educated to uneducated, rich to poor, young to old, general counsel for a large corporation, or executive at a small company.
- The purpose of client emails can be broken down into three general categories: informational letters, opinion letters, and advisory letters.
- Informational letters are the most common type. They do not involve legal analysis, but convey or request information. For example, they could involve confirming deposition dates, updating clients about recent case developments, summarizing what the attorney understood at a recent meeting with the client and asking the client to confirm that the attorney understands the facts correctly, transmitting documents to the client and telling the client what to do with them, requesting documents from the client, etc.
- Opinion letters provide a law firm's opinion as to whether a proposed action by the client is legal or not. They carry the risk of malpractice litigation if the opinion is incorrect, so firms generally have only a few senior attorneys who are experts in that area write the letters, and they are often reviewed by the firm counsel or another senior lawyer.
- Advisory letters are much more common than opinion letters. They typically contain an opening paragraph, the relevant facts, the legal analysis of the issue, the client's options and the attorney's recommendations, and the closing paragraph.
- The opening paragraph introduces the issue, and states when the client asked the attorney to research and advise on that issue; the attorney's conclusion; and often, a brief summary of the client's options and/or the attorney's

recommendation, depending upon what the client had asked the attorney to do.

- Then it contains the relevant facts, and protects the attorney by stating that the advice is based on those facts, and if those facts are incorrect or incomplete, it could change the attorney's conclusion.
- The legal analysis states the general applicable legal rules and then applies them to the facts. If the client is not an attorney, there are no citations, and the attorney should use language that the client will understand.
- Then the letter states the client's strategic options, explains each of them, and provides a recommendation if the client requested it.
- The concluding paragraph reconnects with the patient, shows the attorney's concern, and suggests any necessary follow-up actions, or perhaps suggests a meeting to discuss the client's options.
- Letters to opposing counsel have a narrower audience — attorneys — but there still may be significant differences between the knowledge and personalities of attorneys.
- These letters should be firm but polite and respectful — neither too weak nor too aggressive.
- As with client letters, many letters to opposing counsel are informal. They involve case management or transaction management issues, such as conducting discovery. Like informational letters to clients, they must be respectful, clear, and precise.
- Demand letters or settlement letters attempt to begin negotiations to resolve a dispute. Demand letters usually seek a certain amount of money by a certain date, and threaten consequences such as a lawsuit if the amount is not paid. Certain statutes or contracts may require demand letters as a prerequisite to litigation.
- Settlement letters may offer a certain payment or seek a new demand, and the offer is usually good for only a limited time period.
- Settlement and demand letters that involve specific money demands or offers should contain confidentiality provisions saying that the offer or demand is confidential under Rule 408 of the Federal Rules of Evidence and an analogous state rule.
- The letters may be very short, as with demand letters seeking debt collection (which state the contractual provision under which the debt is owed, when the debt came due, and then make a demand for payment). With more complex issues, a potential plaintiff may choose to tell its story persuasively, explaining how the potential defendant breached a contract, broke the law, or otherwise harmed the writer's client, resulting in damages.
- The letters begin by stating that counsel represents the client, make the demand or offer, and mention the confidentiality provision. After the factual and legal support, they repeat the demand or offer, and state how long the demand or offer is valid.

- Demand letters often conclude by stating what the party will do if the other party does not respond by the deadline, and settlement letters or demand letters may suggest that the parties meet to resolve the dispute.

Chapter 23

OVERVIEW OF CONTRACT DRAFTING

Chapter Preview

This chapter introduces how to draft contracts. The chapter focuses on:

- goals for drafting a good contract;
- converting deal terms into contract language;
- the parts of a contract; and
- contract drafting style tips.

It is a puzzling fact of the U.S. legal system that contract drafting is a fundamental skill that attorneys need, yet many lawyers fail to receive formal training in this area. Traditionally, U.S. law schools focused on the types of legal writing that are more common for litigators, such as memoranda, motions, and briefs, and contract drafting was either not taught at all, or perhaps taught by a part-time faculty member in an elective. More recently, many law schools have developed contract drafting courses that are taught by full-time faculty, but they are still usually electives.

This limited attention to contract drafting does not serve future attorneys well. Most lawyers are likely to draft contracts at various points in their career. For transactional lawyers, it is a central part of what they do, and for litigators, it is necessary to draft certain types of contracts such as settlement agreements, or perhaps agreements related to employment law. Solo practitioners, who are still a large percentage of all U.S. lawyers, must be able to draft many types of agreements.

If your law school offers a contract drafting class, it is a useful course that you should consider taking. This chapter cannot cover the subject in the depth that a specialized course will. Rather, it is intended to introduce you to basic contract concepts and drafting principles.

A. WHAT TO KNOW BEFORE DRAFTING BEGINS

Before you begin to draft contracts, it is important to have background knowledge about the process. First, let's consider the nature of the client, and some differences between litigation clients and transactional clients.

Clients come to litigators when they have a problem, and they need the litigator's help to resolve it. They're already in pain when they see the litigator, and they project some of that pain onto the litigator by associating the litigator with the pain, much as patients do with dentists. Litigation is an adversarial process: We use the term "opposing counsel," and tend to view litigation as a zero-sum gain, where a good result for one party suggests a bad result for the opposing party.

Clients come to transactional lawyers, on the other hand, when they are making a deal and need to memorialize the transaction. Often, the client is excited about the possibilities that the deal represents, and they may associate the transactional lawyer with some of those good feelings, because they see the lawyer as someone who can help them to complete the deal successfully. Those positive feelings may be tempered, however, by worries that the lawyer will create problems when drafting the contract that could endanger or even destroy the deal.

Because the negotiations that lead up to the contract will hopefully result in a "win-win" deal that is good for both parties, we do not use the term "opposing parties." Instead, the parties to a deal are called "principals," "counterparties," or "the other side," which is more neutral language.

For a transaction to be successful, counsel for the parties need to work together to draft a contract that is fair to both parties. This makes sense when we understand that a contract creates private law that governs the relationship between the parties and that courts enforce, provided that it is reasonably fair. Thus, it is in the interest of lawyers for both sides to create a fair contract. One-sided deals may not be enforceable in court, and they might even blow up before the parties sign the contract. This does not help the clients, or the reputations of the lawyers.

In short, the dynamic between transactional counsel is less adversarial and more cooperative than the dynamic between litigators, because counsel for the parties to a deal need to cooperate enough to create a contract that satisfies the parties, leads to a good working relationship between them, and is enforceable in court.

1. Goals When Drafting a Contract

Some lawyers may be thinking primarily of short-term goals when drafting a contract: drafting the document on time, negotiating any changes with counsel for the other side, having the parties execute[1] it, and getting paid for the work.

To draft a well-written contract that leads to a successful working relationship between the parties and avoids litigation, however, attorneys need to think more deeply about the deal, the relationship between the parties, potential problems that may occur further down the road, and how to avoid them. Tina Stark has described the goals as follows:

- To memorialize the terms of a deal accurately.
- To use clear language and to avoid ambiguity.
- To advance the client's goals while reducing its risks.
- To draft a contract that is balanced enough that both parties are satisfied with the deal.
- To balance the need for specific provisions with the need for flexibility.
- To resolve problems pragmatically.
- To draft well enough that the contract is filed away and not read.
- To avoid litigation.[2]

The first three goals are self-explanatory, although new lawyers need to understand that ambiguity is deadly in a contract. Each party will read an ambiguous provision in a way that favors itself, and this can quickly lead to a breakdown in the parties' relationship and an eventual lawsuit. Moreover, under the principle of *contra proferentum*, courts interpret a contract's ambiguous provisions against the interests of the party that drafted the contract. This is why some contracts contain a provision saying that the parties bear equal responsibility for drafting the contract, and ambiguous language should not be construed against either party for being the drafter.

---

[1] U.S. lawyers use the word "execute" to mean "sign": the parties execute the contract by signing it. In other languages such as French, to "execute" means to perform, so parties execute a contract by performing under its terms. This is another problem with translation: even when the same word is used, it may have a different meaning or usage in another language.

[2] Tina L. Stark, *Drafting Contracts: How and Why Lawyers Do What They Do* 4 (Aspen Publishers 2007) (listing eight goals).

The fourth goal may seem surprising. After all, isn't it the attorney's job to do everything possible to favor the client? No, not in this case. As we said above, a contract creates private law between the parties. An unfair contract that favors the more powerful party at the expense of the weaker party may poison the working relationship between the parties, and a court may not enforce the provisions if it sees them as unfair. Courts call that type of agreement an "adhesion contract," and may choose not to enforce inequitable provisions.

The fifth goal, about the need to balance specificity with flexibility, means that the contract must be specific enough that the parties understand what their rights and obligations are, but flexible enough that they have the ability to deal with unforeseen situations and to manage their relationship without feeling constrained by the contract.

Litigators often work on breach of contract cases, and ask each other, "Why didn't the attorneys who drafted the contract foresee this problem?" Although it is possible that the drafters missed the problem — after all, not everything is foreseeable, and no one is perfect — it is also possible that the drafting attorneys intentionally avoided the issue. Most contract relationships between parties proceed successfully, after all. Contracts sometimes remain silent on issues because the parties cannot agree on the language to resolve the issue, or the lawyers do not want to blow up the deal by "inventing" problems that will lead to disagreement, or scare the parties away from completing the deal.

The seventh goal may seem hard to understand at first, but the idea is that if the contract deals with the major potential problems, is clear, and is fair, then the parties will likely have a smooth working relationship, and they will not have any reason to take out the contract and consult it.

2. The Next Step: Converting Deal Terms into Contract Language

After the parties have negotiated the deal, the lawyers need to express the terms of the deal in contract language. Under the terms of a deal, parties have obligations, and they gain rights. They make certain promises to the other party, and they may have the ability to choose what to do in certain situations. Lawyers express all of this by employing the following basic contract concepts:

- declarations;
- covenants;
- representations and warranties;
- conditions precedent; and
- discretionary authority.[3]

---

[3] I am indebted to my former colleague, Prof. Sue Payne, for her clear explanation of the basic contract concepts and the structure of a contract.

a. Declarations

Declarations are factual statements about which the parties agree. They primarily exist in two parts of a contract: the definitions article, and the general provisions, also known as **boilerplate**. The most common declarations are definitions.

Examples:

> "**President**" means the President and Chief Executive Officer of the Purchaser, Ms. Paula Constanzia.
>
> "**Termination Date**" has the meaning assigned in Section 5.1.
>
> *Section 10.2* Governing Law. The laws of the State of New York govern all matters arising out of or relating to this Agreement.

The first two declarations are definitions, and the third declaration is boilerplate. The first definition occurs in the Definitions article, and the second definition provides a cross-reference explaining that the term is defined in Section 5.1. Drafters should always place cross-references for easy reference in the Definitions article for terms that are defined in the text, and they should make sure that the defined term is capitalized uniformly throughout the agreement. If the drafter forgets to capitalize the defined term, it can be ambiguous.

b. Covenants

A covenant is the most common type of contract provision. A party promises to do something for another party. The covenantor — the party who makes the covenant — has a duty to perform, and the covenantee gets the right to receive the performance. In general, it clearer to describe the duty than the right, so it is best to draft a covenant by describing what the covenantor is obligated to do, rather than what the covenantee is entitled to receive.

Example:

> The Seller shall deliver the Goods to the Buyer at the times specified in Schedule 2.[4]

Traditionally, lawyers have used the auxiliary verb "shall" when drafting a covenant. Unfortunately, many lawyers use the word sloppily, to express concepts that are not covenants. Accordingly, some authorities prefer the use of "must" or "will," partly because many so drafters have overused "shall." However, "shall" is still the

---

[4] In the sentence above, "Seller," "Goods," and "Buyer" are all defined terms.

most commonly-used auxiliary verb to express covenants in contracts that are drafted in the United States.

Many authorities believe that because "must" is used to express conditions and "will" is used to make future statements, it avoids confusion and promotes clarity to use "shall" when expressing obligations.[5] The best solution to fix the problems with the overuse of "shall" is to use the word correctly:

- Do not use "shall" with non-parties to the contract, or with inanimate objects. A contract can only create an obligation for the parties to the contract, so you should restrict the use of "shall" to the parties.
- Avoid passive voice with "shall," as it may make it unclear as to who actually has the obligation. "Shall" should always follow the name of a party.

EXERCISE 23 A

Look at the covenants below. If "shall" is used incorrectly, fix the mistake.

1. The Buyer's Consultant shall determine if the Goods are genuine.

2. The Goods shall be in Mint Condition.

3. The Seller will receive payment for the Goods by the dates and times specified in Schedule 3.

4. The Goods shall be maintained in Mint Condition by the Seller until their delivery, by the dates and times specified in Schedule 3.

5. The Seller shall maintain a list that details the source of the Goods ("**List**").

c. Representations and Warranties

Representations and warranties are two related contract concepts that drafters should use together. Although the meanings of these terms are similar, they are not the same.

Example:

The Expert Witness represents and warrants that:

(1) He graduated from Harvard Medical School in 1982;

(2) He has been a board-certified thoracic surgeon since 1993;

(3) He wrote and published a book on thoracic surgery in 2004; and

[5] *See, e.g.*, Stark, supra note 2, at 126–27; Deborah B. McGregor and Cynthia M. Adams, *The International Lawyer's Guide to Legal Analysis and Communication in the United States* 303–04 (Aspen Publishers 2008).

(4) He has testified as an expert witness in the area of thoracic surgery 27 times.[6]

A representation is (1) a statement of fact (2) as of a moment in time (3) that is intended to induce reliance. In the example above, the Expert Witness' statement that he graduated from Harvard Medical School in 1982 is (1) a statement of fact that was true (2) on the date when he signed the contract, and it was (3) intended to induce the plaintiff to hire him as an expert witness.[7]

Misrepresentations (untrue representations) may either be negligent or fraudulent. To prove that the defendant made a negligent misrepresentation, the plaintiff's burden of proof is the preponderance of the evidence, and a successful plaintiff's remedies include rescission (avoiding the contract) and restitution.[8]

To prove that the defendant made a fraudulent misrepresentation (with knowledge of the falsity of the representation), the plaintiff has a heightened burden of proof: by clear and convincing evidence. A successful plaintiff has the choice of rescission and restitution, or damages (either out-of-pocket expenses or the benefit of the bargain). A successful plaintiff may be entitled to punitive damages.[9]

A warranty is simpler than a representation. It is simply a promise that a statement is true. Essentially, the party who provides the warranty indemnifies the other party if the statement is not true. The remedy for breach of warranty is damages.[10]

As the attorney for the party who is receiving the promises, you want the maker of the statement to both represent and warrant the statement, so as to obtain the maximum range of possible remedies and the most flexibility should the client need to sue.

Many drafters make representations and warranties a separate article. The risk with that strategy is that if you inadvertently draft a representation and warranty and do not include it within that article, you potentially create ambiguity.

Finally, do not make representations and warranties about the future, because we do not know what will be true in the future. Instead, use covenants to make promises about the future.

d. Conditions Precedent

A condition precedent is a condition to an obligation: a party promises to do something, but only if something else occurs first. This can be expressed in two ways — either with an "if/then" construction, or by using a tabulation with "must have." If there is only one condition precedent, it's easy to use the "if/then" construction, but it

---

[6] Contract drafters call this type of list a "tabulation."

[7] Stark, supra note 2, at 33.

[8] *See id.*

[9] *See id.*

[10] *See id.*

there is a series of conditions that must occur first, it is likely easier and clearer to draft a tabulation:

Examples:

(1) If/Then Construction

> If the Purchaser pays the Seller the Purchase Price at the Closing, then the Seller shall close the transaction that this Agreement contemplates.

(2) Tabulation Using "Must Have"

> The Seller is obligated to consummate the transactions that this Agreement complicates only if each of the following conditions have been satisfied or waived before the Closing Date.
>
> [a tabulated list of conditions follows, each using language indicating that the Purchaser "must have (done something)"].

If it is a condition precedent to a closing, and the condition does not occur, then the other party has the right to walk away from the deal. If it is a condition precedent to a different right, the party who fails to meet the condition loses that right.

Example:

> If the Associate bills more than 2100 hours of work that Meets Expectations or Exceeds Expectations in a calendar year, then the Associate shall receive a bonus of $15,000 (the "**Bonus**").

If you bill only 2,099 hours in a calendar year, you fail to meet the condition, and you lose the right to receive the Bonus.

e. Statements of Discretionary Authority

The party with the discretionary authority has the discretion to choose between or among the specified options. The contract language includes the auxiliary verb "may" and the conjunction "or."

Example:

> If the Employee earns the Bonus, then the Employee may choose to receive $1,500 or an extra five days of vacation in addition to his or her already-accrued vacation period (the "**Bonus Vacation**").

B. DRAFTING THE CONTRACT

Contracts may vary greatly, depending upon how simple or complex their subject matter is. A short contract may have only a preamble (introduction), recitals (background), words of agreement, and numbered paragraphs that state each provision. (*See* Appendix I, Settlement Agreement and Release, for an example of a short contract.)

On the other hand, a very long and complex contract may be several hundred pages long. A very long contract is likely to have a cover page that states the title and a table of contents that makes it easier for legal readers to navigate through the document. Finally, a long contract is likely to have numerous shorter documents known as schedules and exhibits that follow the contract.

1. Parts of a Contract

While contracts may vary greatly in length and complexity, they tend to have the same parts, even if some of them are omitted in a very short contract. The following section describes each of the parts of a typical contract.

a. Title and Preamble

A very long contract may have a cover page with the title, but medium-length and short contracts typically have the title of the contract centered at the top of the first page, in allcaps.

The title should give some indication as to the type of contract that it is. Simply writing "CONTRACT" or "AGREEMENT" at the top is not useful. Many contracts have basic titles like "SETTLEMENT AGREEMENT AND RELEASE" (*see* Appendix I), "TRANSITION SERVICES AGREEMENT" (*see* Appendix J), "ASSET PURCHASE AGREEMENT," or "DISTRIBUTION AGREEMENT." This has the added benefit of making it easier to do an online search for a model agreement of a particular type at a later date.

The first paragraph after the title is called the "preamble." It introduces the effective date of the agreement and the parties to the agreement:

> ASSET PURCHASE AGREEMENT
>
> This Asset Purchase Agreement ("**Agreement**") is dated as of November 1, 20XX, between Nicolai Shoes, Inc., a Delaware corporation ("**Seller**"), and Shoe-In, Inc., an Illinois corporation ("**Purchaser**").

The date of the agreement is typically the date that the parties sign the agreement, and "as of" is used if one of the parties will sign the contract at a later date. In that case, the parties should have a line in the signature blocks where they may write the date on which they executed the agreement.

The date of the contract is typically also the "effective date," which means the date that the contract takes effect and the parties must follow its terms. The parties can agree upon an effective date that is later than the signing date, but because that is not typical, a later effective date should be spelled out as a provision in the body of the contract, such as in an article stating the term of the contract.

b. Recitals/Background

The second section of a contract was traditionally called the "recitals," and it contained a number of clauses, each beginning with "WHEREAS" in allcaps. Today, some attorneys still use the traditional format, while others use the plain English term "Background" (or perhaps no heading), and provide regular sentences in plain English, without a word that introduces each sentence. Some attorneys have replaced "whereas" by lettering or numbering the sentences in this section, while others simply write short paragraphs without lettering or numbering.

The recitals provide background information about each party and their reasons for entering into the contract. This information is useful for legal readers who may look at the contract months or years after it was drafted, and who may not know the background facts.

The information also may be useful for courts. When construing ambiguous language in a contract, courts give effect to the parties' intent. A Background section can explicitly state the intent, so that the court does not have to infer it (and perhaps make inaccurate inferences).

c. Words of Agreement

This section states that the parties have reached an agreement, and it serves as a transition between the introductory parts of the contract and the articles. Traditionally, lawyers felt that it was essential to provide the "magic words" that asserted that there was consideration for the contract:

> NOW, THEREFORE, in consideration of the foregoing and the mutual agreements contained in this Agreement, and for other good and valuable consideration, the value, receipt and sufficiency of which are acknowledged, the Parties hereby agree as follows:
>
> Or, more simply,
>
> NOW THEREFORE, in consideration of the mutual promises, covenants and agreements contained herein, the Parties to this Settlement Agreement

agree as follows:

Many drafters and clients still insist on using these words today. Some lawyers believe that, should litigation occur, the use of the magic words will satisfy a court that the parties have complied with the formalities and make it less likely to analyze whether there really was consideration to support the contract. Moreover, in certain types of promises such as option contracts or guaranties, a formal promise might be considered binding even where there is no substantive consideration. Thus, some attorneys prefer to retain the language on the ground that it "can't hurt and might help."

Other attorneys, who use the plain English approach, use much shorter and simpler language:

Therefore, the parties agree as follows:

Or

Accordingly, the parties agree as follows:

These drafters do not include the magic words because they are unnecessary if consideration exists. More importantly, the general rule is that if consideration does not exist, magic words are insufficient to create it. Therefore, many drafters eliminate the consideration language as surplusage.

d. Definitions

In a short contract, each provision is simply numbered and the definitions are scattered throughout the provisions (*see* Appendix I). In a longer or more complex contract, the various sections are called "articles," and the Definitions article is the first one, immediately after the words of agreement.

Definitions are in alphabetical order. Some words are defined in the article, and others are defined in the body of the contract and cross-referenced in the Definitions article. As discussed above, once the term is defined, it uses capital letters as the first letter of each word in the term, and the drafter must be sure to be consistent.

When drafting a definition, use the verb "means." If you want to limit a definition, write that it "includes X but does not include Y." Although many drafters still write "means and includes," it is redundant and should not be used.

If there is litigation, courts view definitions simply as declarations, so do not include "operative language" such as covenants in your definitions. Courts will likely not enforce covenants that only exist in the Definitions article.

Other definition rules:

- do not simply use dictionary definitions of words as definitions, as that is unnecessary;

- do not define terms in an unexpected, confusing way (e.g., including food in a definition of "Equipment");
- do not make circular definitions (e.g., defining "Manager" as "a person who manages"); and
- do not use cross-references that send your legal reader all over the document (e.g., stating that a term is defined in Section 5.2, which sends the reader to Section 9.4, which sends the reader to Section 7.3).

e. Action Terms and Term of Contract

After the Definitions article, the body of the contract begins. Depending on the nature of the contract, there may be an article that sets out the contract term (i.e., the period of time in which the contract remains in effect). The other articles at the beginning of the body set out the central parts of the deal — the key provisions that reflect the most important part of the deal, called "action terms."

f. Other Business Provisions

After the key action terms, the next few articles include the other provisions to which the parties have agreed. Drafters express the action terms and the other business provisions by using contract concepts such as covenants, statements of discretionary authority, representations and warranties, and conditions precedent.

g. Termination Provisions

The termination provisions, which some attorneys call the "endgame," describe the parties' obligations, rights, and remedies at the end of the contract. It must provide for both the natural termination of the contract, and the premature termination triggered by a party's breach of a material provision of the agreement.

The contract should distinguish between termination events that automatically terminate the contract, and those that provide a party with the right to terminate the contract if it chooses to do so. It should also specify each party's remedies for certain types of breaches.

h. General Provisions/Miscellaneous Provisions (Boilerplate)

As discussed above, boilerplate is the standard contract language that drafters include in contracts, with little change from one contract to another. Contracts generally include them in an article called "General Provisions" or "Miscellaneous Provisions."

There are many general provisions which parties may include in a contract, including the following:

- notice, which requires the parties to provide each other notice before certain events occur, and which specifies how and when the parties must provide notice;

- the choice of law, also known as the governing law, i.e., which jurisdiction's laws govern the agreement;
- severability, which states that if any portion of the contract is held to be invalid, illegal, or unenforceable, the rest of the contract will remain in full force and effect;
- assignment and delegation, which states that no party may assign its rights or delegate its duties without the approval of the other party; and
- the merger provision, which states that the agreement constitutes the final agreement between the parties, and all prior and contemporaneous negotiations and agreements between the parties on the matters contained in the agreement are merged into and superseded by the agreement.

Typically, parties include many but not all of the common general provisions, as some may not be relevant to the facts of that deal. For example, a contract that involves shipping or transportation will likely include a Force Majeure provision, also called an "Acts of God" provision, which details the effects of a major disruption such as a natural disaster or act of war on the parties' obligations. An employment contract, however, is much less likely to include this provision. The lawyers for each party must determine whether a particular provision is necessary or worthwhile to protect the client's interests.

Drafters must be careful to edit and customize general boilerplate so that it is appropriate for the terms of that deal. For example, a careless drafter may include the wrong addresses from a model contract in the notice provisions if he or she is not careful. Careful proofreading is necessary not just to check for mechanical mistakes such as a spelling, grammar, or punctuation mistakes, but also substantive errors such as incorrect addresses, dates, or amounts.

i. Signature Lines

The format for the signature lines depends upon whether the person who is executing the agreement is an individual who is signing in his or her own capacity, or an executive who is signing in his or her role as an officer on behalf of the corporation, partnership, or other entity.

For an individual, the person's name appears under the signature line. For the entity, the full name of the entity appears above the signature, "By:" appears before the signature line, and the individual's name and position in the entity are below the signature line. There may also be a line for the date, especially if the parties may execute the document on different dates.

j. Schedules and Exhibits (If Any)

Schedules and exhibits are additional documents that go after the signatures, but are still considered part of the contract. Schedules contain information that is drafted for the contract, and they typically involve specific information, such as complex payment terms or a calendar of delivery dates. The drafters include this information in a separate schedule because it is too long and detailed to insert into the body of the contract, and it is easier to read in this form.

Exhibits are typically examples of other important or relevant documents that already exist and were not drafted specifically for the contract.

2. Drafting Style and Advice

a. The Plain English Movement in Contract Drafting

The language in contracts is famous for being difficult to read and for giving non-lawyers headaches. Sometimes the language is so thick and impenetrable that it is very difficult even for lawyers to understand, and we find ourselves having to read the same provision three, four, or even five times to understand what it means. If a lawyer has to read a provision several times to understand what it says, it does not reflect well on the drafter.

The movement toward drafting contracts in plain English mirrors the movement in favor of plain English in other forms of legal writing such as briefs, motions, and memoranda. As we discussed earlier in the book, certain types of writing, such as consumer contracts and federal statutes, must now be drafted in plain English. Also, the Securities and Exchange Commission now requires disclosure documents filed under the Securities Exchange Act of 1933 and registration statements filed under the Securities Act of 1933 to be in plain English.[11] Authorities on legal writing overwhelmingly argue for the use of clearer, simpler writing in contracts, without legalese.[12] Almost all of them use the term "plain English" to refer to the proper modern contract drafting style.

Tina Stark, however, uses the term "contemporary commercial drafting" for business contracts that do not involve consumers.[13] She states that while contemporary commercial drafting is based on plain English principles, several differences exist between the two styles, such as in the use of pronouns. In plain English consumer contracts, an insurance company or bank says "we" to refer to itself and "you" to refer to the consumer, which is too informal for commercial transactions between businesses. Stark also points out a difference in approach: sophisticated business contracts are more likely to include provisions that apply to risks that are conceivable but unlikely.[14]

While the movement toward clearer, more concise contract language has been continuing for decades, examples of traditional contracts are still easy to find. Many transactional lawyers and their corporate clients have pushed back against the

---

[11] George W. Kuney, The Elements of Contract Drafting 18 (3d ed., West 2011).

[12] *See, e.g., id.* at 18–19; Stark, supra note 2, at 4–5, 201; McGregor & Adams, supra note 3, at 313–32; Scott J. Burnham, *Drafting and Analyzing Contracts* 271–96 (3d ed., LexisNexis 2003); Thomas R. Haggard, *Contract Law from a Drafting Perspective* 24–38 (West 2003); Bryan A. Garner, *The Redbook: A Manual on Legal Style* 453–56 (2d ed., West 2006).

[13] Stark, supra note 2, at 4.

[14] *See id.* at 4–5.

movement, and for several pragmatic reasons.

First, many believe in the old saying, "If it ain't broke, don't fix it." They feel that they are familiar with traditional contract-drafting practices, and that they work well enough as is. Second, they are concerned that re-drafting in the newer style when there are acceptable traditional models to use will cost clients too much money and possibly change the meaning of established contract models in unpredictable and possibly unfortunate ways.

While it is true that ignoring traditional contract models and drafting new contracts in plain English or contempory commercial drafting styles may cost clients more money in the short term, the benefits are obvious. The old language *is* often "broken" and archaic, leading to confusion and unnecessary disputes, and the modern style is a significant improvement. Also, drafting contracts in the new style provides a way for lawyers to weed out old language that does not reflect the state of present-day law.

What is occurring at law firms now seems to be a transitional stage, as we see in our two model contracts in the back of the book. Attorneys are likely to draft shorter and simpler contracts, such as the Settlement Agreement and Release in Appendix I, wholly or almost wholly in the modern style, with minimal legalese.

Longer and more complex contracts, such as the Transition Services Agreement in Appendix J, remain something of a hybrid: they are likely to contain aspects of both the modern, simpler drafting style, and of more traditional contract language.

If you work as a transactional associate for a large U.S.-based law firm, what should you do? Try to emulate best practices where possible by drafting in the clear modern style and by eliminating legalese wherever possible. That said, you also need to be pragmatic. If the supervising attorney prefers more traditional contract language or tells you to use forms or models with traditional language, then you need to follow directions.

b. Contract Drafting Style Tips

Most of the tips here are similar to what we discussed in the context of writing office memoranda, but if anything the rules apply even more here. A well-drafted contract is clear, concise, and easy to read. Being concise means stating what is necessary in the fewest possible words. When you see a well-drafted contract, it looks simple and easy to do, but it is not. Here are some tips:

- **Write short sentences.** Keep your sentences to 20 to 25 words or less. Some model contracts have very long sentences. Improve them by chopping very long sentences into three or four shorter ones. If you have to take a breath before reading the sentence out loud, it's probably too long.
- **Use active voice.** Avoid passive voice even more in contracts than in other legal writing: they can make it ambiguous as to which party does what, which can be disastrous.
- **Use action verbs and avoid nominalizations.** Do not write: "The President of the Buyer shall make a determination as to . . . ." Instead,

write "The President of the Buyer shall determine . . ."

- **Avoid confusing words.** For example, avoid words ending in "-ee" and "-or," which tend to confuse most people. "Landlord" and "Tenant" are clearer than "Lessor" and "Lessee."
- **Avoid double negatives, or sentences with several negatives.** Draft affirmative sentences instead.
- **Draft the duty, not the right.** Write covenants, which are typically clearer and more specific than a party's right to receive something.
- **Make complex, multi-part provisions clearer with tabulations.** Tabulations are much easier to read than very long sentences with many semi-colons. Make sure that the sentences or clauses in tabulations have parallel structure.
- **Provide headings and use bold type with them.** Only use numbered provisions without headings for short contracts like the one in Appendix I.
- **Avoid legalese and most Latin terminology.** Legalese survives largely in contracts, but it is usually no more useful in contracts than in other legal writing. Legalese and Latin phrases are archaic, stuffy, and pompous, and you should avoid them.
- **Use defined terms carefully.** Follow proper capitalization with defined terms so that they are clearly used as defined terms.
- **Make sure that contracts have sufficient white spaces.** Contracts are easier to read when there are sufficient white spaces on each page. Do not fill up a page with giant blocks of writing in very small type.
- **Each section or provision should express one idea.** If you are drafting a very long section with many parts, determine whether they are all parts of the same idea. If so, consider using a tabulation. If not, consider breaking it up into several sections.

All of these suggestions help to make a contract clearer and more readable, which of course is our goal. Be creative, be logical, and be concise!

Chapter Review

- Transactional lawyers approach their work with a different perspective from litigators. They work with counsel for the other party in a more cooperative and less competitive way.
- Rather than trying to "win," they want to ensure a contract that is sufficiently fair for both parties to feel satisfied and for a court to find all provisions valid.
- Other goals include memorializing the deal accurately; using clear language and avoiding ambiguity; advancing the client's goals while reducing its risks; making provisions specific enough for clarity yet flexible enough to allow parties sufficient room to operate; anticipating

problems and resolving them pragmatically; and ultimately, avoiding litigation.

- Contract drafters must convert the terms of the deal negotiated by the business people into the basic contract concepts: declarations, covenants, representations and warranties, conditions precedent, and discretionary authority.
- Declarations are true statements that the parties agree on, such as definitions and general provisions.
- Covenants are binding promises to do something for another party.
- Representations and warranties are both promises that something is true, but they are related to different causes of action with different remedies, so use both of them together.
- Conditions precedent involve an event or events that must happen before an obligation is triggered.
- Discretionary authority gives the holder the authority to make choices.
- The parts of a contract include:
  - The title and preamble, which introduce the nature of the agreement, the parties, and the date of the agreement;
  - The recitals or background, which explains why the parties want to make the deal;
  - Words of agreement;
  - In longer contracts, a definitions article;
  - The key action terms that are at the heart of the contract;
  - Other business provisions;
  - Termination provisions;
  - General provisions (also called miscellaneous provisions or boilerplate);
  - The signature lines; and often
  - Schedules and exhibits.
- The general trend is toward drafting contracts in simpler, more concise language, but many lawyers still use model contracts with traditional writing styles.
- It is best to write in clear language, with short sentences in active voice, with action verbs and without double negatives, legalese, or most Latin phrases.
- Use tabulations for clarity.
- Have sufficient white space on a page.
- Limit sections or provisions to one idea.

Chapter 24

LAW SCHOOL SKILLS: PREPARING FOR AND TAKING FINAL EXAMINATIONS

Chapter Preview

This chapter introduces writing skills that will help you to do well in a U.S. law school. The chapter focuses on:

- how to prepare for examinations throughout the semester;
- how to write class outlines; and
- how to write final examinations.

You came to a U.S. law school to learn about the U.S. legal system and its approach to legal problems, as well as to obtain an LL.M. degree. However, those are longer-term goals. At this point in time, you also want to get excellent grades in your classes.

This chapter provides tools to help you with both goals. It discusses study skills that will help you to learn more in your classes and to get excellent grades in them.

A. STUDYING FOR FINAL EXAMINATIONS AND OUTLINING

1. Studying

As a student in an LL.M. degree program at a U.S. law school, you are likely someone who has been an excellent student for many years. You can do even better if you know the skills and techniques that lead to success in law schools here.

We have already discussed basic daily study skills such as how to read cases and other legal materials critically by "attacking" what you read and asking yourself questions as you read, and how to brief cases. What follows are some tips related to preparing for your law school final examinations.

a. Types of Final Examinations

- Law school final examinations typically count for 100% of your grade, or close to it (some professors reserve a small portion of the score for professionalism scores: on-time attendance, class participation, etc.).
- There are several types of law school examinations: essay examinations (the most common kind), multiple-choice and short answer examinations, and some examinations that offer a combination of all three question types: essays, short answers, and multiple choice questions.
- In traditional classes given to first-year law students, all students sit in one room at the same time and take the examinations. Today, many classes at some law schools have self-scheduled examinations, where students may take the exam whenever they want during normal business hours, but within the traditional time limit.
- At some schools, you may be able to get extra time for the test (e.g., one extra hour for a three-hour exam) if English is your second language, but you likely have to apply for the time extension.
- Some classes have "closed-book" exams, where you can bring no materials to the test (other than, perhaps, your laptop). Today, however, most classes have "open-book" exams, when you can bring in outside materials such as outlines or books. Nevertheless, some professors may limit the materials you can bring to the exam; for example, you might only be able to bring an outline that you made yourself.

- A small number of older or more traditional professors may still have you write the essay answers in "Bluebooks" — books of blank lined paper with blue-colored covers — but students take the majority of examinations today online, using their laptops.
- Most classes have the traditional time limit of three hours for a three-credit class, but some classes allow for longer "take-home" exams, where you may have eight or even 24 hours to take the test. In those classes, however, the added time usually means that the professors have a higher grading standard and expect better work.

b. What You Need to Learn About Your Exams

As shown above, there is quite a variety of test procedures, both between law schools, and between classes at the same law school. Thus, you need to learn at the beginning of the semester (ideally in the very first class) how that professor structures his or her class, and what the final examination procedures are: open-book or closed-book; self-scheduled or taken together in a group; written by hand or with your laptop; the standard length of time for an examination, or a longer take-home examination. Each answer to these questions will help to determine how you will study for each class.

Second, listen carefully in each class for small hints that the professor gives about the final examination. If he or she says something like, "this would make a great question on the final examination . . . ," *write it down and underline it.* Then, as you study and review your notes, pay special attention to these hints. In fact, if you have several of them in one class, you can cut and paste them and put them on one page. Then be sure to study and review these areas during the last week or two before the exam period begins.

Third, find out if the professor keeps copies of old final examinations and excellent student answers on reserve in the library. If the answer is yes, look at them early in the semester (when few if any students look at them). What type of questions does the professor like to use? Do you see a pattern in the old tests; i.e., are some subject areas tested more heavily than others? If the professor keeps any "A" exams on reserve, read them and see what they look like. Why is that an excellent examination? You will want to write an exam that shares similar features with it.

c. Getting Practice

Use the old exam questions and write answers to them under the same time limits as the original exam had. You only become good at writing exam essay answers through practice under realistic circumstances!

Finally, consider working with fellow students on exam preparation. Many law students have study groups for each class that meet once per week or so, where the students ask each other questions about that week's readings and materials, or about other areas in the class that they find confusing or difficult to understand. Often, when you try to explain something to other students, you discover that you do not understand it well, and you will likely learn that by working to explain a legal principle to others, you come to understand it more clearly.

2. Outlining

An outline is a summary of the rules of law and the policy that you learned in the course, grouped by the subject area. It focuses on the "black letter law" — the general rules, followed by the more specific rules that explain each of the elements or factors in the major rules, and short examples from key cases in the class that show how to apply the rule to the facts.

The example outline section below from an outline for a torts class discusses an intentional tort called "false imprisonment."

a. Excerpt from Torts Outline

4. False Imprisonment

Elements of a Prima Facie Case:

(1) The defendant's act or omission to act that **confines** or **restrains** the plaintiff to a **bounded** area;

(2) The act or omission to act is **intentional**; and

(3) The act or omission to act **causes** the confinement or restriction.

Confinement: May be accomplished with physical barriers (such as locked doors), physical force, or direct or indirect threats of physical force. Plaintiff must be aware of confinement, or must suffer an actual harm.

Intent: Plaintiff must show defendant's intent to confine plaintiff, or defendant's knowledge that his actions or omission to act would cause plaintiff's confinement.

Defenses:

"Shopkeeper's Privilege"

By statute or case law, many states have given shopkeepers a privilege to detain suspected shoplifters. However, the privilege is limited and only applies if:

(1) The defendant has a **reasonable** belief that the plaintiff committed the theft;

(2) The detention was conducted in a **reasonable** manner, with non-deadly force; and

(3) The detention is for a **reasonable** period of time (about 10 or 15 minutes) and only for the purpose of making an investigation.

You should slowly create your outline throughout the semester. Do not wait until the end of the semester to write the outline; however, you should wait until each area of the law is completed before you make the outline on that area. For example, false imprisonment is an intentional tort. Write the false imprisonment section of the outline as part of the intentional tort section, and write it after you have studied all of the intentional torts.

B. TAKING FINAL EXAMINATIONS

1. Last Preparations for the Final Examination

After you review your outline for the final examination, a great way to prepare for the exam is to reduce it. Some students actually make three versions of the outline: First, they take the complete 35 to 40 page outline and cut the length in half by removing long case explanations or policy discussions. Then, when they are familiar with the reduced version of the outline, they reduce it again to a *very* short, one to three-page version that just includes the black letter law for the major rules in the course, and perhaps some key rules that explain each element or factor.

Also, take the collection of "exam hints" that you assembled from your notes, and review each of those areas of law carefully — there's a very good chance that at least one of them will be tested on the final examination.

2. Taking the Final Examination

The night before you take an exam, make sure that you get a good night of sleep. At this point, stating up most of the night for last-minute studying is counter-productive because it will leave you tired and unable to think clearly at the examination.

a. Before You Write the Examination

When you first open the examination, scroll or flip through the pages to determine the structure of the test. How many questions are there, and what is each question worth? That is how to determine how much time to spend on each question.

For example, let's imagine that you have a three-hour essay examination with three essay questions. The first essay question is worth 50% of the test, and the other two questions are worth 25% each. Then allot the time according to the essay's value: the time limit for the first essay should be 90 minutes and the time limit for each of the other two essays should be 45 minutes.

Essay questions are often long, with very complicated fact patterns, and one or two questions at the end. First read the question(s) at the end. What does it ask you to do? That's called "the call of the question." Figure that out, and then read the question. As you read the facts, highlight or underline key facts that look important.

Many of these essays are what law professors call "issue spotters." They give a long, complicated fact pattern that requires you to identify which legal issues are raised by the facts. Then they expect you to "think like a lawyer" to resolve the issues and conflicts between the parties. As we have learned, you do that by applying the legal rules that you have learned in the class to the facts in the pattern, in a sharp, logical analysis that follows the IRAC pattern (or even better, CRAC, where you state the issue as a conclusion).

Professors are not looking simply for memorization: of course they expect you to know the key rules, and usually allow you to refer to your outline on an open-book test if you get nervous and forget part of them. What they are looking for is your *analysis* — your ability to apply those rules to your client's facts. After all, that's what lawyers have to do.

Before you begin to write each essay, plan it out so that you will write efficiently and in a logical pattern. For example, if the essay asks you to determine a client's possible causes of action (legal claims) against several possible defendants and her likelihood of success for each of them, write an outline as follows:

- Following the order of the problem, take your client's possible claims against each defendant one at a time, organized by the claims. Write down the name of each claim she might have against each possible defendant (*see* example below, "Sample Outline of Essay with Notes"), and any quick ideas about that claim that occur to you.
- These three steps — looking first at the end of the problem to learn the "call of the question," then reading the problem, and finally planning out your response with an outline — should take approximately 25% to 33% of your allotted time for that essay. For example, if you have 90 minutes for the exam's longest, most important essay, you can spend 20 to as much as 30 minutes planning and outlining your answer. It sounds like that will take too much of your time, but it will not. It makes it easy for you to then fill in (populate) each section of your outline.
- For each section, in this type of question, you will describe a potential cause of action by the client against a defendant. Introduce the relevant law for the claim: the rules, and any potential defenses. Then analyze the issue. How do the rules apply to the facts on this issue? Will the defenses work? Why or why not?
- The more you work at a detailed level with the facts that the professor gave you, and the more that you show the best arguments for both parties, the higher your score will be.
- Write objectively, and give your conclusions words like "probably." The questions are often written so that there is no clear answer: you can get an A by taking either position, if you analyze the issues carefully in a balanced, detailed fashion. If you state that an answer is clear or obvious, you are likely incorrect, and may lose points for shallow analysis.
- The professor scores you by giving you points for each issue that you raise that he or she is looking for: each claim, each rule, each analytical point, etc. Write them quickly, and move on. Don't worry about writing elegantly — you don't have time to polish your writing and make it perfect. It's very difficult to finish an essay answer within the time limit.

- You do not have to spend an equal amount of time on each IRAC. For example, if there are similar claims against two parties and you have analyzed the first one in detail, you can basically state that the analysis of that claim against the first defendant also applies to the second defendant. Then move on.
- For example, with the long, complicated torts essay problem below, the outline shows that the client has five claims against the first defendant (false imprisonment, IIED, assault, negligence, and defamation), five claims against the second defendant (battery, false imprisonment, IIED, negligence, and defamation), and two claims against the third defendant. The sample portion of the answer gives a long, detailed IRAC analysis of the first claim (false imprisonment), to show you what a complete IRAC analysis should look like.
- Do not assume that you need to spend an equal amount of writing time on all 12 IRACs. That wouldn't be possible on a 90-minute problem where you only have 60 to 70 minutes of actual writing time. That's an average of only five to six minutes per IRAC, but the long IRAC on false imprisonment in the example took longer than that to write. Because most of the 5 claims for the second defendant are the same as for the first defendant, you can state that the same analysis mostly applies, but focus on the differences of fact between the two defendants and show how that would affect the analysis.

b. Writing the Exam

After outlining the answer, it's time to start populating the answer by filling in the sections of your outline. By following your planned-out structure, it will now be concise and organized, which is what professors want to see. After all, exams test your progress in learning how to think and write like a lawyer, and as we've learned in this book, legal writing involves concise, logical, well-planned writing.

If the name of a case that you studied seems relevant to your answer, state it, but you do not need a full citation, just the name of the case. If you cannot remember the name of the case, just write "A case held that . . ."

(1) Sample Essay Exam Question (Torts)

Essay Number One. This essay is worth 50% of the score.

Nancy Nurse, a potential client, walks into your office and tells you the following story. Nancy knew that her fiancé, Bill Businessman, was going to take her to a jewelry store that weekend to choose an engagement ring, so Nancy decided to go to her local shopping mall a few days before to see what they had.

Nancy walked into Janssen Jewelry and asked to see a beautiful ring with a large diamond in it. Magnus Janssen, the owner, took out a tray with the ring and was about to show it to her, when an obviously pregnant woman shouted, "Help me!" and fell to the floor.

As Nancy Nurse and Magnus Janssen rushed to help her, no one saw a distinguished-looking gentleman in a suit pick up the ring, put it in his pocket, and walk out of the store. While Nancy and Magnus were trying to help the fallen woman, she began behaving strangely, telling them to leave her alone. Confused and disturbed, Nancy forgot about the ring and decided to leave the store. Meanwhile, Magnus Janssen returned to the counter, saw that the diamond ring was missing, and shouted "STOP! THIEF!!" as Nancy left the store.

Nancy assumed that he was talking about someone else and walked away. Magnus ran out of the store, looked at a nearby mall security guard, and screamed, "GO GET HER!!" to the guard, who worked for Ace Security, Inc.

Nancy recognized the security guard, Harry Hoodlum, a juvenile delinquent from her high school days who had asked her on a date and became very angry when she said no. Harry roughly pushed Nancy against the wall, hurting her face. He pulled her hands roughly behind her back and handcuffed her tightly in front of a watching crowd. Harry sneered, "So now you're a thief as well as a slut!" and dragged Nancy back inside the store, where Janssen told him to bring her to a back room.

They locked Nancy in the room for an hour, interrogating her. Janssen shouted at Nancy, saying that he knew that she was working together with the pregnant woman to steal the diamond. Nancy was crying, and begging for them to remove the tight handcuffs and take her to the emergency room of the local hospital, but they refused.

Later, Nancy Nurse went to an emergency room, and learned that Harry Hoodlum had fractured her wrist and dislocated her right shoulder when he roughly grabbed her arm. Nancy said that the pain medication that the doctors gave her for her injuries had "messed her mind up." Nancy went to a psychologist, who told her that she was suffering from post-traumatic stress disorder and depression. Because of these problems, Nancy Nurse lost her good job at the hospital and Bill Businessman decided not to marry her.

Discuss whom Nancy can sue, her various tort claims, and their likelihood of success.

(2) Sample Outline of Essay Answer with Notes

A. Nancy's Claims v. Janssen (Store Owner)

False Imprisonment

IIED (Intentional Infliction of Emotional Distress)

Assault

(Yelling "GO GET HER!" to security guard an intentional causing of an apprehension of harmful or offensive contact?).

Negligence

Defamation

(calling her a thief when he yelled "STOP! THIEF!!" in crowded mall — offensive false publication to many observers)

B. Nancy's Claims v. Hoodlum (Security Guard)

Battery

False Imprisonment

IIED (Intentional Infliction of Emotional Distress)

Negligence

Defamation

(saying "So now you're a thief as well as a slut!" — highly offensive false publication to many observers)

C. Nancy's Claims v. Ace Security, Inc. (Hoodlum's Employer)

Vicarious Liability (Respondeat Superior)

Negligent Hiring

(3) Sample Portion of Essay Answer

Nancy Nurse has causes of action against the jewelry store owner, Magnus Janssen; the security guard, Harry Hoodlum; and his employer, Ace Security. The answer will discuss each claim and its likelihood of success below.

A. Nancy's Claims v. Magnus Janssen (Store Owner)

False Imprisonment

Magnus Janssen is probably liable for false imprisonment when he directed security guard Hoodlum to bring Nancy to a back room, and they locked the door and interrogated her for an hour.

False imprisonment is the intentional infliction of a confinement. Janssen and Hoodlum confined Nancy Nurse when they brought her into a back room of the door, a confined space, and locked the door. The plaintiff must be confined within definite physical boundaries, which Nancy was. She could not leave the room because the door was locked. Janssen intended to keep her confined in the room because they locked her in the room. Moreover, he refused to remove Nancy's handcuffs, which were restraining her. This confirms his intent to keep her confined.

Janssen may assert the "shopkeeper's privilege." A number of jurisdictions have statutes or court decisions that have granted storekeepers a privilege to temporarily detain a person who is reasonably suspected of stealing property. The privilege is limited, however, to a short period of time (about 10 to 15 minutes or less), sufficient to make a quick investigation. The privilege extends to the temporary detention of innocent suspects as long as the suspicion is reasonable, and the manner of detention is also reasonable.

Janssen is unlikely to succeed with this defense. Nancy was innocent of the theft, but Janssen's suspicion was reasonable, because she was near the ring when it disappeared and she left the store as he shouted "Stop! Thief!", which made her look guilty. Thus, his suspicion was reasonable, even though it was incorrect.

However, the privilege is limited to temporary detention only — about 10 to 15 minutes — and Janssen greatly exceeded that by detaining her for an hour. He also likely lost the privilege through the brutal, unreasonable nature of her detention, as Nancy suffered injuries and Hoodlum painfully handcuffed her behind her back, with Janssen refusing to remove the handcuffs.

Finally, it is unclear whether the shopkeeper's privilege extends to dragging Nancy back into the store after she left it. One case found the privilege where the store detective stopped a suspect who had left the store and was walking to the store parking lot, but that was still store-owned property. Here, it occurred in the common area of the mall, which is not store-owned property.

IIED (Intentional Infliction of Emotional Distress)

[analysis of the rest of the claims continues]

Keep an eye on the clock and make sure that you finish the test. If for some reason you did not finish the essay, the professor may give you partial credit for having an unfinished, skeletal outline at the end of the essay that at least shows who the conflict pairs are, and shows their claims.

Chapter Review

- Law school exams are usually 100% of your grade or close to it, so knowing how to study for them is essential.
- There are essay exams, short answer exams, and multiple choice exams, as well as exams that combine all three types of questions.

- Exams may be open-book or closed-book; at a scheduled time in a certain room or self-scheduled; written on paper or on your laptop; three hours (or four, with an ESL allowance); or 8- or 24-hour take-home exams. Find out what type of exam you have at the beginning of the semester, and plan accordingly.
- Listen in class for "exam hints," such as if the professor says that a certain issue "would make a good exam question." Always write down and highlight such a hint, and collect them at the end of the semester for studying.
- Consider joining a study group with other students who are taking the same class.
- Write an outline for the class during the semester. A full outline is usually 35 to 40 pages long.
- The outline contains black letter law: statements of the main rules of law, in elements or factors. Then add more specific rules that interpret each element. Also include any defenses to the rules, any policy justifications or purposes for the rules, and any case summaries of cases discussed in class or appearing in the case book that illustrate the rules.
- In the weeks before the test, study by reducing the outline, first in half, and then to a very short one- to three-page summary.
- Get a good night of sleep the night before the examination.
- When you open the examination, scroll or flip through it quickly to see the organization, such as how many essays there are and how much they are worth. Figure out how much time to allot to each essay according to their worth.
- For each essay problem, look first at the question(s) at the end of the problem to determine the "call of the question" (what it is asking you to do).
- For example, for a common issue-spotting essay problem that gives you a long, complicated fact pattern with several conflicts between potential plaintiffs and defendants, be prepared to determine who can sue whom, and what the potential claims and defenses are, as well as whether the claims are likely to succeed.
- Second, read through the problem, taking notes where facts seem particularly important.
- Third, write an outline for the answer, beginning with the first conflict pair, e.g., client v. first defendant, then client v. second defendant. For each conflict pair, write down all causes of action that apply.
- Altogether, these three pre-writing steps should take 25% to 33% of your allotted time for the answer.
- Then write your answer, populating your outline with each IRAC, one at a time.

- State the issue as a probable conclusion. Then state the relevant rules and defenses. Then apply the rules to the facts of the problem.
- Be balanced and objective. Don't look biased or clearly take sides. Show the arguments for each side, and then conclude with who is likely to prevail.
- Keep checking the time, so that you can finish the test. If time expires and you haven't finished the test, the professor may give you partial credit for at least showing who the conflict pairs are and what their claims are in your unpopulated outline.

APPENDIX A

GLOSSARY

Abrogate To invalidate a law in a formal manner; to repeal.

Affirm To hold that the lower court's decision was correct.

Analogize To show important factual similarities between precedent and our matter, to persuade the legal reader that the precedent is relevant and thus should apply to our issue.

Annotations Short summaries of cases which are relevant to statute sections or entries in legal encyclopedias, treatises, or other secondary sources.

Answer A pleading which responds to a complaint. It admits or denies the facts asserted in the complaint, asserts any affirmative defenses, and may also assert counterclaims against the plaintiff(s).

Appellant The party who appeals from a lower court's decision.

Appellee or **respondent** The party who responds to an appeal.

Bench trial A trial in which the judge determines the legal and factual issues without a jury.

Binding precedent *See* **Precedent.**

Boilerplate A slang term for the general provisions article of a contract. Boilerplate is largely copied from one contract to another, with minor modifications made to fit the terms of the agreement. Contract provisions relating to assignment and delegation, notices, choice of law, severability, modification and amendment, force majeure, and merger are typical boilerplate provisions.

Canon law Church law. It influenced the development of English family and inheritance law, as well as the concept of equity.

Case (1) A lawsuit or other legal matter. (2) A written judicial opinion that announces the court's decision and explains the court's reasons for its decision. (3) The arguments and evidence that support a party. If a lawyer tells a potential client, "you don't have a strong case," it means that in the lawyer's opinion, the potential client does not have strong legal arguments or evidence, and would likely lose in a lawsuit.

Citation In legal writing, a reference to a legal authority that the writer uses to support a statement or position. Generally, the term refers to the entire reference, including the name of the case or statute, such as *Marbury v. Madison*, 5 U.S. 137 (1803). Sometimes lawyers use the term to refer to just the alpha–numeric part that refers to the reporter (for cases) or the code/compiled statutes (for statutes), such as 5 U.S. 137 or 15 U.S.C. § 1125(a).

Citator An electronic system, provided by the major online commercial legal research providers, that tells legal readers whether or not a case, statute, or other legal authority is still good law. It provides the subsequent citing history for the document. For cases, it describes whether opinions gave the case positive treatment, distinguished it, questioned it, or overruled it.

Complaint The initial pleading which begins a trial. The plaintiff states the basis for the court's jurisdiction and venue over the matter, alleges the facts which support its legal claims, asserts its legal claims, and prays for relief.

Concurrence A separate appellate opinion following the majority opinion in which the author explains his or her reasons for agreeing with the majority's decision, but not the reasoning. Concurrences are not law and have no binding precedential value, but later courts may find them persuasive.

Construe To analyze and interpret the meaning: Courts *construe* the language of statutes.

Damages An award of money to be given to a successful plaintiff in a civil suit to compensate the plaintiff for losses.

Defendant (1) In a civil case, the party who has been sued. (2) In a criminal case, the party who has been charged with a crime.

De novo The standard of appellate review for a trial court's findings of law. Under the "de novo" standard, the appellate court makes a "new" determination and gives no deference to the trial court's ruling.

Dicta A short, plural form of *obiter dictum.* Dicta are facts or opinions that were not necessary to form the holding in a judicial opinion, and thus have no precedential value and are not binding. A frequent type of dictum is a hypothetical situation, where a court discusses what it might have done if the facts were different. Later courts may look to dicta if the hypothetical situation in the earlier case becomes the legal issue in the later case.

Discovery The pre–trial process in which the parties investigate disputed facts through such techniques as depositions, document requests, requests to admit, and interrogatories. In the U.S. legal system, this factual investigation is conducted by the parties to the dispute, not by the court.

Discussion In legal writing, the part of a memorandum, brief, or judicial opinion that provides the legal analysis.

Disposition The court's final determination that ends the case.

Dissent A separate appellate opinion following the majority opinion (and concurrence, if there is one) in which the author explains his or her reasons for disagreeing with the majority's decision and reasoning. Dissents are not law and have no binding precedential value, although later courts may find them persuasive.

Distinguish To show important factual differences between precedent and our matter, to persuade the legal reader that the precedent is not relevant and thus should not control our issue.

Double jeopardy The principle, prohibited by the United States Constitution, that a criminal defendant can be subjected to more than one trial for the same offense.

Elements The parts of a legal rule in which all parts must be present for the rule to apply.

En banc An appellate decision that is reached by a large panel of most or all of the sitting judges in that appellate circuit or district.

Equity (1) Fairness and justice. (2) The collection of legal concepts that describe fairness and justice. (3) The system of law that originated in the English High Court of Chancery, separately from the common law courts. When lawyers talk differently about "equity" and "law," they are generally referring to the differences between claims that equitable in nature (for which the remedy is non–monetary, such as an injunction or specific performance), and claims that are legal (for which the remedy is monetary damages).

Ex parte A hearing, motion, or similar occurrence that is done by, or in favor of, one party without the other party being present.

Factors The parts of a legal rule in which not all parts must be present for the rule to apply.

Federal Relating to the national government or laws of the United States.

Federalism The division of the U.S. governmental system into two levels, federal and state, and the relationships between those two levels of government.

Good law Law that is valid. If it is a case, it has not been reversed or overruled; if it is a statute, it has not been held unconstitutional, superseded, repealed, or amended.

Governor The head of the executive branch of a state.

Grant of certiorari When four or more justices of the United States Supreme Court agree to accept an appellant's petition and to review a lower court's decision.

Impeach (1) With public officials, to accuse the official of a crime, and/or to conduct a trial to remove the official from office. (2) In a trial, to attempt to demonstrate that a witness' testimony is untrue or inaccurate.

Injunction An order that preserves the status quo by requiring a party either to act or not to act, to prevent harm to the party that seeks the injunction.
Permanent injunction: An injunction whose duration is permanent.
Preliminary injunction: An injunction whose duration is temporary, often until the disposition of the underlying case.
Temporary restraining order (TRO): An emergency injunction of very short duration, often 10 or 14 days, that preserves the status quo until the plaintiff can move for a preliminary injunction.

Jurisdiction (1) A court's right to bring a defendant into court and to enforce a judgment against him, her, or it. (2) The geographical area over which a governmental authority (such as a court) may exercise its power.
Concurrent jurisdiction: When more than one court (such as a state court and a federal court) has jurisdiction over a matter.
Diversity jurisdiction: When a federal court has jurisdiction over a case with state–law claims because the plaintiff(s) and the defendant(s) are residents of different states.
Exclusive jurisdiction: When only one court has jurisdiction over a matter.
Federal question jurisdiction: When a federal court has jurisdiction over a matter because at least one claim involves federal law.

Jury trial A trial in which the judge determines the legal issues and a jury (which usually consists of 6 or 12 adult citizens who live in the jurisdiction where the trial is held) determines the issues of fact.

Legalese Annoying, pompous jargon used by lawyers, such as "heretofore," "hereinafter," or "said" as an adjective ("said defendant").

Litigant A party to a lawsuit.

Motion A written or oral request to the court to enter an order or a ruling.

Movant The party who makes a motion.

On point Directly relevant to the legal issue (also called **on all fours**).

Opinion A written judicial decision (*see* **case**).
Majority opinion: An opinion that is joined by most of the members of the appellate panel.
Plurality opinion: An opinion where a majority of the judges on the appellate panel agree with the result, but less than a majority agrees with the reasoning. For example, if six out of nine justices on the United States Supreme Court agree on the result but only four of them agree on the reasoning, the resulting opinion is a plurality opinion, meaning that more judges joined with its reasoning than any of the alternatives, but that number was not a majority.
Unanimous opinion: an opinion that is joined by every member of an appellate panel.

Ordinance A municipal or local law or statute.

Party (1) A person or organization who participates in a lawsuit. (2) A person or organization who participates in a transaction.

Per curiam A court's opinion that is released without the name of a judge who authored the opinion.

Plaintiff (1) A party who brings a civil lawsuit.

Precedent A judicial opinion that announces a legal rule. When the legal rule is relevant in a later case, it either may or must be followed by the later court, depending upon the court's level and jurisdiction. A court must follow **mandatory or binding precedent**, such as a holding from a higher court in the same jurisdiction. **Persuasive precedent**, such as a case that was decided in a different jurisdiction, is entitled to respect and consideration, but a court may choose to follow it or not.

Private law (1) To U.S. lawyers, legal documents drafted by individuals or parties that are binding only on those parties, such as wills or contracts, or a narrow class of statutes that is typically enacted to provide compensation for an individual or specific group of individuals. (2) To lawyers from civil–law systems, "private law" refers to the laws that are the focus of the civil code: laws that cover private rights, obligations, and duties.

Promulgate (1) To announce publicly. (2) To put a law into effect, especially regulations.

Public law (1) To U.S. lawyers, almost any statute that is enacted by a legislature (except for the narrow class of statutes that pertains to an individual or specific group of citizens). (2) To lawyers from civil–law systems, "public law" refers to laws that concern the government, or the relationship between the government and the people.

Ratify To confirm a previously–made treaty, agreement, act, etc., so that it becomes valid from the time it was created.

Reception When a country or jurisdiction adopts all or part of the law of another country or jurisdiction as its own.

Remand To return a case to a lower court for further action in accordance with the appellate court's decision, such as to determine attorney's fees or to have a new trial.

Remedy Relief provided by a court in accordance with a party's request. It may be in the form of damages or equitable relief, or it may be the court's enforcing a right.

Remove To transfer a case from one court to another, such as from a state court to a federal court.

Reply The third filing in motion practice: the first party moves, the second party responds, and the first party replies to the second party's response.

Reporter A book that contains published cases. They are organized by jurisdiction and by the level of court, and there are also regional reporters that contain certain published appellate decisions from several states. Reporters are published by the series (typically 1,000 volumes). For example, 360 F.3d 125 refers to a case that begins on page 125 of volume 360 of the third series of the Federal Reporter, which contains the decisions of the intermediate federal appellate courts.

Response The second filing in motion practice: the first party moves, and the second party responds.

Reverse To overturn a lower court's decision.

Specific performance A form of equitable relief, in which a court requires a party to a contract to perform its obligations under the contract.

Standard of review The perspective from which an appellate court reviews the ruling of a lower court.

Stare decisis The doctrine under which courts render judgments that follow the reasoning of earlier judgments that contain similar facts and legal issues. *See* **Precedent**.

Writ A written order from a court that orders the person or organization who is named in the writ to perform or not to perform a certain act.

APPENDIX B

OFFICE MEMO WITHOUT CASE LAW

MEMORANDUM

To: Attorney 1

From: Attorney 2

Re: Possible Company Liability

Question Presented

What civil and criminal penalties does Company potentially face for submitting inaccurate Discharge Monitoring Reports to the State-X Environmental Protection Division and failing to properly inspect two leak detection systems at the Company Plant located in Town-X of State-X?

Short Answer

I. Civil Penalties

At this time, we believe Company's most likely exposure is a cost penalty of between zero and $200,000 assuming that (i) Company voluntarily disclose the violations, (ii) Company institutes a corrective action program to prevent similar errors from occurring in the future, (iii) there is no evidence that there was any actual discharge from either lake into the surrounding environment, and (iv) there is no evidence of a willful or knowing violation of the discharge permit. Maximum cost penalties, which we believe are unlikely, could be about $5 million from State-X and about $3.75 million from the federal government.

II. Criminal Penalties

Based on our current understanding of the facts, we believe it is unlikely that state or federal authorities will seek any criminal penalties against Company. However, the maximum criminal penalties could be about $5 million from State-X and about $10.1 million from the federal government if further factual investigation demonstrates that Company knew it was submitting inaccurate DMRs, knew the contractor responsible for inspecting the leak detection system was falsifying inspection reports, or was negligent in its oversight of the contractor. Even in the event Company is criminally culpable for these acts, it is likely that the fines will still be substantially lower than the maximum.

Background

The Company Plant located in Town-X of State-X has a Discharge Permit issued in Year 1 by the State-X Environmental Protection Division and renewed in Year 5. The Permit governs the discharge limitations, monitoring requirements, and other imposed conditions for operating ponds at Company Plant.

The Permit is a no discharge permit, meaning that although it allows stormwater and plant process water to be discharged into East Lake and West Lake, it prohibits discharges from those lakes to the ground surface, surface waters, or groundwaters of State-X. The Permit requires each of the lakes to have a leak detection system; if the leak detection system detects leakage in excess of 60 gallons per acre per a day in any 25-day period, a corrective action plan to eliminate the leakage must be developed. Among other requirements, the Permit requires Company Plant to monitor the two leak detection systems on a weekly basis to ensure compliance with this limitation. The permit also requires Company Plant to submit quarterly Discharge Monitoring Reports ("DMRs"). The DMRs include information from the weekly inspections of the leak detection systems.

For almost a decade, Company Plant has employed Contractor to perform the required monitoring of the leak detection system. During a periodic environmental and transportation audit at Company Plant, it came to the attention of Company Plant employees that Contractor was not properly performing these inspections. As a consequence, DMRs previously submitted to State-X are likely inaccurate. Company may face liability under both State-X and federal law as a result of these issues.[1] This memorandum provides a preliminary assessment of Company's potential liability.

At this point the investigation is ongoing. Our assessments of the likely penalties faced by Company may change as we gather additional information.

Discussion

I. Failure to Monitor the Leak Detection Systems in Compliance with the Permit Requirements

Company faces potential civil and criminal penalties under both State-X and federal law for the failure to properly monitor the leak detection systems in compliance with the Permit. Based on our current understanding of the facts, we believe the most likely outcome will be a relatively small civil penalty from the State-X Environmental Protection Division ("SXEPD"). We do not believe that Company will face criminal penalties from SXEPD, nor do we believe that Company will face any penalties (civil or criminal) from the federal government.

a. Civil Penalties

The Permit requires Company Plant to inspect the lake leak detection systems on a weekly basis to identify and abate breached containment collections. To our knowledge, Contractor has not conducted proper leak detection system inspections for West Lake since the lake relining project was performed in Year 4. Contractor erroneously believed that the leak detection system for West Lake was located

[1] Although our investigation is ongoing, we have also identified some potential inaccuracies in prior DMRs that were unrelated to Contractor's failure to properly inspect the lakes.

beyond a fence on the north side of the lake. Because Contractor could not access that leak detection system, it recorded previous data from the last proper inspection it was able to conduct.

Contractor usually inspected the leak detection system for East Lake. However, Contractor claims that the leak detection system was occasionally locked and that it could not conduct inspections when the leak detection system was inaccessible. When the leak detection system was locked, Contractor would record previously collected data in the same way it did for West Lake. However, Contractor would not make any notification on its inspection forms concerning the locked system. While we have not been able to find any independent verification that the leak detection system for East Lake was ever locked, Company will have the burden of proving that it complied with the Permit conditions and performed the leak detection system inspections. Because the reports from Contractor cannot be used to verify when the leak detection system may have been locked, Company will have difficulty establishing that the inspections of East Lake were properly performed.

The laws of State-X provide that violating a permit condition is punishable by a penalty of up to $50,000 per day (for each day that the permit condition is violated). Stat. § 800(b). Because inspecting the leak detection system in compliance with the Permit is a permit condition, the law allows State-X to assess a penalty up to $50,000 per incorrectly performed inspection.[2] There were 100 weeks between the date the permit was issued and the date Company Plant discovered the problems with Contractor. Therefore, State-X could assess a maximum penalty of $5,000,000.[3]

Under the Clean Water Act, the federal government could also penalize Company for violating a permit issued by a state under authority delegated by the EPA. 33 U.S.C. § 1319(d). The maximum federal penalty for violations of the Permit conditions is $37,500 per day for each violation. 33 U.S.C. § 1319(d); 40 C.F.R. § 19.[4] The cumulative maximum federal penalty is $3,750,000 ($37,500 for each of the incorrectly performed inspections). This could be in addition to any penalty assessed by State-X.[5]

---

[2] State-X could also impose up to a $50,000 penalty for each day of violation for the late submission of the DMR. Submission of the DMR itself is a permit condition. We believe a fine for submitting a late DMR is unlikely given the circumstances leading to the late submission of the DMR. Company Plant has previously submitted late DMRs without penalty and Company Plant's rationale for submitting a late DMR is to ensure the DMRs accuracy after identifying issues with its accuracy. If Company Plant had submitted the DMR on time, State-X would have stronger arguments to support a criminal violation for knowingly submitting an inaccurate report.

[3] State-X could potentially argue that the incorrect inspection of each lake is a separate violation. However, the permit places a single condition requiring inspection of the leak detection systems. We believe that the most persuasive reading of the permit is that any failure to correctly perform a weekly inspection is a single violation, regardless of how many problems Company Plant had performing the weekly inspection. But State-X may make this argument and if it prevails, the maximum penalty would double for each category of fine discussed in this section. For example, in the case of civil penalties under the State-X statute, the potential fine would be $10,000,000.

[4] As enacted, the maximum penalty under the Clean Water Act for civil violations is $25,000. 33 U.S.C. § 1319(d). However, the Federal Civil Penalties Inflation Adjustment Act requires federal agencies to adjust civil penalties to account for inflation at least once every four years. 28 U.S.C. § 2461 note.

[5] EPA could also elect to seek administrative penalties under 33 U.S.C. § 1319(g). Under the Act, an administrative penalty cannot exceed $177,500. 33 U.S.C. § 1319(g)(2)(B); 40 CFR § 19.4 (adjusting for inflation). If EPA were to seek to collect higher penalties, it would need to institute a civil enforcement proceeding. Examples of enforcement proceedings that EPA has identified which would warrant an

However, the Clean Water Act penalties would only apply if the federal government elects to overfile, meaning the federal government files an environmental enforcement action where the state environmental enforcement agency has not sufficiently prosecuted a violator of a federal environmental statute. Overfiling is unlikely in the present situation. The federal government usually chooses to overfile when it believes that a state will not adequately address the violation or where violations are extraordinarily egregious. There is no evidence that State-X will not properly respond to any violation, nor is any violation especially egregious. The violation at issue relates to inspection and Company Plant is in the process of correcting the problem. Although there may be a dispute on that point, and more investigation is necessary, we are also hopeful that we can establish that there has been no release from either West Lake or East Lake.

b. Criminal Penalties

The laws of State-X and the Federal Clean Water Act both provide criminal penalties when a corporation violates a permit condition with some scienter. Under State-X law, a corporation that intentionally or with criminal negligence violates the terms or conditions of a discharge permit can be punished by a fine of no more than $50,000 for each day of the violation.[6] Stat. § 805. The maximum criminal penalty under the State-X statute would thus be $5,000,000 (the same calculation used above for the civil penalty).

As with the laws of State-X, the Clean Water Act provides that negligent violations of permit conditions are punishable by a fine of no less than $2,500, but no more than $25,000 per day of violation.[7] 33 U.S.C. § 1319(c)(1).[8] The maximum federal penalty for a negligent criminal violation would thus be $2,500,000 ($25,000 times number of incorrectly performed inspections). The Clean Water Act provides higher penalties for knowing violations. Knowing violations of permit conditions are punished by a fine of no less than $5,000, but no more than $50,000 per day. *Id.* § 1319(c)(2).[9] The maximum penalty for knowing criminal violations of permit conditions would be $5,000,000 ($50,000 times number of incorrectly performed inspections).

The State-X criminal penalties would be in addition to any civil penalties obtained.

---

administrative penalty are issues relating to DMRs. *See EPA Guidance on Choosing Among Clean Water Act Administrative, Civil, and Criminal Enforcement Remedies*, April 1987.

[6] Under the State-X statute, an individual can also be imprisoned for up to two years. Stat. § 805.

[7] Criminal penalties are not adjusted for inflation like civil penalties. However, under the Criminal Fine Improvements Act, the maximum criminal fine a court may impose may be up to the greater of the amount specified in the law setting forth the offense or various alternative ceilings in the Criminal Fine Improvements Act. 18 U.S.C. § 3571. For negligent violations, this would be a maximum penalty of $200,000. *Id.* For knowing violations, the maximum penalty would be $500,000. It is unclear whether each weekly inspection would constitute a separate offense, but the per day language of the Clean Water Act implies that each failed inspection is a single offense with increasing penalties based on the duration of the failure. Therefore, the Clean Water Act penalties are more likely the upper limit on liability.

[8] Under the federal statute, an individual can also be imprisoned for up to one year. 33 U.S.C. § 1319(c)(1). A person previously convicted of a negligent violation faces double the fine and maximum prison term. *Id.*

[9] Under the federal statute, an individual can also be imprisoned for up to three years. 33 U.S.C. § 1319(c)(2). A person previously convicted of a knowing violation faces double the fine and maximum prison term. *Id.*

Similarly, the federal government can pursue both civil and criminal penalties. However, in practice, the government pursues only one type of penalty.

Based on our present understanding of the facts, there is little credible evidence that Company intentionally or knowingly violated any permit condition.[10] Contractor claims that Company was aware of its practices, but we have not been able to corroborate its assertions. Furthermore, Contractor claims that it has e-mail backing up its assertion that Company knew it was falsifying reports. However, none of the emails produced by Contractor support these allegations. Nonetheless, State-X or the federal government could potentially argue that Company's failure to exert oversight and monitor Contractor was negligent and justifies imposing a criminal penalty.

Based on our experience, we believe it is unlikely that State-X or the federal government would pursue criminal penalties against Company for failure to monitor the leak detection systems. This analysis could change as we gather more facts.

II. Failure to Submit Accurate DMRs

Company would face separate penalties under State-X and federal law if it knowingly[11] submitted inaccurate DMRs. Under the laws of State-X, "[a] person who knowingly makes a false representation in a report required by a permit under these laws... shall be punished by a fine of not more than $30,000[.]" Stat. § 820.[12] The Clean Water Act contains nearly identical language and provides for a maximum fine of $10,000. 26 U.S.C. § 1319(c)(4).[13]

Additionally, the federal False Statements Statute, 18 U.S.C. § 1001, provides that a corporation that, in any matter within the jurisdiction of the executive, legislative, or judicial branch of the Government of the United States, knowingly and willfully falsifies a material fact, makes any materially false statement or representation, or makes any false writing knowing it to contain any materially false statement, shall be fined up to $500,000 or imprisoned not more than five years, or both. 18 U.S.C. §§ 1001, 3571(c). Courts broadly interpret "Government of the United States" to include state agencies where a program is either federally funded or the federal government has delegated authority to the states to enforce federal law. *See, e.g., United States v. White*, 270 F.3d 356 (6th Cir. 2001) (false statements made to state water agency came within jurisdiction of EPA for purposes of prosecution under 18 U.S.C. § 1001, since EPA retained authority to enforce its regulations and actively

---

10 Arguably, Company intentionally and knowingly failed to timely submit a third quarter 2011 DMR. Submission of the DMR itself is a permit condition. We believe that a fine is unlikely given the circumstances leading to the late submission of the DMR. *See* note 3 above.

11 Regulators may cite Company for unintentionally submitting incorrect DMRs and attempt to assess civil penalties. We believe these citations would be inconsistent with the laws of State-X and the Clean Water Act. Both bodies of law separately penalize knowingly submitting false reports and provide a lesser penalty for knowingly submitting a false report than for a civil violation. Penalizing a corporation at a higher level for unintentional acts than for intentional acts would lead to absurd results. Furthermore, unintentionally submitting an inaccurate report is usually the result of a violation of some other permit condition. Regulators can asses a civil penalty for violating the permit condition that led to the inaccurate report. Allowing a penalty for also submitting an inaccurate report would permit the regulator to penalize the same conduct twice.

12 Under the State-X statute, an individual can also be imprisoned for up to two years. Stat. § 820(b).

13 Under the federal statute, an individual can also be imprisoned for up to two years. 33 U.S.C. § 1319(c)(4). A person previously convicted of a knowing violation faces double the fine and maximum prison term. *Id.*

ensure state compliance with national safe water standards); *United States v. Wright*, 988 F.2d 1036 (10th Cir. 1993) (false water quality data reports which water treatment plant manager filed with state health department were within jurisdiction of EPA, even though EPA had granted primary authority for safe drinking water standards to state, since such grant was not exclusive, EPA having retained authority to enforce its regulations). Here, the EPA has delegated primary enforcement of the Clean Water Act to the SXEPD, but it has retained its authority to enforce its own regulations, including violations of permits issued by state agencies. Therefore, Company could be convicted under 18 U.S.C. § 1001 if it knowingly and willfully submitted a false DMR to the SXEPD.[14] Each DMR is arguably a separate violation of 18 U.S.C. § 1001.

Based on our current knowledge, we do not believe that Company knowingly or intentionally submitted a false DMR. However, if further investigation changes these conclusions, Company could face up to $300,000 in fines under State-X law ($30,000 times 10 false DMRs) and $5,100,000 in fines under federal law ($10,000 times 10 false DMRs violating the Clean Water Act plus $500,000 times 10 false DMRs violating the False Statements Statute).

CONCLUSION

Based on our current understanding of the facts, we believe that the most likely scenario would be for State-X to impose civil penalties on Company of between zero and $200,000 for failure to properly inspect the leak detection systems on East Lake and West Lake and submitting previously inaccurate DMRs. Our estimate assumes Company conducts a full investigation into the permit compliance failure, creates a corrective action plan, and makes a full disclosure to state authorities. Based the present status of our investigation, we do not believe that State-X or the federal government will pursue criminal charges against Company, nor do we believe that the federal government will assess civil penalties.

---

[14] In fact, the DMR itself acknowledges that submitting false information could be a violation of the False Statements Statute.

APPENDIX C

OFFICE MEMO WITH CASE LAW

MEMORANDUM

JUNE 25, 2012

To:	Attorney 1 Attorney 2
From:	Attorney 3
Re:	Big Corp (TCPA Litigation)
Subject:	Availability of Common Law Defenses To TCPA Actions

Introduction

In Year 3, Small Corporation ("Small Corp") filed a complaint in state court on behalf of itself and a class of similarly situated individuals and entities allegedly challenging Big Corporation's ("Big Corp") "policy and practice" of sending unsolicited advertising facsimiles under the Telephone Consumer Protection Act ("TCPA"). Small Corp's individual claim rests on its alleged receipt of nine advertising faxes received between Year 1 and Year 2.

The Telephone Consumer Protection Act ("TCPA") provides substantial statutory damages for, among other things, sending unsolicited advertising facsimiles. A fax is "unsolicited" if it is sent without the recipient's express permission. The only defense enumerated in the statute is if the sender can demonstrate an Established Business Relationship ("EBR") with the recipient.

An investigation performed by Big Corp and its counsel has shown that Small Corp is a professional TCPA plaintiff with dozens of TCPA lawsuits pending. Big Corp has been sending Small Corp advertising faxes for at least the past five years, and has occasionally sold Small Corp products from one of its offices. Some of these products may have been advertised on the very faxes at issue in Small Corp's suit. Small Corp appears to have filed suit now — after letting some of its individual claims expire under the applicable statute of limitations — solely to maximize the damages that may be available in a class action.

This memorandum analyzes the availability of common law defenses to a TCPA action. This memorandum begins by surveying the existing case law on common law defenses under the TCPA and identifying common law defenses that could theoretically bar Small Corp's claims. Because the availability of common law defenses to TCPA actions is an open question, this memorandum continues by setting out a framework for arguing for the recognition of various non-statutory common law defenses. This memorandum concludes by explaining the content of potentially applicable common law defenses and articulating theories under which those defenses could apply to bar Small Corp's claims.

Executive Summary

Few if any courts have specifically considered the extent to which non-statutory common law defenses will bar a claim arising under the TCPA. Two courts have adopted non-statutory defenses — laches and assumption of risk — but neither addressed the threshold question of the TCPA's susceptibility to non-statutory defenses. In this case, plausible non-statutory common law defenses to Small Corp's claims include implied waiver, equitable estoppel, implied acquiescence, and laches.

Whether such defenses can serve to bar a TCPA claim is likely a matter of Congressional intent and the defenses' consistency with the statutory scheme. Under this standard, implied waiver, equitable estoppel, implied acquiescence, and laches probably would be recognized as legitimate defenses to TCPA claims — such defenses are likely to advance a statutory scheme designed to prevent random advertising phone calls and faxes by focusing enforcement on abusive fax practices and excluding from the punitive statutory damages faxes to which the plaintiff had expressly or impliedly assented.

Analogous implied waiver, equitable estoppel, implied acquiescence, and laches cases are rare. Existing case law, however, provides enough guidance to articulate workable theories under each defense. Whether any particular defense is likely ultimately to preclude Small Corp's claims is difficult to assess without further fact development.

Discussion

I. To Date, Few If Any Courts Have Adopted Common Law Defenses To TCPA Actions; Plausible Common Law Defenses To Small Corp's Claim Include Implied Waiver, Equitable Estoppel, Implied Acquiescence, And Laches.

A. Two courts have recognized common law defenses to TCPA claims.

Several courts have noted that defendants have raised one or more common law defenses to an action arising under the TCPA. However, none of these courts undertook a detailed analysis of whether the common law defense claimed, if proven, would actually defeat the plaintiff's claim. For example, in *The Flag Co. v. Maynard*, 2006 WL 2225816, at *2 (D. Or. 2006), the court dismissed a defendant's common law defenses with leave to replead without addressing the question of whether such defenses were viable:

> [Defendant's] affirmative defenses raise the following issues: unclean hands (fifth), failure to mitigate damages (seventh), waiver and estoppel (eighth), assumption of risk (eleventh), and release (twelfth). Plaintiff moves to strike all as being inadequate "barebones" legal assertions which do not satisfy Federal Rule of Civil Procedure 8(b).... I recommend that plaintiff's motion as

to these affirmative defenses be granted, but that defendants be given leave to amend and replead them to include sufficient facts to explain the nature of the defense.

See also Stern v. Bluestone, 47 A.D.3d 576, 577 n.1 (N.Y.A.D. 2008) (noting that the defendant had raised the defense of laches but declining to address the defense on appeal because it found the defense waived).

Arguably, two courts have expressly adopted a common law defense in the context of a TCPA claim:

- In *Kinder v. Allied Interstate, Inc.*, 2010 WL 2993958, at *6 (Cal. App. 4 Dist. 2010), the trial court dismissed plaintiff's TCPA claim on the basis of California's assumption of risk doctrine. In upholding the dismissal on appeal, the court explained that by reconnecting his pager after disconnecting it due to the volume of unwanted calls, and "with[out] any valid contention that he wished to utilize it to engage in any legitimate business other than that of filing successive law suits," plaintiff had "intentionally subject[ed] himself to unwanted telephone calls." *Id.* The court found that plaintiff's conduct satisfied California's common law assumption of risk defense and "precludes recovery under the TCPA." *Id.*
- In *Boehm, Kurtz & Lowry v. Interstate Ins. Servs. Agency, Inc.*, the trial court dismissed plaintiff's TCPA claim on the basis of laches. 900 N.E.2d 1075, 1077 (Ohio App. 1 Dist. 2008). On appeal, plaintiff argued that laches was inapplicable because the defendant had not demonstrated prejudice. The court agreed and remanded the case back to the state court. *Id.* at 1078. Without expressly addressing the issue, the court's analysis indicates that dismissal on the basis of laches would have been proper if prejudice had been shown.

B. Plausible common law defenses to Small Corp's claim include implied waiver, equitable estoppel, implied acquiescence, and laches.

Here, Small Corp, as a professional TCPA plaintiff, was aware of its rights under the TCPA from the time it received its first fax, and yet waited over five years to bring suit against Big Corp. In the meantime, Small Corp purchased at least some products from Big Corp — possibly off of the very faxes now at issue. Furthermore, it is possible that Small Corp has established a fax line, and supplies that line with paper and toner, solely for the purpose of receiving "junk" faxes on which it then sues under the TCPA.

As discussed in more detail below, the above facts suggest that the following widely used common law defenses may be applicable to Small Corp's claim: implied waiver, equitable estoppel, implied acquiescence, and laches.

II. If Given An Opportunity, The Court Will Probably Conclude That Common Law Implied Waiver, Equitable Estoppel, Implied Acquiescence, And Laches Constitute Defenses To TCPA Claims.

A. Courts are divided on the precise standard for recognizing common law defenses to statutes.

The Supreme Court has never definitively resolved the question of whether federal courts are permitted to recognize non-statutory defenses to statutory causes of action. *United States v. Oakland Cannabis Buyers' Co-op.*, 532 U.S. 483, 490 (2001) ("[W]e note that it is an open question whether federal courts ever have authority to recognize a necessity defense not provided by statute."). The Court has, however, explained that Congress "legislates against a background of Anglo-Saxon common law." *United States v. Bailey*, 444 U.S. 394, 415-16 n. 11 (1980). Lower courts have thus found it appropriate in some instances to recognize certain defenses not explicitly authorized by statute. *See, e.g., United States v. Gore*, 592 F.3d 489 (4th Cir. 2010) (recognizing common law justification defense to 18 U.S.C. § 111). This recognition is done as a matter of federal common law.[1] *See Official Comm. of Unsecured Creditors of PSA, Inc. v. Edwards*, 437 F.3d 1145, 1152 (11th Cir.2006) ("The federal law of affirmative defenses governs the enforcement of causes of action created by federal statutes."); *Thurber v. W. Conference of Teamsters Pension Plan*, 542 F.2d 1106, 1108 (9th Cir.1976) ("Where federal statutes determine rights and liabilities, the federal common law, rather than state law, is controlling with respect to whether the defense of estoppel is available.").[2]

Lower courts are arguably divided on the precise standard used to recognize non-statutory defenses. *Compare United States v. Gore*, 592 F.3d 489 (4th Cir. 2010) ("Any inquiry into whether a common-law defense to a federal criminal statute may be recognized must focus on the particular circumstances and in the end turn on whether it can be said that Congress contemplated the defense when it enacted the statute.") *with Official Committee of Unsecured Creditors of PSA, Inc. v. Edwards*, 437 F.3d 1145, 1154-55 (11th Cir. 2006) ("[T]he application of the defense of in pari delicto to causes of action created by federal statutes depends on... the policy goals of the federal statute."). However, the core inquiries appear to be Congressional intent and consistency of the proposed defense with the statutory scheme.[3]

B. Common law implied waiver, equitable estoppel, acquiescence, and laches defenses appear to be consistent with Congressional intent and the statutory scheme.

Along with other circuits, the Tenth Circuit has explained that "the TCPA protects a species of privacy interest in the sense of seclusion" by preventing unwelcomed disruptions in the form of unwanted phone calls and faxes. *Park University Enterprises, Inc. v. American Cas. Co. Of Reading, PA*, 442 F.3d 1239, 1249 (10th Cir. 2006).

---

[1] Prior to *Mims v. Arrow Financial Services, LLC*, several courts, including the Tenth Circuit, concluded that the TCPA's use of the phrase "if otherwise permitted by state law" in Section 227(b)(3) incorporates state substantive law. *US Fax Law Center, Inc. v. iHire, Inc.*, 476 F.3d 1112, 1118 (10th Cir. 2007). The *Mims* Court's determination that "federal law gives rise to the claim for relief [under the TCPA] and specifies the substantive rules of decision" has probably implicitly abrogated these decisions. 132 S. Ct. 740, 744-45, 48 n.8, 52, 53 (2012).

[2] In contrast to the *availability* of common law defenses to federal causes of action, the *content* of such defenses is often derived from state common law absent a need to craft a uniform national rule. *See Steffes v. Stepan Co.*, 144 F.3d 1070, 1075 (7th Cir. 1998) ("A standard way in which federal courts make federal common law is by adopting the law of the state whose law would govern in the absence of federal law, subject to the implicit proviso that the adopted state law be consistent with federal policy.").

[3] Courts have articulated these principles in various ways. *See, e.g., Clark v. Capital Credit & Collection Services, Inc.*, 460 F.3d 1162 (9th Cir. 2006) ("With respect to rights secured by federal statute, 'absent some affirmative indication of Congress' intent to preclude waiver, we have presumed that statutory provisions are subject to waiver by voluntary agreement of the parties.'"); *United States v. Panter*, 688 F.2d 268, 271 (5th Cir. 1982) ("The right to defend oneself from a deadly attack is fundamental. Congress did not contemplate that § 1202 would divest convicted felons of that right.").

Federal legislation was necessary as a supplement to state legislation "because telemarketers could avoid state legislation by engaging in interstate operations." *ErieNet, Inc. v. Velocity Net, Inc.*, 156 F.3d 513, 517-18 (3d Cir. 1998) *abrogated by Mims*, 132 S. Ct. 740 (2012). Rather than target all advertising phone calls and faxes, the TCPA only targeted phone calls and faxes made without permission and, in 2005, codified an exception for phone calls and faxes between individuals and entities with a business relationship.

First, the TCPA was not designed to protect individuals from all advertising phone calls and faxes. Rather, the Act focuses on communications that recipients are unlikely to want — random solicitations from individuals with whom the recipients have no relationship — and protects the recipients with a large statutory penalty. Recognition of waiver, equitable estoppel, acquiescence, and laches arguably facilitates this statutory scheme in two ways: (1) by excluding claims in which the plaintiff has assented to the communication in some way, these defenses focus enforcement on truly abusive faxing; and (2) these defenses narrow the scope of a highly punitive statutory penalty that presumably Congress wanted sparingly applied.

Second, federal statutory rights are almost always subject to waiver. *See Clark v. Capital Credit & Collection Services, Inc.* 460 F.3d 1162 (9th Cir. 2006) (noting waiver defense to FDCPA claim). Because nothing in the TCPA's plain language or legislative history indicates an intent to preclude waiver, the common law defense of waiver is almost certainly available. Equitable estoppel, acquiescence, and laches are closely related to waiver in that each involves relinquishment through words or conduct of a known right. To the extent that the Court accepts that TCPA claims can be impliedly waived, the analogous doctrines of equitable estoppel, implied acquiescence, and laches should be adopted as well.

III. Without Additional Fact Development, It Is Unclear If Big Corp Would Prevail On Any Common Law Defense; Analogous Case Law Is Rare As To Each Possible Defense.

A. Implied Waiver

1. Case Law

Waiver is the most firmly entrenched common-law defense to statutory rights. *See, e.g., Ebling v. United States Dept. of Justice*, 2011 WL 2678935 (D.D.C. 2011). It is well established that "[w]aiver, as defined by federal common law, requires an 'intentional relinquishment of a known right,'" — i.e., that "the parties were aware of their rights and made the conscious choice, for whatever reason, to waive them." *New York Tel.*, 930 F.2d at 1011 (waiver under Maritime law); *Apponi v. Sunshine Biscuits, Inc.*, 809 F.2d 1210, 1217 (6th Cir. 1987) (waiver under Labor Management Relations Act); *Gonyea v. John Hancock Mut. Life Ins. Co.*, 812 F. Supp. 445, 450 (D. Vt. 1993) (waiver under ERISA).

Although most cases involve waiver by express agreement, waiver of a right may also be implied from the conduct, acts, or words of a party. *Delta Consulting Group, Inc. v. R. Randle Const., Inc.*, 554 F.3d 1133 (7th Cir. 2009) (applying Illinois law); *see also Am. Airlines, Inc. v. United States*, 77 Fed. Cl. 672, 681 (2007) ("A waiver need not be express, but may be inferred from a pattern of conduct."). Implied waiver arises "where a person against whom the waiver is asserted has pursued such a course of conduct as to sufficiently evidence an intention to waive a right or where his conduct is inconsistent with any other intention than to waive it." *Delta Consulting Group, Inc.*, 554 F.3d at 1140 (emphasis added); *see also PPM Finance, Inc., v. Norandal USA, Inc.*, 392 F.3d 889, 895 (7th Cir. 2004) (waiver implied when a party's conduct is inconsistent with an intention to assert that right). Inaction or silence can be the basis for implied waiver where that inaction or silence is inconsistent with an intent to claim a right. *Patrons Mut. Ins. Ass'n v. Union Gas System, Inc.*, 250 Kan. 722 (Kan. 1992). However, implied waiver is disfavored, and courts usually require that the act relied on to constitute the waiver must be clear. 31 C.J.S. Estoppel and Waiver § 88.

The circumstances under which courts have concluded that a course of conduct constituted an implied waiver of a right are varied. For example:

- **Passage Of Time:** In *Hidalgo Properties, Inc. v. Wachovia Mortgage Co.*, the Tenth Circuit considered a defense of implied waiver in the context of a breach of contract claim. 617 F.2d 196, 199–200 (10th Cir. 1980). Wachovia had entered into a standby loan commitment with Hidalgo that required Hidalgo to complete certain conditions prior to disbursement of the loan upon completion of Hidalgo's construction project. One condition was provision of a "foundation completion certificate." *Id.* at 199. Hidalgo never provided the required certification, and Wachovia refused to release the funds at the agreed time. However, evidence showed that Wachovia representatives had viewed the project at various stages of completion and there was no dispute "that Wachovia knew the foundations had been completed." *Id.* According to the court, Wachovia's "[failure] to demand performance when it knew the time for performance had arrived and passed created... waiver [issues] for the jury." *Id.*
- **Failure To Object To Prior Violations:** In *Schuster v. Dragone Classic Motor Cars, Inc.*, an S.D.N.Y. court considered a claim of implied waiver of a statutory right arising under New York law. 98 F. Supp. 2d 441, 448–49 (S.D.N.Y. 2000) (applying NY waiver law). Schuster had obtained automobile repair work from Dragone Classic on fifteen occasions, with each repair done under an oral agreement. When a dispute arose over the cost of four repairs, Dragone Classic sued for breach of contract. *Id.* at 445. As a defense, Schuster argued that Dragone had failed to comply with a New York statute requiring the issuance of a written estimate prior to the repair work and moved for summary judgment. *Id.* at 448. The court denied the motion: "Defendants' allegations regarding the parties' prior course of dealing [suggests] that plaintiff, in failing to object to the lack of a written authorization or record of his consent to the estimates in the prior eight transactions, waived his right to both the authorization and the record of his consent." *Id.* at 449.

Waiver cases are highly fact specific and ultimately turn on the intent of the party alleged to have waived its right. Although no court appears to have addressed a claim of waiver of a statutory right under circumstances identical to Small Corp, cases like *Hidalgo* and *Schuster* suggest that a waiver theory could be successful.

2. Theory

Small Corp was well aware that its statutory rights were being violated when it received faxes from Big Corp. Small Corp nevertheless chose not to object to Big Corp's conduct, instead choosing to accept the benefits of Big Corp's faxing and to enter into business with Big Corp on the basis of those faxes. Accepting this trade off shows an intent on the part of Small Corp not to enforce its statutory rights.[4] That Small Corp waited years to enforce its rights — and, indeed, even let some of its claims lapse — shows that Small Corp's delay cannot be explained by anything other than an intent to relinquish its claims.[5] Small Corp cannot now change its mind.

B. Equitable Estoppel

1. Case Law

Courts often consider estoppel and waiver together, and occasionally will blend the two. *See, e.g.*, *Jones v. Sunset Oil Co.*, 118 Cal. App. 2d 668 (2d Dist. 1953) (explaining that under California law implied waiver requires a showing of reliance). However, the doctrines are distinct: "[E]stoppel involves the conduct of both parties, whereas waiver depends upon what only one intends to do." *Corbett v. Garland*, 228 Fed. Appx. 525, 531-532 (6th Cir. 2007). Specifically, under federal law, equitable estoppel requires a showing of:

> (1) conduct or language amounting to a representation of material facts; (2) the party to be estopped must be aware of the true facts; (3) the party to be estopped must intend that the representation be acted on or act such that the party asserting the estoppel has a right to believe it so intended; (4) the party asserting the estoppel must be unaware of the true facts; and (5) the party asserting the estoppel must detrimentally and justifiably rely on the representation.

Apponi, 809 F.2d 1210, 1217 (6th Cir. 1987) (citing *Acri v. International Association of Machinists*, 781 F.2d 1393, 1398 (9th Cir. 1986) and *Hass v. Darigold Dairy Products*, 751 F.2d 1096, 1099 (9th Cir. 1985)); *see also F.D.I.C. v. Hulsey*, 22 F.3d 1472 (10th Cir. 1994).

The central theory underlying estoppel is that a party who acts in a manner "calculated to mislead or deceive" will be precluded from asserting the true facts in subsequent legal proceedings. *Frontier Ins. Co. in Rehabilitation v. RLM Const. Co.*, 2012 WL 833655 (6th Cir. 2012). Silence can constitute the action necessary to give rise to estoppel if combined with other misleading conduct. *A.C. Aukerman Co.*, 960 F.2d at 1042.

Equitable estoppel defenses appear to be less common than defenses based on a theory of waiver. However, several federal courts have sent equitable estoppel claims to juries for resolution. For example:

- In *Apponi v. Sunshine Biscuits, Inc.* the Sixth Circuit considered a claim of equitable estoppel in the context of a dispute over pension benefits owed to union employees. 652 F.2d 643, 649-50 (6th Cir. 1981). Although the parties'

---

[4] Small Corp's likely response will be to point to its collection and preservation of faxes as evidence of its continuing intent to stand on its rights under the TCPA. Research has not identified a clear response to this argument.

[5] An implied waiver argument could be strengthened by evidence that Small Corp only sued after Big Corp stopped sending its faxes; such evidence would support an inference that Small Corp re-evaluated its decision not to sue once it stopped receiving the benefits conferred on it by Big Corp's faxing.

> contract clearly disclaimed pension benefits for employees under a certain age, the union introduced affidavits that company representatives had represented during collective bargaining negotiations that pension benefits would accrue based only on years worked and regardless of the employee's age. *Id.* at 649. In remanding for trial, the court explained: "If company representatives did make the statements they were alleged to have made during the labor negotiations, then the company shall be precluded from arguing that it is not liable. The company will simply be held to its word." *Id.* at 650.

Unfortunately, research has yet to uncover a successful claim of equitable estoppel based on misleading conduct, as opposed to misleading statements.

2. Theory

Small Corp was well aware that its statutory rights were being violated when it received faxes from Big Corp. Small Corp nevertheless chose not to object to Big Corp's conduct, and instead chose to lead Big Corp to believe that Small Corp valued the information it was receiving. Coupled with its ongoing business relationship and long delay in filing suit, Small Corp's silence arguably constituted a representation that Small Corp would not press its rights under the TCPA. This interpretation is reinforced by Small Corp's decision to let some of its claims lapse. Big Corp was entitled to rely on that representation, and did so to its determent.[6] In fact, Small Corp always intended to sue under the TCPA, and was merely accumulating damages. Having mislead Big Corp to Big Corp's detriment, Small Corp cannot now claim that Big Corp's faxes were without permission.

C. Implied Acquiescence

1. Case Law

Acquiescence is closely related to laches, and the two defenses are often considered together. *See* 27A Am. Jur. 2d Equity § 113 (explaining that courts find "acquiescence to an alleged wrong or situation supportive of a finding of laches"). "The difference between acquiescence and laches is that laches denotes passive consent and acquiescence denotes active consent." *Coach House Rest.*, 934 F.2d at 1558. Specifically, acquiescence requires "a finding of conduct on the plaintiff's part that amounted to an assurance to the defendant, express or implied, that plaintiff would not assert his [claims] against the defendant." *Creative Gifts, Inc. v. UFO*, 235 F.3d 540, 547-48 (10th Cir. 2000); *see also Sweetheart Plastics, Inc. v. Detroit Forming, Inc.*, 743 F.2d 1039, 1046 (4th Cir. 1984); *Elvis Presley Enterprises, Inc. v. Elvisly Yours, Inc.*, 936 F.2d 889, 894 (6th Cir. 1991). In this way, acquiescence is also closely related to waiver and equitable estoppel (and is sometimes called "estoppel by acquiescence"). As with the other common law defenses discussed above, showing delay in filing suit alone is not enough to make out an acquiescence defense. *See Creative Gifts, Inc. v. UFO*, 235 F.3d at 547-48. Successful acquiescence defenses appear to be exceedingly rare.[7]

---

[6] Importantly, unlike waiver Big Corp would not have to show that Small Corp intended to relinquish its right to suit — only that its conduct indicated an intent not to sue.

[7] This may be because of the doctrine's overlap with other defenses, such as waiver, that are more widely employed.

2. Theory

Big Corp sent Small Corp dozens of faxes over the course of five years. Rather than file suit, Small Corp engaged in business with Big Corp and let several of its claims lapse. In so doing, Small Corp impliedly assured Big Corp that it would not press its rights under the TCPA, thereby acquiescing in Big Corp's course of conduct. Small Corp cannot now complain about conduct that it assented to for such an extended period of time.

D. Laches

1. Case Law

Laches is an equitable doctrine that historically served as an equitable counterpart to statutes of limitation, which only applied in courts of law to legal actions. The doctrine of laches will bar a claim when three elements are present:

> (1) a delay in asserting a right or a claim; (2) that the delay was not excusable; and (3) that there was undue prejudice to the party against whom the claim is asserted.

Venus Lines Agency, Inc. v. CVG Intl Am., Inc., 234 F.3d 1225, 1230 (11th Cir. 2000); *see also Costello v. United States*, 365 U.S. 265, 282 (1961) (focusing on lack of diligence and prejudice). *NAACP v. NAACP Legal Defense & Educational Fund, Inc.*, 753 F.2d 131, 137 (D.C. Cir. 1985); *Oneida Indian Nation v. County of Oneida*, 617 F.3d 114, 127 (2d Cir. 2010). Common forms of prejudice to defendants include:

> loss of evidence to meet the claim of plaintiff, change in situation induced by the delay, and change in the value of the subject-matter involved, especially where plaintiff had the privilege of waiving or asserting his claim so that he could take advantage of either a decrease or an increase in the value.

TransWorld Airlines, Inc. v. American Coupon Exchange, Inc., 913 F.2d 676, 696 (9th Cir. 1990).

Unlike defenses such as waiver and equitable estoppel, there is considerable disagreement among courts about the types of claims to which laches can serve as a defense. Some federal courts have concluded that laches is only a defense to equitable relief. *UA Local 343 United Ass'n of Journeymen & Apprentices of Plumbing and Pipefitting Industry of U.S. and Canada, AFL-CIO v. Nor-Cal Plumbing, Inc.*, 48 F.3d 1465 (9th Cir. 1994). Still other federal courts have concluded that laches can be applied to a claim seeking legal relief, but is unavailable if monetary relief is pursued within the applicable statute of limitations. *Lyons Partnership, L.P. v. Morris Costumes, Inc.*, 243 F.3d 789, 797 (4th Cir. 2001) ("[S]eparation of powers principles dictate that an equitable timeliness rule adopted by courts cannot bar claims that are brought within the legislatively prescribed statute of limitations.").

The dominant view appears to be that laches does apply to both legal and equitable claims and that there is merely a strong presumption that "plaintiff's delay in bringing the suit... is reasonable [if the] statute of limitation has not elapsed." *Tandy Corp. v. Malone & Hyde, Inc.*, 769 F.2d 362, 365 (6th Cir. 1985). Under this approach, laches claims made prior to the expiration of the applicable limitations period are rarely successful. *See* 27A Am. Jur. 2d Equity § 163. Still, such claims occasionally prevail where the prejudice is severe. For example:

- In *Chirco v. Crosswinds Communities, Inc.*, the Sixth Circuit considered a laches defense to a claim for legal and equitable relief under the Copyright Act. 474 F.3d 227, 231–36 (6th Cir. 2007). There, plaintiffs alleged that defendant copied certain architectural plans and used those plans in constructing its residential development. Despite having learned of the alleged infringement before the defendant broke ground on the offending development, plaintiffs waited over 18 months to sue — enough time for 168 of the planned 252 units to be constructed, 141 units to be sold, and 109 to become occupied by the buyers. Plaintiffs sought money damages, an injunction preventing additional construction, and destruction of the offending units. Although the claim was brought within the copyright act's 3-year statute of limitations, the trial court dismissed plaintiffs' entire suit on laches grounds. *Id.* at 230–31. On appeal, the court explained that only extraordinary circumstances would justify barring plaintiffs' claims on the basis of laches within the limitations period. The court reasoned that notwithstanding plaintiffs' "deliberate delay," laches would not bar their claims for money damages and certain injunctive relief because "we cannot conclude that the defendants were *unduly* prejudiced by the plaintiffs' delay in filing this cause of action." *Id.* at 235. By contrast, plaintiffs' request for destruction of the offending units was properly barred: "[T]he plaintiffs' inordinately lengthy delay in filing this suit makes any effort to procure the destruction of buildings already occupied, sold, or substantially constructed unduly prejudicial to the defendants." *Id.* at 236.

2. Theory

Big Corp personnel have been sending advertising faxes to Small Corp for years. As a professional TCPA plaintiff, Small Corp was well aware of its rights under the TCPA and understood that Big Corp's conduct amounted to a violation. Instead of suing to enforce its rights, Small Corp deliberately delayed filing suit. That delay was not for any legitimate reason, but instead was calculated to maximize Small Corp's ultimate recovery and undermine Big Corp's ability to defend the suit. Small Corp was successful in both respects — not only has Big Corp been exposed to considerable liability, but critical pieces of testimonial evidence have been irretrievably lost. Delaying suit to cause the opposing party to accumulate substantial statutory damages and obtain a litigation advantage is just the sort of "inequity... the judicial system should abhor" and the doctrine of laches should prevent. *Chirco*, 474 F.3d at 235. The extreme prejudice incurred makes this a proper case to bar relief within the statutory period.[8]

---

[8] Small Corp's likely answer will be that Big Corp cannot rely on damages to other parties to demonstrate prejudice for the purposes of a laches defense to Small Corp's claim. Research has not identified a clear response to this argument.

APPENDIX D

MULTI-ISSUE EMAIL MEMO

Attorney 1,

This email summarizes some of Truck Co.'s possible defenses in the event Insurance Co. brings a breach of contract action pursuant to the parties' claim servicing agreements. I have focused primarily on Texas law because of Insurance Co.'s connections to that jurisdiction. However, much of the law discussed evokes general contract principles that would be applicable in most jurisdictions. The one notable exception is the statute of limitations for breach of contract claims, which is four years in Texas and five years in Arkansas.

Factual Overview

Starting in Year 1, Truck Co. purchased insurance policies from Insurance Co. covering workers' compensation, automobile liability, and general liability. The policies have been renewed annually since then, including a recent renewal for Year 7. Truck Co. also hired Insurance Co. to perform claim servicing for the claims related to these policies. Both the insurance agreements and the claim servicing agreements were incorporated into written binders laying out the parties' obligations to one another. Because the agreements were renewed annually, there were seven or so claim servicing agreements between Truck Co. and Insurance Co.

Until the fall of this year, Insurance Co. has purportedly failed to bill Truck Co. for the fees related to the claim servicing agreements. Insurance Co. now seeks roughly $750,000 for the fees it says it has accrued under the claim servicing agreements dating back until Year 2. Truck Co. has several possible defenses, some of which apply to all of Insurance Co.'s potential claims and some of which apply only to claims for specific years.

1.) Because Insurance Co. failed to make a demand for payment under the Year 1 and Year 2 claim servicing agreements within a reasonable time, the statute of limitations bars any breach of contract claim based on those agreements.

The statute of limitations for breach of contract actions in Texas is four years. *Continental Casualty Co. v. Dr. Pepper Bottling Co. of Texas, Inc.*, 416 F. Supp. 2d 497, 506 (N.D. Tex. 2006). Texas law is clear that "where a demand is a condition precedent to suit, the plaintiff may not, by failing or refusing to perform the condition, toll the running of the statute and reserve to himself the right to sue within the statutory period from such time as he decides to make a demand." *United States v. First City Capital Corp.*, 53 F.3d 112, 115 (5th Cir. 1995). The general rule in cases in which a demand for payment is a condition precedent to a suit is that "[a] demand must be made within a reasonable time after it may lawfully be made." *Id.* The reasonableness of any delay is typically a question of fact, but "the law will ordinarily consider a reasonable time as being coincident with the running of the statute[.]" *Stevens v. State Farm Fire and Cas. Co.*, 929 S.W.2d 665, 671 (Tex. App. Ct. 1996). Thus, in Texas, a party has four years as of the date the right to payment accrues to demand it. "[A]n action will be barred if a demand is not made within that period." *Id.*

In this case, Truck Co. can assert that Insurance Co. has failed to make a demand for payment for the Year 1 and Year 2 claim servicing agreements within a "reasonable time." The Year 2 agreement (and presumably the Year 1 agreement, which I have not seen) put the onus on Insurance Co. to bill Truck Co. At the top of the Fee Schedule, there is a clause stating that "[t]he following fee schedule [is] [*sic*] to be billed to you by Insurance Co. Risk Management." This agreement was in effect until the end of Year 2. At that point in time, Insurance Co. could demand payment from Truck Co. for the claim servicing arising from the term of the Year 2 agreement. Insurance Co. had until the end of Year 6 to make that demand for payment. Because Insurance Co. failed to do so, the Texas statute of limitations would bar Insurance Co. from seeking recovery under the Year 2 claim servicing agreement.

In Arkansas, however, the statute of limitations for breach of contract actions arising from written contracts is five years. *Zufari v. Architecture Plus*, 323 Ark. 411, 419 (Ark. 1996). Thus, if Arkansas law applies to this case, Truck Co. will probably be unable to invoke the statute of limitations as a defense to any claim arising from the Year 2 agreement. The statute of limitations defense may still apply to the Year 1 agreement, however, because even the five-year statute of limitations has run for any claim based on that agreement.

2.) The Year 6 claim servicing agreement lists the estimated claim servicing fees as "$0" for the term of that agreement, so Insurance Co. cannot recover damages for that year.

As you pointed out in our meeting yesterday, the Fee Schedule for the Year 6 claim servicing agreement has all zeroes for the columns on the Fee Schedule titled "Estimated No. of Claimants" and "Estimated Fee." The "Estimated Rate per Claimant Fees" is also listed as "$0." The box at the top of the page next to "Claims Service Fees" is not checked, even though it had been in all the prior agreements.

These facts could support an argument that Insurance Co. cannot recover anything under the Year 6 claim servicing agreement. The law in Texas is clear that "[a]n unambiguous contract will be enforced as written, and parol evidence will not be received for the purpose of creating an ambiguity or to give the contract a meaning different from that which its language imports." *Sacks v. Haden*, 266 S.W.3d 447, 450 (Tex. 2008). Here, the written agreement between the parties is unambiguous: Truck Co. agreed to pay $0 in claims servicing fees for the term of the Year 6 claim servicing agreement. Of course, Insurance Co. would likely respond that listing the estimated fees as "$0" was a mistake. But in order to show that, Insurance Co. would have to rely on parol evidence, which it cannot do. Furthermore, a contract must be strictly construed against the drafter, which, in this case, is Insurance Co..

3.) By failing to bill Truck Co. in a timely manner, Insurance Co. breached the claim servicing agreements and obviated Truck Co.'s obligation to pay.

All of the claim servicing agreements include a clause at the top of the Fee Schedule stating that Truck Co. "will be billed" by Insurance Co. Although the language varies among the agreements, the idea remains the same: Insurance Co. was obligated to bill Truck Co. The later agreements (Year 5, Year 6, Year 7) also state that the amount Truck Co. owes for claims service fees "will be adjusted based upon the actual number of claims as of the annual loss valuation date."

These clauses imposed an obligation on Insurance Co. to bill Truck Co. and to do so in a timely manner. As Insurance Professional told us yesterday, the industry standard is monthly billing. At the very least, the statement in the later agreements that the amount Truck Co. owed would be adjusted "as of the annual loss valuation date" creates an expectation of annual billing. Insurance Co.'s failure to provide timely billing was a breach of each of the agreements. Texas courts have held that "[w]hen one party to a contract commits a material breach of that contract, the other party is discharged or excused from any obligation to perform." *Compass Bank v. MFB Fin. Servs.*, 152 S.W.3d 844, 852 (Tex. App. Ct. 2005). Truck Co. can argue that Insurance Co.'s failure to timely bill was a material breach, because Truck Co. was unable to accurately assess (or, if need be, contest) its liability at the time specified for doing so: the annual loss valuation date. The claims adjustment period was an important aspect of the contract. Insurance Co.'s late billing has substantially impaired Truck Co.'s ability to obtain this benefit. Thus, Insurance Co. has materially breached each of the claim servicing agreements, and Truck Co. is no longer obligated to perform under them.

4.) The claim servicing agreements are invalid, because Insurance Co. fraudulently failed to disclose a 1.5% fee that it has been applying to all of Truck Co.'s policy payments.

Employee informed us yesterday that she and her colleagues have been under the impression that Truck Co. has been paying for Insurance Co.'s claims handling services all along. This impression is based on otherwise inexplicable fees that have been included in the bills Truck Co. has been receiving from Insurance Co. pursuant to the policy agreements. Employee and her colleagues have calculated that the fees amount to 1.5% of the policy payments. Thus far, the contractual basis for these fees has not been identified.

Fraud in the inducement is a defense to breach of contract in Texas. *Nichols v. YJ USA Corp.*, 2009 U.S. Dist. LEXIS 22450, at *57-58 (N.D. Tex. Mar. 18, 2009). This defense requires the party asserting it to show that the other party "engaged in misrepresentation or concealment." *Id.* It is also not enough for the party accused of fraudulent inducement to have included disclaimers and merger clauses in the fraudulent agreement. *Id.* Courts in Texas have held that "[a]lthough the law charges parties with knowledge of the contends of the contracts they sign, proof of fraudulent misrepresentations and reliance on such misrepresentations may permit parties to void their contracts." *Id.* at *57.

In this case, the mystery 1.5% fee could be the basis for a fraud defense. Unless this fee is for claim servicing, as Employee has believed until recently, there is nothing in the binder explaining what it is. The inclusion of such a mystery fee without explanation is concealment on Insurance Co.'s part. Similarly, the failure to include this fee in the binders was a misrepresentation of what Truck Co.'s obligations are under the agreements.

5.) The 1.5% fee that Insurance Co. has been paying is an accord and satisfaction of whatever Truck Co.'s obligations may have been under the claims servicing agreements.

Under Texas law, "[a]n accord is an agreement where one party agrees to give or perform something different from what he is obligated to give or perform, and the other party agrees to accept the substituted performance in satisfaction of the obligation." *Stevens v. State Farm Fire and Casualty Co.*, 929 S.W.2d 665, 676 (Tex.

App. Ct. 1996). “A satisfaction is the performance of such an agreement.” *Id.* Truck Co. could argue that its payment of the unknown 1.5% fee and Insurance Co.’s acceptance thereof is “accord and satisfaction” for Truck Co.’s obligations under the claims servicing agreements. Insurance Co.’s failure to seek additional payment from Truck Co. for going on six years is acceptance through silence of this modified agreement.

I am happy to continue with my research tomorrow if you would like. I wanted to get you what I have in the meantime though. Please let me know if there are revisions you would like me to make or if there are other tasks you would like me to pursue.

Thanks,
Attorney 2

APPENDIX E

SINGLE-ISSUE EMAIL MEMO

Attorney 1,

This memo addresses whether Buyer is barred from bringing a fraud claim against Seller by the provisions of the purchase agreement that disclaim reliance on prior representations and provide that the property is sold "as is." We have a reasonable argument that Buyer should not be barred from bringing a fraud claim, but there is strong contrary authority.

The relevant clause of the purchase agreement states:

> "SELLER IS NOT, AND SHALL NOT BE, LIABLE OR BOUND IN ANY MANNER WHATSOEVER BY ANY WRITTEN OR VERBAL STATEMENT, REPRESENTATION, REPORT, SURVEY OR INFORMATION FURNISHED TO BUYER, OR MADE BY ANY PARTY WITH RESPECT TO THE PROPERTY. BUYER SPECIFICALLY AGREES THAT HAVING BEEN GIVEN THE OPPORTUNITY TO CONDUCT SUCH TESTS, STUDIES AND INVESTIGATIONS AS BUYER DEEMS NECESSARY AND APPROPRIATE, BUYER IS RELYING SOLELY UPON HIS OWN INVESTIGATION OF THE PROPERTY AND NOT ON ANY INFORMATION PROVIDED BY SELLER. BUYER FURTHER AGREES THAT EXCEPT FOR THE REPRESENTATIONS AND WARRANTIES EXPRESSLY SET FORTH IN SECTION 7, BUYER HAS AGREED TO PURCHASE THE LAND IN ITS CURRENT, "AS IS," WITH ALL FAULTS CONDITION . . ."

This clause contains what are described in the case law as "disclaimer-of-reliance" and "as-is" provisions, and I will refer to them as such throughout.

The Texas Supreme Court has held that "a disclaimer of reliance on representations, where the parties' intent is clear and specific, should be effective to negate a fraudulent inducement claim." *Forest Oil Corp. v. McAllen*, 268 S.W.3d 51, 56 (Tex. 2008), *quoting Schlumberger v. Swanson*, 959 S.W.2d 171, 179 (Tex. 1997). The Court looks at five factors to determine whether the parties' intent is clear and specific, examining whether "(1) the terms of the contract were negotiated, rather than boilerplate, and during negotiations the parties specifically discussed the issue which has become the topic of the subsequent dispute; (2) the complaining party was represented by counsel; (3) the parties dealt with each other in an arm's length transaction; (4) the parties were knowledgeable in business matters; and (5) the release language was clear." *Id.* at 60. Generally speaking, the test examines the "totality of the circumstances." *Id.* at 60.

In our case, it is likely that all five factors are present to some extent. With respect to the first factor, the purchase agreement presumably was negotiated and not a contract of adhesion — although we probably do not know at this point whether the parties specifically negotiated the disclaimer-of-reliance and as-is provisions. The second through fourth factors are also likely present, since Buyer is a large, sophisticated company that was presumably represented by counsel and negotiated at arm's length with the seller. The fifth factor is probably also present, since the clause above contains express disclaimer-of-reliance and as-is provisions. With respect to this factor, the Supreme Court held in *Forest Oil* that a disclaimer-of-reliance clause was clear where the parties disclaimed reliance upon "any statement or any representation of any agent of the parties." *Forest Oil*, 268 S.W.3d at 54. Similarly, in *Schlumberger*, the Supreme Court held that a party was barred from bringing a fraudulent inducement claim where it had entered into a contract stating that "none of us is relying upon any statement or representation of any agent of the parties." *Schlumberger*, 959 S.W. 2d at 180. The language in Buyer's clause above is similar to those.

There are two cases that provide us with a reasonable basis to argue that Buyer should not be barred from bringing a fraudulent inducement claim: *Duke Energy Intern., LLC v. Napoli*, ___ F. Supp. 2d ___, 2010 WL 3749298 (S.D. Tex. Sept. 21, 2010) and *Baker v. City of Robinson*, 305 S.W.3d 783 (Tex. App. 2009).

The defendant in *Duke Energy* was a company that had purchased a power plant from Duke executives. The defendant and the executives were allegedly involved in a scheme in which the executives secretly had formed a company that purchased the power plant and sold it to the defendant, who had then sold it to Duke at an inflated price. Duke alleged that the defendant had concealed the executives' role and split the profit with them.

The defendant here moved to dismiss on the grounds that the purchase agreement contained an "as is" clause that "clearly expressed the parties' intent to waive a fraudulent inducement claim." The court denied the motion. The court held, first, that the "as is" clause did not relate to the alleged fraud. The court found that the "as is" clause related to the "malfunctioning of the plant or its unsuitability," whereas the alleged fraud was that Duke was induced into purchasing the power plant at a higher price by the defendant's concealment of the executives' role in purchasing the plant. The court also distinguished *Forest Oil* and *Schlumberger* on the grounds that those cases involved "settlement agreements — agreements highly favored by law," whereas the agreement here related to the purchase of a power plant. *Id.* at *6. The court further noted that while the contract here contained "as is" and "entire agreement" provisions, it did not contain a disclaimer-of-reliance provision. *Id.* at *4. Finally, the court stated that "most significantly, Duke alleges that essentially the Purchase Agreement was not in fact negotiated at arm's length," because of the scheme of its executives. *Id.* at *7

Duke Energy is somewhat helpful to us, particularly in pointing out that *Forest Oil* and *Schlumberger* involved settlement agreements, which are "highly favored by law," whereas the contract in our case is for the purchase of real property. As will be discussed below, however, other cases have found that disclaimer-of-reliance provisions in purchase agreements can bar fraudulent inducement claims. In addition, *Duke*

Energy is probably distinguishable on the grounds that the alleged fraud there did not relate to an aspect of the property covered by the "as is" clause, the parties did not expressly waive reliance on prior representations, and the case involved a breach of fiduciary duty by Duke executives that made it such that negotiations were not at arms' length.

The other helpful case I found is *Baker v. City of Robinson*, 305 S.W.3d 783 (Tex. App. 2009). In that case, the plaintiff had purchased real estate from a city at an auction. He alleged that the city defrauded him when a city employee told him the property was zoned for commercial use when it actually was not. The Court denied the defendant summary judgment, finding that the disclaimer-of-reliance and merger clauses in the purchase agreement did not preclude a fraud claim. The Court noted that the plaintiff was not represented by counsel and did not negotiate any terms of the contract besides the purchase price. While the Court found that the plaintiff was a sophisticated purchaser of real estate, it concluded that this fact alone was not enough to find that he had clearly waived his right to bring a fraud claim.

Baker is a decent case for us, but again probably distinguishable on the grounds that Buyer was represented by counsel and was a more sophisticated party.

A court would probably more likely conclude that our case is similar to *RAS Group, Inc. v. Rent-A-Center East, Inc.*, ___ S.W.3d ___, 2010 WL 4400511 (Tex. App. 2010). The plaintiff here was a company that had purchased accounts receivable from Rent-A-Center that ended up being worthless. It sued for fraudulent inducement based on Rent-A-Center allegedly having misrepresented that no previous attempts to collect on the accounts had been made, and Rent-A-Center had used its best efforts to remove accounts in pending litigation. The contract contained provisions stating that the buyer (1) "relied solely on its own investigation and it has not relied upon any oral or written information provided by Seller" and (2) that the assets are being sold "'as is' and 'with all faults.'" *Id.* at *3

The Court here granted summary judgment to Rent-A-Center, finding that the plaintiff had waived its right to bring a fraudulent inducement claim. The Court stated that (1) the parties were sophisticated and represented by counsel; (2) they negotiated at arm's-length on the scope of the no-reliance provision; and (3) the people who negotiated the contract for the plaintiffs testified that they could have requested that certain language be added to the agreement, showing that the agreement was not adhesive. *Id.* at *4.

Another bad case for us is *McDougal v. Stevens*, 2009 WL 1664600 (Tex. App. 2009).

In this case a buyer of a construction business under an "as is" sale contract sued the seller for fraudulently misrepresenting the amount of real property owned by the seller and the condition of the equipment. The court held that the "as is" clause itself — without a disclaimer-of-reliance clause — clearly and unequivocally waived any reliance on the misrepresentations. The Court noted that the parties had negotiated at arm's length and "specifically discussed" some of the issues relating to the size of the property and condition of equipment which were the subject of the fraud suit. *Id.* at *4.

Sincerely, Attorney 2

APPENDIX F

SHORT DEMAND LETTER

VIA OVERNIGHT MAIL

To the Offices of Opposing Counsel

Dear Opposing Counsel:

Our firm represents Business Agency.

Our client has informed us that each of you, as makers, executed and delivered to Business Agency a Promissory Note dated Day 1, Year 1 in the principal amount of $200,000 with a maturity date of Day 5, Year 2. The note provides for interest at the rate at 8%. The note also provides that there would be no extensions of the maturity date, and we have been advised that Business Agency has not granted any extension.

Although the maturity date has long since passed, Business Agency informs us that you have not paid the note. Accordingly, Business Agency has asked us to communicate to you that it demands payment, in full, of the principal amount of the note and all accrued interest by Day 10, Year 3.

On behalf of Business Agency, we urge you to give this matter your prompt and serious attention so there will be no need for legal proceedings which will cause all parties to incur unnecessary expense.

Yours truly,
Attorney

APPENDIX G

LONGER DEMAND LETTER

TO THE OFFICES OF OPPOSING COUNSEL

Re: Notice of Blue Company's Breach and Termination of the Green-Blue Agreement

Dear Counsel for Blue Company:

Green Company (Green Co.) has retained my firm to address Blue Company's (Blue Co.) breaches of the Green-Blue Agreement dated Day 80, Year 3, which incorporates terms from the parties' Initial Agreement. All capitalized terms used herein have the definitions assigned to them in the Green-Blue Agreement and Initial Agreement unless otherwise stated.

As explained below, Blue Co. breached the Green-Blue Agreement by, among other things:

1. Intentionally delaying the certification and government approval of Green Co.'s Product, rather than using good faith efforts to achieve those goals, by: (a) unilaterally modifying the parties' agreed-to specifications, and (b) imposing upon Green Co. a series of pretextual certification requirements, all designed to ensure the Green-Blue Agreement would terminate on Day 60, Year 4 and attempt to avoid paying Green Co. the $6 million Payment Promise;
2. Failing to inform Green Co. of the specific reasons, supported by sufficient data, for its eleventh hour imposition of the pretextual certification requirements; and
3. Imposing upon Green Co. certification requirements that it did not impose on other suppliers of similar products.

Based on Blue Co.'s breaches of the Green-Blue Agreement, Green Co. hereby terminates the Green-Blue Agreement and in accordance with its terms demands payment of the Payment Promise.

I. BACKGROUND.

A. The Parties Execute the Initial Agreement.

Green Co. has been supplying Product to Blue Co. for many years. On Day 1, Year 1, the parties formalized their supply relationship in the Initial Agreement. In that agreement, Green Co. agreed to supply Blue Co. specific products in certain quantities and according to agreed-to Specifications defined in the agreement.

The parties agreed that unless earlier terminated, the Initial Agreement would stay in effect for as long as Blue Co. purchased Product. The parties identified several events of termination, including a material breach of the agreement by either party. The parties also agreed that Green Co. could terminate the Initial Agreement, upon four months notice to Blue Co., if it decided to exit the business of making Product.

B. Green Co. Notifies Blue Co. Of Its Intent To Exit The Business.

On or about Day 30, Year 2, Green Co. notified Blue Co. that it intended to exit the business of making Product and would cease supplying Product to Blue Co. on Day 30, Year 3. On Day 60, Year 2, the parties entered into an "Amendment to the Initial Agreement." In addition, in exchange for Blue Co. giving Green Co. certain consideration, including a Payment Promise, Green Co. agreed to extend its operations an additional eight months through Day 270, Year 3.

C. The Parties Execute the Conversion Agreement and Green-Blue Agreement.

In or about Day 20, Year 3, Blue Co. asked Green Co. to consider extending the Initial Agreement beyond Day 30, Year 3. Green Co. was reluctant, as it had already decided to exit the business and had taken steps towards doing so. Furthermore, Green Co.'s supplier of Compound — a raw material used in Green Co.'s creation of Product — ceased making Compound. Green Co. nevertheless agreed to consider a proposal to continue supplying Product to Blue Co., so long as it fairly compensated Green Co. for staying in the business solely to supply Blue Co. and included a transition plan for Green Co. to exit the business.

Blue Co. then began discussing the Green-Blue Agreement as a certification and supply agreement. In consideration for the significant expense and risks Green Co. would incur to stay in the business of making Product exclusively for Blue Co., Blue Co. agreed to a take-or-pay arrangement pursuant to which it would pay Green Co. $3 million in each year of the Blue-Green Agreement regardless of how many instruments Blue Co. actually ordered subject to the maximum volumes noted below (the "Payment Promise"). Also, Blue Co. agreed to a step-down in the maximum number of technical instruments it could order under the Green-Blue Agreement from 10,000,000 instruments in Year 3, to 5,000,000 instruments in Year 4, to 2,500,000 instruments in Year 5. Because the arrangement provided Green Co. guaranteed revenue and allowed Green Co. to ramp down production and exit the business within three years, Green Co. executed the Green-Blue Agreement on Day 80, Year 3.

The Green-Blue Agreement also set forth a detailed plan for the parties to certify Product made with the new Compound and for Blue Co. to obtain government approval of Product. The parties agreed that upon identification and approval of the new Compound, Green Co. would send to Blue Co. ten lots each of six Technical Instruments that met the specifications that the parties jointly defined in the Green-Blue Agreement. Blue Co., in turn, would test the Technical Instruments according to its internal processes ("Certification Procedure") and if satisfactory, submit the results to the government for approval. Blue Co. expressly agreed that if the Technical Instruments met the Specifications and passed Blue Co.'s Certification Procedure, then the government should approve the Product for sale within 100 to 200 days, and further that testing and government approval of the Technical Instruments would be sufficient to consider all Product to be qualified and government-approved and ready for purchase in accordance with the supply portion of the Green-Blue Agreement. The parties also agreed that if government approval was not received by Day 200, Year 4, the Green-Blue Agreement would terminate.

Due to the significant investment Green Co. would make to stay in the business of making Product beyond its scheduled exit date, it negotiated numerous protections against Blue Co. using its Certification Procedure or the government approval deadline as a means to back out of the Green-Blue Agreement and attempt to avoid paying the Payment Promise. Those protections included Blue Co.'s express agreement to:

1. Use good faith efforts to certify the new Compound;
2. Use good faith efforts to secure government approval for Product; and
3. Inform Green Co. of the specific reasons explaining any failure in certification with sufficient data demonstrating the failure and comparative data showing the reasons for the failure relative to previous instruments supplied by Green Co.

The Green-Blue Agreement expressly provides that if Green Co. terminates the Green-Blue Agreement due to Blue Co.'s material breach of those provisions or any other, Blue Co. will still be obligated to pay the full Payment Promise.

II. BLUE CO. BREACHED THE GREEN-BLUE AGREEMENT.

Blue Co. materially breached at least three provisions of the Green-Blue Agreement. On that basis, and because Blue Co. has indicated to Green Co. that it intends to let the Green-Blue Agreement expire on Day 60, Year 4 and not pay Green Co. the Payment Promise, Green Co. hereby terminates the Green-Blue Agreement and in accordance with its terms demands payment of the Payment Promise.

A. Blue Co. Breached Its Obligations To Exercise Good Faith Efforts To Certify New Compound And Secure Government Approval For Product.

Blue Co. first breached its obligations under the Green-Blue Agreement to use good faith efforts to Certify new Compound and obtain government approval for Product. Blue Co. did so by unilaterally modifying the parties' agreed-upon Specifications and imposing upon Green Co. new and pretextual certification requirements at the eleventh hour, to guarantee Blue Co. would not be able to obtain government approval for Product by the Green-Blue Agreement's deadline and attempt to avoid paying the Payment Promise.

First, Blue Co. unilaterally decided that the mutually agreed upon test in the Green-Blue Agreement to measure the chemical composition of the Technical Instruments was inadequate. This delayed the Certification Process and government approval for at least four months. In the Green-Blue Agreement Specifications, the parties expressly agreed to measure Chemical-A using an analytical test. On Day 150, Year 3, Green Co. submitted Technical Instruments to Blue Co. that satisfied the Specifications in all respects, including Chemical-A as measured with the analytical test. Had Blue Co. tested the Technical Instruments for Chemical-A using an analytical test, as it agreed in the Green-Blue Agreement to do, the Technical Instruments would have passed Blue Co.'s Certification Procedure, Blue Co. would have received government approval for Product, and Green Co. would have been entitled to the full Payment Promise long ago.

Rather than test the Technical Instruments with an analytical test as required by the Green-Blue Agreement, however, Blue Co. used a non-analytical test. Using a non-analytical test, Blue Co. found that one of the lots submitted by Green Co. — which satisfied Blue Co.'s Chemical-A chemical characteristic requirements when Green Co. tested it with an analytical test — had too much Chemical-A, and on that basis rejected that lot.

Second, Blue Co. ignored Green Co.'s repeated requests for direction on what else it needed to do to certify the new Compound. Green Co. sought that direction while the parties worked through the Chemical-A issue, rather than after resolution of that issue, to avoid delay. But in a calculated effort to miss the deadline for government approval, Blue Co. dismissed Green Co.'s requests, and only began addressing them after Green Co. threatened to cease work for Blue Co.

Third, less than four months prior to the Green-Blue Agreement's deadline for government approval, Blue Co. unilaterally imposed upon Green Co. at least four additional requirements:

1. Supplemental Certification
2. Chemical-B analysis and certification
3. Elasticity documentation and procedures
4. Viscosity measures

Green Co. believes the new requirements were pretextual and intended to delay certification. The time for Blue Co. to request these requirements was during the parties' lengthy negotiations over Specifications that were incorporated into the Green-Blue Agreement, but Blue Co. did not do so. Indeed, Blue Co. had never before imposed upon Green Co. these requirements during the parties' longstanding relationship. Blue Co. knew that by creating this obstacle course, it would virtually guarantee it would not obtain government approval by the Green-Blue Agreement deadline.

Fourth, over five months after Blue Co. improperly rejected Green Co.'s Technical Instruments, Blue Co. demanded that Green Co. submit documentation explaining the reasons for the failure of the one lot. Blue Co. was well aware at that time, however, that the only reason why the single certification lot failed was because Blue Co. measured Chemical-A with a non-analytical test, rather than the agreed-upon analytical test. This was just another delay tactic, as there was no reason why Green Co. could not have proceeded with making the additional Technical Instruments at that time.

Despite the unreasonableness and pretextual nature of Blue Co.'s demands, Green Co. complied with each one.

B. Blue Co. Breached Its Obligation To Provide A Reasonable Explanation For Imposing New Requirements.

Blue Co. also breached its obligation under the Green-Blue Agreement to inform Green Co. of the specific reasons, supported by sufficient data, explaining the reasons for imposing its eleventh hour requirements. The only explanation Blue Co. offered was in its brief letter to Scientist. However, Blue Co. has never provided any explanation for why it believed — after many years of accepting Product from Green Co.— Green Co.'s processes were inadequate, nor any data supporting the same. Its failure to do so is a violation of the Green-Blue Agreement.

C. Blue Co. Has Not Imposed Any Of The New Certification Requirements On Other Suppliers.

In addition, Blue Co. breached its obligation under the Green-Blue Agreement to use at least the same degree of effort that it uses to certify other suppliers for similar products. Blue Co. has not imposed upon any of its other suppliers any of the new requirements it imposed upon Green Co. Blue Co. had never before imposed those requirements on Green Co. and when Green Co. asked Blue Co. to provide written descriptions of the new requirements as given to third parties, Blue Co. was unable to do so.

* * *

Green Co. demands Blue Co.'s payment of the Payment Promise by Day 90, Year 4.

If you have any questions, please feel free to contact me. Green Co. also is amenable to a meeting if Blue Co. believes it would be productive.

Very truly yours,
Attorney for Green Company

APPENDIX H

SETTLEMENT LETTER

VIA ELECTRONIC AND U.S. MAIL

To the Offices of Opposing Counsel

Re: *Party 1 v. Party 2*

Dear Opposing Counsel:

We write to inform you that in response to your recent request, the appellants in the above captioned matter are willing to meet with you and your clients to discuss immediate resolution of the parties' dispute on the morning of Day 1, Year 1, at the Bank.

In anticipation of the meeting, please provide us with a settlement term sheet that outlines your clients' proposed terms and conditions for resolution. We agree to treat the term sheet as confidential.

We look forward to hearing from you.

Sincerely,

Attorney

APPENDIX I

SETTLEMENT AGREEMENT AND RELEASE

SETTLEMENT AGREEMENT AND RELEASE

This Settlement Agreement and Release ("**Settlement Agreement**") is entered into as of Day 1, Year 2, by and between TENANT 1, a limited liability company, and TENANT 2, a limited liability company. Tenant 1 and Tenant 2 are sometimes referred to herein together as the "Parties" and each individually as a "Party".

RECITALS

A. Tenant 1 and Tenant 2 are both commercial tenants at Shopping Center in Town-X of State-X.

B. On or around Day 1, Year 1, water infiltrated Tenant 2's storage space located in Shopping Center, and as a result of this infiltration, Tenant 2 sustained damages amounting to approximately Fifty Thousand Dollars ($50,000.00).

C. Certain disputes have arisen between the Parties as to the cause of the water infiltration in the storage space rented by Tenant 2 (the "**Disputes**").

D. The Parties agree that it is in their mutual interest to avoid litigation arising out of the disputed matters.

NOW THEREFORE, in consideration of the mutual promises, covenants and agreements contained herein, the Parties to this Settlement Agreement agree as follows:

1. Payment to Tenant 2. In exchange for the release, covenant not to sue and other covenants contained in this Settlement Agreement, Tenant 1 shall pay to Tenant 2 Twenty Thousand and No/100 Dollars ($20,000.00) (the "**Settlement Amount**"). The Settlement Amount will be paid upon the execution and delivery of this Settlement Agreement by both Parties.
2. Release and Covenant Not to Sue. Tenant 2, on its behalf and on behalf of its attorneys, assigns, agents, officers, directors, predecessors in interest, affiliates, representatives, and all persons acting by or through any or all of them, does hereby irrevocably and unconditionally covenant not to sue for any reason, and releases and forever discharges, Tenant 1, and its members, officers, trustees, administrators, executives, attorneys, assigns, predecessors in interest, affiliates, employees, agents, representatives, and all persons acting by or through them (individually and collectively, the "**Released Persons**") from any and all claims, demands, obligations, actions, inactions, grounds for complaint and or any cause or causes of action, in law or in equity, suits debts, liens liability including, but not limited to, direct or indirect

liability, vicarious liability, claims for compensatory or punitive damages, or for declaratory or injunctive relief, whether past or present, known or unknown, asserted or unasserted, fixed or contingent, whether based in tort or contract or other theories of recovery (individually and collectively, "**Claims**") through and including the date of this Settlement Agreement. The released Claims do not include any rights or obligations under, or any Claims with respect to, a breach of any provision of this Settlement Agreement.

3. Taxes. Tenant 2 is responsible for all taxes (if any) that may be applicable or payable with respect to the Settlement Amount.

4. Claims. Each Party represents and warrants to the other that (a) except for the Claims arising out of the Disputes which Disputes are being fully settled as provided in this Agreement, said Party has no Claims of any nature against the other Party or any of the other Released Persons as of the date of this Settlement Agreement; and (b) said Party has not assigned any interest in or to the Claims.

5. Entire Agreement; Integration Clause. This Settlement Agreement is the entire agreement between the Parties and supersedes and replaces all prior negotiations or proposed or actual agreements, written or oral. This Settlement Agreement may not be modified except in a writing signed by the Parties.

6. Counterparts. This Settlement Agreement may be signed in multiple counterparts, all of which together shall constitute one original agreement. Likewise, signatures may appear on separate pages without affecting the validity of this Settlement Agreement.

7. Choice Of Law. THIS SETTLEMENT AGREEMENT SHALL BE CONSTRUED IN ACCORDANCE WITH STATE-X LAW, WITHOUT GIVING EFFECT TO ANY LAW OR RULE THAT WOULD CAUSE THE LAWS OF ANY JURISDICTION OTHER THAN STATE-X TO BE APPLIED. Each of the Parties hereby irrevocably and unconditionally consents to submit to the exclusive jurisdiction of the state and federal courts located in State-X ("**State-X Courts**") for any dispute arising out of or relating to this Settlement Agreement and the matters contemplated hereby (and agrees not to commence any litigation relating thereto except in such courts) and agrees not to plead or claim in any State-X Court that such litigation brought therein has been brought in an inconvenient forum.

8. No Admission. The Parties to this Settlement Agreement agree and understand that the execution and delivery of this Settlement Agreement, or the exchange of the consideration provided for by this Settlement Agreement, is made in compromise and that one of the benefits to entering into this Settlement Agreement is that the Parties can avoid the cost of lengthy discovery and litigation. This Settlement Agreement shall not be construed or act as an admission by either Party with respect to the merit of the Claims or the Disputes. Except as otherwise expressly set forth in this Settlement Agreement, nothing in this Settlement Agreement shall, or shall be deemed to, relieve a Party of its obligations under this Settlement Agreement.

9. Successors; Assigns; Third Party Beneficiaries. This Settlement Agreement will be binding upon and inure to the benefit of the Parties and their respective successors and assigns. This Settlement Agreement will not confer upon any person, other than the Parties, any rights or remedies of any nature

whatsoever under or by reason of this Settlement Agreement.

10. Non-disclosure. The Parties hereto and their counsel agree not to disclose to any person or entity, directly or indirectly, or by or through any agent, employee, or other representative, the terms or conditions of this Settlement Agreement other than as necessary to effectuate the provisions of this Settlement Agreement or as may be required by law.

11. Attorney Reviews and Arm's-Length Agreement. By signing this Settlement Agreement, the Parties acknowledge that they have been advised with respect thereto by their respective attorneys, that they have been afforded ample opportunity to review this Settlement Agreement, that they have negotiated and bargained for the terms of this Settlement Agreement at arm's length and in good faith, that they have read and understand this Settlement Agreement, and that they have executed this Settlement Agreement freely and voluntarily with advice of counsel. The Parties specifically acknowledge that they have reviewed this Settlement Agreement with their legal or other advisors, and are fully aware of all of their rights and alternatives. In executing this Settlement Agreement, the Parties acknowledge that their decisions and actions are entirely voluntary and free from any economic duress.

12. Authorization. The undersigned individual signatories each represent that they are authorized to execute this Settlement Agreement on behalf of the Party or Parties identified with respect to each. At the request of either Party, the other Party shall deliver a copy of the resolution or other document authorizing such Party to enter into and perform its obligations under this Settlement Agreement.

[Signature Page Follows]

IN WITNESS WHEREOF, the Parties have executed this Settlement Agreement as of the date first above written.

TENANT 1:
By: ___________
Name: ___________
Its: ___________

TENANT 2:
By: ___________
Name: ___________
Its:___________

APPENDIX J

TRANSITION SERVICES AGREEMENT

TRANSITION SERVICES AGREEMENT

This TRANSITION SERVICES AGREEMENT (this "Agreement"), dated as of Year 1 (the "Effective Date"), is entered into by and among ***Parent***, a Delaware corporation ("Parent"), ***S Corporation***, a Delaware corporation ("S Corporation"), ***S Distribution***, a Delaware corporation ("S Distribution" and together with Parent and S Corporation, collectively, "Sellers" and each a "Seller"), and ***Purchaser***, a Delaware corporation ("Purchaser").

WHEREAS, pursuant to that certain Sale and Purchase Agreement, dated as of Year 1 (the "Purchase Agreement"), by and among Sellers, Purchaser and *Sponsor*, Purchaser is, among other things, acquiring the Purchased Assets and assuming the Assumed Liabilities on the terms and subject to the conditions set forth in the Purchase Agreement; and

WHEREAS, Sellers require certain transition and other services from Purchaser and Purchaser is willing to provide or cause to be provided such transition and other services on the terms and subject to the conditions contained herein.

NOW, THEREFORE, in consideration of the foregoing and the mutual agreements contained in this Agreement, and for other good and valuable consideration, the value, receipt and sufficiency of which are acknowledged, the Parties hereby agree as follows:

ARTICLE 1

INTERPRETATION; DEFINITIONS

Section 1.1 Definitions. All capitalized terms used but not defined in this Agreement shall have the same meanings as are given to such terms in the Purchase Agreement. As used in this Agreement, the following terms have the meanings set forth below or in the sections set forth below:

"Additional Services" has the meaning specified in Section 2.5(a).

"Agreement" has the meaning specified in the Preamble to this Agreement.

"Base Cost" has the meaning specified in Section 1 of Schedule C.

"Default Rate" has the meaning specified in Section 1 of Schedule C.

"Defaulting Party" has the meaning specified in Section 4.3.

"Disputed Amount" has the meaning set forth in Section 2.9.

"Early Termination Consequence" has the meaning specified in Section 4.2.

"Effective Date" has the meaning specified in the Preamble to this Agreement.

"Force Majeure Event" has the meaning specified in Section 2.7.

"Liability Cap" means the amount by which the (i) aggregate Usage Fees received by Purchaser (from the Effective Date until the date Purchaser is first notified of a Claim by a Receiving Party) exceeds (ii) the aggregate Base Cost with respect to such Usage Fees; provided that in no event shall the Liability Cap be less than $1 Million or greater than $5 Million.

"Net Recovery" has the meaning specified in Section 5.2(a).

"Neutral Arbitrator" has the meaning set forth in Section 2.9.

"Parent" has the meaning specified in the Preamble to this Agreement.

"Parties" means Sellers and Purchaser together, and "Party" shall mean Sellers or Purchaser, individually, as the case may be.

"Purchase Agreement" has the meaning specified in the Recitals to this Agreement.

"Purchaser" has the meaning specified in the Preamble to this Agreement.

"Receiving Parties" has the meaning set forth in Section 2.1.

"Regular Shut Down Periods" has the meaning specified in Section 2.6.

"S Corporation" has the meaning specified in the Preamble to this Agreement.

"S Distribution" has the meaning specified in the Preamble to this Agreement.

"Seller" and "Sellers" each have the meaning specified in the Preamble to this Agreement.

"Service Providers" has the meaning specified in Section 2.1.

"Termination Date" has the meaning specified in Section 4.1.

"Termination Notice" has the meaning specified in Section 4.2.

"Third Party Act or Omission" has the meaning specified in Section 5.2(a).

"Third Party Service Provider" means any Unaffiliated Third Party that a Service Provider has designated as a direct or indirect provider or supporter of Transition Services.

"Transition Services" has the meaning set forth in Section 2.1.

"Unaffiliated Third Party" has the meaning specified in Section 5.2(a).

"Usage Fee" has the meaning specified in Section 1 of Schedule C.

"Withheld Amount" has the meaning set forth in Section 2.9.

Section 1.2 Interpretation. The words "hereof," "herein" and "hereunder" and words of similar import when used in this Agreement refer to this Agreement as a whole (including any Schedules hereto) and not to any particular provision of this Agreement, and all Article, Section and Schedule references are to this Agreement unless otherwise specified. The words "include," "includes" and "including" are deemed to be followed by the phrase "without limitation." The meanings given to terms defined herein are equally applicable to both the singular and plural forms of such terms. Whenever the context may require, any pronoun includes the corresponding masculine, feminine and neuter forms. Except as otherwise expressly provided herein, all references to "dollars" or "$" are deemed references to the lawful money of the United States of America. Each Party hereto has participated in the drafting of this Agreement, which each Party acknowledges is the result of extensive negotiations between the Parties, and consequently this Agreement shall be interpreted without reference to any rule or precept of law to the effect that any ambiguity in a document be construed against the drafter.

ARTICLE 2

TRANSITION SERVICES

Section 2.1 Provision of Transition Services.[1] On the terms and subject to the conditions of this Agreement, Purchaser and its Subsidiaries (the "Service Providers") shall provide or cause a Third Party Service Provider to provide to Sellers and their Subsidiaries on the Closing Date (the "Receiving Parties") each of the transition services and support functions set forth on Schedule A as reasonably required by the Receiving Parties (i) to wind down and liquidate and (ii) to operate in bankruptcy prior to liquidation (collectively, the "Transition Services"); provided, however, that no Service Provider will have any obligation to provide to any Receiving Party any type of service described on Schedule B. Each Service Provider shall provide Transition Services in substantially the same manner such services are then provided or obtained by such Service Provider for its own account or to one or more of its Subsidiaries, and in accordance with any applicable specifications and limitations set forth on Schedule A. With respect to Transition Services not provided by a Service Provider for its own account or to one or more of its Subsidiaries, the Service Provider shall provide such Transition Services in a commercially reasonable manner, and in accordance with any applicable specifications and limitations set forth on Schedule A. Notwithstanding the foregoing, with respect to Transition Services provided by a Third Party Service Provider, the Service Providers shall use commercially reasonable efforts to cause such Third Party Service Provider to provide Transition Services in accordance with the terms of this Agreement and the applicable service agreement obligating such Third Party Service Provider.

---

[1] Between the signing of the Purchase Agreement and the signing of this Agreement in connection with the Closing, the Parties will work diligently, in good faith, to identify and list additional types of services (and specifications and limitations) on Schedule A and Schedule B, as mutually agreed by Sellers and Purchaser.

Section 2.2 Modification of Transition Services. A Service Provider may make changes from time to time in the manner of performing Transition Services if the Service Provider is making similar changes in performing or receiving similar services for itself or its Subsidiaries; provided that the Service Provider furnishes or uses commercially reasonable efforts to cause to be furnished to the Sellers reasonable advance written notice regarding such changes and such changes do not materially degrade the applicable Transition Services. Notwithstanding anything herein to the contrary, the Service Providers shall not be required to maintain any business, subsidiary, asset or employee principally in order to continue to provide Transition Services under this Agreement.

Section 2.3 Compliance with Law. Notwithstanding anything herein to the contrary, the Service Providers shall not be responsible for providing any Transition Service if and to the extent such Transition Service would violate applicable Law. No Service Party shall have any responsibility or liability for failure to provide any, or part of any, Transition Service unable to be provided as contemplated by this Section 2.3.

Section 2.4 Third Party Consents and Providers.

(a) Sellers acknowledge that Service Providers may be required to obtain third-party consents and approvals following the Effective Date in order to provide certain Transition Services. The Service Providers shall use commercially reasonable efforts, and the Receiving Parties shall cooperate with the Service Providers, to obtain such consents or approvals (which shall not include the payment by or on behalf of any Service Provider or Receiving Party of any consent fee or other fees or expenses of or to any third party) that may be required from any third parties in order to provide the Transition Services. The obligation to provide any Transition Service hereunder, which Transition Service is provided or supported by the products or services of a Third Party Service Provider as of the Effective Date, is subject to and conditioned upon obtaining any required third-party consent or approval.2 No Service Party shall have any responsibility or liability for failure to provide any, or part of any, Transition Service unable to be provided pursuant to this Section 2.4.

(b) Sellers acknowledge that as of the Effective Date certain Transition Services are and will continue to be provided by Third Party Service Providers. A Service Provider may also subcontract with Unaffiliated Third Parties to directly or indirectly provide or support other Transition Services (or otherwise cause an Unaffiliated Third Party to provide Transition Services) to the Receiving Parties if Purchaser, in good faith, expects that the Usage Fees payable for such Transition Services, as provided or supported by the Third Party Service Provider (as of the date of subcontract) will not exceed the Usage Fees that would otherwise have been payable for such Transition Services as performed by the Service Providers.

Section 2.5 Requests for Additional Services.

(a) Except for services of the type listed on Schedule B, at any time after the Effective Date and before the Termination Date, Sellers may request in writing that additional services be provided and Schedule A be amended to reference such additional services. Schedule A shall be amended to include and the Service Providers shall use commercially reasonable efforts to provide (or cause to be provided through a Third Party Service Provider) such requested services if such requested services are reasonably required by Sellers (i) to wind down and liquidate or (ii) to operate in bankruptcy during liquidation (the "Additional Services"); provided, however, that no Service Provider shall be obligated to perform or cause to be performed any such Additional Services unless and until the Parties agree in writing as to the specifications (and other terms and conditions) under which the Service Providers shall provide (or cause to be provided) such Additional Services. Upon such agreement of the Parties, such Additional Services shall be deemed to be Transition Services under this Agreement.

(b) At any time after the Effective Date and before the Termination Date, Sellers may request that Schedule A be amended to reference additional or modified specifications, and Purchaser and Sellers shall thereupon negotiate in good faith regarding the provision of Transition Services in accordance with such additional or modified specifications; provided, however, that the Service Providers shall not be obligated to perform or cause to be performed any Transition Services in accordance with such specifications unless and until mutually agreed by the Parties.

Section 2.6 Modifications and Shutdowns. If at any time a Service Provider determines that it is necessary or appropriate to temporarily suspend a Transition Service due to scheduled or emergency repairs, maintenance and/or modification, the Service Provider shall give the Receiving Party reasonable prior notice of such shutdown (including information regarding the nature of the shutdown and the projected length of such shutdown), unless it is not practical to give such prior notice because the shutdown is due to an emergency. Sellers are hereby notified that the Service Providers currently intend to shut down operations for five weeks, twice annually during the periods (i) around the end of December and the beginning of January and (ii) in the month of July (the "Regular Shut Down Periods"), which may result in substantially diminished availability of Transition Services during such periods. In addition, the Service Providers may utilize the same regularly scheduled information technology support and maintenance windows (during which information systems are not fully available) as were utilized by Sellers prior to the Closing. Purchaser shall provide Sellers reasonable prior written notice of any change in the Regular Shut Down Periods or such support and maintenance windows.

Section 2.7 Force Majeure; Reduction of Services. Each Service Provider (including with respect to services performed through Third Party Service Providers) shall be excused from the performance of its obligations under this Agreement, for any period and to the extent that such performance is prevented, in whole or in part, as a result of delays caused by a Receiving Party or any act of God, public enemy, war or threats of same, terrorism or threats of same, epidemic, fire, flood, embargoes, severe weather, civil disturbance, act of government, court order, labor dispute or other cause beyond its reasonable control (a "Force Majeure Event"), and such non-performance shall not be a breach or default hereunder or grounds for termination hereof. Such affected Service Provider shall give written notice to Sellers of any such Force Majeure Event as soon as reasonably practicable, and the respective Service Providers (including with respect to services performed through Third Party Service Providers) and Receiving Parties will use commercially reasonable efforts to mitigate the effect of any such Force Majeure Event and its consequences on performance hereunder.

Section 2.8 Fees for Transition Services. The fees to be charged to Sellers for the Transition Services and the billing and payment terms therefore are set forth on Schedule C.

Section 2.9 Disputes. The Parties shall exercise commercially reasonable efforts to resolve disputes in good faith as promptly as practicable. If Sellers in good faith dispute the accuracy or legitimacy of any portion (the "Disputed Amount") of an invoice or charge, (i) Sellers may, without being in breach of this Agreement, withhold one-half of the Disputed Amount when paying such invoice or charge pending resolution of the dispute (such half of the Disputed Amount, the "Withheld Amount") and (ii) Sellers will thereupon provide written notice thereof to Purchaser, and the dispute resolution process set forth below in this Section 2.9 shall become applicable. Promptly following receipt of such written notice, Purchaser and Sellers shall discuss the resolution of such Disputed Amount. If a full resolution of the Disputed Amount has not occurred within 30 days of the initial discussion described in the foregoing sentence, Sellers and Purchaser shall cooperate to promptly submit for resolution such matter (or the portion thereof remaining in dispute) to a mutually agreed person (the "Neutral Arbitrator"). The Parties each agree to execute, if requested by the Neutral Arbitrator, an engagement letter reasonably satisfactory to such person. The Parties shall direct the Neutral Arbitrator to render a resolution of such disputed matter within 30 days after its engagement (or such other period agreed upon by the Parties). The resolution of the Neutral Arbitrator shall be set forth in a written statement delivered to each of the Parties and shall be final, binding, conclusive and non-appealable for all purposes hereunder. All fees and expenses of the Neutral Arbitrator shall be promptly advanced (on a 50-50 basis) to the Neutral Arbitrator, upon its request, by the Parties, subject to the award of such fees and expenses in accordance with this Section 2.9. The Neutral Arbitrator shall determine the amount of the Disputed Amount due to Provider, which amount shall not exceed the Disputed Amount or be less than zero. If the Neutral Arbitrator determines Purchaser was due an amount equal to or exceeding half of the Disputed Amount, then the Neutral Arbitrator shall award to Purchaser (i) the amount of the Withheld Amount determined by the Neutral Arbitrator to be payable to Purchaser, (ii) all of its out-of-pocket costs and expenses paid to third parties in connection with the subject dispute, including the out-of-pocket costs borne by Purchaser with respect to the Neutral Arbitrator, and (iii) interest, from the date of the invoice giving rise to the dispute, at a rate of 4 percent per annum on the amount of the Withheld Amount to which Purchaser is entitled. If the Neutral Arbitrator determines Purchaser was due an amount equal to less than half of the Disputed Amount, then the Neutral Arbitrator shall award to Sellers (i) the amount by which the portion of the Disputed Amount determined by the Neutral Arbitrator to be not properly payable by Sellers exceeds the Withheld Amount, (ii) all out-of-pocket costs and expenses paid to third parties in connection with the subject dispute, including the out-of-pocket costs borne by Sellers with respect to the Neutral Arbitrator, and (iii) interest, from the date of the invoice giving rise to the dispute, at a rate of 4 percent per annum on such amount of the Disputed Amount in excess of the Withheld Amount to which Sellers are determined to be entitled. Any amount awarded by the Neutral Arbitrator shall be paid by either Purchaser or Sellers, as applicable, by wire transfer of immediately available funds to the account or accounts designated in writing by the other Party or Parties within five

Business Days after the date on which the resolution of the Neutral Arbitrator is delivered to the Parties. Subject to compliance with the other terms and conditions of this Agreement by the Receiving Parties, the Service Providers will continue performing the Transition Services in accordance with this Agreement pending resolution of any such dispute.

Section 2.10 Personnel.

(a) Designation of Personnel. The Service Providers shall have the right, in their reasonable discretion, to designate which personnel shall be assigned to perform the Transition Services, and shall have the right, in their reasonable discretion, to remove and replace any such personnel at any time and/or designate a Third Party Service Provider.

(b) Financial Responsibility for Personnel. The Service Providers shall be responsible for the payment of all personnel expenses, including wages, required travel and travel related expenses, of their employees performing the Transition Services.

Section 2.11 Status of Service Providers. In all matters relating to this Agreement, each Service Provider shall be acting as an independent contractor and not as an agent, representative or joint venture partner of the Receiving Party. The Service Providers shall not be liable for any debts, obligations or liabilities of the Receiving Party.

Section 2.12 Protective Acknowledgements. Sellers acknowledge that the Service Providers are not insurers or guarantors of the Transition Services they provide. Sellers acknowledge that the Service Providers are not in the business of providing Transition Services and are providing the Transition Services only as an accommodation to Sellers. In order to facilitate their compliance with their financial reporting requirements, Sellers acknowledge and agree that the Service Providers may decide not to make changes to any or all of their systems during the last calendar quarter of any year and, therefore, unless otherwise set forth in a plan agreed to by all Parties, the Service Providers are not obligated hereunder to make any such changes during the last calendar quarter of any year.

Section 2.13 Receiving Party Obligations. The Receiving Party shall fully cooperate with the Service Providers and the Third Party Service Providers with respect to the provision of Transition Services. Without limiting the foregoing, as necessary to enable the provision of Transition Services by the Service Providers and the Third Party Service Providers, the Receiving Parties shall: (a) adhere in all material respects to the policies of the Service Providers with respect to the protection of proprietary information and other policies regarding the use of information technology resources, to the extent relevant to the Transition Services provided; (b) provide timely responses to any information requested by the Service Providers or the Third Party Service Providers; and (c) provide access to the facilities and assets of the Receiving Parties as requested by the Service Providers or Third Party Service Providers. The Receiving Parties shall promptly notify Purchaser of any problems or failures with respect to the Transition Services, or any breach or default by any Service Provider or Third Party Service Provider under this Agreement, which notice shall describe the foregoing in reasonable detail, and the Receiving Parties shall cooperate with the

Service Providers and the Third Party Service Providers to correct the foregoing. The Service Providers and the Third Party Service Providers shall be entitled to rely on any instructions or other information provided by the Receiving Parties, and the Service Providers shall not be in breach of or in default under this Agreement as a result of any such reliance; provided that no such instructions shall expand the obligations of the Service Providers hereunder. The Service Providers shall be excused from their obligation to perform or cause to be performed a Transition Service if and to the extent that (i) such failure to perform or cause to be performed such Transition Service was due to the Receiving Party's failure to perform its responsibilities under this Section 2.13 and (ii) the Service Providers use commercially reasonable efforts to perform or cause to be performed such Transition Service notwithstanding Receiving Party's failure, if practicable.

ARTICLE 3
CONFIDENTIALITY

Section 3.1 Confidentiality. All information shared in the course of providing or receiving Transition Services, including information related to employees, customers or suppliers, will be considered the Confidential Information of the Person disclosing the information, and will be subject to the confidentiality provisions set forth in Section 6.18 of the Purchase Agreement; provided that, notwithstanding the term set forth in Section 6.18 of the Purchase Agreement, the term of the confidentiality obligation with respect to the Confidential Information covered by virtue of this Section 3.1 shall extend until the second anniversary of the Termination Date.

Section 3.2 Survival. The provisions of this Article 3 shall survive any expiration or termination of this Agreement. Each Party shall use commercially reasonable efforts not to, and shall cause their Subsidiaries, successors and permitted assigns to use commercially reasonable efforts not to, attempt at any time to access any data, information or system of the other Party or Parties except as required to provide or receive Transition Services, as the case may be.

ARTICLE 4
TERM AND TERMINATION

Section 4.1 Term and Final Termination. This Agreement shall commence on the Effective Date and continue until the termination of all Transition Services pursuant to Section 4.2 (the "Termination Date").

Section 4.2 Early Termination. Notwithstanding anything to the contrary, (i) Sellers may terminate all or any Transition Services on not less than 30 days prior written notice to Purchaser, unless another notification period is specified on Schedule A (each such notice a "Termination Notice") and (ii) the Parties may terminate this Agreement or any Transition Services by mutual agreement at any time. As soon as a Transition Service is terminated, Sellers shall no longer be obligated to pay any fees for the terminated Transition Services with respect to the period following the effective date of such termination. As soon as reasonably practicable following receipt of a Termination Notice, Purchaser shall provide Sellers with a written notice as to whether the termination of any of the Transition Services that are the subject of the

Termination Notice will require termination or partial termination of any of the other Transition Services and/or will result in any early termination costs and expenses and, if so, a good faith estimate of the aggregate amount of such costs (each, an "Early Termination Consequence"). If Purchaser notifies Sellers of an Early Termination Consequence, Sellers may withdraw or modify their Termination Notice within 10 days of such notification. If Sellers do not withdraw or modify such Termination Notice (in writing) within such period, termination of such Transition Services will be final, including with respect to the termination of any other Transition Services identified by Purchaser as an Early Termination Consequence and Sellers shall have the obligation to pay the actual amount of any early termination costs and expenses identified by Purchaser as an Early Termination Consequence (notwithstanding that any such actual amount may be greater than the estimated amount). Notwithstanding anything to the contrary, Sellers shall not have the right to unilaterally reinstitute any Transition Service if such Transition Service has been terminated.

Section 4.3 Early Termination by Non-Defaulting Party. Purchaser on the one hand or Sellers on the other hand may terminate this Agreement (i) upon 15 days prior written notice to the other Party, if such other Party (the "Defaulting Party") is in breach of its payment obligations hereunder (it being understood that a Party will not be deemed to be in breach of such obligations with respect to an invoice or charge so long as it is disputing such invoice or charge in good faith in accordance with Section 2.9) or (ii) upon 60 days prior written notice to the Defaulting Party, if the Defaulting Party is in material breach of any of its non-monetary obligations hereunder, and, in the case of either of clause (i) or (ii), the Defaulting Party fails to cure such breach within the applicable notice period specified above. Other than as provided in Section 4.2 and 4.3, this Agreement may not be terminated by either Party under any circumstances.

Section 4.4 Effect of Termination. If this Agreement is terminated in its entirety pursuant to Section 4.1, 4.2 or 4.3, all obligations of the Parties under this Agreement shall terminate, except for (i) Articles 3, 5, 6 and 7, the terms and conditions of which shall survive any termination or expiration of this Agreement and (ii) the obligation of Sellers to pay all unpaid amounts in respect of Transition Services provided under this Agreement prior to the date of termination, whether or not invoiced prior to such date, and other costs and expenses expressly required by the terms of this Agreement to be borne by Sellers, including Early Termination Consequences.

ARTICLE 5
INDEMNIFICATION; EXCLUSIVE REMEDY

Section 5.1 Purchaser Indemnification. Subject to Article 6 and the other limitations set forth in this Agreement, Purchaser shall indemnify, defend and hold harmless the Receiving Parties from, against and in respect of any and all Losses incurred by Receiving Parties, or any of them, as a result of the performance of the Transition Services, but only if such Losses result from the gross negligence or willful misconduct of a Service Provider.

Section 5.2 Third Party Act or Omission.

(a) In the event a Receiving Party seeks indemnification from Purchaser for Losses that result in whole or in part from any act, omission, product or service of any Person other than Purchaser and its Subsidiaries (an "Unaffiliated Third Party") and Purchaser is obligated to indemnify such Receiving Party under Section 5.1 for Losses resulting from such act, omission, product or service, or such Losses result from a breach by an Unaffiliated Third Party of its respective agreement with the Service Provider (a "Third Party Act or Omission"), then Purchaser shall use commercially reasonable efforts to obtain recovery of such Losses from such Unaffiliated Third Party, and the liability of Purchaser under Section 5.1 in connection with such breach shall be limited to, and shall in no event exceed, the Net Recovery with respect to such Losses. In connection with the preceding, Purchaser agrees to obtain the consent of the respective Receiving Party (which shall not be unreasonably withheld or delayed) prior to any settlement between Purchaser and the Unaffiliated Third Party. "Net Recovery" means the net amount that Purchaser actually and finally collects from such Unaffiliated Third Party pursuant to a final, non-appealable award by a Governmental Authority or under an arbitration award in favor of Purchaser or a final, valid and enforceable settlement between Purchaser and the Unaffiliated Third Party in respect of such Third Party Act or Omission, in each case after the deduction of all costs and expenses incurred by Purchaser in connection with such action and not previously reimbursed to Purchaser. Sellers shall be jointly and severally liable for reimbursing Purchaser, on a monthly basis, for all reasonable costs and expenses of Purchaser and its Subsidiaries (including reasonable legal expenses and arbitrator fees) incurred in connection with their efforts to obtain recovery of such Losses. At Purchaser's request and option, Sellers shall pay to Purchaser the estimated amount of such costs and expenses in advance on a monthly basis, which shall be subject to reconciliation with the actual amount of such costs and expenses. Purchaser shall reasonably consult with Sellers in connection with its efforts to obtain any such award or settlement and shall not enter into any such final settlement without the prior written consent of Sellers.

(b) Purchaser may, in its sole discretion, elect not to seek recovery of Losses from an Unaffiliated Third Party pursuant to Section 5.2(a) by providing written notice of such election to the Sellers. Upon making such election: (i) Section 5.2(a) shall no longer apply to the applicable Third Party Act or Omission; and (ii) Purchaser's aggregate liability to the Receiving Party for such Third Party Act or Omission shall be limited to the Net Recovery that Purchaser would reasonably have been expected to recover from the applicable Unaffiliated Third Party (as determined in good faith by Purchaser) under the applicable agreement with such Unaffiliated Third Party.

Section 5.3 Exclusivity of Remedy. Notwithstanding anything to the contrary herein, the indemnification set forth in this Article 5 shall be the sole and exclusive remedy of the Receiving Parties with respect to any breach of this Agreement or any Losses otherwise arising out of or relating to the Transition Services. In no event shall such remedies be deemed to have failed of their essential purpose.

ARTICLE 6
LIMITATION OF LIABILITY; EXCLUSION OF CONSEQUENTIAL DAMAGES

Section 6.1 Limitation of Liability. IN NO EVENT SHALL THE AGGREGATE LIABILITY ARISING UNDER OR IN CONNECTION WITH THIS AGREEMENT OF PURCHASER, ARISING UNDER ANY LEGAL THEORY, EXCEED THE LIABILITY CAP.

Section 6.2 Exclusion of Consequential Damages. WITHOUT LIMITING THE GENERALITY OF SECTION 6.1, IN NO EVENT SHALL SELLERS OR PURCHASER BE LIABLE FOR ANY INCIDENTAL, SPECIAL, PUNITIVE OR CONSEQUENTIAL DAMAGES OR LOSSES OF ANY KIND ARISING UNDER OR IN CONNECTION WITH THIS AGREEMENT, REGARDLESS OF LEGAL THEORY, INCLUDING ANY SUCH DAMAGES OR LOSSES RESULTING FROM BUSINESS INTERRUPTION OR LOST PROFITS.

ARTICLE 7

MISCELLANEOUS

Section 7.1 Notices. Any notice, request, instruction, consent, document or other communication required or permitted to be given under this Agreement shall be in writing and shall be deemed to have been sufficiently given or served for all purposes (a) upon delivery when personally delivered; (b) on the later of the scheduled delivery date or the first Business Day following such delivery date (if scheduled for Saturday delivery) after having been sent by a nationally or internationally recognized overnight courier service (charges prepaid); (c) at the time received when sent by registered or certified mail, return receipt requested, postage prepaid; or (d) at the time when confirmation of successful transmission is received (or the first Business Day following such receipt if the date of such receipt is not a Business Day).

Section 7.2 No Right of Setoff. Except as expressly provided under Section 2.9 in this Agreement, no Party nor any of its Affiliates shall have any right of holdback or setoff or assert any Claim or defense with respect to any amounts that may be owed by such Party or its Affiliates to any other Party (or Parties) hereto or its or their Affiliates as a result of and with respect to any amount that may be owing to such Party or its Affiliates under this Agreement or any other commercial arrangement entered into, between or among such Parties and/or their respective Affiliates.

Section 7.3 Taxes. The Receiving Party shall pay any and all sales, use or value-added taxes due for the respective Transition Services.

Section 7.4 Assignment; Successors and Assigns. Neither this Agreement nor any of the rights, interests or obligations provided by this Agreement may be assigned by any Party (whether by operation of law or otherwise) without the prior written consent of the other Parties, and any such assignment without such prior written consent shall be null and void; provided, however, that, without the consent of Sellers, Purchaser may assign its obligations hereunder to one or more Affiliates of Purchaser; provided, further, that no such assignment shall relieve Purchaser of any of its obligations under this Agreement. Subject to the preceding sentence and except as otherwise expressly provided herein, this Agreement shall be binding upon and inure to the benefit of the Parties hereto and their respective successors and permitted assigns.

Section 7.5 Amendment. This Agreement may not be amended, modified or supplemented except upon the execution and delivery of a written agreement executed by a duly authorized representative or officer of each of the Parties.

Section 7.6 Waiver. At any time prior to the Termination Date, the Parties may (a) extend the time for the performance of any of the obligations or other acts of the other Parties or (b) waive compliance with any of the agreements or conditions contained herein (to the extent permitted by law). Any such waiver or extension by a Party (i) shall be valid only if, and to the extent, set forth in a written instrument signed by a duly authorized representative or officer of the Party to be bound and (ii) shall not constitute, or be construed as, a continuing waiver of such provision, or a waiver of any other breach of, or failure to comply with, any other provision of this Agreement. The failure in any one or more instances of a Party to insist upon performance of any of the terms, covenants or conditions of this Agreement, to exercise any right or privilege in this Agreement conferred, or the waiver by said Party of any breach of any of the terms, covenants or conditions of this Agreement shall not be construed as a subsequent waiver of, or estoppel with respect to, any other terms, covenants, conditions, rights or privileges, but the same will continue and remain in full force and effect as if no such forbearance or waiver had occurred.

Section 7.7 Severability. Whenever possible, each term and provision of this Agreement will be interpreted in such manner as to be effective and valid under law. If any term or provision of this Agreement, or the application thereof to any Person or any circumstance, is held to be illegal, invalid or unenforceable, (a) a suitable and equitable provision shall be substituted therefore in order to carry out, so far as may be legal, valid and enforceable, the intent and purpose of such illegal, invalid or unenforceable provision and (b) the remainder of this Agreement or such term or provision and the application of such term or provision to other Persons or circumstances shall remain in full force and effect and shall not be affected by such illegality, invalidity or unenforceability, nor shall such invalidity or unenforceability affect the legality, validity or enforceability of such term or provision, or the application thereof, in any jurisdiction.

Section 7.8 Counterparts. This Agreement may be executed in one or more counterparts, each of which shall be deemed an original, and all of which taken together shall constitute one and the same Agreement. All signatures of the Parties may be transmitted by facsimile or electronic delivery, and each such facsimile signature or electronic delivery signature (including a PDF signature) will, for all purposes, be deemed to be the original signature of the Party whose signature it reproduces and be binding upon such Party.

Section 7.9 Headings. The descriptive headings of the Articles, Sections and paragraphs of, and Schedules to, this Agreement are included for convenience only, do not constitute a part of this Agreement and shall not be deemed to limit, modify or affect any of the provisions hereof.

Section 7.10 No Third-Party Beneficiaries. Except for the Receiving Parties pursuant to Article 5, this Agreement is for the sole benefit of the Parties hereto and their respective successors and permitted assigns, and nothing express or implied in this Agreement is intended or shall be construed to confer upon or give to any Person, other than the Receiving Parties, the Parties, their Affiliates and their respective permitted successors or assigns, any legal or equitable Claims, benefits, rights or remedies of any nature whatsoever under or by reason of this Agreement.

Section 7.11 Governing Law. The construction, interpretation and other matters arising out of or in connection with this Agreement (whether arising in contract, tort, equity or otherwise) shall in all respects be governed by and construed (a) to the extent applicable, in accordance with the Bankruptcy Code, and (b) to the extent the Bankruptcy Code is not applicable, in accordance with the Laws of the State of New York, without giving effect to rules governing the conflict of laws.

Section 7.12 Forum Selection; Consent to Service of Process; Waiver of Jury Trial. Except as provided in Section 2.9, the Parties irrevocably and unconditionally submit to the exclusive jurisdiction of the federal courts in the Southern District of New York and state courts of the State of New York located in the Borough of Manhattan in the City of New York for any litigation arising out of or in connection with this Agreement and the Transition Services (and agree not to commence any litigation relating thereto except in the federal courts in the Southern District of New York and state courts of the State of New York located in the Borough of Manhattan in the City of New York, other than actions in any court of competent jurisdiction to enforce any judgment, decree or award rendered by any such court as described herein).

Section 7.13 Waiver of Jury Trial. EACH PARTY WAIVES THE RIGHT TO A TRIAL BY JURY IN ANY DISPUTE IN CONNECTION WITH OR RELATING TO THIS AGREEMENT OR ANY MATTERS DESCRIBED OR CONTEMPLATED HEREIN, AND AGREES TO TAKE ANY AND ALL ACTION NECESSARY OR APPROPRIATE TO EFFECT SUCH WAIVER.

Section 7.14 Entire Agreement. This Agreement (together with the Purchase Agreement and the Schedules) contains the final, exclusive and entire agreement and understanding of the Parties with respect to the subject matter hereof and thereof and supersedes all prior and contemporaneous agreements and understandings, whether written or oral, among the Parties with respect to the subject matter hereof and thereof. Neither this Agreement nor any other Ancillary Agreement shall be deemed to contain or imply any restriction, covenant, representation, warranty, agreement or undertaking of any Party with respect to the transactions contemplated hereby or thereby other than those expressly set forth herein or therein, and none shall be deemed to exist or be inferred with respect to the subject matter hereof.

Section 7.15 Disclaimer. EXCEPT AS EXPRESSLY SET FORTH IN THIS AGREEMENT, NONE OF SELLERS, PURCHASER, THE OTHER SERVICE PROVIDERS OR THEIR RESPECTIVE AFFILIATES OR ANY PERSON ACTING ON BEHALF OF ANY SUCH PARTY MAKES ANY REPRESENTATIONS

OR WARRANTIES OF ANY KIND, EXPRESS OR IMPLIED, AT LAW OR IN EQUITY WITH RESPECT TO THE TRANSITION SERVICES OR THE SUBJECT MATTER OF THIS AGREEMENT, INCLUDING ANY WARRANTY OF MERCHANTABILITY, FITNESS FOR ANY PARTICULAR PURPOSE OR USE, TITLE OR NON-INFRINGEMENT, OR THE ACCURACY, AVAILABILITY, TIMELINESS OR COMPLETENESS OF, OR THE RESULTS TO BE OBTAINED FROM, SUCH TRANSITION SERVICES, AND SELLERS, PURCHASER, THE OTHER SERVICE PROVIDERS AND THEIR RESPECTIVE AFFILIATES HEREBY DISCLAIM THE SAME.

SCHEDULE A

TRANSITION SERVICES

- public reporting,
- communications and public relations,
- payroll,
- cash management,
- treasury,
- timekeeping,
- accounts receivable and accounts payable processing,
- fixed assets administration,
- real estate management services,
- finance and financial reporting,
- accounting,
- budgeting,
- expense reporting,
- insurance,
- litigation and other legal support,
- purchasing,
- tax,
- human resources,
- pension and OPEB,
- health and welfare plan administration,
- IS&S (information technology)
- environmental

SCHEDULE B

EXCLUDED SERVICES

- engineering,
- manufacturing,
- quality,
- distribution and
- customs and export compliance.
- any service that would expose a Service Provider to potential statutory liability, including owner/operator liability under environmental protection laws.

SCHEDULE C

PAYMENT TERMS

1. *Definitions.*

   "Default Rate" means the prime rate as quoted in the Wall Street Journal from time to time plus 2 percent per annum.

   "Usage Fee" means an amount equal to the actual, fully-burdened cost incurred by the Service Providers in providing a service (the "Base Cost"), including, as applicable, actual amounts of direct labor, direct materials, direct purchased services and subcontractor charges associated with the service provided, together with a portion of indirect costs to reflect labor, administrative and general and other overhead amounts, plus 5 percent of such base cost; provided that if a Transition Service is of a type provided and allocated to a division or Subsidiary of Purchaser, the Usage Fee shall be an amount determined in a manner consistent with its internal transfer cost allocation policies, plus 5 percent of such base amount. In any case, fixed costs, including general and other overhead amounts, are to be fairly allocated in a manner consistent with internal transfer cost allocation policies.

2. *General Consideration.* Sellers shall pay the respective Usage Fee for each Transition Service. All payments indicated in this Schedule C and all other amounts payable under this Agreement are exclusive of federal, state, provincial and local sales tax, goods and services tax, and any other applicable taxes.

3. *Invoices.* Except as otherwise provided in this Agreement, within 30 days after the end of each calendar month, Purchaser or the respective Service Provider shall submit one or more reasonably detailed invoices to Parent or the respective Receiving Party for all Transition Services provided during such calendar month pursuant to this Agreement.

4. *Time of Payment.* Invoices for Transition Services shall be due and payable in accordance with the MNS-2 system, which provides, on average, for payment on the second day of the second month following the date of the invoice or if such MNS-2 system is not utilized, within 40 days after receipt.
5. *Interest Arrears.* If the Receiving Party fails to pay when due any invoiced amounts in respect of Transition Services, the Receiving Party shall pay interest on the unpaid amount at the Default Rate from the date due until the date paid, without prejudice to and in addition to any other remedy available to the Service Provider under the Agreement or at law.
6. *Currency Conversions.* Usage Fees shall be invoiced and payments shall be made in U.S. dollars. If a Usage Fee includes Base Costs that are accounted for or incurred in a currency other than U.S. dollars, such amounts of Base Cost shall, for purposes of invoice and payment, be converted into U.S. dollars based on the average rate of exchange for the month to which the invoice relates, based on daily noon buying rates for cable transfers in New York City certified for customs purposes by the Federal Reserve Bank of New York, available on the website for the Board of Governors of the Federal Reserve System (or any successor entity).

APPENDIX K

TRIAL BRIEF

IN THE UNITED STATES DISTRICT COURT FOR THE NORTHERN DISTRICT OF ILLINOIS EASTERN DIVISION

BLUE CORP.,	
Plaintiff,	
v.	
RED CORP.,	
Defendant.	

MEMORANDUM IN SUPPORT OF DEFENDANT'S MOTION TO DISMISS FOR IMPROPER VENUE AND FAILURE TO STATE A CLAIM

Attorney 1

Attorney 2

Attorney 3

LAW FIRM

Attorneys For Defendant Red Corp.

TABLE OF CONTENTS

TABLE OF AUTHORITIES

FEDERAL CASES

TABLE OF AUTHORITIES

FEDERAL CASES

STATE CASES

STATUTES

OTHER AUTHORITIES

Defendant Red Corp. ("Red") respectfully submits this memorandum in support of its motion to dismiss for improper venue and failure to state a claim.

INTRODUCTION

There are two separate, independent reasons why the Complaint should be dismissed with prejudice. First, by filing its Complaint in this jurisdiction, plaintiff Blue Corp. ("Blue") violated the forum selection clause of the Supplemental Agreement that governs the parties' relationship as corporate shareholders of non-party Joint Venture Corp. ("JVC"). That agreement requires that any legal action Blue pursues against Red be filed in Japan. The Seventh Circuit has held that, absent very unusual circumstances not present in this case, forum selection clauses are *prima facie* valid and should be enforced. Accordingly, Blue's Complaint should be dismissed with prejudice for lack of proper venue.

Second, although styled as a claim for breach of fiduciary duty, Blue's Complaint alleges unfairness in the terms of the New Supply Agreement and is a disguised attempt to reform that agreement. However, that agreement is between Red and JVC; Blue is not a party. Blue has no standing to seek to reform a contract to which it is not a party.

FACTUAL BACKGROUND

Blue's Complaint alleges that Red breached joint venture fiduciary duties Red allegedly owes to Blue as a result of the parties' joint ownership of JVC. Before addressing the legal deficiencies of Blue's Complaint, Red briefly addresses the factual background relevant to the Court's analysis.

1. The Basic And Supplemental Agreements Between Blue And Red.[1]

In Year 1, Red and Blue formed a general partnership named Early Joint Venture, JVC's predecessor, the purpose of which was "to perform research and development on certain Blue and Red compounds." Basic Agreement at 2, App. 2 to Declaration, attached as Ex. A. That partnership was created through a Basic Agreement between Red and Blue. *Id.*

In Year 2, Red and Blue executed a Supplemental Agreement "to supplement the provisions of the Basic Agreement." Supplemental Agreement at 1, App. 3 to Ex. A. The Supplemental Agreement governs the basic elements of the Red/Blue relationship with respect to JVC. Section 10.1 of the agreement states that Blue and Red agree "to utilize their voting power in [the joint venture] in such a manner as to effectuate the intent of the Basic Agreement and this Supplemental Agreement." *Id.* at ¶ 10.1. The Supplemental Agreement contains no limit of duration or expiration date. *Id.*

Section 9.2 of the Supplemental Agreement memorializes the parties' agreement to expand the business of JVC to establish "manufacturing, distribution, marketing or

[1] In deciding a motion challenging venue pursuant to Fed. R. Civ. P. 12(b)(3), a court is not obligated to limit its consideration to the pleadings; rather, the Court may examine facts outside the complaint to determine whether venue is proper. *See Cont'l Cas. Co. v. Am. Nat'l Ins. Co.*, 417 F.3d 727, 733 (7th Cir. 2005); *Faur v. Sirius Int'l Ins. Corp.*, No. 04 C 7640, 2005 WL 1139634, *5 (N.D. Ill. Apr. 25, 2005). All cited unpublished cases are attached as Exhibit C.

sales organizations" for JVC's operations. *Id.* at ¶ 9.2. That same provision also authorizes either Red or Blue to sell "bulk product" to JVC for use in those activities. *Id.* The agreement requires Blue and Red to cause JVC to give its shareholders "the first opportunity to quote on supplying such bulk product to... [JVC]," but provides "the selection of the supplier shall be made on the basis of the economic advantage to [JVC]." *Id.*

The Supplemental Agreement remains in effect as a binding shareholders' agreement between Blue and Red. Ex. A, ¶ 7. The Supplemental Agreement has been amended twice. Both Amendments applied to corporate transactions through which JVC evolved (as explained below in Part 3) and made minor changes to the agreement, none of which is significant to this action. Both Amendments state that "[e]xcept as modified by this Amendment, the Supplemental Agreement is ratified and confirmed in its entirety." App. 4 to Ex. A at 1; App. 5 to Ex. A at 2.

2. The Forum Selection Clause Of The Supplemental Agreement.

The Supplemental Agreement contains mandatory, reciprocal forum selection clauses that require any actions filed between Red and Blue "arising from, concerning or in any way related to" the Supplemental Agreement to be filed in the adversary's home forum. Section 10.5 of the Supplemental Agreement (App. 3 to Ex. A) provides in full:

> (a) BLUE and RED agree that, in the event of a dispute between them arising from, concerning or in any way related to this Agreement, the parties shall undertake good faith efforts to resolve the same amicably between themselves. In the event that any such dispute cannot be resolved amicably within ninety (90) days after notice by either party to the other, and either party files an action, suit or proceeding ("action") following such ninety (90) day period to resolve such dispute, the parties shall proceed exclusively in accordance with the following provisions of this section.
>
> (b) If RED is the party which files such action, it shall do so in the Circuit Court of County, Illinois, or in the United States District Court for the Northern District of Illinois, Eastern Division, Chicago, Illinois as RED shall determine. RED hereby covenants and agrees to refrain from filing any such action in any other court, either within or outside of the United States.
>
> (c) If BLUE is the party which files such action, it shall do so in the Osaka District Court in Osaka, Japan, or in the Tokyo District Court in Tokyo, Japan, as BLUE shall determine. BLUE hereby covenants and agrees to refrain from filing any such action in any other court, either within or outside of Japan.
>
> * * *
>
> (e) RED and BLUE each hereby waive and agree not to assert by way of motion, as a defense, or otherwise in any such action brought in accordance with paragraph (b) or (c) of this section, any claim... that the action is brought in an inconvenient forum, that the venue of the action is improper, or that this section may not be enforced in or by such court.

3. **The Structure Of JVC Was Changed From a Partnership to a Corporation.**

The Supplemental Agreement provided for a series of corporate transactions through which the Red-Blue partnership was restructured into its current corporate form, JVC, a close corporation. App. 3 to Ex. A at 3-11. Blue and Red each own 50% of the shares of JVC. Compl., ¶¶ 3-4. JVC's Board of Directors has 10 members, four elected by Red, four elected by Blue, and two elected jointly by Red and Blue. Ex. A, ¶ 2.

JVC's Certificate of Incorporation acknowledges that the Supplemental Agreement shall be on file with the records of JVC and that it memorializes "the basis upon which [Blue and Red each] agreed to become a stockholder" in JVC:

> Article 5. (a) The two (2) entities [Red and Blue] which are to become the stockholders of this corporation upon the formation thereof have set forth in a separate instrument the basis upon which each such entity has agreed to become a stockholder of this corporation. Such separate instrument is the Supplemental Agreement, as amended, between such entities, which instrument shall be on file with the records of this corporation.

Certified Documents for JVC, attached as Ex. B, at 9.[2]

The stock certificate memorializing Red's ownership in JVC Predecessor, Inc.[3], which bears the signatures of JVC's then-President and then-Assistant Secretary, similarly acknowledges that the Supplemental Agreement is the controlling JVC shareholders' agreement between Blue and Red:

> The two (2) entities [Red and Blue] which are the stockholders of this corporation have set forth in a separate instrument the basis upon which each such entity has agreed to become a stockholder of this corporation. Such separate instrument is the Supplemental Agreement, as amended, between such entities, which instrument shall be on file with the records of this corporation.

Red Stock Certificate at 2, App. 8 to Ex. A.

4. **The Supply Agreements Between JVC And Red.**

In Year 3, consistent with Section 9.2 of the Supplemental Agreement authorizing Blue and Red to supply JVC with "bulk product" for use in JVC's operations, JVC entered into a ten-year agreement with Red (the "Original Supply Agreement") whereby Red supplied bulk X-Compound to JVC. JVC markets the X-Compound under the brand known as Brand 1. Blue is not a party to the Original Supply Agreement. Compl., ¶¶ 9, 11; Original Supply Agreement, App. 6 to Ex. A.

---

[2] JVC's current structure is the result of a series of corporate evolutions, including several name changes. Ex. B at 1. For example, the Certificate of Incorporation bears one of JVC's prior names. Because the charter documents adequately demonstrate the various evolutions of JVC, and for ease of comprehension, references in this memorandum to "JVC" include, where necessary, JVC's prior corporate identities.

[3] JVC Predecessor, Inc. is the immediate corporate predecessor to JVC.

In Year 12, again consistent with Section 9.2 of the Supplemental Agreement, JVC and Red entered into a new supply agreement (the "New Supply Agreement") by which Red currently supplies bulk X-Compound to JVC.[4] JVC's Board of Directors, including the directors elected by Blue, approved the New Supply Agreement; albeit the Blue-elected directors stated they "reserved all of [Blue's] rights" related to that agreement. Blue is not a party to the New Supply Agreement. Compl., ¶ 27; New Supply Agreement, App. 7 to Ex. A.

5. This Action.

Although the Complaint carefully avoids any reference to the Basic or Supplemental Agreements, this lawsuit is based on fiduciary duties existing between Blue and Red arising out of their joint venture in JVC, which in turn is governed by the Basic and Supplemental Agreements, as amended. This is clear from Paragraphs 3 through 11 and 30 of the Complaint, as well as Blue's prayer for relief. Compl., ¶¶ 3-11, 30. As noted above in Part 2, the controlling forum selection clause is contained in Section 10.5 of the Supplemental Agreement.

Among the remedies the Complaint seeks are an accounting of all profits Red has obtained and expects to obtain under the New Supply Agreement. Compl. at 8. Blue also seeks to enjoin Red from its alleged "self-dealing," in other words, from charging the prices bargained for in the New Supply Agreement. *Id.*

ARGUMENT

I. BLUE'S COMPLAINT SHOULD BE DISMISSED FOR LACK OF PROPER VENUE.

Blue alleges that Red breached fiduciary duties it purportedly owed to Blue as a joint venturer in JVC by engaging in self-dealing with respect to the Original and New Supply Agreements. Because the Complaint focuses on the alleged breach of a fiduciary relationship between Red and Blue as joint venturers in JVC, the forum selection clause of the Supplemental Agreement, which governs the relationship between Red and Blue as shareholders in JVC, applies. That clause expressly requires Blue to bring this action in Japan.

A motion to dismiss asserting that a forum selection clause requires litigation in another jurisdiction raises the issue of improper venue and is appropriately brought pursuant to Fed. R. Civ. P. 12(b)(3). *Cont'l Ins. Co. v. M/V ORSULA*, 354 F.3d 603, 606-07 (7th Cir. 2003). The party resisting application of a forum selection clause bears the burden of establishing that it has chosen the proper venue and that the forum selection clause is unenforceable. *Penn, L.L.C. v. New Edge Network, Inc.*, No. 03 C 5496, 2003 WL 22284207, *1 (N.D. Ill. Oct. 3, 2003).

A. The Supplemental Agreement Governs The Red/Blue Relationship.

The Supplemental Agreement remains in effect between the parties. Ex. A, ¶ 7; Ex. B at 9; App. 8 to Ex. A at 2. Under Delaware law, the Supplemental Agreement is a

---

[4] The Original and New Supply Agreements include forum selection clauses that require any lawsuit JVC pursues against Red to be brought in Japan. Apps. 6, 7 to Ex. A at ¶ 13.6(c).

valid stockholders' agreement between Red and Blue. *See Zion v. Kurtz*, 405 N.E.2d 681, 684-86 (N.Y. 1980) (upholding stockholders' agreement under Delaware law).

The Supplemental Agreement contains no limit of duration or expiration date. App. 3 to Ex. A. Section 10.1 of the Supplemental Agreement acknowledges that Blue and Red would agree "to utilize their voting power in [JVC] in such a manner as to effectuate the intent of the Basic Agreement and this Supplemental Agreement," which is to develop and market compounds. *Id.* at ¶ 10.1. Consistent with that intent, JVC continues today to market and sell, among other products, the product known as Brand 1.

B. Blue's Fiduciary Duty Claim Against Red Falls Within The Broad Scope Of The Supplemental Agreement's Forum Selection Clause.

The Complaint stresses that Blue's claim arises out of a joint venture relationship between Red and Blue, which is JVC. Blue alleges that "Red and Blue remain equal joint venturers that are entitled to share equally in the profits of JVC. Red owes Blue fiduciary duties... in its dealings with Blue and JVC." Compl., ¶ 5. Blue also alleges that "Red has no right to take advantage of its special role as JVC's supplier and thereby divert to itself profits that rightly belong jointly to Blue and Red as equal joint venturers in JVC." *Id.*, ¶ 10. Blue's request for relief asks the Court to "enjoin[] Red from its self-dealing and related misconduct that breaches Red's fiduciary duties to Blue as a joint venturer in JVC." *Id.* at 8. Those allegations all relate to the duties Red and Blue owe to each other as joint venturers in JVC, and thus are governed by the Supplemental Agreement.

The Blue/Red relationship in JVC, and any fiduciary duties owed by the parties to each other, are defined, created, and controlled by the Supplemental Agreement. The Supplemental Agreement is the joint venture agreement between Red and Blue; but for that agreement, JVC would not exist and no fiduciary duties would be owed by either party. Indeed, both JVC's Certificate of Incorporation and Red's JVC stock certificate state that the Supplemental Agreement identifies "the basis upon which [Blue and Red each] agreed to become a stockholder of [JVC]." Ex. B at 8; App. 8 to Ex. A at 2.

Moreover, Blue's claim relates directly to an aspect of Red's dealing with JVC that is expressly addressed in the Supplemental Agreement. Section 9.2 of the agreement authorizes either Red or Blue to enter into contracts with JVC to supply bulk products. App. 3 to Ex. A at ¶ 9.2. Blue claims that Red engaged in improper self-dealing by entering into the New Supply Agreement, which is a bulk supply agreement subject to Section 9.2. Compl., ¶¶ 9, 11; App. 3 to Ex. A at ¶ 9.2. Blue contends that JVC could have found a lower-price bulk supplier and that the prices in the New Supply Agreement are too high. Compl., ¶¶ 11-12.

Blue's claim falls squarely within the broad scope of the Supplemental Agreement's forum selection clause. Section 10.5 of the Supplemental Agreement covers disputes "arising from, concerning or in any way related to" the Supplemental Agreement. App. 3 to Ex. A at ¶ 10.5. The Seventh Circuit has held that a forum selection clause using this type of language is extremely broad: "all disputes the resolution of which arguably depend on the construction of an agreement 'arise out' of that agreement...." *Omron*

Healthcare, Inc. v. Maclaren Exps. Ltd., 28 F.3d 600, 603 (7th Cir. 1994); *see also Kiefer Specialty Flooring, Inc. v. Tarkett, Inc.*, 174 F.3d 907, 909 (7th Cir. 1999) (arbitration clauses containing "arising out of" and "relating to" language "have been characterized as extremely broad and capable of an expansive reach.").

Blue's claim relies directly on duties Red allegedly owes to Blue "arising out of" their status as owners of JVC, which status is controlled by the Supplemental Agreement. Blue's claim also "concerns" and "relates to" Section 9.2 of the Supplemental Agreement, which contemplates that Red and Blue will enter into bulk supply agreements with JVC.

Blue cannot evade Section 10.5's forum selection requirements simply by styling its claim as one for breach of fiduciary duty rather than breach of contract. Forum selection clauses apply beyond contract claims. *See Omron*, 28 F.3d at 602-04; *Penn, L.L.C.*, 2003 WL 22284207, at *2. Finding otherwise would permit Blue "simply [to] avoid its contractual obligations through sophistry." *Penn, L.L.C.*, 2003 WL 22284207, at *2.

Omron is particularly instructive. Maclaren terminated Omron as Maclaren's distributor, then sold a number of baby strollers bearing Omron's trademark. *Omron*, 28 F.3d at 601. Omron sued Maclaren for trademark infringement. Maclaren moved to dismiss the complaint based on a forum selection clause in the parties' distributorship agreement, which stated that "the parties hereto agree that all disputes arising out of this Agreement... shall be referred to the High Court of Justice in England which will have exclusive jurisdiction to determine such disputes." *Id.* at 601-02. The District Court dismissed Omron's complaint and the Seventh Circuit affirmed, rejecting Omron's argument that the trademark infringement claim did not arise out of the parties' agreement. *Id.* Specifically, the court held that "Omron's claim engages both the parties' compact and the rules of trademark law" because the determination whether Maclaren properly sold Omron's trademarked strollers "depend[s] on an understanding of the parties' written bargain and all of its implied terms." *Id.* at 602. As in *Omron*, Blue "signed a contract promising to litigate in [a specified forum], or not at all. It broke that promise." *Omron*, 28 F.3d at 604. Blue should be held to its contractual bargain to pursue this claim against Red in Japan.

C. The Forum Selection Clause Is Enforceable Under Federal Law.

A forum selection clause is "*prima facie* valid and should be enforced unless enforcement is shown by the resisting party to be unreasonable under the circumstances." *Bonny v. Soc'y of Lloyd's*, 3 F.3d 156, 159 (7th Cir. 1993) (quoting *M/S Bremen v. Zapata Off-Shore Co.*, 407 U.S. 1, 10 (1972)). A clause may be considered "unreasonable under the circumstances" only if: (1) it was agreed to as a result of fraud, undue influence or unequal bargaining power; or (2) the selected forum is so gravely difficult and inconvenient as to deprive the resisting party of its day in court; or (3) enforcement of the clause would contravene a strong public policy of the forum in which the suit was originally brought. *Bonny*, 3 F.3d at 160. Blue cannot demonstrate any ground on which to avoid the unambiguous language of Section 10.5's forum selection clause.

Before analyzing the *Bonny* factors, a court first must consider whether a forum selection clause contains mandatory or permissive language. *Paper Express Ltd. v. Pfankuch Maschinen GmbH*, 972 F.2d 753, 755 (7th Cir. 1992). Section 10.5 of the Supplemental Agreement "clearly manifests an intent to make venue compulsory and exclusive." *Id.* at 756. According to Section 10.5, Red and Blue "*shall* proceed *exclusively*" in the designated venues, and "*shall*" file any action arising from or in any way relating to the Supplemental Agreement in those venues. App. 3 to Ex. A at ¶ 10.5. The word "shall" denotes that the stated forum is exclusive. *Paper Express*, 972 F.2d at 756. Moreover, the parties specifically agreed not to file any action outside the designated venues. App. 3 to Ex. A at ¶ 10.5(e). Indeed, they expressly agreed that they would not contend that the forum selection clause "is improper, or that this section may not be enforced in or by [a] court." *Id.* That language is mandatory.

Turning to the first of the three *Bonny* factors, there was no fraud, undue influence, or unequal bargaining power in the formation of the Supplemental Agreement or the forum selection clause.[5] Red and Blue have been equal partners in JVC since Year 1. Both have legal staffs of experienced lawyers. The Supplemental Agreement, including Section 10.5, was "freely negotiated between sophisticated international corporations." *AAR Int'l, Inc. v. Nimelias Enters. S.A.*, 250 F.3d 510, 526 (7th Cir. 2001) (enforcing forum selection clause). The reciprocal nature of Section 10.5 shows that the parties received equal benefits and shared equal burdens. *See Warner & Swasey Co. v. Salvagnini Transferica S.p.A.*, 633 F. Supp. 1209, 1213 (W.D.N.Y. 1986). The forum selection clauses of the Original and New Supply Agreements also require that any claim JVC brings against Red related to those agreements be pursued in Japan. Apps. 6, 7 to Ex. A at ¶ 13.6(c). The forum selection clause of the Supplemental Agreement thus is not an anomaly in the relationships among Red, Blue, and JVC.

Nor can Blue demonstrate that enforcement of Section 10.5 is so gravely difficult and inconvenient as to deprive Blue of its day in court. *Bonny*, 3 F.3d at 160. Enforcement of forum selection clauses in international contracts is strongly favored, *id.* at 159-60, and Blue bears a "heavy burden" to show that it will suffer a grave difficulty or be deprived of its day in court if it is required to litigate in Japan. *Eisenmann Corp. v. Tek-Mor, Inc.*, No. 03 C 4375, 2004 WL 547253, *2 (N.D. Ill. Feb. 5, 2004). Executives and employees of both parties have for years traveled between the United States and Japan for JVC business. Ex. A, ¶¶ 3, 4. Neither the additional expense to Blue of litigating in Japan nor the location of witnesses is enough to show that Blue will suffer a grave difficulty. *Paper Express*, 972 F.2d at 758; *Joy v. Hay Group, Inc.*, No. 02 C 4989, 2004 WL 719389, *14 (N.D. Ill. March 31, 2004) (Guzman, J.), *aff'd in part, rev'd in part on other grounds*, 403 F.3d 875 (7th Cir. 2005); *Cafcas v. Radisson Seven Seas*, No 00 C 7936, 2001 WL 558049,*3 (N.D. Ill. May 21, 2001) (Guzman, J.). Litigating Blue's claims in Japan, just as litigating Red's claims against Blue in the United States, obviously was foreseeable at the time the parties entered

[5] Some courts have held that this analysis is unnecessary where a forum selection clause was freely entered into by sophisticated parties with equal bargaining power; those courts hold the inquiry into the enforceability of the clause is limited to whether the objecting party would be deprived of its day in court. *Roberts & Schaefer Co. v. Merit Contracting, Inc.*, 99 F.3d 248, 254 (7th Cir. 1996); *Faur*, 2005 WL 1139634, *5. Here, Red simply seeks to hold Blue to its contractual bargain to litigate those claims in Japan, as the parties agreed.

into the Supplemental Agreement, and each party reciprocally agreed to litigate in the other's "home court" if it brought suit. *AAR Int'l*, 250 F.3d at 526; *Karlberg European Tanspa, Inc. v. JK-Josef Kratz Vertriebsgesellschaft mbH*, 618 F. Supp. 344, 349 (N.D. Ill 1985) ("Litigating international disputes is always going to be inconvenient for one (or both) of the parties, and we find that the parties allocated this burden in a contract that the court is in no position now to modify.").

Enforcement of Section 10.5 will not contravene the public policy of Illinois. *Bonny*, 3 F.3d at 160. Both Japan and Illinois have a public policy interest in protecting their citizens and contracts that are formed in the state. *See, e.g., Faur*, 2005 WL 1139634, at *7. "Competing policy arguments" are not strong enough to "overcome the heavy burden that is required to disregard a forum selection clause." *Id.*

In sum, none of the three factors identified in *Bonny* warrants disregard of the bargained- for venue in this case.

D. The Forum Selection Clause Is Enforceable Under Illinois Law.

Although courts generally apply federal law to determine the enforceability of forum selection clauses, *see, e.g., Northwestern Nat'l Ins. Co. v. Donovan*, 916 F.2d 372, 374 (7th Cir. 1990), some courts have applied Illinois law to the analysis. *See, e.g., IFC Credit Corp. v. Burton Indus.*, No. 04 C 5906, 2005 WL 1243404, *3 (N.D. Ill. May 12, 2005) (Guzman, J.). As shown above, Section 10.5 is enforceable under federal law. It is equally enforceable under Illinois law, which applies six factors to determine the enforceability of a forum selection clause:

> (1) which law governs the formation and construction of the contract; (2) the residency of the parties involved; (3) the place of execution and/or performance of the contract; (4) the location of the parties and the witnesses participating in the litigation; (5) the inconvenience to the parties of any particular location; and (6) whether the clause was equally bargained for.

Id. at *3 (quoting *Calanca v. D&S Mfg. Co.*, 510 N.E.2d 21, 23 (1st Dist. 1987)).

As to the first factor, United States law governs Blue's claim. Courts have enforced similar contractual provisions even when there is concern that a foreign court may have difficulty deciding complex areas of American law. *See Mitsubishi Motors Corp. v. Soler Chrysler-Plymouth, Inc.*, 473 U.S. 614, 633-34 (1985) (enforcing arbitration clause requiring Japanese arbitration panel to apply U.S. antitrust law[6]); *Scherk v. Alberto-Culver Co.*, 417 U.S. 506, 519-20 (1974) (enforcing arbitration clause requiring French arbitration panel to apply U.S. securities law); *Omron*, 28 F.3d at 602-03 (collecting cases and enforcing forum selection clause requiring English court to apply U.S. trademark law). In any event, Blue's claim against Red involves the alleged breach of fiduciary duties, not a particularly complicated area of the law.

The second and third factors are evenly split and, thus, do not weigh against enforcement. *IFC Credit*, 2005 WL 1243404, at *5-*6. Red resides in Japan, and Blue in the United States. Execution and performance of the Supplemental Agreement have

[6] An arbitration clause is one particular kind of forum selection clause. *Id.* at 630.

occurred in both Japan, where Red is located, and the United States, where Blue is located. Ex. A, ¶¶ 3-4, 7. This is an even split and does not provide a basis upon which to reject Section 10.5.

The fourth, fifth, and sixth *Calanca* factors also weigh in favor of enforcement. The witnesses reside and work in both Japan and the United States. The executives of both parties meet in both the United States and Japan to conduct JVC's business. *Id.* at ¶¶ 3-4. Both parties are sophisticated international companies, and the reciprocal nature of the clause shows that the parties knowingly split the burden of international litigation. *Cf. Sompo Japan Ins. Inc. v. Alarm Detection Sys., Inc.*, No. 03 C 2322, 2003 WL 21877615, *3 (N.D. Ill. Aug. 6, 2003). Blue and Red knew precisely what they were committing to when they agreed to Section 10.5 of the Supplemental Agreement.

The forum selection clause mandates that any claim Blue pursues against Red which arises from, concerns, or in any way relates to the Supplemental Agreement be brought in Japan. Under either federal common law or Illinois law, Blue's fiduciary duty claim should be dismissed with prejudice for lack of proper venue.

II. BLUE CANNOT SEEK REFORMATION OF A CONTRACT TO WHICH IT IS NOT A PARTY.

Blue's Complaint also should be dismissed because Blue does not have standing to pursue what essentially is a thinly-disguised claim for contract reformation. The Complaint alleges that Red's prices under the New Supply Agreement are impermissibly high. Compl., ¶¶ 18, 27. For its remedy, Blue seeks an accounting of all profits Red has obtained and expects to obtain under the New Supply Agreement, and also seeks to "enjoin[] Red from its self-dealing" — in other words, from charging the prices bargained for in the New Supply Agreement. *Id.* at 8.

Effectively, Blue is attempting to reform the price provisions of the New Supply Agreement, a contract to which Blue is not a party. But an action to reform a contract can be maintained only by a party to the contract or one in privity with a party. *See, e.g., Uhlmann Grain Co. v. Fid. & Deposit Co. of Md.*, 116 F.2d 105, 108 (7th Cir. 1940); *Hartford Fire Ins. Co. v. A. Block Mktg., Inc.*, No. 04 C 5523, 2005 WL 1838447, *6 n.7 (N.D. Ill. Aug. 2, 2005); *CJS Reformation of Instruments*, § 49 (1994).

Blue's Complaint does not allege that Blue is in privity with either Red or JVC, nor does it allege that Blue is a third-party beneficiary of the New Supply Agreement. Because it is not a party to the New Supply Agreement, in privity with either Red or JVC, or a third-party beneficiary, Blue cannot sustain a claim seeking to enjoin enforcement of the price provision of the New Supply Agreement. *Uhlmann*, 116 F.2d at 108; *Hartford Fire Ins. Co.*, 2005 WL 1838447, at *6 n.7.

CONCLUSION

Blue, hardly a victim of unequal bargaining power or a lack of sophistication, seeks to undo an agreement that it apparently now believes was unwise — an agreement to sue Red only in Japan. No basis exists for the Court to disregard the forum selection clause of the Supplemental Agreement. For this reason, and because Blue improperly seeks to reform a contract to which it is not a party, Red respectfully requests that the Court dismiss Blue's Complaint.

Respectfully submitted,
RED CORP.
By: __________
One of Their Attorneys

Attorney 1
Attorney 2
Attorney 3
LAW FIRM

APPENDIX L

APPELLATE BRIEF

IN THE UNITED STATES COURT OF APPEALS FOR THE SEVENTH CIRCUIT

CONSULTING FIRM, Plaintiff-Appellee/Cross-Appellant, v. COMPANY Defendant-Appellant/Cross-Appellee.	Appeal from the United States District Court for the Northern District of Illinois, Eastern Division

REPLY AND CROSS-RESPONSE BRIEF OF COMPANY

Attorney

Counsel for Defendant-Appellant/Cross-Appellee

ORAL ARGUMENT REQUESTED

TABLE OF CONTENTS

TABLE OF CONTENTS

TABLE OF AUTHORITIES

Cases

TABLE OF AUTHORITIES

SUMMARY OF ARGUMENT

1. The jury had no legal basis to award Consulting Firm ("CF") $5 million in lost profits for the following three reasons: *First*, in the ten months that CF marketed Company's Programs, it established itself as an unprofitable business. *See, e.g., SK Hand Tool Corp. v. Dresser Indus., Inc.*, 284 Ill. App. 3d 417, 428 (1st Dist. 1996) (barring "hypothetical profits of an established, unprofitable business"). CF's track record of making program sales says nothing about its ability to generate profits in the future because the rate at which dealers cancelled, refused to pay, or demanded refunds on Company's Programs was high (reaching 80% on Program-X), and, under the initial agreement, CF forfeited its commissions "for any cancellations, credits, unpaid accounts, or refunds across all programs" it sold.

Second, contrary to CF's contention, Company's inability to provide Program-Y dealers with an average of ten leads per dealer per month was due not only to delay in developing the sorting technology, but also because Reviews.com did not generate a sufficient number of leads to service the enrolled dealers. The business model guaranteeing dealers an average of ten internet leads per month from a single website was not feasible.

Third, CF's *pro forma* sales projections do not lay a reasonable ground for the jury's multi-million dollar lost profits award because they: (a) do not take into account actual dealer cancellations, non-pays, and refunds; and (b) assume subscription-based contracts when the industry trend was towards paying on a per lead basis.

2. CF has not refuted the fact or significance of the erroneous evidentiary rulings. *First*, because the initial agreement was valid and unambiguous and did not contain any references to CF's sales projections, the district court erred by admitting CF's projections and the drafts of the initial agreement into evidence. *Second*, CF cannot support the admission of its principals' improper opinion testimony regarding prospective attrition rates in Company's Programs because it is uncontested that CF's principals did not have firsthand knowledge of actual attrition rates in Company's Programs. *Third*, CF cannot justify excluding Company CFO's testimony about the actual performance of Company's Programs after the termination because the case law, which CF fails to distinguish, states that a business's actual performance is directly relevant to estimating plaintiff's lost profits.

3. The district court did not abuse its discretion in refusing to award prejudgment interest on the jury's lost profits award. *First*, CF failed to request prejudgment interest before judgment, thereby violating the Rule 59(e) requirements. *Second*, Illinois law bars an award of prejudgment interest here because CF's alleged lost profits damages were neither liquidated, nor subject to easy calculation.

ARGUMENT

As late as Year 3, CF Principal described Company's Program-Y as "a new product line and no existing product." (Pl.Ex.32.) Although CF's brief completely ignores this candid contemporaneous assessment, CF Principal's admission explains two key facts that demonstrate why CF's lost profits award must be reversed and judgment entered for Company. First, CF Principal's statement explains why CF experienced the success in attracting the "500 dealers" that it trumpets in its brief (CF Br.22)[1]: CF was selling 'pie-in-the-sky' -- programs promising ten Reviews.com leads on average for every one of its Program-Y dealers every month -- a non-existent product that was too good to be true because it required more leads than the Reviews.com website could ever produce. (Tr.1353-55,1385-93.) Second, CF Principal's statement also explains why cancellations, non-pays, refunds, and unilateral contract modifications by dealers reached staggeringly high levels: the dealers' rampant dissatisfaction when they discovered that these programs were, in fact, too good to be true.

Although CF disputes the cancellation rates for the failed Program-X -- which CF designed and persuaded Company to implement -- the hard facts of record are that virtually any Program-X dealers who were willing to continue working with Company

---

[1] CF Br.__ refers to Consulting Firm's Brief; Company Br.__ refers to Company's Opening Brief; A__ refers to the Appendix filed with Company's Opening Brief; Pl.Ex.__ refers to Plaintiff's Trial Exhibits; Def.Ex.__ refers to Defendant's Trial Exhibits; Tr.__ refers to the Trial Transcript; and R__ refers to the Record on Appeal.

insisted on being transferred to other programs (80% of all Program-X dealers); others simply quit for good (about 15%). (Pl.Exs.69,70.) Despite the uncontested facts that most of the Program-X dealers deserted that program within months, forcing the program to shut down, CF still based a substantial portion of its lost profits on *future* Program-X sales, which CF claims Company might have renewed in Year 4. (CF Br.28.)

Further, perhaps recognizing the speculative nature of its projections -- forecasting more than $30 million in total revenues in two years from the sale of "a new product line," which CF Principal admitted the Company Programs were -- CF endeavors to support its projections by arguing that Advisor 1, whom Company had hired to launch its ill-fated retail internet leads programs, was very experienced with retail internet leads and accepted those projections. (CF Br.24, Pl.Ex.83A, R187-9 at 20.) This argument is factually incorrect.

Although CF argues in this Court that Advisor 1 had extensive experience with retail internet leads in Year 1, CF successfully argued absolutely the opposite to the district court: that Advisor 1 had *no* experience with retail internet leads at that time. (Tr.235-38,259-68.) Advisor 1 acknowledged that his first experience with retail internet leads was not until Year 2. (Tr.261.) Based in part on that fact, the court barred Advisor 1 from explaining to the jury aspects of the retail internet leads market. (Tr.261-63.) Therefore, CF cannot save its guesswork projections, and the lost profits award that relies on this speculation, from application of the Illinois rule against speculative damages.

Indeed, the district court should have excluded CF's projections from evidence altogether. The court recognized that CF's principals had no experience with retail internet leads programs before working with Company; it found that Company was their "first internet leads program." (A26-27.) But while the court barred Advisor 1's testimony, it allowed CF's principals to testify about *their* expectations of multi-million dollar profits from Company's retail internet leads programs. (*E.g.*, A13-21, Tr.165-73; A24-27, Tr.470-74; A28, Tr.485.) Had the court ruled consistently, CF's case for lost profits never would have gone to the jury. Therefore this Court should vacate CF's damages award and enter judgment for Company.

I. CF Has Failed To Establish That The Jury's Award Of $5 Million In Lost Profits Rests On Anything But Speculation.

In its opening brief, Company demonstrated that the jury's multi-million dollar lost profits award was speculative because the programs CF marketed had a track record of losing, not making, money. (Company Br.21-29; Pl.Ex.32.) CF responds by arguing that CF was an established business (because it sold Company-related programs for nine months before termination) that met or exceeded its sales targets. (CF Br.22,25-32,35-36.) CF, however, has mistakenly equated making sales with making profits. In fact, CF had agreed to return its commissions when a dealer to whom it sold a program cancelled, failed to pay, or demanded a refund: "Monthly commissions due CF shall be reduced to account for any cancellations, credits, unpaid accounts, or refunds across all program contracts sold by CF." (A1, Pl.Ex.3.) Given the large number of cancellations and refunds on these programs, CF's projected sales figures grossly overstate profits.

Under Illinois law, "hypothetical profits of an established, unprofitable business" are too speculative to award lost future profits. *SK Hand Tool Corp. v. Dresser Indus., Inc.*, 284 Ill. App. 3d 417, 428 (1st Dist. 1996). Yet, as further shown below, the record is clear that CF was unprofitable in the nine months it was marketing Company's Programs; and, hence, its hypothetical projection of $5 million in future lost profits is too speculative under Illinois law.

A. The Law Did Not Permit The Jury To Award Lost Profits To CF Because CF Did Not Demonstrate Any Track Record Of Generating *Profits* From Its Sales Of Company's Programs.

Although CF can show that it sold subscriptions to Company's Programs, it did not -- and cannot -- show a track record of generating any profits from marketing these new programs. That dooms its claims to lost profits, even under the cases CF cites. For example, CF relies on *Tri-G, Inc. v. Burke, Bosselman & Weaver*, 222 Ill. 2d 218 (2006). (CF Br.22,35-36.) There, the Illinois Supreme Court explained that proving lost profits "with a reasonable basis" may be done "through evidence of past *profits* in an established business." *Id.* at 248 (emphasis added). Likewise, in *Oakleaf of Illinois v. Oakleaf & Associates, Inc.*, 173 Ill. App. 3d 637, 649-50 (1st Dist. 1988), on which CF also relies (CF Br.38), the Court upheld a lost profits award where a plaintiff distributor presented *evidence of profits it actually earned in the first half of the contract period*, and where the plaintiff's profit margin was uncontested. In *BE&K Constr. Co. v. Will & Grundy Counties Bldg. Trades Council*, 156 F.3d 756, 770 (7th Cir. 1998), another CF case (CF Br.40), the Court affirmed a lost profits award where the plaintiff established that it received "a $4.00 per hour *profit*" on labor it subcontracted. (emphasis added.)

In contrast, CF did not show any history of generating profits in the nine months before its termination. To the contrary, several months before termination, CF Principal sent Company an email attaching CF's "most recent profit and loss statement demonstrating how devastating financially it has been thus far to us to be in business with Reviews.com." (Pl.Ex.32.) *After* termination, CF's Profit & Loss Statement still showed a year-to-date *loss* of $200,000 on Company's Programs. (Pl.Ex.76.) CF sustained these losses despite withholding at least $100,000 in commissions from the payments received directly from dealers. (Tr.733-34, Def.Ex.11.)

The Illinois Supreme Court has noted: "Jurors do not possess a roving commission to find such damages as they please." *Tri-G*, 222 Ill. 2d at 252. The standard barring awards of speculative damages provides courts with a means to issue judgment (even summary judgment) for a defendant when a plaintiff cannot adduce evidence demonstrating lost profits with reasonable certainty. *See, e.g., Mindgames, Inc. v. Western Publ'g Co.*, 218 F.3d 652, 658-59 (7th Cir. 2000) (affirming summary judgment where plaintiff failed to provide evidence to show future damages with reasonable certainty). In Illinois, the courts have phrased this standard as follows: "a business which has not been profitable generally will be unable to provide competent proof by which the profits can be estimated with reasonable certainty." *SK Hand Tool Corp.*, 284 Ill. App. 3d at 427.

Here, CF projected that over the two years of the initial agreement, the Programs' gross revenues would have reached $40 million, entitling CF to $12 million in commissions. (Pl.Ex.83A, R187-9 at 20; Tr.762-63.) Reduced by expenses and present value calculations, CF requested $8 million in lost profits damages. (Tr.780.)

These astronomical figures contrast starkly with CF Principal's complaint that months of working with Company had proven "devastating financially" to CF (Pl.Ex.32) and with the fact that CF was half-a-million dollars in the hole at termination, after several months of working with Company (Pl.Ex.76).[2] CF's brief contains no fact or argument that can rebut the inexorable conclusion that CF did not prove $5 million of lost profits with any certainty, but "just dreamed" those damages. *See Mindgames*, 218 F.3d at 658.

B. The Record Does Not Support CF's Assertion That But For The Termination It Would Have Sold Enough Programs To Justify Its Lost Future Profits.

In its opening brief, Company demonstrated that Program-X and Program-Y both substantially underperformed CF's projections. (Company Br.25-29.) In its response, CF ignores the programs' actual track record and argues that, "but for Company's breach [by terminating CF], the programs would have performed as the parties forecast." (CF Br.25.) CF's contention is not supported by the record.

(a) The Record Reveals That Program-X Failed.

CF erroneously contends that "there is no such evidence" that many dealers cancelled Program-X. (CF Br.28.) Contrary to CF's contention, CF's Principal acknowledged in Year 1 that, out of all the dealers whom CF signed up for Program-X, at least 80% were converted to Program-Y because they no longer wished to remain in Program-X, and another 15% "received a credit for monies paid." (Pl.Ex.69, CF Principal e-mail to Company Executive; CF Br.29.) Moreover, the spreadsheet that CF forwarded to Company shows that many Program-X dealers "cancelled," while others were "upsold" to Program-Y. (Pl.Ex.70 at RDC06030-32, RDC06034-34B.) In light of these dealers' cancellations, and the fact that CF admittedly did not market Program-X at the time, CF had no reason to calculate lost profits assuming over 100 dealers would be enrolled in Company's Program-X at the end of Year 1. (Pl.Ex.83A, R187-9 at 18.)

Furthermore, CF cannot dispute that despite some initial success selling about 75 contracts between March and June of Year 1, CF sold only three Program-X contracts in July, six in August, one in September, and none in October or November. (Pl.Ex.83A, R187-9 at 21; Tr.408.) The number of converts from Program-X to Program-Y demonstrates that the former was not viable without leads.

Indeed, CF Principal testified that the parties did not contemplate resuming Program-X until after "Program-Y got rolling and leads were going to dealers and dealers were happy." (Tr.544-45.) This never came to be because Program-Y never

---

[2] These figures also would have contrasted starkly with the improperly excluded evidence that Company's actual gross revenues from both Programs during the entire period were approximately $2 million. (Tr.1107.)

delivered to dealers as many internet leads as it was contractually obligated to deliver. (Tr.980, Company Executive testifying that Program-X does not exist today.)

In short, nothing in the record suggests that Program-X would rise again and produce $12 million in CF commissions over the term of the initial agreement. (Pl.Ex.83A, R187-9 at 20.)

(b) Program-Y Was "A New Product Line With No Existing Product."

Perhaps the most serious of its several acts of willful blindness to the facts is CF's refusal to address in its brief the contemporaneous admission of CF Principal that CF was selling "a new product line and no existing product." (Pl.Ex.32.) CF ignores CF Principal's admission and instead argues that CF was selling an "established product." (CF Br.25.) But CF took the opposite tack at trial, embracing CF Principal's "no existing product" position, for example, when cross-examining Company's Advisor 1 (Tr.332, emphasis added):

Q: In other words, since they [CF] started selling Program-Y until they were terminated, there was no program that was actually functioning that they could sell the dealers. They were selling the dealers the ability to receive leads *that never were implemented*, correct?

A: Which was patently clear to them when they began selling the programs. All of them.

Indeed, CF's final cross-examination question for Advisor 1 re-emphasized this very point: "Q: The 'no existing product' would be a reference to leads?

Advisor 1: Correct." (Tr.981.) As CF Principal's admission and Advisor 1's testimony combine to demonstrate, CF's position before this Court -- that CF was selling an "established product" -- contradicts CF's position at trial and misstates the trial evidence.

CF bases its contention solely on Pl.Ex.7, an e-mail from Company's Advisor 1 to CF Principal, predicting that, "[i]n February of Year 1, Reviews.com *will generate* 9,000 leads per month through Reviews.com and other affiliated properties." (emphasis added.) Based on Pl.Ex.7, CF contends that, "9,000 Reviews.com leads *were sold to dealers* in February of Year 1" and that this fact purportedly demonstrates "that Company lacked neither a valuable product nor an established market." (CF Br.25, emphasis added.) But Pl.Ex.7 says nothing about the number of Reviews.com leads *actually sold* to dealers in February of Year 1. It is not even a statement of fact, but Advisor 1's prediction, when he was new to CF and to retail internet leads. The record contains no evidence of how many leads Reviews.com actually generated that month. (Tr.857, Advisor 1: "I don't know how many leads per month we were generating at that point.") Company Expert, however, testified that as late as Year 3, Reviews.com was generating only half that many leads. (Tr.1354.)

Furthermore, in February of Year 1, Company did not have sorting technology and its Reviews.com leads were wholesale, not retail. Company sold wholesale leads only in bulk to wholesalers, "at a lesser price." (A5, Tr.71.) As late as November of Year 1, CF acknowledged that thousands of Reviews.com leads could not be sold to dealers: "Reviews.com had approximately 4,000 unplaced leads in October of Year 1."

(Pl.Ex.67.) Hence, Pl.Ex.7 does not refute the fact that Company had no established retail internet leads product as of mid-September of Year 1 and, hence, no established market for it.

CF likens its case to *Milex Products, Inc. v. Alra Labs., Inc.*, 237 Ill. App. 3d 177, 193 (2d Dist. 1992) (CF Br.37), in which the Court upheld a lost profits award for a generic drug manufacturer, finding that the generic drug had "an established market." CF's reliance on *Milex*, however, is misplaced. The generic drug at issue in *Milex* had "an established market" because it "contain[ed] the equivalent active ingredients" and "work[ed] as well as" the brand drug Clomid and two other equivalent drugs. 237 Ill. App. 3d at 179. The plaintiff's expert performed extensive market analysis and presented evidence at trial on the volume of prescriptions and pricing of those equivalent drugs, based in part on actual audit data. *Id.* at 184-85.

In contrast, CF presented no evidence that Company's Program-Y had equivalents in the market, or evidence of profits generated by competitors marketing similar products. Indeed, Company Expert (the only retail internet leads expert called at trial) testified that a business model guaranteeing dealers a substantial number of monthly leads generated from a single website was not sustainable. (Tr.1354-55.) Company Expert's own business contracted with *more than 160 publishers* to supply internet leads on a regular basis to dealers. (Tr.1330.)

CF's reliance on *Mid-America Tablewares, Inc. v. Mogi Trading Co., Ltd.*, 100 F.3d 1353 (7th Cir. 1996), also is misplaced. There, this Court reversed a jury's award of more than $2.6 million in lost profits for a brand new dinnerware pattern that never made it to store shelves. Although this Court upheld the district court's decision to submit plaintiff's lost profits claim to the jury, it did so based on Wisconsin law, which is less stringent than Illinois law in the level of certainty it demands of lost profits evidence. *Compare id.* at 1365-67 *with, e.g., SK Hand Tool*, 284 Ill. App. 3d at 426-29. This Court also affirmed the denial of defendant's motion for judgment as a matter of law because defendant did not preserve it properly, and in dictum noted again Wisconsin's more liberal standards. 100 F.3d at 1363-68. But even under Wisconsin's standards, this Court did *not* "find[] sufficient evidence to support lost profits from dinnerware pattern that was never sold," as CF argued. (CF Br.36.) Rather, the Court reversed the lost profits award as "unreasonably speculative, excessive and unsupported by the evidence." *Id.* at 1368.

(c) Program-Y Promising An Average Of 10 Reviews.com Internet Leads Per Dealer Per Month Was Not Feasible.

CF presses the mistaken view that Program-Y dealers did not receive sufficient leads solely because of Company's delay in developing and implementing the sorting technology, which it contends was "fully implemented by December" of Year 1. (CF Br.25.) The record proves this statement incorrect. Even though Company's Advisor 1 testified that, by the second week of December, Company "got the program basically ready to go" and could provide "a better flow of leads" to the dealers (Tr.299), no evidence whatsoever suggests that, at any time following CF's termination, Company supplied all, or even most, Program-Y dealers with an average of ten Internet leads per month. To the contrary, the record shows that the number of retail leads the Reviews.com website was generating as of Year 3 (approximately 5,000 leads per month, (Tr.1354) was insufficient to service even the 300 dealers that CF enrolled into Program-Y prior to termination, R187-9 at 21: a promise of an average of ten leads per dealer per month required at least 7,000 retail leads -- a shortfall of over 24,000 leads annually). Indeed, as of early November of Year 1, CF discovered that, out of 220 dealers then enrolled in the Program-Y, only *five* received the number of leads that they contracted to receive. (Pl.Ex.64.) This huge disparity strongly suggests that the problem was not in sorting but in supply.

Additionally, CF contends that the only reason Company did not make some $40 million on Program-Y was because it stopped marketing that program after terminating CF, *i.e.*, that the admittedly "sophisticated businesspeople" at Company simply turned their backs on the opportunity to make huge sums from the sale of the program. (CF Br.31-32, Pl.Ex.83A, R187-9 at 20.) This argument is economic nonsense. Rather, confronted with a Program-Y already filled well past the point at which Company could meet its demands, with dealers canceling and demanding refunds, Company did what any rational business would do: stop expanding to focus on providing service to those already in the program. (Tr.300.) So, even though, months later, Company ultimately implemented a variation of the internet leads program (*Id.*), Company was never able to generate as many internet leads for as many dealers as CF initially had forecasted. (Tr.1340-41.)

Indeed, Company Expert testified that Reviews.com could not possibly generate the number of leads sufficient to service the 2000+ dealers CF planned to sign into Program-Y during the two-year contractual period. (Pl.Ex.83A, R187-9 at 19; Tr.1340-41,1354.) CF attacks Company Expert's credibility based on his age: "Company Expert was in high school when CF Principal began his career in dealer marketing." (CF Br.23.) Company Expert, however, was the only witness at trial with previous experience developing a retail internet leads program. For more than eight years, Company Expert has operated a sales and marketing company that provides dealers with Internet leads. (Tr.1328-1330.) CF Principal may have spent more years marketing traditional leads programs to dealers, but as the district court recognized, he had no experience developing and marketing a retail internet leads program. (A26-27.) Consequently, Company Expert's testimony was the only competent evidence on the issue of the retail internet leads market at the relevant time.

CF seeks to undermine Company Expert's testimony on several grounds. None has merit. *First*, CF criticizes Company Expert for assuming that Reviews.com was the only source of leads for Program-Y. CF cites Advisor 1's testimony that in July of Year 1, before launching Program-Y, the parties contemplated "fill[ing] in the holes" with other leads available on the market. (Tr.892.) CF Principal himself, however, acknowledged that the "high quality" of Reviews.com leads was "[t]he hook" of Program-Y (Tr.441; Pl.Ex.12 at 2), and the pricing of Program-Y was based on the quality of Reviews.com leads (Tr.102). Further, Company Expert explained on cross that Program-Y contracts "only described leads from Reviews.com." (Tr.1380.) Company Expert was right: the standard Program-Y contract guaranteed "qualified leads each month *that are generated from Reviews.com.*" (Pl.Ex.79, emphasis added.)

Second, in rendering his opinion, Company Expert relied on the fact that, for the last four years, Reviews.com averaged between 500,000 and 700,000 visitors per month. (Tr.1385-87.) This information was based on website industry rankings conducted by Nielsen NetRatings. (Tr.1385.) In response, CF points out that, in an e-mail to CF Principal, Advisor 1 estimated that Company had "1.5 million users each month." (Pl.Ex.9.)

As an initial matter, not all website visits result in users entering their personal contact information, thereby generating an internet lead. (Tr.1340, Tr.63-64.) Indeed, less than 2 percent of website visits generate an internet lead. (Tr.1388.) Further, Advisor 1's projection of user visits to Reviews.com was not based on Nielsen sampling surveys, but rather was "a marketing plan to get to that number." (Tr.1387.) More importantly, Company Expert explained on cross that, even if the 1.5 million number were accurate, it would not have changed his ultimate conclusions (Tr.1387-88):

Q: In your opinion, it's extremely unlikely that they would have ever had 1.5 million visitors?

A: The opinion I was trying to make certain that came through is that even with 1.5 million unique, you're so far off from being able to produce a $40 million business it's categorically wrong.

Q. So . . . even if the basis for your assumption is understated by three times, your opinion doesn't change a bit that Reviews.com just could not have provided enough leads, correct?

A: Correct.

Third, Company Expert testified from his personal experience selling Company's internet leads program that, since Year 3, Reviews.com has generated approximately 4,000 retail leads per month. (Tr.1354.) In response, CF once again cites Advisor 1's *projection* that in February of Year 1, Reviews.com "will generate 9,000 leads per month." (Pl.Ex.7.) There is, however, no contradiction here: Advisor 1 was predicting the future at a time when he was new to the internet leads market, while Company Expert testified to actual past performance. (Tr.1354.) Furthermore, Advisor 1 projected the number of *wholesale* leads, while Company Expert testified about the number of *retail* leads Reviews.com generated. As CF principal acknowledged, these numbers are not the same: thousands of Reviews.com wholesale leads did not get placed with any dealers. (Pl.Ex.67.)

Fourth, CF contends that its estimate of ten internet leads per dealer per month was reasonable because Company Expert's own business delivers an average of 25-30 leads per month to each dealer. (CF Br.25.) Company Expert, however, explained that those leads are "coming from many website publishers," which strengthens his conclusion that no single website could support a retail internet leads program of the scale CF needed to justify its lost profits numbers. (Tr.1380-83.)

C. CF Never Demonstrated That Its Projections Reasonably Predicted Future Profits.

In its opening brief, Company demonstrated that CF failed to introduce non-speculative evidence to support its lost profits calculations. In response, CF contends that the jury's lost profits award is supported by "much additional evidence" (CF Br.23) but points only to its program sales and pro forma projections (CF Br.25-32).

CF's many arguments concerning projections boil down to three key contentions: first, that its actual sales met its projections; second, that at the time CF showed these projections to Company, Company did not object to them; and, third, that CF Principal -- who provided assumptions for the projections -- purportedly had experience "with similar products." None of these contentions supports CF's lost profits award.

(a) Actual Sales Are Meaningless Without Accounting For Dealer Cancellations, Refunds, And Non- Payment.

CF contends that its projections were reasonable because it met and exceeded its projected sales and sold contracts to dealers on the pricing terms similar to the ones it initially projected. (CF Br.25-29,31-32.) The actual sales and pricing terms, however, are meaningless without also knowing how many of those dealers cancelled, requested refunds, simply never paid, or unilaterally changed the terms of their contracts -- because, in these instances, CF forfeited its commissions. (A1; Pl.Ex.3, Initial Agreement.)

Indeed, as noted above, dealer cancellations were a big problem in both programs, right up to termination (and beyond), with Company repeatedly informing CF that its commissions were reduced because of that. For instance, in October of Year 1, Advisor 1 informed CF Principal that $100,000 Company owed to CF in commissions "[was] not inclusive of credits or cancellations of which we've had a few." (Pl.Ex.48.) In early November of Year 1, Advisor 1 wrote to CF Principal that Company was "running into issues with the cancel/conversion programs in Program-X" (Pl.Ex.65), and that the "program revenue [was] down considerably because of cancels and no-pays." (Pl.Ex.69.) A few days later, Company stated that it owed no additional commissions to CF because of "significant cancellations within Program-X." (Pl.Ex.71.) This high attrition defeats the notion that CF could predict its lost future profits with reasonable certainty.

Additionally, CF's lost profits calculation assumes 12-month subscription-based contracts, but the industry trend was to switch to pay-per-lead contracts. CF contends that "nearly all Program-Y contracts had twelve-month terms," (CF Br.31fn.6), but ignores that, in August of Year 1, based on its interactions with dealers, CF itself suggested reducing the contract length: "[I]f necessary, we will drop the length of contract from 12 months to 6 months to even 3 months in order to add more dealers." (Pl.Ex.18.)

Indeed, as of early November of Year 1, more than 40% of Program-Y dealers were paying on a per lead basis. (Pl.Ex.64.) Further, in November of Year 1, CF Principal stated that, going forward, CF planned to market only pay-per-lead contracts to dealers. (Pl.Ex.68.) This evidence supports Company Expert's testimony that the trend was for dealers to switch to paying on a per-lead basis. (Tr.1393-94.) Again, it defeats the notion that CF's projections, which depended upon steady subscription fees from 12-month Program-Y contracts, provide a realistic and reasonably certain basis for assessing lost profit damages.

(b) The Fact That Company Did Not Object To CF's Projections At The Time Does Not Lend Credence To These Projections.

Perhaps realizing that its projections are unreliable on their own, CF tries to support them by arguing that Company agreed to them. Specifically, CF claims that: (1) it discussed its projections with Company, (2) Company initially offered a cash advance to CF after the parties' meeting in August of Year 1, and (3) early drafts of the initial agreement mentioned CF's projections. (CF Br.22-23, 25-31,39.) These contentions do not support using CF's projections to determine lost future profits.

CF claims that Advisor 1's testimony "could alone provide a sufficient basis" for CF's lost profits calculations because, when shown those projections, Advisor 1 did not object to them. (CF Br.24,30-31,39.) CF argues that Advisor 1 had "the extensive experience . . . with new leads and . . . was hired by Company to develop its internet-based business and build a leads program." (CF Br.24.) This was *not* CF's position at trial, where Advisor 1 testified that he had only "been working with retail leads since Year 1" -- in other words, this was his first retail internet leads experience. (Tr.239, 260-61.) CF objected to Advisor 1's testimony about internet leads technology and dealer cancellation rates based on his lack of experience.

In sustaining CF's objection, the district court held: "[H]e [Advisor 1] doesn't have any relevant experience. He had no program. They were not set up to have a program." (Tr.260-63.) Because Advisor 1 did not have relevant experience with internet leads programs before Year 1, the fact that he did not object to CF's projections at that time does not lend any credence to those projections, and does not provide an independent basis for CF's assumptions. No evidence suggests that Company President and Advisor 1's superior had experience with internet leads programs and thus their lack of comment on CFs projections also does not lend credence to these projections. In any event, "the entrepreneur's 'cheerful prognostications' are not enough" to show the existence of lost profits. *Schonfeld v. Hilliard*, 218 F.3d 164, 173 (2d Cir. 2000) (quoting 1 *Dobbs Law of Remedies* § 3.4) (plaintiff not entitled to lost future profits despite the fact that both parties initially "*believed* that profits from [the new business] were reasonably certain.") (Court's emphasis.)

CF mistakenly relies on *In re Arbitration Between Eljer Mfg., Inc. v. Kowin Dev. Corp.*, 14 F.3d 1250 (7th Cir. 1994), and *Havoco of America, Ltd. v. Sumitomo Corp. of America*, 971 F.2d 1332 (7th Cir. 1992), both involving long-term supply contracts, in contending that its projections were reasonable. *Eljer* involved a 20-year contract obligating a metal files manufacturer "to purchase a certain number of files every year." 14 F.3d at 1252, 1256. *Havoco* involved a 10-year contract for a purchase of 2.4 million tons of coal per year for a specific price, with a plaintiff subsequently selling its rights under the contract for $3 million. 971 F.2d at 1334, 1345. In these circumstances, where the contracts obligated the parties to supply or purchase specific quantities of products over time at specific prices, this Court held that lost profits could be calculated with reasonable certainty. 14 F.3d at 1256; 971 F.2d at 1346.

The initial agreement, in contrast, was purely a commissions-based contract, which did not obligate CF to sell any specific number of dealer contracts, and, most importantly, did not require Company to accept any specific number of dealer contracts sold by CF. To the contrary, the initial agreement expressly provided that, "Reviews.com retains the right to accept or reject any dealer contract for any reason." (A1, Pl.Ex.3.)

CF draws the wrong inference from the fact that early drafts of the initial agreement -- unlike the final agreement -- mentioned CF's projections and provided for a cash advance to CF. The final agreement between the parties did *not* incorporate CF's projections and did *not* provide for any cash advance based on CF's business plan, demonstrating that Company rejected both CF's projections and business plan. Indeed, because provisions in early term sheets contradicted the provisions of the initial agreement, they should have been excluded from evidence by the district court under the parol evidence rule. CF's continued reliance on this improper evidence highlights the significance of the district court's error in admitting this evidence. *See* Section II, below.

(c) CF Identifies No Prior Experience With Retail Internet Leads Programs.

Finally, CF contends that its projections were reliable because CF's principals, who provided assumptions for those projections, purportedly had experience "with similar products." (CF Br.23.) Even if CF's principals had prior experience with retail internet leads, the fact that actual events disproved their key market assumptions, including cancellation and renewal rates, growth, and dealers' program preferences, would invalidate their projections and lost profits damages. In *SK Hand Tool*, for example, the Court reversed the lost profits damage award despite plaintiff's expert's computer modeling and calculations because the expert "failed to show that the analysis was based on a true premise...." 284 Ill. App. 3d at 429.

In fact, though, CF identified no prior experience with retail internet leads. Although CF contends that "CF Principal had 'plenty' of experience selling internet lead contracts to dealers" (CF Br.23), CF's contention is based on a single, self-serving statement CF Principal made during cross-examination (Tr.682-83):

Q. . . . if I understood your testimony correct under direct examination, prior to July of Year 1 you had no experience in selling internet leads contracts to dealers.

A. I never said that. That would be crazy. I had plenty of experience delivering internet leads to dealers.

Q: Selling internet leads contracts to dealers?

A. Oh, yes.

This is all of the evidence concerning CF Principal's alleged experience "delivering internet leads to dealers" before working with Company, admitted during the entire two-week trial. One must wonder why -- if CF Principal had "plenty" of experience delivering internet leads to dealers – CF did not bother to elicit a single example of such a program in two weeks of trying a case that focused on the delivery of internet leads. Indeed, the district court observed that Company's Program-Y was CF Principal's "first internet leads program." (A26, Tr.472.)

(d) CF's Efforts To Distinguish Controlling Caselaw Fail.

Although Illinois case law setting the standard for lost future profits damages does not demand mathematical certainty, it does require that a plaintiff's evidence comport with reality. CF recognizes this fact. For instance, it attempts to distinguish *Midland*

Hotel Corp. v. Reuben H. Donnelley Corp., 118 Ill. 2d 306 (1987), on which Company relied, as follows: "rejecting lost profits where key assumption of plaintiff's proof was disproven by actual performance." (CF Br.39.) Similarly, it disputes Company's citations to *SK Hand Tool Corp. v. Dresser Indus., Inc.*, 248 Ill. App. 3d 417 (1st Dist. 1996) as follows: "rejecting lost profits where key assumption of expert calculations was disproven by actual events." (CF Br.39.) Yet as the discussion above demonstrates, CF's projections also must fail precisely because actual events demonstrate that they are incorrect. Under controlling caselaw, therefore, CF's lost profits damages must be reversed and judgment entered for Company.

* * *

Therefore, this Court should vacate the jury's award of $5 million in lost profits and enter judgment for Company because CF failed to present competent evidence of its damages. At a minimum, this Court should remand this case for a new trial limited to the issue of damages, where the jury would not be exposed to improperly admitted evidence and where Company would be able to explain its case to the jury by introducing evidence which had been improperly excluded by the district court.

II. CF Has Not Refuted The Fact Or Significance Of The Evidentiary Errors At Trial.

A. The Court Should Have Excluded Pre-Contractual Sales Projections And Early Term Sheets Incorporating Those Projections.

In its opening brief, Company demonstrated that the district court erred by admitting into evidence CF's pre-contractual sales projections and early term sheets of the initial contract that referenced those projections, for two key reasons: First, CF's projections were speculative because the assumptions, on which they rested -- in particular the dealer attrition rates -- were unreasonable. Second, the parol evidence rule barred the projections and term sheets because the final agreement did not mention them or set any sales targets. (Company Br.38-40.)

In response, CF contends that its projections were not speculative because they were "based on both parties' experience with similar products in an established market and validated by actual performance." (CF Br.42.) But as demonstrated above, neither Company (*see* pp. 22-23 above) nor CF (*see* pp. 24-26 above) had prior experience with developing and marketing a retail internet leads program. Moreover, the "actual performance" of Company's two programs was dismal in financial terms -- "devastating financially" in CF Principal's contemporaneous words (Pl.Ex.32) -- as many dealers cancelled, requested refunds, failed to pay their invoices, or re-negotiated their contracts. (Tr.1078-79; Pl.Exs.65,69,70,71.) Hence, reality refuted CF's "rosy" projections. *See Fishman v. Estate of Wirtz*, 807 F.2d 520, 552 (7th Cir. 1986) ("a *forecast* of tomorrow's weather is always subject to confirmation or modification by tomorrow's *observation*") (quoting *A.C. Becken Co. v. Gemex Corp.*, 314 F.2d 839, 840 (7th Cir. 1963)).

Second, CF claims that the parol evidence rule does not apply here because neither the projections nor the term sheets that reference them were admitted to contradict the terms of the initial agreement. According to CF, they were admitted "to show the amount of business the parties reasonably expected to conduct under the initial agreement." (CF Br.43.) But the fact that Company refused to sign an agreement that included those projections is the point. Not only did the final agreement *not* reference CF's projections and *not* set sales targets, it expressly provided Company with "the right to accept or reject any dealer contract for any reason." (A1, Pl.Ex.3.) In Illinois, if a contract is not found ambiguous -- and there was no finding of ambiguity here -- evidence of pre-contractual negotiations is not admitted to explain the contract's terms. *See Lease Mgmt. Equip. Corp. v. DFO P'ship*, 392 Ill. App. 3d 678, 686 (1st Dist. 2009). Rather, under the "four corners rule," the parties' intentions are adduced from the four corners of the contract. *Id.*

CF tries to distinguish *TAS Distrib. Co. v. Cummins Engine Co.*, 491 F.3d 625 (7th Cir. 2007), by stating that the Court there excluded projections because plaintiff sought to hold defendant "bound" by them, while here, projections were relevant to the question of damages. (CF Br.43.) A closer reading of *TAS*, however, reveals that the *TAS* Court rejected the very same arguments that CF is making here. Specifically, plaintiff in *TAS* argued that defendant's pre-contractual projections, which set forth prospective sales targets, provided a reasonable basis for finding how many sales defendant was likely to make under the parties' contract. The contract itself, however, did not set any sales targets; it required defendant only to exercise "reasonable efforts" in promoting the sales of the plaintiff's product; and contained an integration clause. In its brief, plaintiff argued, just as CF does here: "TAS does not assert that [defendant's] projections establish [defendant's] breach. Rather, TAS asserts that once the breach is established, the projections provide a reasonable basis on which a jury could award TAS damages. The integration clause in the License Agreement is, for this purpose, irrelevant." TAS Br., 2006 WL 951808, at *44 (citation omitted).

This Court disagreed, affirming the exclusion of the sales projections under the parol evidence rule: "Illinois courts have interpreted the parole evidence rule to bar the introduction of evidence relating to understandings not reflected in the terms of the contract, reached either before or at the time of the contract's execution, where those terms would vary or modify the terms of the contract itself." 491 F.3d at 637. Here too, the terms of CF's pre-contractual projections vary from the terms of the initial agreement because they set forth specific sales targets; the agreement does not. Hence, the district court erred by admitting CF's projections into evidence.

CF mistakenly relies on *Danville Polyclinic, Ltd. v. Dethmers*, 260 Ill. App. 3d 108 (4th Dist. 1994), in which a hospital sought an injunction against a physician based on a non-compete agreement. The physician challenged the validity of the non-compete agreement, claiming that he was induced into signing it by fraud. In those circumstances, the Court upheld the circuit court's admission of evidence surrounding the parties' signing of the non-compete agreement. *Dethmers* follows a well-established exception to parol evidence rule, that evidence of pre-contractual negotiations is admissible when a party challenges the validity of the contract. *See, e.g., O'Brien v. Cacciatore*, 227 Ill. App. 3d 836, 845 (1st Dist. 1992) (parol evidence admissible to establish the affirmative defenses of fraud, duress, mistake or illegality). Here, the district court upheld the validity of the initial agreement before trial (R123 at 14-15), so validity was not at issue at trial, and this exception to the parol evidence rule did not apply.

CF also makes two other arguments in footnotes. First, it argues that, because Company did not appeal exclusion of Pl.Ex.33, it was not substantially prejudiced by admission of similar Pl.Exs.24 and 27. (CF Br.42n.8.) Because Pl.Ex.33 is also a term sheet, it is included in the category of documents that Company identified as having been erroneously admitted. (Company Br.40-42.) Indeed, the trial objections Company cited in its Opening Brief (*id. citing* Tr.491-93) addressed all term sheets including Pl.Ex.33, to which Company specifically objected at trial. (Tr.518.) Consequently, Company has preserved and presented to this Court its objection to Pl.Ex.33.

Second, CF claims that the term sheets purportedly related "to the question of breach," but the only example it gives concerns the parties' negotiation of the contract duration (Company proposing a month-to-month arrangement, but CF insisted on a two-year term). (CF Br.43n.9.) Hence, CF never explained how the draft provisions incorporating CF's projections related to the question of breach.

In any event, because CF raises these arguments only in footnotes, they are waived. *See Long v. Teachers' Ret. Sys. of Illinois*, 585 F.3d 344, 349 (7th Cir. 2009); *United States v. White*, 879 F.2d 1509, 1513 (7th Cir. 1989).

Because the initial agreement was valid and unambiguous and did not contain any references to CF's sales projections, the district court erred by admitting CF's projections and the drafts of the initial agreement into evidence. The admission of these exhibits substantially prejudiced Company because they formed the basis of the jury's excessive lost profits award against Company.

B. CF Cannot Support The Admission Of CF Principal's Improper Opinion Testimony Regarding Prospective Attrition Rates.

The district court improperly allowed CF Principal to testify about cancellation (attrition) rates in Company's programs though he acknowledged that he had no personal knowledge regarding actual dealer attrition and did not qualify as an expert. (Tr.363,645-46.)

CF does not dispute that CF Principal lacked firsthand knowledge of Company's programs' attrition rates. (CF Br.44-46.) Nonetheless, it contends that the court properly allowed him to testify to his assumptions concerning the attrition rates based on his "extensive past experience" and on his discussions with Advisor 1, "who himself had extensive industry experience" and who "was responsible for implementing the programs CF was selling." (CF Br.24,44-45.) CF forgets, however, that at trial, it prevented Advisor 1 from testifying about prospective attrition rates in Company's Programs on the grounds that he lacked experience in the retail internet leads market and that he was not qualified as an expert. (Tr.260.) Surely CF cannot justify admitting its testimony on the topic based on hearsay conversations with Advisor 1 having barred Advisor 1's own testimony on the very topic. Furthermore, having barred Advisor 1 from testifying about prospective attrition rates, the district court plainly should have barred CF Principal's foundationless lay opinion testimony on the same topic. (Tr.260-63.)

CF mistakenly relies on *Allied Sys., Ltd. v. Teamsters Local 604*, 304 F.3d 785, 790 (8th Cir. 2002), in which the court allowed a company's internal accountant to testify "as to his personal knowledge of the company's books and financial status." The Eighth

Circuit explained that the accountant's testimony was properly admitted because it was "limited to his firsthand knowledge." *Id.* at 792. CF Principal had none.

CF also mistakenly relies on *Compania Administradora de Recuperacion de Activos Administradora de Fondos de Inversion Sociedad Anonima v. Titan Int'l, Inc.*, 533 F.3d 555, 560 (7th Cir. 2008). But in quoting this Court's statement of the rule there, CF omits the crucial word "only": "[A] business owner or officer is allowed to testify without being qualified as an expert only because that testimony is tied to his or her personal knowledge." *Compare id. with* CF Br.44. Having no firsthand knowledge of attrition rates in Company's Programs, CF Principal could not properly testify regarding those attrition rates.

Additionally, CF contends that its Year 1 projections were not based on "industry averages," unlike the projections it prepared in the course of litigation in Year 4. (CF Br.46.) CF's contention is without merit. Both the projections prepared in August of Year 1(Pl.Ex.23) and the projections prepared in response to an interrogatory in Year 4 use the same monthly attrition rates for Company's programs. Moreover, CF Principal testified that he used the same methods in arriving at the attrition rates in both his Year 1 and Year 4 projections (Tr.686):

Q: Did you arrive at the attrition rate that you used in answering the interrogatory answers in the same way that you arrived at the attrition rate in preparing Exhibit 23?

A: Yes, in general, yes.

This approach included reliance on supposed "industry averages" that CF Principal apparently got "off the internet," not from his personal knowledge. (Tr.689-90.) When asked if he took attrition rates for the August projections from industry averages, CF Principal equivocated, stating that, even though he "generally" took it based on his experience, "I'm always looking at industry averages." (Tr.684.)

Because CF Principal did not have personal knowledge of actual cancellation rates in Company's Programs, the district court erred by allowing him to testify about those rates at trial.

C. CF Cannot Justify Excluding Company CFO's Testimony About The Actual Performance Of Company's Programs Post-Termination.

The district court erred by barring Company CFO from testifying that from Year 3 to Year 5, Company generated only $1.5 million in gross revenues from Company's Programs, vastly less than the $40 million CF projected and even substantially below the $5 million that the jury awarded to CF as its lost future profits. In response, CF contends, without citing any authority and without distinguishing any of Company's cases, that Company CFO's excluded testimony was not relevant because Company purportedly failed to market the two programs after terminating CF.

Both Company CFO and Advisor 1 testified that, even though Company did not have anyone "lined up" to replace CF immediately upon its termination, Company did eventually resume marketing six to eight months after terminating CF. (Tr.300,977-78; A38, Tr.1099.) Equally important, Company's decision not to enroll more dealers into Program-Y immediately after terminating CF was reasonable: even setting aside its issues with developing the leads-sorting technology, Reviews.com simply could not generate enough leads to fulfill its existing dealer contracts, let alone assume obligations to new dealers. (Tr.328,1353-55.)

Moreover, the proferred testimony regarding the programs' actual financial performance was highly relevant to the damages issue; it demonstrated that Company's Programs were never as profitable as CF projected them to be. CF acknowledges that Company management consisted of "sophisticated businesspeople" with "extensive industry experience," who worked for "a publishing company that sells hundreds of millions of dollars of books and periodicals each year." (CF Br.2,31.) If these programs were as successful as CF projected them to be, and if Company indeed was capable of "fully delivering" both programs starting in Year 1, as CF alleges without citation (CF Br.25), then Company would not deliberately have foregone the opportunity to make $40 million from the sale of these programs after terminating CF. The fact that Company did not actively market the two programs at first and that, when it did, it earned only $2 million in gross revenues from them over almost two-and-a-half years, demonstrates that the programs were not nearly as successful as CF projected. Consequently, this testimony was highly relevant to the jury's calculation of damages, and Company was prejudiced by its exclusion.

CF ignores this Court's decision in *Fishman v. Estate of Wirtz*, 807 F.2d 520, 552 (7th Cir. 1986), but that case held that where, as here, a business continued in the hands of defendant, defendant's *actual* gain gave a court "an exceptionally helpful guide to [plaintiff's] damages."

CF argued that Company was not prejudiced because the evidence that its $2 million in Company's gross revenues was comparable to projections that Company would earn approximately $3 million under the contracts that CF had sold before termination. This comparison is inapposite. CF sold contracts with contractual terms of 12, six, and three months, and even some month-to-month contracts. Hence, the latest of those contracts would have expired in Year 2, with most of the contracts expiring much sooner. Company CFO, however, testified to Company's actual gross revenues for a much longer time period, between Year 1 and Year 3. The fact that Company took two-and-a-half years to generate what CF projected it should have generated from already-existing contracts in one year merely highlights the fallacy of CF's projections.

III. The District Court Properly Denied Prejudgment Interest.

CF cross-appeals the district court's denial of its request for prejudgment interest on the underlying judgment under the Illinois Interest Act, 815 ILCS 205/2.

In denying CF's request for prejudgment interest, the district court first noted that CF may have requested prejudgment interest too late: CF's request for prejudgment interest "was not presented to the jury through evidence or jury instructions and was not included on the verdict form." (A55 fn.1 citing *First State Bank of Monticello v. Ohio Cas. Ins. Co.*, 555 F.3d 564 (7th Cir. 2009)). CF first requested prejudgment interest by filing a motion on the date of the verdict, but it didn't file a notice of motion until the date judgment entered, and that notice set a hearing for several days after. (R188, 189.)

The court noted that Illinois law allows prejudgment interest only when the amount due is "fixed or easily calculated," and held that CF's lost future commissions were neither fixed by the initial agreement nor easily calculated. (A56) (quoting *First Nat'l Bank of LaGrange v. Lowrey*, 375 Ill. App. 3d 181, 214-15 (1st Dist. 2007).) The court observed that CF sought lost profits based on future projections, which made damages "particularly difficult to determine." (A57-58.) The district court also noted that the parties' calculation of damages differed dramatically. (A58.) In awarding $5 million in damages, the jury "disagreed with both parties as to the appropriate sum due CF." (A58.)

A. The Decision To Award Prejudgment Interest Is Reviewed For Abuse Of Discretion.

Under Illinois law, whether to award prejudgment interest "is a matter within the trial judge's discretion." *Dallis v. Don Cunningham & Assocs.*, 11 F.3d 713, 718 (7th Cir. 1993). This Court will not disturb a district court's decision to deny prejudgment interest "unless that decision constitutes an abuse of discretion." *Liu v. Price Waterhouse LLP*, 302 F.3d 749, 757 (7th Cir. 2002) (affirming denial of prejudgment interest under the Illinois Interest Act).

Here, the district court did not abuse its discretion in denying prejudgment interest on CF's underlying lost profits award because CF's purported lost profits were neither liquidated nor subject to easy calculation.

B. CF Requested Prejudgment Interest Too Late.

This Court should affirm the denial of CF's request for prejudgment interest because CF failed to request prejudgment interest before judgment. In *Uphoff v. Elegant Bath, Ltd.*, 176 F.3d 399 (7th Cir. 1999), this Court ruled that plaintiffs' Rule 59(e) motion for prejudgment interest was "untimely and improper" where the plaintiffs failed to move for prejudgment interest before the district court entered summary judgment: "the Plaintiffs should have requested the prejudgment interest *prior* to judgment, but they did not." *Id.* at 410. (Court's emphasis.) *Uphoff* explained that "prejudgment interest, unlike post-judgment interest, normally is considered an element of the judgment itself" and, hence, is "subject to the requirements of Rule 59(e)." *Id.* (quoting *Healy Co. v. Milwaukee Metro. Sewerage*, 60 F.3d 305, 308 (7th Cir. 1995)). Further, "Rule 59(e) may not be used to raise novel legal theories that a party had the ability to address in the first instance." *Id.*

Recently, this Court reaffirmed that post-judgment motions for prejudgment interest are governed by the same standards as any other Rule 59(e) motion to alter or amend judgment. In *First State Bank of Monticello v. Ohio Cas. Ins. Co.*, 555 F.3d 564, 572 (7th Cir. 2009), this Court affirmed the district court's denial of prejudgment interest where plaintiff failed to request prejudgment interest under the Illinois Interest Act, 815 ILCS 205/2, before the entry of judgment. This Court reiterated that Rule 59(e) "may not be used by 'a party to complete presenting his case' to the district court," and denied plaintiff prejudgment interest requested after summary judgment entered in its favor. *Id.*

Like the plaintiffs in *Uphoff* and *First State Bank of Monticello*, CF failed to raise the issue of prejudgment interest in a timely fashion despite multiple opportunities to do so: CF did not request prejudgment interest in its motion for summary judgment (R.102,103), at any time during the jury trial, in jury instructions, or on the verdict form. Rather, CF moved for prejudgment interest for the first time in Year 7, after the jury returned its verdict, and even then failed to notice the motion for hearing properly. (R188.) CF filed its notice of motion on the same day the district court entered judgment on the jury's verdict. (R189, 191.) This Court should affirm the denial of prejudgment interest.

C. CF Is Not Entitled To Prejudgment Interest.

CF's request also does not meet the requirements for recovery of prejudgment interest under the Illinois Interest Act.

1. CF Misstates Illinois Law On Prejudgment Interest.

CF states, erroneously, that, to receive prejudgment interest, "the damages amount need not be liquidated, but rather *capable of calculation*." (CF Br.49, emphasis added.) This is not the standard under Illinois law.

Illinois courts have held consistently that, "Prejudgment interest will only be awarded for amounts due on an instrument of writing if the amount due was liquidated or subject to *easy* computation." *Oldenburg v. Hagemann*, 207 Ill. App. 3d 315, 327 (2d Dist. 1991) (emphasis added). "Easy" is the key: "for recovery of prejudgment interest, the sum due must be liquidated or subject to *an easy* determination by calculation or computation." *Couch v. State Farm Ins. Co.*, 279 Ill. App. 3d 1050, 1054 (3d Dist. 1996) (emphasis added). *Accord Spagat v. Schak*, 130 Ill. App. 3d 130, 138 (2d Dist. 1985) (the amount due must be "fixed or *easily* ascertainable") (emphasis added); *Cushman & Wakefield of Illinois, Inc. v. Northbrook 500 Ltd. P'ship*, 112 Ill. App. 3d 951, 963 (1st Dist. 1983) (same).

This Court has held the same: "[U]nder Illinois law, litigants are entitled to prejudgment interest if the damages are liquidated and capable of *easy* calculation." *Stanley Gudyka Sales Co., Inc. v. Lacy Forest Products Co.*, 915 F.2d 273, 279 (7th Cir. 1990) (emphasis added); *Dallis v. Don Cunningham & Assocs.*, 11 F.3d 713, 718 (7th Cir. 1993) (same). CF does not even argue that its damages were liquidated or subject to easy calculation. Indeed, they were not.

2. CF's Damages Were Not Liquidated.

Under Illinois law, "[a]n amount due under a contract is liquidated if the parties agree on the amount." *Oldenburg*, 207 Ill. App. 3d at 327. Here, the parties sharply disputed the amount of lost profits, if any, that CF stood to earn if the initial agreement remained in force. Specifically, Company's damages expert calculated that, after the dealers' cancellations were taken into account, Company owed nothing to CF on the contracts that CF sold before its termination. (Tr.1154-59, Def.Ex.12.) The damages expert also opined that, even if CF continued to enroll new dealers into Company's Programs in the two years following its termination, the maximum it might have earned in commissions was less than $200,000 (Tr.1166, Def.Ex.13) -- substantially less than the $7 million that CF projected for the same period of time. Plainly, CF's damages were not liquidated.

3. CF's Damages Were Not Easy To Calculate.

As the district court correctly observed after hearing the trial evidence on damages, CF's lost future profits were not easy to calculate. (A56-58.) CF appears to concede this point: it argues only that its damages were "*capable* of calculation," not that calculation was easy. (CF Br.50-51.) CF also acknowledges that the commissions schedule set in the initial agreement was insufficient, by itself, to calculate its lost profits damages; rather the lost profits calculation was "based on the assumptions that required legal ascertainment." (*Id.*)

CF does not cite a single case in which a court awarded prejudgment interest on lost future commissions. This is not surprising: courts applying Illinois law consistently deny prejudgment interest in cases involving lost future commissions. For instance, in *Cushman & Wakefield of Illinois, Inc. v. Northbrook 500 Ltd. P'ship*, 112 Ill. App. 3d 951, 963 (1st Dist. 1983), the Court affirmed a circuit court's denial of prejudgment interest on the underlying leasing commissions, explaining that the amount of commissions was not "readily ascertainable" because it was disputed by defendants and "dependent upon many factors such as amount of rent, length of the lease, and the procuring broker."

Likewise, in *Stanley Gudyka Sales Co. v. Lacy Forest Products Co.*, 915 F.2d 273 (7th Cir. 1990), plaintiff sought lost commissions pursuant to the parties' contract for the sale of lumber. This Court affirmed the district court's denial of prejudgment interest because the amount of commissions due plaintiff was not capable of easy calculation, even though the parties agreed on the applicable formula, *i.e.*, "50% of the net between the amounts claimed by [plaintiff] and the amounts acknowledged by [defendant]." *Id.* at 279. This Court noted that, like here, the final damages amount was not close to plaintiff's or defendant's calculations and the proper measure of damages remained "central" to plaintiff's appeal. These were "more than adequate reasons" for denying prejudgment interest. *Id.* at 279.

Likewise, in *Dallis v. Don Cunningham & Associates*, 11 F.3d 713 (7th Cir. 1993), a sales representative sought to recover commissions he earned prior to his termination. This Court ruled that plaintiff could not recover prejudgment interest on the underlying award of lost sales commissions before the parties stipulated to their amount. The Court explained that, before the parties' stipulation, the amount of plaintiff's lost commissions was "not easily calculable" because it was based on a lengthy exhibit, with each page containing "up to 30 specific entries for various accounts." *Id.* at 718-19. This Court further stated that, "'if judgment, discretion, or opinion, as distinguished from calculation or computation is required to determine the amount of the claim, it is unliquidated'" and thus not subject to an award of prejudgment interest. *Id.* at 719 (quoting *First Nat'l Bank of Clinton, Ill. v. Ins. Co. of North America*, 606 F.2d 760, 770 (7th Cir. 1979)).

CF's lost profits were "not easily calculable" -- as noted above, they are the product of speculation, not calculation. They rest on speculative projections involving hundreds of individual dealers' contracts, each with varying terms. (*See* Pl.Exs.82,83.) Even more importantly, to calculate CF's lost commissions, several witnesses offered their personal opinions regarding multiple assumptions, including prospective sales volumes and dealer cancellation rates, renewal rates, and preferences for subscription vs. pay-per-lead contracts. The witnesses' opinions differed sharply: to give one example,

CF's principal opined that Company's Programs would have experienced a 2-3 percent monthly attrition rate, (Tr.685) while Company's damages expert believed that a 12 percent monthly attrition rate was more realistic. (Tr.1200.) The parties also disagreed about the average length of future contracts, their renewal rates, how many contracts could have been sold on a monthly basis, and on what terms.

Indeed CF offered no explanation of how the jury calculated $5 million. That figure is not close to either CF's or Company's calculations. Nor does it follow logically and directly from any exhibit or testimony at trial. This award is the result of speculation, not easy calculation.

D. CF's Cases Are Inapposite.

CF's cases do not support it. In several, the parties disputed only liability, not the amount of plaintiff's damages, making those damages liquidated. For instance, in *Kehoe v. Wildman, Harrold, Allen & Dixon*, 387 Ill. App. 3d 454 (1st Dist. 2008), the parties stipulated to the amount of the lawyer's separation payments, but disputed whether the payout was required. In *Mut. Serv. Cas. Ins. Co. v. Elizabeth State Bank*, 265 F.3d 601, 629 (7th Cir. 2001), plaintiff's damages "corresponded directly" to the amount of the check that the defendant bank cashed without plaintiff's authorization. Although the parties disputed the bank's liability, "the damages themselves were always subject to quick calculation." *Id.* Likewise, in *Residential Mktg. Group, Inc. v. Granite Investment Group*, 933 F.2d 546, 547-49 (7th Cir. 1991), the parties disputed whether a promissory note constituted defendant's "gross income" from the sale of property, but did *not* dispute the note's amount or that the plaintiff was entitled to 11/2 percent of the note as commission if the note was considered "gross income."

In the other cases on which CF mistakenly relies, the amount of plaintiff's damages was easily determinable because of specific terms of the underlying contracts. For instance, in *SNA Nut Co. v. Haagen-Dazs Co., Inc.*, 302 F.3d 725 (7th Cir. 2002), plaintiff's contract damages were subject to easy calculation because they were based on supply contracts that obligated defendant "to purchase [from plaintiff] a set volume of nut products over a set period of time for a set price." *Id.* at 728. In *Ash v. Georgia-Pacific Corp.*, 957 F.2d 432, 439 (7th Cir. 1992), plaintiff's damages on a shipping contract were "mechanically computed" as the difference between the contractual tariff rates and the rates plaintiff actually paid. In *Platinum Tech., Inc. v. Federal Ins. Co.*, 282 F.3d 927 (7th Cir. 2002), an insurance coverage case, plaintiff PTI entered into a settlement with defendant's insured, which involved an award of $6 million in product credits available for future use. Even though PTI and its insurer, Federal, disputed the current cash value of those product credits, their figure ($6 million) was made "clear" by the settlement and thus was "known to Federal" once the parties settled. *Id.* at 933-35.

The initial agreement did not set any volume of prospective sales, did not set the pricing terms of the dealers' contracts, and did not specify whether future contracts would be signed on a subscription or pay-per-lead basis. Moreover, many of the assumptions necessary for calculating CF's alleged lost profits depended upon market conditions, such as competition from other companies, dealers' cancellation and renewal rates, and dealers' preferences for shorter contract terms. These were matters of considerable dispute between the parties, before, at, and after trial. Hence,

CF's lost future commissions were neither fixed nor subject to easy calculation, and the district court acted within its discretion in denying prejudgment interest.

CONCLUSION

Company respectfully asks this Court: to reverse the district court's judgment and either enter judgment for Company or remand for a new trial on damages; and to affirm the district court's denial of prejudgment interest.

Respectfully submitted,
COMPANY

By: ______________________

One of Its Attorneys
Counsel for Defendant-Appellant/Cross-Appellee

CERTIFICATE OF COMPLIANCE WITH FED. R. APP. P. 32(a)(7)

1. This reply brief complies with the type-volume limitation of Fed. R. App. P. 32(a)(7)(B).

2. This reply brief complies with the typeface requirements of Fed. R. App. P. 32(a)(5) and Circuit Rule 32 and the type style requirements of Fed. R. App. P. 32(a)(6) because this brief has been prepared in a proportionally spaced typeface using Microsoft Office Word 2003 in Bookman Old Style, Font Size 12.

__________________________Attorney

CIRCUIT RULE 31(e)(1) CERTIFICATION

The undersigned hereby certifies that I have filed electronically, pursuant to Circuit Rule 31(e)(1), a version of this reply brief in non-scanned PDF format.

__________________________Attorney

CERTIFICATE OF SERVICE

Attorney hereby certifies that she caused an original and 15 copies and an electronic version of the foregoing Reply Brief of Defendant-Appellant/Cross-Appellee Company to be transmitted to the Court for filing via hand delivery, and two copies and an electronic disk version of the Reply Brief of Defendant-Appellant/Cross-Appellee Company to be served on the opposing party, via messenger.

__________________________Attorney

INDEX

[References are to sections.]

[References are to sections.]

D

[References are to sections.]

[References are to sections.]

[References are to sections.]

V

W

[References are to sections.]